A True Story of Sorrows and Joys

Margaret 2017

By Margaret Beggan Dowling

Copyright © Margaret Dowling, 2017
First Published in Ireland, in 2017, in co-operation with
Choice Publishing, Drogheda, County Louth,
Republic of Ireland.
www.choicepublishing.ie

Paperback ISBN: 978-1-911131-26-7

All rights reserved. No part of this publication may be reproduced, stored in a retrieval system, transmitted in any form, or by any means, electronic, mechanical, photocopying, recording or otherwise, without the prior permission of the copyright holder.

A CIP catalogue record for this book is available from the National Library.

MY WRITTEN CONTRIBUTIONS TO THE BOOK WORLD

2008 - Fireside Nostalgia Poetry

2010 - From Clare to Texas

2012 - A Patchwork of Short Stories

2013 - Recapturing Bygone Days

Contributions requested for the following books:

"Down Memory Lane - Ballybane and Its People"

"Women of Our Time" - Ballybane Beg Writers Group

"Galway a City of Strangers - Voices of the New Galway"

"Reflections by the River" - Creative Writers, Croi na Gaillimhe

ACKNOWLEDGEMENTS

I could not have written this book of my life story without the encouragement and assistance of my awesome family and helpful friends.

My thanks to Fergal Fahy, patient tutor of computer skills.

To Grainne Gilmore and Angela Whelan, computer class tutors at Ballybane Library, Galway.

My sincere thanks go especially to:

My daughter Caroline Dowling, who has patiently dedicated hours of her time structuring and correcting my many errors.

My daughter Margery Fahy for her help in contributing necessary information.

My granddaughters Lisa Ruffley and Caroline Dowling Jr. in the selecting of photographs.

My granddaughters Kristina Beggen and Cassandra Beggen in forwarding interesting articles of their busy lives, from the USA.

My dear son Mike Beggen for his hours of help by phone, also his wife Mary.

My grandsons Michael, Gary, and Ian Beggen, USA, for their help.

My son Leo Beggen and his wife April for their help by phone and e-mail.

My cousin Sister Margaret Hurley, Dublin, for her help.

Mrs Anne Flower and Terry Higgins, Co. Clare - without their help I wouldn't know where some of my relations were buried.

To Mrs Margaret Donnellon and Mrs Mary Lally, Ballybane.Galway

Mrs.Eileen Carrick, Mervue, Galway

To Mr Joe McCarty, Renmore.Galway

To Mr John Costello, City Centre. Galway

DEDICATION

I'm dedicating this book to the many parents, but especially mothers, who have given countless voluntary hours and endless days to the young children of their area. Hours spent amusing and entertaining them, being the childrens' chaperone on trips and outings, and taking responsiblity for their safety, without question. Parents who were never recognised for their years of unselfish dedication.

CONTENTS

WRITTEN CONTRIBUTIONS TO THE BOOK WORLD III
ACKNOWLEDGEMENTS IV
SHARING MY LIFE'S HISTORY .... - 1 -
A TRUE STORY OF SORROWS AND JOYS .... - 1 -
OUR PARENTS EDWARD ABBERTON AND BRIDGET HURLEY .... - 1 -
1930 - MOVING INTO THE LODGE .... - 2 -
FIRST CHILD .... - 2 -
I WAS BORN .... - 3 -
1936 - SCREAMING .... - 4 -
ARRIVING IN KILNACREE .... - 4 -
GRANNY'S HOUSE .... - 6 -
A LONG-AWAITED LETTER .... - 6 -
1937 - GRANNY STAYING IN BED .... - 7 -
1938 - STARTING SCHOOL .... - 8 -
RURAL IRELAND .... - 9 -
1939 - GRANNY PASSED AWAY .... - 10 -
GRANNY'S COFFIN .... - 12 -
1940 - FIRST HOLY COMMUNION .... - 13 -
SHOWING OFF MY DRESS .... - 14 -
O'NEILLS HOUSE .... - 16 -
1941 - THERE WERE CHANGES .... - 16 -
HONEY BEES .... - 17 -
CHANGING SCHOOLS .... - 18 -
1942 - SET DANCING .... - 19 -
MY WHITE COW .... - 19 -
VERY, VERY SAD NEWS .... - 20 -
1943 - NEWS OF A NEW BABY .... - 22 -
ANOTHER CHANGE .... - 22 -
SAYING GOODBYE .... - 23 -
THE JOURNEY .... - 24 -
BROKEN HEARTS .... - 24 -
AUGUST .... - 25 -
AN EYE-OPENING EXPERIENCE .... - 26 -
BRIARHILL SCHOOL .... - 27 -
1943 - THE LETTERS THAT NEVER CAME .... - 28 -
EYE OPERATION .... - 28 -
1944 – THE AROMA OF FISH .... - 32 -
CONFIRMATION .... - 32 -

MAY ALTAR	- 33 -
THE BULLIED GOOSE	- 34 -
WHOOPING COUGH	- 35 -
1945 - COOKING CLASS	- 37 -
LEARNING STEP DANCING	- 38 -
1946 - APRONS ARE NOT WORN IN TOWN SCHOOLS	- 38 -
1947 - SIGNING OFF THE ROLLBOOK	- 40 -
I'M A YEAR AT HOME	- 40 -
GETTING READY	- 41 -
MOTHER RECEIVES A LETTER	- 42 -
1949 - A NEW BABY	- 42 -
HOME ON MY BREAK	- 43 -
1950 - AGE SEVETEEN	- 44 -
1951 - TAKING A BIG STEP	- 45 -
SHE DID TALK TO ME	- 46 -
PACKING UP TO LEAVE	- 46 -
I WAS CURIOUS ABOUT MY DAD	- 47 -
A NEW BEGINNING	- 48 -
1952 - EMIGRATION	- 49 -
MAKING PREPARATIONS	- 50 -
SAYING MORE GOODBYES	- 51 -
FAREWELL TO FRIENDS OF THE TEAROOM	- 52 -
A LIVE WAKE	- 53 -
DECEMBER DEPARTURE	- 54 -
17TH DECEMBER, HAVING ARRIVED	- 56 -
A STRANGE NEW WORLD	- 56 -
FIRST CHRISTMAS IN THE USA	- 58 -
JANUARY 1953 - EMPLOYMENT	- 58 -
ST. PATRICK'S DAY	- 59 -
CONNACHT TRIBUNE	- 60 -
OUT IN THE COUNTRY	- 60 -
EVERYONE IS COMING BACK	- 64 -
IT'S BACK TO THE CITY	- 65 -
1954 - A JOB CHANGE	- 66 -
FIRST PLANE FLIGHT	- 67 -
FUTURE HUSBAND	- 69 -
1955 - OUR WEDDING	- 70 -
OUR HOME ON TAYLOR AVENUE	- 72 -
WAITRESS	- 73 -
SURGERY	- 73 -
ELDERLY LADYS' COMPANION	- 73 -

MY BROTHER EDDIE'S ANNOUNCEMENT	- 74 -
1956 - IRISH HOLIDAY	- 75 -
CROSS-BORDER SEARCH	- 76 -
GALWAY	- 77 -
1957 - COUNTY CLARE	- 78 -
RETURNING TO GALWAY	- 80 -
JANUARY 3RD 1957	- 80 -
BACK TO MONAGHAN	- 80 -
BACK TO GALWAY	- 81 -
JULY - A BABY BOY	- 82 -
BABY'S FIRST CHRISTMAS	- 85 -
1958 - ONE YEAR OLD	- 85 -
COUSIN MAUREEN'S PLANS	- 86 -
1959 - AUNT MARGIE'S FIRST GRANDCHILD	- 87 -
MOTHER'S ARRIVAL	- 88 -
DUSTING LOCKERS	- 89 -
CHRISTMAS IS APPROACHING	- 90 -
1960 - NEW YEAR'S DAY	- 91 -
AN APRIL WEDDING	- 92 -
MOTHER GOES HOME	- 93 -
A MORNING JOB	- 93 -
ATLANTIC CITY	- 95 -
UNCLE LEO	- 96 -
1961 - WE ARE GIVEN THE NEWS	- 96 -
IT IS NOT GOING TO BE A GOOD YEAR	- 96 -
WE ARE BACK TO ROUTINE	- 98 -
I HAVE NEWS	- 99 -
1962 - UNCLE LEO IS LEAVING	- 99 -
OUR VISITORS	- 100 -
BEST MAN AND A NEW BABY	- 100 -
MY BROTHER PADDY	- 102 -
MY HUSBAND PASSES AWAY	- 102 -
HIS FUNERAL	- 103 -
FIRST CHRISTMAS	- 104 -
1963 - MOUNT SINAI HOSPITAL	- 105 -
GOING BACK TO IRELAND	- 105 -
LEO'S FIRST BIRTHDAY	- 106 -
AMERICAN LINER	- 106 -
FAREWELL WEDDING DRESS	- 107 -
BOARDING THE S.S. AMERICAN	- 108 -
MEETING THE YOUNG MOTHER	- 109 -

ARRIVING IN COBH	- 111 -
MOTHER WAITING AT THE DOOR	- 112 -
HUNGRY	- 112 -
I AM BACK IN GALWAY	- 113 -
SCOTSTOWN	- 114 -
HIRING A CARAVAN	- 115 -
PRESIDENT KENNEDY	- 117 -
FIRST CHRISTMAS IN GALWAY	- 117 -
1964 - A MINI MINOR CAR	- 118 -
MICHAEL GOES TO SCHOOL	- 118 -
NEWS OF ANOTHER ADDITION TO THE ABBERTON FAMILY	- 119 -
LEGION OF MARY	- 120 -
TOO RICH	- 121 -
RENTING A FLAT	- 122 -
LIVING IN A THATCHED COTTAGE	- 123 -
SEWING MACHINE	- 124 -
OCTOBER	- 125 -
CELEBRATING CHRISTMAS	- 127 -
1965 - FELL FROM HER BIKE	- 128 -
A SAD MOMENT	- 130 -
OUR OWN HOME	- 130 -
B&B	- 131 -
CONCERT	- 131 -
HISTORY	- 132 -
EDDIE MAKES A SUGGESTION	- 132 -
AT AGE THIRTY-TWO	- 133 -
DAD SHOWS US HIS GARDEN	- 134 -
MARY'S WEDDING	- 135 -
GOING TO A WEDDING	- 135 -
A BARBER	- 136 -
1966 - DATING	- 137 -
MANY WERE THE TRIPS	- 138 -
ANOTHER GRANDCHILD	- 139 -
1967 - VISITING OUR DAD	- 139 -
PADDY A GARDENER	- 139 -
NOSTALGIC DAY	- 140 -
WE ARE PLANNING	- 141 -
OUR SECOND MARRIAGES	- 141 -
GOING TO ST. PATRICK'S SCHOOL	- 142 -
1968 - VISITING DAD	- 143 -
1969 - ANOTHER FAMILY WEDDING	- 144 -

ST. PATRICK'S DAY	- 144 -
LADIES CLUB	- 146 -
1970 - OUR NIGHTS OUT	- 148 -
PADDY WAS A FEATHERWEIGHT	- 150 -
AFTER WE WERE MARRIED	- 150 -
1970 - CABARET	- 150 -
1971 - NEWS FROM BALLINASLOE	- 152 -
MAKING A FIRST COMMUNION DRESS	- 152 -
CONFIRMATION	- 153 -
1972 - PADDY'S INJURY	- 154 -
OUR SECOND DAUGHTER	- 154 -
USA VISITORS	- 154 -
CHRISTENING	- 156 -
MY TEETH	- 156 -
SLEEPLESS NIGHTS	- 157 -
1973 - JANUARY	- 158 -
CUB SCOUTS	- 159 -
AUGUST	- 159 -
FIRST COUSIN'S PROFESSION	- 160 -
DECEMBER - CLARE TRIP	- 161 -
TRADING IN THE MINI	- 164 -
REGIONAL COLLEGE	- 164 -
EUGENE'S CONFIRMATION	- 165 -
1974 - DENTURES	- 165 -
A SCOUT	- 165 -
EUGENE RETURNS TO BOHERMORE	- 166 -
MONASTEREVIN EASTER	- 167 -
BUILDING A CHALET	- 168 -
STEEPLE JACKS	- 169 -
MONASTEREVIN SIEGE	- 173 -
1975 - A HERNIA	- 174 -
MOTHER'S FIRST BIRTHDAY PARTY	- 174 -
A DEATH	- 176 -
TULLA, COUNTY CLARE	- 176 -
1976 - FIRST HOLY COMMUNION	- 178 -
GRANNY'S TREAT FOR MARGERY	- 179 -
TULLOW, CO CARLOW	- 181 -
1977 - GERMANY	- 183 -
AUNT MARY HURLEY	- 184 -
1978 - CONVENT OF MERCY, SPIDDAL	- 185 -
MERCY CONVENT, GALWAY	- 187 -

MORRIS MINOR	- 188 -
MY HUSBAND CONTINUED SMOKING	- 189 -
1979 - SECOND OPERATION	- 190 -
THE LITTLE ONE'S FIRST COMMUNION	- 190 -
THE END OF PADDY'S CAREER AS A BARBER	- 191 -
DRIVING THE VAN	- 192 -
SCOUTING AND GUIDING	- 192 -
GIRL GUIDE MOVEMENT	- 192 -
MICHAEL'S NEWS	- 193 -
SPARE ROOM	- 195 -
A FIRST TRIP HOME AFTER FIFTY YEARS	- 195 -
CALLAGHANS' ARRIVAL	- 197 -
AUNT MARGIE SEES HER HOME COUNTY	- 199 -
1979 – SEPTEMBER, POPE'S VISIT	- 201 -
A FLEETING GLANCE	- 201 -
1980 - NEED FOR A PLAYSCHOOL	- 202 -
"ROCK DALE" PLAYSCHOOL	- 202 -
"ROCK DALE" PLAYSCHOOL IS NOW OFFICIALLY OPEN	- 203 -
BROWNIES	- 204 -
BROWNIES ENROLMENT	- 204 -
DANCING CLASSES	- 205 -
1980/81 - A COMHALTAS CEOLTÓIRÍ BRANCH	- 205 -
CÉILÍ	- 207 -
CAROLINE ON CALL	- 207 -
CARD PLAYING	- 208 -
A RED OPEL CADET	- 208 -
MUSIC CLASS – ENTER-CLASS COMPETITION	- 209 -
BUYING THE TROPHIES	- 209 -
1981 – 6TH JANUARY	- 210 -
COMHALTAS COMPETITIONS	- 211 -
AFTERMATH	- 212 -
PLAYSCHOOL	- 214 -
MOTHER PASSED AWAY	- 214 -
IN DIRE NEED OF A CAR	- 215 -
APRIL WEDDING	- 215 -
MOTHER'S HEADSTONE	- 216 -
PLAYSCHOOL SUMMER HOLIDAYS	- 216 -
IN ALL WALKS OF LIFE	- 217 -
CAMP BALLYLANDERS	- 217 -
LEO GOES TO DUBLIN	- 219 -
JULY - USA	- 220 -

THE BRONX	- 221 -
SIGHTSEEING IN MANHATTAN	- 222 -
COUSIN MAUREEN	- 223 -
SHANNON AIRPORT	- 225 -
ACTIVITIES	- 226 -
SEPTEMBER - MY OPERATION	- 227 -
HIT BY LIGHTNING	- 228 -
THINKING OF A BROWNIE CONCERT	- 229 -
A TERRIBLE THIRST	- 229 -
HALLOWEEN PARTY	- 230 -
PLANING THE CONCERT	- 230 -
1982 - AFTER SHOCK OF THE HYSTERECTOMY	- 231 -
FEBRUARY - BABY MICHAEL	- 232 -
BALLYBANE GUIDE UNIT	- 232 -
ST. PATRICK'S DAY PARADE	- 233 -
DISAPPOINTING NEWS	- 234 -
GALWAY IGG	- 234 -
DECEMBER - CHRISTMAS CAKES	- 234 -
MICHAEL'S SUCCESS	- 236 -
1983 - BALLYBANE MUMMERS	- 237 -
THE JOY OF GUIDING	- 238 -
DEATHS IN CO. CLARE	- 238 -
"ROCK DALE"	- 239 -
1984 - WITHOUT A CAR	- 240 -
FINALLY WE RISE	- 241 -
DECEMBER CHOIR	- 242 -
PLAYSCHOOL SUPERVISORS TRAINING	- 242 -
1985 - FINE GAEL SOCIAL	- 243 -
BUYING A VANETTE	- 244 -
GREAT SOUTHERN HOTEL	- 244 -
FIRST AID TRAINING	- 245 -
BEAVERS	- 246 -
LARCH HILL OUTING	- 247 -
NATIONAL SCOUTS JAMBOREE	- 247 -
BEAVERS QUIZ COMPETITION	- 248 -
BUILDING FUND	- 248 -
LORD AND LADY BADEN POWELL	- 249 -
ANOTHER DEATH	- 249 -
1986 - THE LAST OF THE CONFIRMATIONS	- 250 -
CAMP BALLYFINN	- 251 -
1987 - RENMORE PANTO	- 253 -

PADDY PASSES AWAY	- 254 -
PADDY AT REST	- 256 -
HELP FROM A GOOD NEIGHBOUR	- 257 -
GETTING ON WITH LIFE	- 259 -
CONTINUING WITH THE BEAVERS	- 260 -
A SECOND GRANDSON	- 260 -
MARGERY GRADUATES	- 261 -
SON MIKE HAS SOMETHING TO TELL	- 261 -
MIKE'S FIRST JOB	- 262 -
FAMILY ALL TOGETHER	- 263 -
ISLE-OF-MAN GUIDE CAMP	- 263 -
BALLYBANE'S NEW CHURCH	- 266 -
1988 – APRIL, MY VISIT TO HAYWARD'S HEATH	- 266 -
PREPARATIONS WENT INTO ACTION	- 267 -
ENTERTAINMENT AND ACTIVITIES	- 269 -
LEAVING TO GO HOME	- 270 -
LEO'S WEDDING PLANS	- 271 -
RACE WEEK	- 272 -
A VERY WET DAY	- 272 -
THE YEAR IS NOT OVER	- 273 -
ENGAGEMENT	- 274 -
INVITATION	- 274 -
LEO AND JOEY	- 275 -
1989 - WEDDING MORNING	- 276 -
CLOSING THE PLAYSCHOOL	- 277 -
PLAYSCHOOL'S LAST MASS	- 278 -
IT IS HARD TO TRY	- 279 -
LEO AND JOEY ARE READY	- 280 -
1989 - PACKING	- 281 -
ARRIVING	- 281 -
1989 - AMERICAN WEDDING	- 282 -
RACE WEEK	- 284 -
IT WAS NOW TIME	- 284 -
1989 - GUIDES ARRIVAL	- 285 -
CASTLEGAR HURLING CLUB	- 288 -
1990 - IN SEARCH OF A NEW HOME	- 288 -
THE VANETTE SOLD	- 289 -
CAROLINE'S GRADUATION	- 289 -
1990 - CHOIR OUTING	- 290 -
LEO PHONES	- 291 -
BALLYBANE DOG SHOW	- 292 -

FLOWER ARRANGING	- 293 -
MY NEXT VENTURE	- 295 -
GOOD NEWS	- 298 -
A GRANDDAUGHTER	- 298 -
BRENDAN TOURS	- 299 -
NEWS FROM ACROSS THE SEA	- 300 -
AN AWARD	- 300 -
1991 – JANUARY, A DISMAL MONTH	- 301 -
I'M PLANTING VEGETABLES	- 302 -
FLOWER GARDEN	- 303 -
ANOTHER GRANDDAUGHTER L.I.	- 304 -
ST. PATRICKS BRASS BAND	- 305 -
1992 - KENNEDY AIRPORT	- 306 -
AN AMERICAN CHRISTENING	- 307 -
COMMITTEE MEETING	- 308 -
NO END TO PREGNANCIES	- 309 -
1993 - THE LATE BRONWYN	- 309 -
A GARDEN OF THISTLES	- 310 -
GRANDDAUGHTER KRISTINA	- 311 -
SET DANCING	- 312 -
BRINGING SOME OF MY PATCHWORK TO THE STATES	- 314 -
THE CHOIR NIGHT OUT	- 315 -
1994 - DAUGHTER CAROLINE DOWLING	- 316 -
SON MICHAEL APPLIES	- 317 -
1995 - I AM PLANING ANOTHER HOLIDAY	- 318 -
A PLEASANT FLIGHT	- 319 -
1995 - ATLANTIC CITY	- 321 -
ARIZONA	- 322 -
WELL HERE WE ARE	- 324 -
SIGHTSEEING IN SEDONA	- 327 -
RED CLAY	- 331 -
SHANNON AIRPORT	- 332 -
1995 - SEPTEMBER	- 332 -
ANCIENT ORDER OF HIBERNIANS	- 333 -
HERE I AM AND BLESSED	- 333 -
CAROLINE COMES HOME	- 334 -
SAVED BY A DOG	- 335 -
LEO NEEDS A FAVOUR	- 335 -
MEETING MY GRANDSON IAN	- 336 -
LANDING AT SHANNON	- 339 -
A WEDDING ANNIVERSARY	- 340 -

CHRISTMAS IN MARGERY'S	- 340 -
1996 - A SAD JOURNEY TO DUBLIN	- 341 -
FEBRUARY - ESKER RETREAT	- 342 -
1996 BROKEN HEARTED FAMILY	- 343 -
MADELINE'S LAST FAREWELL	- 344 -
GRANDDAUGHTER LISA	- 345 -
FEBRUARY	- 345 -
1996 - ART CLASS	- 347 -
A WEDDING INVITATION	- 347 -
AN UNFORGETTABLE DAY IN AUGUST	- 347 -
POOCHY'S NOSE	- 350 -
1997 - ANOTHER LITTLE GRANDDAUGHTER	- 351 -
NIECE MARIE'S WEDDING	- 352 -
1998 - THE BIG PRAM	- 353 -
FEELING SORRY	- 353 -
1997 - THEIR OWN PLACE	- 354 -
1997 - AN ACCIDENT	- 354 -
1998 – FEBRUARY, THE PASSING	- 356 -
1998 - FIRST COMMUNION	- 357 -
THE DEATH OF OUR COUSIN	- 358 -
1998 - IN TODAY'S IRELAND	- 358 -
1998 - I AM ECSTATIC	- 359 -
1999 - IT IS FIRST COMMUNION DAY	- 360 -
JOINING THE RENMORE ACTIVE RETIREMENT	- 360 -
2000 - ELECTED CHAIRPERSON	- 361 -
ZIMBABWE	- 361 -
MEETING COLM	- 362 -
MY SON MIKE	- 363 -
RENMORE ACTIVE RETIREMENT	- 364 -
MORE ACTIVITIES	- 365 -
ANTICIPATING COLM'S PHONE CALL	- 366 -
KALLUM'S CHRISTENING	- 366 -
2001 - POOCHY GONE TO DOGGIE LAND	- 367 -
SAD NEWS IN BALLINROBE	- 367 -
A TALENTED LADY	- 368 -
OUR WEEK ENJOYING THE RACES	- 368 -
2001 - AN AUGUST I WON'T EVER FORGET	- 369 -
SON LEO PHONES	- 371 -
SURPRISE VISITOR	- 371 -
2001 - MY PRAYERFUL THOUGHTS	- 373 -
2001 - THE SADDEST SEPTEMBER	- 374 -

IT'S MY FIRST VISIT	- 376 -
2001 - TRYING TO RELAX AT HOME	- 377 -
2001 - ONE MONTH LATER	- 378 -
WILL DEAR MARY HAVE GOOD NEWS?	- 379 -
2002 - REMEMBRANCE MASS	- 381 -
HIGHEST AWARD IN GIRL GUIDES	- 382 -
GRADUATING FROM COLAISTE COIRIBE	- 383 -
MY VISIT TO MORAN'S	- 384 -
SAD NEWS IS HARD	- 385 -
I AM THINKING OF MRS MORAN	- 386 -
2002 - CHURCH FLOWERBEDS	- 386 -
REACH-OUT	- 387 -
TAKING MY SON'S ADVICE	- 388 -
AN OFFER	- 388 -
2003 - GETTING THE KEY	- 389 -
GRADUATING	- 390 -
A BIRTHDAY PARTY FOR ME	- 390 -
NEXT DOOR NEIGHBOURS	- 391 -
A BEAUTIFUL SUNDAY	- 391 -
LAUNCH OF BALLYBANE ACTIVE RETIREMENT	- 392 -
2004 - "ROCK DALE" IS SOLD	- 396 -
TAKING A TRIP TO SEE MY SON	- 397 -
KEEPING ME UP TO DATE	- 398 -
GRANDSON GARY	- 398 -
MORE EXCITING NEWS	- 400 -
NOMINATIONS	- 401 -
2005 - LEAVING NEW JERSEY	- 402 -
I AM ONE YEAR LIVING HERE	- 403 -
WEDDING INVITATION	- 404 -
I WAS NOT AWARE	- 405 -
I HAVE ANOTHER SURPRISE	- 407 -
THE PHONE IS RINGING	- 408 -
THE MAYOR'S AWARD	- 409 -
2006 - FIRST CIVIL CERMONY WEDDING	- 409 -
WORKING AT SURVIVAL	- 410 -
GRANDSON GARY	- 411 -
BOBBIE AND I TAKE A HOLIDAY	- 411 -
OUR N.C. HOLIDAY	- 412 -
CALLING TO SEE BERNIE	- 413 -
JOEY SALES LADY	- 414 -
INVITATION	- 414 -

MAYOR'S AWARD	- 415 -
CREATIVE WRITERS	- 415 -
2007 – ST. BRIGID'S CHURCH	- 415 -
JOEY'S FUNERAL	- 417 -
A REMEMBRANCE MASS	- 418 -
KRISTINA AND IAN	- 418 -
I BOOKED THREE MONTHS	- 419 -
OCTOBER	- 420 -
2008 - RETURNING HOME	- 423 -
BOOK LAUNCH	- 423 -
KALLUM	- 424 -
NEXT DOOR NEIGHBOUR'S FIRE	- 425 -
LAUNCHING 'FIRESIDE NOSTALGIA POETRY'	- 426 -
EMPLOYED	- 427 -
RETURNING TO CNOC NA CILLE	- 428 -
ANOTHER PHONE CALL	- 428 -
2009 - THE WEDDING RECEPTION	- 429 -
LEFT HIP REPLACEMENT	- 429 -
GRANDCHILDRENS LETTERS	- 430 -
KILLARNEY	- 431 -
A TRUE MEMBER PASSES AWAY	- 431 -
COMPUTER SKILLS	- 431 -
WORKING HARD	- 432 -
PATRICA MADE A SUGGESTION	- 432 -
FLOWER GARDEN PRIZE WINNING	- 433 -
2010 - LAUNCH FROM CLARE TO TEXAS	- 433 -
JOINING THE CREATIVE WRITERS	- 435 -
SOME SAD NEWS	- 436 -
2011 - I FLY OUT	- 437 -
MY FIRST VISIT TO MY BROTHER	- 438 -
CÚIRT FESTIVAL	- 439 -
SPRING BREAK	- 441 -
FOR A LONG TIME	- 441 -
BOOK SELLING IN CLARENBRIDGE	- 443 -
WHAT WILL THIS YEAR HOLD	- 443 -
2012 - REMEMBRANCE MASS	- 444 -
I CONTINUED TO ATTEND	- 445 -
2013 - THIS WILL BE AN EXTRAORDINARY	- 446 -
THE LAUNCH OF 'RECAPTURING BYGONE DAYS'	- 446 -
GRANDSON KALLUM	- 447 -
WHITE COLLAR BOXING	- 448 -

MEDJUGORJE	- 449 -
USA GRADUATIONS	- 449 -
IT WAS A LONG AND BEAUTIFUL DRIVE	- 450 -
AT LAST, WE HAVE ARRIVED	- 451 -
KRISTINA	- 451 -
AFTER A FEW DAYS' REST	- 453 -
CASSANDRA JANE BEGGEN	- 454 -
SOMETHING GOING ON	- 459 -
A PARTY	- 460 -
2014 - A MIRACULOUS MIRACLE	- 463 -
MIDNIGHT MASS	- 463 -
JOINING THE ST. JOSEPH'S	- 464 -
MAYOR'S AWARDS AGAIN	- 465 -
MEETING A FIRST COUSIN	- 465 -
ANOTHER GRADUATION	- 467 -
MODEL PLANE FLYING CLUB	- 468 -
A MOST PLEASURABLE INNER FEELING	- 469 -
CHRISTMAS HOLIDAYS	- 469 -
DECEMBER	- 470 -
2015 - WE ARE IN LONG ISLAND	- 472 -
PREPARING FOR A MEMORABLE WEEK	- 473 -
DAN O'HARA COTTAGE	- 474 -
THE FASTEST WEEK	- 476 -
AFTERNOON WALKS	- 477 -
2016 - WONDERFUL NEWS	- 478 -
I AM BOOKING THROUGH FAHY TRAVEL.	- 478 -
I RECEIVE SAD NEWS	- 479 -
ON THE GO BUS	- 480 -
MEETING OUR NEW RELATIONS	- 480 -
INSTRUCTIONS FOR THE BIG DAY	- 481 -
THE WEDDING DAY	- 482 -
MASS IN ST. PATRICK'S CATHEDRAL	- 485 -
IT WAS A WEDDING WEEK	- 485 -
2016 - GOING TO NEW YORK	- 486 -
A BLUE MASS	- 486 -
QUEEN'S COLLEGE	- 486 -
A LARGE HEADING	- 489 -
ODE TO PATRICK KAVANAGH	- 489 -
2017 - THE GREATEST SHOW ON EARTH	- 490 -
MOTHER'S DAY	- 491 -
CLOSING MY LIFE STORY	- 492 -

A True Story of Sorrows and Joys

SHARING MY LIFE'S HISTORY

As I travel back through this journey of my life, I am sharing passages of experiences I had while climbing up the ladder of old age.

A TRUE STORY OF SORROWS AND JOYS

With help from my many journals that I have kept throughout the years, journals that I often thought of putting a match to (yet each time, I place them into their box and up they go on the top shelf), I will be sharing reminiscences of my childhood growing up in County Clare. I will share a cavalcade of memories with you. There is a reason for everything. I will refer occasionally to the journals as I endeavour to share the ups and downs of a life so far well spent.

OUR PARENTS EDWARD ABBERTON AND BRIDGET HURLEY

Our parents Edward and Bridget were married in St. Joseph's Church in Limerick on the 4th of February in 1930. My mother's brother Michael, and sister Mary Hurley, were their witnesses. Edward/Ned and Bridget met at Glenlow, County Clare where they both worked. Ned worked on the farm and Bridget as the housekeeper. Ned was originally from Derryvonlan, Powers Cross, Woodford, Portumna, County Galway. Bridget was from Kilnacree, Six-Mile-Bridge, County Clare.

After they married, Mr and Mrs Edward Abberton came to live in County Galway. Ned got a job in the Marble Quarry in Ballyinew. This was a large wooded area. Colonel Waitman was the owner of the woods and surroundings. Dad and Mam were in search of a house of their own. There was a vacant lodge on the grounds. Dad approached the colonel and asked him if he and his wife could live in the lodge until they got a house. It was a satisfactory arrangement.

1930 - MOVING INTO THE LODGE

The lodge was fully furnished and had an open fireplace with plenty of turf, as it was in the heart of the woods. There were enough logs for burning to last years. Their possessions were few. Two brown suitcases held their personal belongings. Mother had two extra parcels, wrapped in one was a handmade knitted quilt, a gift from her mother and her sister Mary. She also had a basket; this contained a precious wedding gift from the people she worked for, a pair of guinea fowl. There was a small shed at the back of the lodge. "Nice and handy, for my guinea fowl", she said to herself.

FIRST CHILD

My brother Edward/Eddie was born in 1930, while they were still living in the lodge. Two years later, a council cottage became vacant in Ballybrtt. It was one of seven, and was an end-house with over an acre of ground. The other six cottages were already occupied. In 1932, Dad and Mom moved in and made it their home. Having so much ground, Ned bought a cow, saying there was plenty of grass for her to graze. Mother, having come from farming stock, had no problem with milking this cow. That same year, Dublin was hosting the Eucharistic Congress and they both decided to take the train and attend it. Mother often talked about that wonderful day, the memory of which lasted with her all of her life. Their young son was in the safe hands of Kate Long, Ballinew.

I WAS BORN

I was born in the Central Hospital (now called University Hospital Galway) on 29th of September in 1933 and christened Margaret Mary. During those years, few parents would have godparents at the ready to stand for their children when baptised. In my case it was a Sr. M. Euquinas and Dr. Power, who were hospital staff.

For the first two years of my life I lived with Mam, Dad and my brother Eddie in Ballybrit, Galway. Mother was a shy, quiet person; she didn't know many of her neighbours, who were friendly but kept to themselves. When she discovered she was expecting her third child, her thoughts turned to her family, a long distance away in County Clare. At dinner one evening, she made the suggestion to Dad: "We will need someone to mind baby Maggie, she is very cross cutting her teeth and her arm is still not fully better after the smallpox vaccination." Back then it was important for babies to be vaccinated while very young against smallpox, and in some cases, a baby would get very sick and the arm would swell up and be very painful. I was one such baby. My poor mother told me once about how they thought I would lose my arm. They walked the floor day and night with me for at least a month. It wasn't an injection the doctor gave the baby, but three or four scrapes with an object like a piece of broken glass on the upper part of the little arm, then he would put a coat of iodine over each scrape to prevent infection.

Mother was worried about me. She decided on what she thought the best thing to do, which was to write to her sister Mary and ask her to come and take me to Clare for two or three months until after the baby was born. "That is the best thing to do," my dad agreed. In the course of conversations when I enquired as to how I came to be raised in Granny Hurley's in County Clare for so long, Mam told me that she asked my Aunt Mary to bring me to my granny's to mind me until the baby was born. I never thought the three months would turn out to be eight years. Mam explained to me how Eddie was five years old and would stay with friends in Ballinew and then with his Dad after his day's work. That was how the arrangement of the few months living in Granny Hurley's with Aunt Mary and Uncle Paddy, turned out to be eight years, which was alright with everyone, especially me.

1936 - SCREAMING

It was coming into the busy time of the year for farmers when Aunt Mary came to bring me with her on the bus to Limerick. I was told by Aunt Mary that on the morning she was taking me from my mother, I kicked and screamed while clinging to my mother.

"Even with all the coaxing of the two of us, you still held on, you didn't want to leave. We finally calmed you down for long enough to get you into the hackney waiting at the gate to take us to the bus. There, you began to cry again and vomited on my lovely coat.

"It was a sorrowful morning for both you and your mother. You eventually fell asleep and woke up when we arrived in Limerick. Your Uncle Paddy was waiting with the pony and trap. He took you in his arms. You were about to cry, but seeing the pony, you stopped."

ARRIVING IN KILNACREE

Aunt Mary continued telling me what happened at that period of time, "Everything looked strange to you in the house. You started to cry again. You were looking around for your mother, who wasn't there. I sat you on your granny's lap and she rocked you to and fro, trying to hush you from crying. The collie dog came to lick your face; you got down on the floor and cuddled into the collie's fur. Granny turned to me saying, "She will settle down now, Mary". This part of my young life must have been crushing for me and my Mam, but I had people who loved me. I shudder when I think of mothers and babies forced apart and who spend their lives searching for each other.

Granny, Mary Hurley, her sons Michael and Patrick (Paddy), her daughters Bridget (Our mother) and Mary seated.

Grandad Michael Hurley

GRANNY'S HOUSE

Grandmother Mary Hurley lived in a thatched farmhouse in Kilnacree, Six-Mile-Bridge in County Clare. Her daughter Mary and son Paddy lived with her (Her husband Michael, our grandad, had passed away in 1920 from a burst appendix, fifteen years prior to me being brought to Kilnacree). The house was situated on a small farm of land. It was well equipped with the necessary produce - hay haggard, sheds for fowl of every breed, cattle, cows, a work horse, a pony for the trap, and always a pig to be fattened for the table. For a time, they kept goats, a puck, a nanny and two kids. They also had vegetables, potatoes and some fruit trees. The pony trap was put away in the cart house after Saturday's shopping and Sunday Mass. The springwell was half-way up the field in front of the house. A lovely stream flowed down the hill, past the side of the house, and the bog kept the open fire well supplied with turf. There was concern in case I would fall into the open fire. Granny assured everyone there was no fear of that happening while she was sitting by the fire on her rocker, with her black shawl wrapped around her shoulders. "'Don't worry, I'll mind Maggie when ye are out on the land",' she would say to me," said Aunt Mary.

A LONG-AWAITED LETTER

Granny was watching for the postman to bring a certain letter. Aunt Mary would tell her it will come, "Be patient, Mam." In those years, the post was delivered once every two weeks. It was hard work for the postman, cycling up the mountain on a push bike. In Granny's house, he could be sure of getting a cup of hot tea and a slice of homemade bread and butter.

This morning, the dog was barking and Granny was very excited. "Hurry Maggie, bring me the letter." She was unable to open it as her hands were shaking with excitement. "Here Maggie, open it for me." She started to read down the page, "Mary, Mary, Bridget had another son born in August, he is a month old. I am a granny to two grandsons and a granddaughter. That's you Maggie, you have a baby brother." I didn't pay heed to babies; in fact, for a long time I hated them.

1937 - GRANNY STAYING IN BED

There was a sad feeling about the house. "Why is Granny staying in bed so much?" I asked Aunty. "She is old Maggie, and needs rest," was her reply. Aunty would prepare her stirrabout/porridge in the morning and give it to me to spoon-feed Granny while they were out working in the farm. We would talk away. Granny had lots of stories of her younger days, she would tell me about dreams she had when she sat in the field making daisy-chains, making and wrapping one around her head, then pretending she was a fairy princess. Other times she would go quiet and her lips would be moving. These were the times she would be talking to God. There was a monthly visit from the priest; the rattle of his old car could be heard coming up the dirt road. We would stand in respect of the Blessed Eucharist he was carrying, as he passed through the kitchen to Granny's bedroom. He would hear her confession, pray over her, and then serve her Holy Communion.

Afterwards the tea and cake would be ready for him. Uncle Paddy would ask how he thought Gran was looking. "Great," the priest would always say.

Gran insisted on getting up in the evenings. She liked the company of the neighbours dropping in with a bit of gossip. It was now coming to my turn to mind Granny from the fire. I would go to bed when she was going. Uncle Paddy would light the candle which was in an old candle holder that had a handle; I held the handle as I carried it to the bedroom. Granny would come in behind me. After placing it on a little table, I would help Granny into her bed. She would say, "God bless you, child," and then shake the holy water on me. I would then make ready and go to bed myself. The last thing said was, "Blow out the candle." It was important not to leave the candle lighting for long because it would be needed for many nights. There was no electricity in those times. A paraffin oil lamp was used in the kitchen; a handy little lamp hung high on the wall, one side of the fireplace, with a shiny tin plate at the back of the glass globe to throw a bright light over the kitchen.

1938 - STARTING SCHOOL

At the age of five, Aunt Mary brought me to Oatfield School. This was a long distance by road. She popped me up on the carrier of her bicycle and cycled to Oatfield. Meeting the teacher was a new thing, and as I was not in the habit of being in the company of a group of children, I was not willing to go into the classroom when I saw so many children; I pulled back behind my aunt. The teacher was very nice and asked one of the children from the small/junior infants class to bring a box of sweets for me to pick out one. Too shy, I looked into the box, but would not put my hand in. The little girl tried handing me one, but I pulled back behind my aunt again. The teacher said to Aunt Mary to take me home and bring me back the next Monday with the promise of that sweet. At home, Aunty Mary was in a big discussion with Granny who would say, "She will be alright, Mary, she will get used to it." I was outside, thinking of that box of sweets.

Starting school, Oatfield, the first school I attended.
Now it is someone's home.

RURAL IRELAND

In rural Ireland, farmhouses were situated long distances from each other. Children could seldom get together except for young lads that played hurling. The nearest village to Kilnacree was Reinaskomoge, about two miles away. The O'Neill family lived there. Maureen was the only daughter and the youngest of three brothers. Each day she would pass Granny's house on her way to Oatfield School, across bog land. Maureen was five years older than me. Aunt Mary was good friends with her mother; they would meet on Saturdays in the Limerick market selling their farm produce.

It was arranged for Maureen to call for me on Monday morning to bring me to school. It would be my first real day at school. I waited for her and kept thinking of that sweet in the box. Granny and Aunt Mary were thanking Maureen for coming to the house to get me. "It's no trouble at all," said Maureen.

She brought me to school, holding my hand all the way as we crossed the fields and bog land. I had a small school bag that held a bottle of milk, two thick slices of homemade brown bread and butter, and a pencil and copy book. Going into the classroom, the teacher allowed Maureen to sit in the desk beside me for a while, but, as she was in fifth class, she soon had to go into the next room. I, of course, started to cry. The little girl brought down the box of sweets and, as everyone picked one out, I did too, and from then on I was fine with going to school. Maureen and I had great fun in the summer time, when we went bare foot and the soft bog ground squished up between our toes like velvet (We remained life-long friends until she passed away in 2013 at the age of eighty-five. I was sad but happy when I was able to attend her funeral in Six-Mile-Bridge. May she rest in peace. Maureen was married to Joe Costello; they had two sons, Martin and Joseph. Joe passed away in the 1980's about the same time as my husband Paddy).

Our days crossing the bog are long gone now. But I cannot help reflecting back to the months of April and May. After a night's fall of rain; the purple heather would turn a deeper purple, the furze bush flower was a sparkling honey gold, the bog cotton more fluffy, the black thorn and the white thorn would begin to blossom, all in preparation for summer time.

1939 - GRANNY PASSED AWAY

At night, before Aunt Mary would get into bed, she would tuck Granny in and wish her a good night's sleep. On this night, as we were about to fall asleep, Granny spoke: "Mary, I see a collie dog running through the meadow."

"You're dreaming, Mam," Aunty Mary answered.

In a while she spoke again. "I see a little girl running through the meadow, her hair is tied in two bunches with pink ribbons."

"That's Maggie, Mam, now go to sleep, or I won't be able to get up in the morning." Early in the morning, the first thing Aunty would do was ask Gran, "Will I make you some stirrabout Mam?" Only this morning she got no answer. I sat up in the bed and stared at Gran's face, I thought she looked whiter than usual. I wanted to say something but the words wouldn't come. Aunty called out to Uncle Paddy, his bedroom was across to the other side of the kitchen, "Paddy, Paddy, its Mam, come quick!" He hurried into the room and began calling, "Granny!" I started crying. "Go out and sit near the fire Maggie, your Granny is gone to meet her Maker." What did all that mean? The only thing I could do was stand by the fire. I could hear Aunty saying, "She must have just slipped away, she is still warm." Then, closing the bedroom door, they came into the kitchen. They were both crying and at the same time talking about what they had to do in preparation for Granny's funeral. "You will have to cycle around and tell the neighbours, Paddy. Go to Six-Mile-Bridge post office and have a telegram wire sent to Galway to tell Maggie's mother, and you will need to send word to our sister Margaret/Margie in America. They will do that in the post office too. And go to Oatfield and let the priest know, tell the neighbours to pass the word around. There's men working on the road, let them know; they will tell passers-by." (Word sent in those years to America on the death of a family relation was sent in a black rimmed envelope; the receiver would know immediately that a close relation had passed away.) Aunt Margie told me she knew the moment she saw the black border of the envelope, that she would never see her mother again. "It was a black day for me, Peggy."

There was a lot of preparation going on making ready for Granny's wake and funeral. A bed for my mother, and my two brothers, a cot for the baby, when they arrived from Galway. Someone went to Limerick and brought home a long orange box. Aunt Mary tucked a blanket around the insides of it and put a pillow in the bottom, then she said, "A cot fit for any baby," and stood back to admire her handiwork. Uncle Paddy went to Limerick with the pony and trap to meet Mam and family. It was only when they were coming in the door that I was told who they were. I didn't know them, for I was only two years old when I was brought to Clare in 1935. My mother was crying. Aunt Mary took the baby from mother and placed her in the orange box which was now a baby's bed. Mother went back to the room behind the fire to where Granny was laid out in a brown shroud. She also wore the brown Carmelite Scapular, which was the tradition for many years. (We would be enrolled in the brown Scapular on our first Communion Day and wore it always as a pledge of our salvation; somewhere along the way, this sacred habit ceased.)

Granny's nieces, Mary and Brigid Boland, prepared a meal for Mam and the children. I stood staring at the two boys. Being shy, I was keeping my distance. Mam took my hand and said, "You have grown since I saw you last. I'm your mother and this is your baby sister, Mary. She is just three months old." I couldn't take my eyes off her. I had never seen a small baby before. The two boys are your brothers, Eddie and Paddy. Now Maggie, you have met us; what do you think?"

I was mesmerised and just six years old. I now had a family, two brothers and a baby sister. She then got Eddie and I to shake hands; he was just as shy as I was.

Aunt Mary encouraged everyone to sit into the table and eat; "I'm sure you are all starving." Neighbours were sitting in the bedroom where Granny was laid out on her bed. The women were sniffing a yellow powder up their noses, a yellow dribble would drip down their chins and they would wipe it off with pieces of rags. When no-one was looking, I took a pinch and sniffed it up my nose; I almost sneezed my head off. Aunt Mary was cross with me. "Were you at the snuff?" she scolded. One of the women said, "It will do her no harm."

After they had finished eating, Eddie and I went outside to play. We really got to know each other. He was nine and he told me that he had a sheepdog at home and they would go hunting for rabbits. "What would you do with the rabbits?" I asked. "Mam would clean them and cook them for dinner."

"I wouldn't eat a rabbit," I said, making a face. Eddie insisted I would love the soup. We had great fun playing with the two sheepdogs.

GRANNY'S COFFIN

Granny's coffin was placed in a horse-drawn hearse. Family members came behind in two horse-drawn buggies. So many people were shaking hands at the St. Vincent de Paul Oatfield chapel. The priest saying Mass gave a talk about Granny on how she reared a family of seven on a small farm in Kilnacree by herself after the sudden death of her husband, Michael, in 1920. Her youngest son, Paddy, was only eleven years old at the time. After the Mass, everyone went to the graveyard in Broadford where she was buried with her husband Michael, our granddad, whom we never knew. Soon, everyone was packing to go home after the funeral. I was very lonely to see my family leave. Promises were made that we would soon meet again. "Indeed we will," said Aunt Mary.

I was very lonely for my mother, who was crying a lot. I remembered her the most. When things settled down, and Aunty and I were on our own, I asked her "Why was my Mam crying so much?"

"She has a lot of troubles Maggie. When you are older, she will tell you," was her answer. Aunty and I had slept in the same room as Granny. When it came time for me to go bed, I didn't want to go into the room. Aunty made up a small bed in the room for me next to the window and facing the door; she fixed Granny's bed for herself. "We will be alright now." she told me. "Granny is in heaven, so go to sleep, Maggie." In my sleep, I could see Granny sitting by the fire. I woke up calling "Aunty, Granny is not dead at all, she is sitting by the fire."

"You have been dreaming, go back to sleep," came her reply. I went to sleep and again had the same dream. I got up and went to see if she was sitting in her old chair, but it was vacant. I sat down on it. When Aunty came to find me, I was fast asleep. "You miss her, don't you? I miss her too Maggie, and so do we all."

"Is she really in heaven?" I asked.

"She is. You stay there and I will make the stirabout. You will feel better after you eat."

1940 - FIRST HOLY COMMUNION

At the age of seven, I made my first Confession and Holy Communion in St. Vincent De Paul Chapel, Oatfield, County Clare. Aunt Mary brought me to Limerick to buy my First Holy Communion dress, veil and everything necessary in white for First Holy Communion, except for black patent leather shoes with silver buckles. These shoes were called 'Hornpipes'. "Why do you want hornpipes?" Aunty asked, "Because that is what Maureen wore for her First Communion," I answered. While getting dressed on the morning of my First Holy Communion and wearing my First Holy Communion medal on a chain around my neck, I felt very important. Aunty had put my hair in ringlets, using rags to wrap each one. In the morning, they fell on my shoulders; just beautiful. Maureen O'Neill's brother Pa brought her on the bar of the bike as far as Uncle Paddy's. She was coming with us in the pony and trap to see me making my

First Communion. She sat next to Uncle Paddy in the trap. Aunt Mary and I sat on the opposite side. Aunty was telling Maureen she was going to take me to Limerick on Saturday to have my photo taken and send it to my mother. "She will love to see Maggie in her First Communion dress." They talked about Granny, how sad it was she hadn't lived to see me on this great occasion. She had passed away the year before. I was happy thinking of another day in Limerick and eating in a restaurant. After Mass, some people gave me coppers or pennies and Maureen gave me a shilling. Aunt Mary was saying, "That is too much Maureen."

"Why are people giving me money?" I asked.

"Because it is your First Holy Communion day."

"Oh! Can I spend it when we go to Limerick on Saturday?"

"You can, but buy something nice," Aunty said.

First Holy Communion – Confession box

SHOWING OFF MY DRESS

Aunty Mary promised we would visit O'Neill's the next Sunday. "I'll dress you up in your First Communion dress for Mrs O'Neill to see." I was very excited about this. 'Knock, knock' on the door. Mrs O'Neill, on opening it, was full of amazement. "Mary where did you get this lovely angel?"

"Mam," said Maureen, "that's Maggie, the First Communion girl."

"Oh, you look like a little angel, come in until I get a good look at you."

Giving me a birdie (kiss) on the cheek, she pressed half a crown (of money) into my hand, which I was shy to take.

"Open up your little purse and put it into it."

I whispered, "Thanks."

"Sit into the table and have the tea," said Mrs O'Neill. There was lovely homemade sponge cake and biscuits, and Mrs O'Neill placed a tea towel across my lap to keep my dress clean. "There now, eat up," and I did. Maureen and I played snakes and ladders, it was great fun. Then Maureen showed me her first Holy Communion photo you are wearing hornpipe shoes like mine, I am Maggie;There was a lot of chat going on between Mrs O'Neill and Aunt Mary as they sat by the open hearth fire. Walking out the road home, Aunty said, "You have a lot of money now to spend on Saturday." I was wondering in my mind what I would buy, I had never bought anything before.

Showing of my dress: Maureen O'Neill, Margaret Abberton

O'NEILLS HOUSE

Maureen lived with her parents and three brothers in a cosy thatched house, situated at the bottom of the mountains. The road to her house was a dirt road stretching two miles from the main road. Several streams ran down the mountain and across the road. Watercress grew in abundance around the streams. People from Limerick would come out to gather the watercress. As a natural-grown plant, it was known to have healing properties. In the winter the road would be flooded; the only way to get through was by horse and cart. The O'Neill house was surrounded with fuchsia and rhododendrons, and around the door was an arch of rambling pink roses. Inside, it was a true, welcoming country farmhouse, with gleaming, white-washed walls and an open fire. The Sacred Heart picture was on the wall and the little Sacred Heart lamp hung in front of it, forever lighting, with its red globe giving off a welcome glow. This was typical of every home in Ireland in those times. The dresser was laden with platters and a variety of delph. Hanging on the chimney was the shot gun, and to the side was Pa's fiddle, upon which I often heard him play many lively tunes.

1941 - THERE WERE CHANGES

Coming to Kilnacree, Granny had left the house and farm of land in her will to Uncle Paddy, who was now making plans to get married.

Aunt Mary and I moved out to grand-uncle Mick O'Mara's old house (grand-Uncle Mick was a twin brother to Granny Hurley; he outlived her by about fourteen years). He lived alone and would be glad of our company. Aunt Mary packed all her possessions into boxes, including the hens and chickens and also the ducks. They were all loaded up on the horse and cart. I made sure that my doll, in her shoebox bed, was coming too. The geese were marched out the road to this old house, a half a mile away. It was a very old two-story house, dark and scary. I was unhappy about the move. The gramophone, with its big horn, needed special packing, so this was another trip. "I don't think I will be winding it up any more," said Aunty sadly. "No more Sunday evening house dances Maggie."

"Why?" I asked. She made some excuse about the kitchen floor.

Aunt Mary didn't have the time to give much heed to my complaints; she had a lot of work in getting accustomed to the change herself. Her fowl were upper-most in her mind. The hens, geese, and ducks needing housing; there were plenty of old sheds, but they were in need of doors and perches. The ducks were my worry, as they were used to wandering off all day, coming home in the evening and making straight for their shed. "They won't know where to go when they come back in the evenings," I complained. Grand-uncle Mick said he would be on the look-out for them. "Don't worry; ducks have a good sense of finding their own way," he said. There was one happy situation about living in Reinaskomoge; Maureen and I were nearer to each other now.

Among the many enjoyable memories I had from Kilnacree was the haymaking season. Aunty would send me out to the meadow to bring Uncle Paddy his bottle of tea, a couple of slices of soda bread, and a wedge of bacon wrapped in newspaper placed in a cardboard box. "I'm ready for this!" he would say. When he was finished eating, he would light up his cigarette. Then he'd teach me a song, 'The Ould Bog Road'. I wasn't to tell anyone I knew the song. By the time winter came and the fireside stories and sing-song sessions started, I too would have a party piece.

HONEY BEES

There was a new excitement in Reinaskomoge that I wasn't aware of before. It was the swarming of the honey bees. They would be buzzing loud up in the trees. Grand Uncle Mick, with Uncle Jimmy would wear hats with nets on their heads and down over their faces; they looked a bit frightening to me. It was a lot of work, coaxing the bees down into the beehive boxes. Aunty and I watched from a safe distance behind a wall, with a warning not to make a sound. Uncle Jimmy was talking about the yield of honey they would get this year. Honeycombs would be removed from the hives and placed in curtain nets hung on stallions (a wooden frame without shelves), to let the honey drip into dozens of basins, then potted and sold in the Limerick market.

CHANGING SCHOOLS

"My next job," says Aunty, "is to meet the parish priest in Six-Mile Bridge and get you changed into school there."

"I don't want to change to a different school, it's an awful long walk from here," I said. It was indeed a long walk for a little one of eight years old. Five miles down to Six-Mile-Bridge and five miles home uphill, ten in all. In the morning, I left home at eight a.m., to be in school by nine thirty. When I first started, Aunty would walk a distance with me. School day was over at three p.m. I was told to be at Collins's house when the Cratloe hooter with loud hoots signalled for the woodcutters to finish their work at five o'clock. I would be almost home then after walk, walk, and walk. Bridget and Michael Collins were about my age and went to the same school. I would be with them most mornings but they were in different classes to me, so we would miss each other for coming home. On my way up to the school through Six-Mile-Bridge town, there was a house with a lot of steps up to the front door. The family who lived there had children about my age, who I discovered were my first cousins. But, because of a family dispute I was forbidden to speak to them. One of the girls would stand on the top step and wave to me. I would put my head down and keep on walking like I was told to do. Years later, the same cousins are now my very good friends. I never found out the reason why such a harsh punishment was put upon us. With the passing of time, things did settle down. I got used to the house and it wasn't so scary at all. It was summer time and I was on school holidays. I had persevered for two years walking the ten miles, five to and five from, school. In the winter time I missed a lot of school days, and it must have been a big worry to Aunt Mary as she would say, "You are getting no schooling." The worst sickness I got while I was living there was the mumps.

1942 - SET DANCING

There was a little cottage just up the road from O'Mara's house. It was known as the nun's house. Two women who had lived there had long since left it. A local farmer had a key to it. One Sunday Aunty said, "Do you hear the music Maggie?"

I said, "It's coming from the nun's house." Taking my hand, she said, "Come on, I think someone is holding a bit of a dance there." Sure enough, locals had come with their musical instruments. They were about to start the Clare half-set and Aunty was first on the floor, dragging me with her. I did my best to follow her steps. When it was finished, she said, "Now Maggie, you will know it the next time." There was no next time for me for I ran home. On Sundays, Aunty would rush the dinner and the washing-up to be ready in time for the céili. "Are you coming Maggie?" I'd shake my head. "Keep an eye to her," she would say to grand-uncle Mick, "until I get back." Uncle Mick would sit and read the Sunday paper then fall asleep; the paper would slip down onto the floor by his side, while I played with my doll, making her bed over and over again in the shoe box.

MY WHITE COW

When we lived in Kilnacree one of the cows was pure white; she was my cow, not because of her colour, but because she was so docile. She would hold her head down for me to rub it and stay standing quietly. Out in the field she would walk behind me. I just loved her and missed her when we moved to O'Mara's.

It was winter time and a very thick mist had descended down over the mountains. I vaguely remember someone coming to O'Mara's half door and shouting, "Quickly, you're needed at Hurley's." Aunt Mary and Uncle Jimmy put old coats and caps on and hurried out the door. Grand-uncle Mick was left to mind me. We looked at each other. "What's wrong?" I asked.

"I don't know, but whatever it is, it has to be bad," said my grand-uncle, "and the weather that's in it." He took out his rosary beads and started to pray, "God bless the people this night and grant no harm will come to anyone."

"There is no news coming, it's very late and you should be in bed. I will light the candle and you get ready, call me when you're in bed." I called him, "I'm in bed now." He looked in the door at me, "Say your prayers and go to sleep. Whatever has happened, we will hear about it in the morning." Then he quenched the candle. "Good night Maggie," he said.

"Good night Mick," I said, and soon went to sleep.

VERY, VERY SAD NEWS

Next morning, I raced to the kitchen. The three of them were at their breakfast, but no one was eating or talking. Aunt Mary had tears in her eyes. "What's wrong?" I demanded to know. Still no one spoke. Uncle Paddy had been very sick and was in bed a long time. "Is Uncle Paddy dead?"

"No, no, he is fine," said Uncle Jim. I was getting no satisfaction, so I ate my stirabout and went back to bed. An argument started in the kitchen, I could hear Aunt Mary saying, "I haven't the heart to tell her, she was stone mad about that cow." I got out of the bed and stood at the bedroom door, When Aunt Mary saw me, she asked, "Are you listening to us?"

"What has happened to my cow?" I asked.

"Maggie, it is sad news about poor Bessy; she was walking behind the four cows down the hill to be milked and in the heavy mist she didn't see where she was going and fell down a narrow trench. A lot of help was needed to get her up out of it. We couldn't leave her there all night." Uncle Jim was telling me the full sad story. "What is going to happen to poor Bessy now?" I asked.

"We don't know, the vet will tell us today if he can save her."

"If he can save her; is she that bad?" I asked. Before I could take another breath, I began to cry like I had never cried in my nine years.

It was a long day and I was not allowed to see my cow. I lay on the bed and Aunt Mary sat with me. "Here, play with your doll. I have some work to do," she hurried outdoors. The news came: Uncle Jim had been at Uncle Paddy's waiting for the vet to come. I could hear him coming in the door. I waited to hear what he was going to say. Then I got it full belt. "Mary, are you in there? They are taking the cow to the slaughterhouse soon." When he got no answer, he looked into the bedroom and saw me lying on the bed. "Maggie! Jesus, what have I done? Her aunt will kill me," I could hear him say when leaving. The argument coming down the yard was loud. Aunty was saying, "Could you not wait?"

"No, of course not." As they came in the door, I was standing in the kitchen. "You heard everything?"

I nodded my head, "Is Bessy dead?"

"She died quietly during the night," said my Aunt. "Now Maggie, get dressed and we will go over to see your Uncle Paddy and Anne."

Walking over the road, Aunty is telling me not to cry, "They are feeling sad about it being your cow, but that is how things go." They were both in the kitchen. Looking at me, Uncle Paddy said, "She was a great cow and a great milker." For some reason, I didn't cry or even feel like crying.

"Are you better now, Uncle Paddy?"

"Indeed he is not," said his wife, "he shouldn't be out of bed."

"I'll go back now," he said. I went with him and sat on his bed a while. As he lay down he said, "Maggie, things happen for a reason, maybe it was meant to be me, but God took Bessy instead."

"I'm glad Paddy, you are alright now?"

"I will be, I need a few more days to get my strength back."

"I was afraid it was you, Paddy," I said to him. Aunt Mary took my hand and, as Annie opened the door for us, she said, "Maggie, Uncle Paddy will be better in a few days, come back then."

I nodded my head saying, "I will."

1943 - NEWS OF A NEW BABY

Born in Kilnacree, Uncle Paddy and his wife Annie had a baby son. I was brought to see him; I loved him and wanted to stay in Kilnacree with him. His mother Annie told me I could come to see him any time. "What is his name?" I wanted to know; "Pa Jo," said Annie. Going back to O'Mara's, Aunt Mary and I were full of talk about baby Pa. Jo.

I had news for some friends in school next day about my new cousin. I could run over the road in the evenings anytime I wanted to, and often stay with the baby while his parents were out milking the cows. I liked the times I was allowed to hold him and feed him the bottle. He would fall asleep and his Mammy would put him in his cradle and I would run out the road home again. I just loved him, me that once hated the sight of a baby.

ANOTHER CHANGE

In 1943, it was the month of July, and my Aunty Mary says, "I'm taking you back to Galway. I had a letter from your mother and she says it's time you got to know your two brothers Eddie and Paddy, and your young sister Mary; she is four years old now. Your mother would like to have you with herself too." "What do you think of that Maggie?" I made no answer; the lump in my throat was almost choking me.

"I know we will miss each other Maggie, we have been together for over eight years". I knew I would be missing my friend Maureen and my baby cousin Pa. Jo too.

"Your mother says that your sister Mary will be starting school and it's only ten minutes walk from the house." I felt a little better hearing that.

"You will be happy to be with your own family, Maggie. It's hard here and the walk to Six-Mile-Bridge is getting too much for you, and you miss a lot of time out of school in the winter time."

"I know, Mary," I said, "I hate it." We gave each other a hug. "When will we be going to Galway, Mary?"

"At the end of the month". I want to see Maureen."

"I know you do; we will go visit them before you go." Maureen and her mother met us at the door, and they put their arms around me. "You are going back to your mother, Maggie. She will be so happy to have you at home with your family." I began to cry. I wasn't sure what to say. "I'm going to be lonely for you."

"You will, and we are going to be lonely for you too. Now, Maureen, make the tea and let ye sit at the table." Maureen's mother dried my tears with the end of her apron. She was a true Irish mother and treated me as one of her own.

SAYING GOODBYE

Saying our goodbyes was giving me a feeling in my tummy I didn't like, especially when it came to Uncle Paddy. In all my young years, he had been a big part of my life; the years that would stand out in my memory. There were tears in his eyes; Annie was standing aside while he hugged me. Then it was her turn. I got to hold baby Pa. Jo. for the last time. I was all choked up to have to leave little Pa Jo. Still, the time had come when I had to go. But it was a surprise to me that my time in County Clare had come to an end.

Uncle Jimmy had the horse and cart ready to take us to Limerick Station, to get the bus to Galway. He had a few parting words to say. "It's hard to see the little one leaving after getting used to seeing her running around the yard for so many years".

"Say goodbye quick, or we will miss the bus," said Aunt Mary. "I'll be back in a few days Jim, so keep an eye to the fowl for me." Now it was Grand-uncle Mick's turn, holding my hand and muttering his last words: "I don't think we will meet on this earth again."

"For God's sake, will you stop upsetting the child, Mick and say your goodbyes!" shouted Aunty. He hugged me into his flannel shirt, where he had dribbled some soup down on it. Aunty grabbed my hand, and then lifted me up on to the cart. The last I saw of him, he was walking in that bent way with his two hands behind his back as he headed over to the Haggard.

THE JOURNEY

In the bus, it felt very long. After getting off at the bus depot in Galway, we climbed on to a horse-drawn sidecar or 'back-to-back' with four other people who never stopped arguing about horses for the rest of the journey to Ballybrit. It was the two-day races in Ballybrit.

I was confused with all the coming and going of people to my mother's house. I was only ten years old and knew nothing about the Ballybrit Races. My mind was full of meeting my sister, who was no-way like me. She was four years old and had the most beautiful long red curly hair, which, in time I loved to brush. My two brothers had changed too, looking older than when I had seen them at Granny Hurley's funeral. Mother hugged me but she seemed to be very busy making tea for a lot of people. I asked Eddie "Is your house a restaurant?" He laughed, "Mam does this for the two race days; she makes a few pounds to help pay bills." I had never heard of bills, except the goose's bill she ate with.

BROKEN HEARTS

As Aunt Mary was leaving to go back home to County Clare we hugged until I thought our hearts would break.

Week after week I cried in bed. I missed my cat and dog, Shep. I missed the horses, the rattle of the cartwheels on the cobble stones, the lift to Mass in Six-Mile-Bridge and the Saturdays to Limerick in Uncle Paddy's pony and trap, and also the milking of the cows. Above all, I missed Maureen; I was missing it all so much I wanted to go back to Kilnacree. I was tempted to run away some night and find my way to Clare. I had no idea of which road to take. My poor mother put in a hard time consoling me, especially when she discovered I went to bed early for the sheer purpose of crying. "Maggie, I want you to help me put the geese into the shed and make sure all the hens are in too."

"They are all in, Mam."

"Did you count them? You need to count them. If one is still out the fox will get her."

"I will count them now."

"How many did you get?"

"I counted thirty."

"Very good." From then on it was my job to help mother every evening to see the fowl were locked up for the night. There was also the rosary to be said, and I had the decade after Eddy to say. My crying stopped. Looking back, I think my mother was a genius for figuring out a way to ease my loneliness.

AUGUST

Mother was sitting on a chair in the kitchen with a letter in her hand and the tears were running down her face. I walked over to her. "What is wrong?" I asked. "Thank God you are here!" She said through her tears. "An accident," she said, "A bad accident. Your Aunt Mary fell of her bicycle as she was going to Mass on the fifteenth of August, and one of the spokes from the front wheel went into a vein in her leg. She would have bled to death but for Pa O'Neill finding her. He was on his way to Mass in the pony and trap. He stopped the bleeding by tying his tie tight around her leg and got her into the trap, then he took her to Six-Mile-Bridge to the doctor, where they both put her into the doctor's car. She was unconscious. The guard's barracks was near, and the doctor ran and told them a car was needed, that an accident had occurred and he needed to rush the patient to Limerick Regional Hospital. One of the guards put on the siren and your Aunt was rushed in. She is alive but she doesn't know where she is." I started to cry.

"Who is the letter from, Mam?"

"Your Uncle Jimmy. That's a week ago now." Then another letter came with worse news. Aunt Mary had lost her mind and was in Ennis Mental Hospital. "Jim wants me to go see her and bring you with me. When she sees you she might snap out of it."

AN EYE-OPENING EXPERIENCE

Going to Ennis on the bus, Mother was explaining to me as best she could, "Don't take any notice of Aunt Mary if she doesn't know you, the shock of the fall off her bike and the loss of blood must have upset her whole system." Of course, I understood nothing of what she was saying. This was a bad time for both my mother and me. Poor Aunt Mary didn't know either of us. The nurses were nice and one gave me a sweet that I wasn't able to eat. Was this the Aunt I lived with? Why doesn't she know me? Aunty sat quietly with her head down and not talking to anyone. This was not the way I knew her. "You go home now and take the little one with you," said the nurse who was talking to Mom.

"We will keep you informed of your sister's progress."

"That's a terrible place, Mam," I said.

"It is Maggie. Are you hungry? I would love a cup of tea, I thought they would give us one, but they were busy. I couldn't ask them to make tea for us. I don't have much money; not enough for a restaurant." As we walked through Ennis, Mam said, "I'm going to knock at this door and maybe we will get a cup of tea here."

The lady of the house said, "I don't serve teas." But after Mam explaining our situation, the lady brought us into a lovely little parlour. "How much money do you have?" She asked. "Three shillings," said Mam.

"I will make you a small pot of tea and a slice of buttered bread each." Mam was grateful to the lady. When she brought the tray of tea to the table there was four small biscuits on it. Mam wouldn't let me take one in case we had to pay she didn't have the price of them. The lady came in just as we were finished eating and Mam went to hand her the three shillings. As she was taking it, she asked, "Do you like biscuits?" I said, "I do."

"Then take them with you." We thanked her. We kept the biscuits to eat on the bus.

BRIARHILL SCHOOL

It's September, and I'm holding my sister Mary's hand going the short walk to school. It gave me a grown-up, sisterly feeling. Eddy introduced me to the schoolmaster, Tom Donnellon. He shook hands and welcomed me by my Irish name 'Mairead'. He asked one of the girls to show me to my desk next to Maureen Egan, who lived near us. We became friends and I settled into this new life.

Brier Hill School, I'm wearing the apron with straps.

1943 - THE LETTERS THAT NEVER CAME

The letters from Aunt Mary telling the news about Baby Pa Jo and my dog and cat never came. Coming in from school, I would ask Mam if there was a letter for me. Her answer was always no. One day, she had a letter from Uncle Jimmy. He wrote to explain he was roofing churches in Limerick and was getting home very late in the evenings. With the weather getting wintry, he would be staying the weeknights in digs in Limerick, and it would be impossible for him to take care of Mary's fowl. "I got a man to take them all away, especially the geese (Aunt Mary was very proud of her geese. At Christmas time she would kill, pluck and truss them and have them ready to sell at the Limerick Christmas market). Ould Mick is in poor health; he won't go outside the door for the winter. In fact, I think he has forgotten all about the fowl." He continued; "I went to the hospital to see Mary; it was the first time she showed signs of knowing me."

Mother said, "That gives us hope." Then she told me to write a letter to Maureen O'Neill. "I will," I said. I sat down one Sunday after Mass and spent the day writing half a page to Maureen.

EYE OPERATION

I had what was called a cast in my right eye. It was turned into the corner by the side of my nose and didn't move like the left one. I also wore glasses. Mother took me to the Central Hospital Galway to meet an eye specialist who was known to be the best. His name was Dr. Conor O'Malley. I was admitted to the eye section for an operation to straighten my eye. I was taken to theatre by a nurse who was telling me what a brave girl I was, "There is nothing to be afraid of, you will be asleep and won't feel a thing. Good girl, climb on to the table and lie flat."

As I lay flat on my back looking up at the ceiling, a very strong light was shining down on me. The nurses asked me to put my hands down by my sides. Then I felt them strapping down my arms and legs tight to the table. Before I could ask, "What are ye doing?" A soft cloth was placed over my mouth and drops from a bottle were slowly coming into my mouth. I wanted to call my mother and tried kicking to get away, but I could do neither. The last I saw was that big light coming down closer to me. I was given Ether to put me to sleep. It was an awful experience, especially as no one prepared me for it. Five days after the operation, Dr. Conor O' Malley removed the bandages from my eyes. He asked me what I could see. I said, "Two of everything." He then said to nurse Shaughnessy, who was always with him, "We should be able to remove the bandages permanently in a few days; it will take a while for the double vision to go."

"The operation is a success. I will be back in a day or two, Margaret," he said, as he patted me on the hand. I was very happy to hear that I would be able to see again. One night, when everyone was settling down to sleep, a nurse came and said, "Margaret, we need your bed, I have a mattress on the floor for you. You won't mind sleeping with another little girl." I was upset but could say nothing, and so the nurse put me down on the mattress. Lying flat down, I tried to find a pillow, but there was none. The top of the mattress was raised on the heating pipes that ran along the bottom of the wall. I couldn't sleep. The girl I shared this type of a bed with, said, "Did the nurse tell you we are not to tell that they are giving our beds to others and taken us out of them at night?"

"No," I said. She then went to sleep. As it happened, a nurse would come in in the mornings to check my bandages and get me back to my bed as fast as she could. Because of the bandages, I never got to see who slept in my bed for the night. But this one morning, nurse Shaughnessy herself came in early. She shouted at the nurses, "Who took that child out of her bed, and put her on a mattress on the floor and without a pillow, after a serious eye operation? She should not have been disturbed. Whoever did this, I hope for your sake there is no damage done." Then she picked me up and carried me to the bed. Before putting me down, she ordered a nurse to change my sheets. "What nurse took you out of your bed?"

"I don't know, nurse." I did know her voice, but I was too afraid to tell. It was three days before Dr. O'Malley came to remove the bandages. My body was sore from sleeping on crumbs, my bed had not been changed since the night on the floor; someone must have blamed me that I told about the bed swap. Dr. O'Malley and nurse Shaughnessy came to remove the bandages. "She can stand on the floor while we do this," said the doctor. When nurse Shaughnessy went to help me out of the bed, she saw the sheet full of crumbs and said, "Excuse me." She called a nurse to freshen up my bed. The crumbs went flying everywhere. Dr. O'Malley very slowly removed the bandages, there were some other doctors looking on. "Don't mind these men in white Margaret, I'm showing them the success of your eye operation, we will leave the bandages off. Can you still see two of everything?" he asked.

"No, doctor," I answered. Nurse Shaughnessy helped me back to bed. I could see everything. Some nurses came to talk to me and were very happy that I could see. But I never heard the voice of the nurse who put me sleeping on the floor again. The week before I left the hospital, a lot of tests and exercises were done on my eyes. Dr O'Malley held up a mirror for me to see my eye. "What do you think of your eye now Margaret?" he asked.

"It's all red, doctor."

"It is, but do you see that your eye is not turned into the corner any more?"

"I see that now," I answered. "I won't be called crocked eyes anymore in school."

"You poor little girl, was there a lot of name calling?"

"Yes, doctor."

"You can go home now. There is no need for you to wear glasses, your sight is perfect."

Mother was so happy to be taking me home. She thanked the doctor and nurses for all they had done for me. Nurse Shaughnessy came to the ward, just as we were about to leave and handed me a small box of chocolates. I was reluctant to take it. "Here Margaret, this is a little something from me; you have been such a good patient."

"Say 'thank you' to the nurse, Maggie," said Mam.

"Thank you, nurse," I whispered. I had never seen a box of chocolates before, never mind having one in my hand. It was four miles to our house. "I'm taking you home in a hackney; you are not fit to walk that far," Mam said. She was also happy I didn't need glasses.

My brothers and sister were happy to have me home and happier still when I gave them each a chocolate. I was tired and Mam put me to bed. The next morning there were red spots on my arms and legs; during the night they got very itchy, they had watery bubbles on them and were very red. Mam went for a neighbour, Mrs O'Flaherty to look at them. She advised her to take me back to the hospital. "I will need to get the hackney again and I can't afford it," said Mam.

"I will get my husband, Mattie to take you in his van," said our good neighbour. He was only too glad to oblige. Going in through the hospital door, we met nurse Shaughnessy. "What is wrong Mrs Abberton?" She asked.

"Look at Maggie's legs and arms, nurse," said Mam. She took us into a room and put me on a stretcher. "What are the spots, nurse?" she asked.

"They are scabies and I am going to put some purple dye on them. It won't sting. Tonight, I want you to make a bowl of starch, let it cool, then cover each one with a blob of it and wrap her legs and arms in bandages for the night. In the morning pull them off quickly and you will take the scabies from the root."

Mattie Flaherty was waiting for us. I was so sick and tired. At home, Mam made me tea and put me to bed. Then she set to work making up the starch like the nurse had told her. It wasn't so bad, and the starch was cool and eased the itch. Came the morning and the painful job took place. Each strip Mam pulled, it hurt. "That's the starch bringing out the root" she said, "and I had to tear up one of my good sheets to do this job." When she was done I said, "Mam, do you remember me telling you I was put into a bed on the floor with a girl? I bet I got them scabies from her."

"It's very likely you did," said Mam, "it's over you now." We both said, 'Thank God.' It was after the Christmas holidays before I was able to go back to school. I was no longer called crocked eyes.

1944 – THE AROMA OF FISH

cooking in mother's kitchen on a Friday hit our noses as we came home from school (meat was not allowed to be eaten on Fridays in those years).

Women would come out early from Galway on Friday mornings, wheeling hand carts laden with fish. They could be heard shouting coming up the road, "Herring's alive and their eyes wide open."

Mother would be waiting at the gate with her 2/6 to buy some mackerel. She would clean them, place them over the boiled potatoes in the pot and there they would cook. It was the meal of the week.

CONFIRMATION

The month of April, Eddie and I made our Confirmations in St. Columba's Chapel, Castlegar. Eddie was fourteen and I was eleven. Mother was worried that I wouldn't be ready for Confirmation for I had missed so much school because of my eye operation. Going down across the racecourse fields and over stiles to the Castlegar Chapel, four evenings a week for eight weeks, was very tiring. We had to know the long and the short Catechism for the religious test before Confirmation. Read a chapter of the Catechism and then explain what it meant to the examiner. There was no end to the pages we had to learn.

The day before our Confirmation we had to answer what we had learned. Canon Hyland examined three of us; it was about an hour of questioning. English was taught in Briarhill School. The Castlegar School did their lessons in the Irish language and Canon Mitchell preferred the Irish speaking school and so he was their examiner. For my Confirmation, mother bought me a nice blue coat and red cap. Eddie had a tweed jacket and grey short pants. We were very proud of our style, going up to Bishop Brown to be confirmed, to kiss his ring and get a slap on the jaw/cheek. He would say some words in Latin and then say, "You are now a soldier of Christ".

After being confirmed, we walked home, up across the racecourse. It was a lovely day. The ceremony was very long and we were starving. Mam made us up a big fry of eggs, rashers, black and white pudding with slices of her home-baked brown bread. It was a delicious meal. Eddie decided it was the last time he would wear a pair of short pants! He said, "I'm a man now" as he put on a pair of long pants. I thought they made him look taller.

MAY ALTAR

It was the month of May. I was thinking of my friend Maureen O'Neill and how the two of us would create an Altar to Our Lady for the Month of May in their kitchen. I told Mam about it. "Do you want to make one?" She asked.

"I do, but I need a small table and there is none."

"Leave it with me and I will find something," said Mam. The next evening when I came in from school she had a small table ready with a floral cloth spread on it. "Oh Mam, that's lovely. Where did you get it?"

"I had the battery wireless left on it and I have put it up safely on a shelf; I put what was on the shelf into a drawer."

"You went to a lot of trouble, Mam."

"I did it for Our Lady and you can set to work now." The first thing I needed was her statue, "I don't have one of her, but I have a holy picture of Our Lady." It showed her with one hand at her heart and the other pointing her finger towards heaven. Next, I found two small brass candle sticks, and two used candles to be lit, only while we were saying the rosary. I needed two vases for flowers. "Here are two little jugs," said Mam, "now get the flowers." That was no trouble as there were plenty of buttercups and daises. I put a little water in and arranged the flowers, then stood back and admired our Altar. We placed our rosary beads in front of the picture. When my brothers and sister saw it, they were between being amused and looking serious. But they soon got used to it, especially when we knelt down to say the rosary in front of it. Each year I would prepare the May Altar with the help of my sister Mary.

May Alter

THE BULLIED GOOSE

Mother always kept four geese for laying and a gander, so that she would have plenty of goslings to rear and fatten up for the Christmas market, where she would sell them and keep one or two for our Christmas dinner. One Saturday she bought a goose to increase her flock. She hadn't expected the rejection this new intruder would get from the resident geese. They pecked and chased her and would not let her near their food pan. "The geese don't want that goose here Mam," I said.

"They will settle down after a few nights in the shed together," she replied.

But it got worse, you could hear the fight going on in the shed, and geese can be very loud. "I can't put her in with them, I will leave her in the hall and you get up early in the morning to let her out so she can eat and have some water, before I let the others out," Mam said.

"As soon as they see her, they will kill her, Mam."

"I will put her into their shed until they go up the field for the day. We will keep her down here near the house, they might get used to her after a while."

WHOOPING COUGH

Mother was thanking God that I didn't have the whooping cough when I was getting ready for my Confirmation. I would get a bad fit of coughing occasionally; gradually it got worse. It was the month of May and every year about this time a family of tinkers/travellers would come with their little horse and covered-wagon, and each year there would be another baby. They would stay a few weeks at the end of the road near the water pump in Ballybane, close to a row of houses known as the ten cottages, where they would beg for milk for their baby and ask for bread for the breakfast. The people would hand them whatever they requested. They never caused any trouble but loved music.

The father played the accordion. I loved listening to it, and one evening I asked my mother if I could sit out on the wall to listen to the music. "You can," she said, "but dress warm and don't stay there long."

It was getting dark and Mam told me to come in. She made me a mug of cocoa and told me to go to bed. She had put a hot water bottle in the bed, it was cosy. I was glad to be told I didn't need to stay up for the rosary. Early morning, I got up and let the goose out, then I went into the kitchen to get a drink of water, but when I tried to swallow a mouthful I couldn't. I called Mam and told her I could not take a breath without pain in my back. "Go into bed and I will make you hot tea."

No, I could not swallow. As the day went on, I got worse. Mam told Eddie to cycle into town for Doctor Powell, to tell him how sick I was. Doctor Powell came and listened to my chest. "She has double pneumonia," he said. He gave Mam some large penicillin tablets and told her to give me a whole one every four hours with a drink of water and to make sure I stayed in bed. Mam could not keep me in bed, I wanted up every few minutes and I was unable to swallow the tablets. Mam sent Eddie for our good neighbour, Mrs Flaherty. She came running. She told Mam to send Eddie for the priest, and she would get her husband Mattie to go for the ambulance. Mam was weak with worry. Fr Maroney, the Parish Curate of Castlegar, anointed me saying: "This will make you strong Margaret." While praying over me, he made the sign of the cross on the palms of my hands, on my forehead and on the soles of my feet with oils of crissum. The ambulance came and two men brought me out on a stretcher. I was looking around; everything seemed strange to me. One man put his hand on Mam's shoulder saying: "She will be alright Mrs Abberton, we will look after her." Mam was unable to come in the ambulance with me, but the last image I had of her, she was saying goodbye to me and crying.

It took days for the doctors to get me through the crisis; I was told my mother came to see and talk to me, but I kept asking her who she was.

At last, I was drinking milk. The nurses took me out to stand on the floor; I felt pins and needles going up through my legs and after a few more times standing on the floor, they could finally take me for walks down the corridor. Then one day a nurse said, "We want you to get up yourself today and go to the toilet, take your walk on your own. We will be with you, but you must do everything on your own." From then on, I was getting stronger. After four weeks in hospital, I was sent home in the ambulance. My poor mother was the happiest woman in the world. The house looked so strange to me. Mam said, "It's because you were in hospital for so long." My sister Mary wanted to sleep with me, but Mam thought it better I to sleep on my own.

Eddie worked for the local farmers and when he came home that evening and saw me, he said, "God Maggie, I thought you were never coming home."

"Well here she is," said Mother. Something occurred to me. I said to Eddie, "Before I got sick, I think I was minding a goose; was that a dream?"

"No, it was real alright."

"Is she still here?"

"Mam said I was not to tell you, but we had an early Christmas dinner."

"Ye ate my poor goose!"

"Shhhh, don't let on I told you," he said. That first evening, my sister, two brothers and I played a game of cards, but after one game of old maid I got tired. I went to sleep while they still played. Mam peeped around the bedroom door, "You won't be going to school until September, Maggie, you will be good and strong by then." My daily tonic was a glass of half milk and half stout to build me up. I drank it, but hated it.

1945 - COOKING CLASS

It was announced at Mass that a cooking class would be set up in the old school in Castlegar. Mother asked me, "Would you like to join it?"

"I would love to," I said.

"You will need to go on Friday evening to get instructions." The ages ranged from twelve to fifteen. Our first lesson was how to make custard. We were given a list of items, a tablespoon, some custard powder, a little sugar and a half pint of milk, a bowl to mix the custard in and a little saucepan to cook it in. I had all my ingredients and felt very pleased with myself. The cooking would be done on an open fire in the grate. The fire was already on when we arrived at the school. I didn't know it, but a couple of girls would be selected each week to set and light the fire. This would not be one of my good points. Each one had to wait her turn to do her cooking. When my turn came I tried to get my custard to thicken, but I failed. My friend and neighbour, Maureen Feerick made a nice pot of custard. The tutor said I had put too much milk in mine. When I arrived home mother laughed at my saucepan of milk. She added more custard powder and made a lovely thick bowl of custard.

"What are ye doing next Friday?"

"We are making a soda bread Mom, I have to bring about two cups of white flour, one cup of brown, a half teaspoon of bread soda and a mug of buttermilk in a bottle and bring a bowl to mix the ingredients in and then bring our soda cake home and bake it."

The following Friday's cooking class, I brought my bread home for baking. Mother was pleased with how nice I had rounded off the bread and cut the cross on it. She placed it on the baking tray and put it in the oven. No matter how long we waited, it wouldn't rise. It was then we found the bread soda still in the paper bag. It was the end of the cooking class for me.

LEARNING STEP DANCING

A couple of older girls said at school they were going to teach Irish dancing in the old School. I was allowed to attend. First, we learnt the one, two, and three.

I was good at the steps, but when it came to learn the three-hand reel, I kept going the wrong way around. I was replaced. Then it was the two-hand reel. Maureen Feerick was my partner. I went just so far in that too and again lost my spot. I went home crying to mother. "You're not going anymore," she said. "Get a basin of water and wash up the delph, do something useful about the house," she ordered. I unwillingly obeyed her.

1946 - APRONS ARE NOT WORN IN TOWN SCHOOLS

At the age of thirteen, mother changed me from Briarhill School to the Convent of Mercy in Galway town. My friend Maureen Egan was starting on the same day as me. I was already with my school bag waiting at my gate for Maureen. As she approached me she said, "Is that an apron you are wearing?"

"It is," I said. "Mam bought it on Saturday."

"They don't wear aprons in the town schools, you should take it off or they will all laugh at you in the class." I quickly pulled it of and threw it into the kitchen. "Thanks Maureen for telling me, I don't want to get laughed at on my first day." It was a three mile walk to the Convent of Mercy in Galway town. Maureen and I were in the same Fifth Class. Sr Mary Borrgea was our teacher, a lovely nun. The children walking in from the country got her special attention. I used to look forward to most Fridays, when we would have knitting or sewing classes. I learned how to knit socks. Turning the heel was tricky but I managed it. At sewing class, hands had to be washed well first, to keep our test piece of pure-white cotton spotless. Learning to cut out and make a buttonhole was hard work. The stitches must be small and the same length, and after a lot of practice and several new pieces of white cotton, I mastered it. It was among the best on the test table. I also loved the Friday singing class; people that were able to sing could leave their class a half-hour early to join this class. We had a lovely nun for this, she taught us the scales' highs and lows and then we would sing 'veer mè ò'. The Friday evening learning class was algebra; this was the principal's class. She would flounce into the classroom; wearing her long black habit, she was less than five feet tall. Carrying her algebra lesson copy under her arm and the thick slapper, she would go on about the A, B and C's of algebra, and then do a sum on the blackboard. We were to write down its meaning. Most of the class would have their heads down writing. I had no idea what to write. For my lack of knowledge, I would receive a couple of hard slaps across the fat part of my thumb. It would stay swollen for a day or two and I would be unable to use it. After a couple of turns of this treatment, my mother got worried that I would lose the use of my right thumb. She threatened to go into the Convent and 'pull the veil of that nun's head'. I begged her not to, for I would soon be age fourteen and I would finish school.

1947 - SIGNING OFF THE ROLLBOOK

It was permissible those years to leave school at the age of fourteen. On the day I turned fourteen I went to the Principal's office to sign off my name from the register. Some of my friends departed company that year too. Mother had to also come to the Principal's office to sign her name to show she approved of me leaving school at fourteen. As we were walking up the street I said, "Mam, that's the nun who slapped me across my thumb."

She stood up sharply; "Why didn't you tell me before we went into her office? I had the perfect opportunity to tell her what I thought of her and her slapper. I've a good mind to go back."

"Don't Mam; I'm out of there now."

I'M A YEAR AT HOME

Mother thought I was long enough idling my time, so one Saturday after doing her weekly shopping, coming in the door she told me she had news for me.

"Maggie," she called, "I have a job for you!"

"Tell me quick what is it?"

"It's a job minding two children for a family in Roscommon." I felt grown up all of a sudden, me working, making money! Mother sold eggs to a Mrs Mahon, who had a grocery shop in Prospect Hill in Galway. She was the children's granny. I would be working for her daughter, who was married to Mr Tim O'Keeffe, a solicitor in Roscommon. Mrs O'Keeffe cycled out from Galway to our house to see and talk to me. She explained what my work would be and I would be paid £2 monthly. Mam asked, "Could you pay her a little more?"

Mrs O'Keeffe explained all the extras I would have with the two pounds. "She will have her own bedroom and her meals and I will have to train her." Mam just nodded her head. When we were on our own I said, "Mam why did you ask for a bit more money?"

"You will be sending me one pound ten shillings. If you got a few shillings more, you could send me the £2," was her answer.

GETTING READY

Getting ready to travel to a new life and work for wages in Roscommon, my sister Mary was watching me pack. I had some lovely dresses, suits with matching jackets and skirts and blouse all from the American parcels our Aunt Margie sent. I had to have two aprons, including a special one for answering the door. I was feeling very important. I had a warm fawn coat and a green beret, one good pair of shoes and a well-worn pair. I would wear that pair for working and a couple of old skirts and tops. Mother said I was taking too much clothes. "Your case is going to be heavy," she said

Mother carried my case as far as the Tuam Road, where the O'Keeffe's stopped the Roscommon bus for me to get on. I kissed mother goodbye. "Be sure and write soon," she said.

"I will Mam."

I'm on my way to Roscommon and work. I was feeling very happy at age fourteen and a half. I wore one of my special suits, a lovely aqua green colour with four unusual buttons down the front and a cream blouse, black shoes and white ankle socks. Sitting on the bus with Mr and Mrs O'Keeffe were the two children who would be in my care. The little girl was four and the boy was two, they both had lovely curly hair like their mother.

Their house was an old two-story thatched house, the front was covered with ivy. The front door was a heavy, wooden dark brown with brass knocker and latch. It was very quaint. My room was off the kitchen. It was without a window and very dark. I didn't like it and the bed was very low. I guessed I'd get used to it. The first thing I was told to do was put on an apron; there was no time to change out of my nice clothes. Well, I got on with being obedient and doing the work.

MOTHER RECEIVES A LETTER

Soon after I started working, I got a letter from mother telling me she had a received a letter from Aunt Mary's doctor in Ennis. It was telling her that she should come and sign her sister out of the hospital, as it was a pity for her to be in there. She was in perfect health and spent her time knitting for the nurses and serving the evening teas. Mam in her reply said that she'd written to the doctor to tell him she would gladly sign her sister out. As she was signing the discharge document, Aunt Mary said, "I don't want to go back to that house again in Resicamogue."

"You can come and stay with us in Galway," said Mam.

"Well, the blessings of God on you, Bridget," said Mary. "I was afraid I would have to look for digs in Limerick."

Mam filled me in on everything; "She is asking for you. I told her you won't be home until after Christmas. She is in great health, it's hard to believe she is fifty-one years old and with all she has gone through she hasn't a grey rib of hair, and now she is looking for a job. I don't know what sort of work she will do, the only work she ever did was farming. That's my news Maggie." It was easy to tell by Mam's letter that she was very happy.

1949 - A NEW BABY

An increase in the O'Keeffe family came when they had a third baby, a little girl whom they named Mary. Now they had two girls and a boy.

I worked very hard with very little free time, except to go to Mass on a Sunday. One of my jobs was taking the two children to the library every second Saturday. On one occasion the librarian told me to join the library and I could take out three books at a time. I made an excuse that I wasn't good at reading. "Sign your name there," she said so I did.

"You are able to write and you will be able to read." She excused herself and came back with three children's books to me. "Take these and next time you come in, change them and make your own choice at selecting three."

I was very excited telling Mrs O'Keeffe that I had joined the library. She was pleased! "Reading is a great pastime," she said. Going to the library took on a new meaning for me, browsing through the stacks of books. One book caught my eye: 'Little Women' by Louisa May Alcott. This was a lovely story about the four March sisters. I read it over and over.

HOME ON MY BREAK

Going home for my four days off after Christmas was thrilling. It was a freezing cold morning as I boarded the bus in Roscommon for Galway. I didn't feel a bit of it, as I was looking forward to meeting Aunt Mary after all that had happened in the past five years. I wondered how she would look. Walking from Galway to Ballybrit, I thought the road had gotten longer than I remembered. Opening the gate gently, I hoped I could sneak into the house. Peeping around the kitchen door I said, "Surprise!" There was a rush for me; Mam hadn't seen me in five months. But Aunt Mary hadn't seen me in five years. "Here," said Mam, "you go first." Aunt Mary pulled me tight to her bosom in hugs. Mam gave me a quick kiss on the cheek. I said, "Aunt Mary, you have put on weight!"

She laughed, saying, "Middle-age spread." Looking at me up and down she remarked: "You have grown into a young lady. How old are you?"

"I'm fifteen, Mary."

"I wouldn't know you if I met you on the road, Maggie." I thought to myself, 'it wouldn't be the first time you wouldn't have known me.' Then I checked myself, "Don't you be nasty." She looked well and had a job working in the Garda barracks in Eglington Street serving up their meals. She was back to cycling again. Mam told me to say nothing about Auntie's accident.

"Do you go to work everyday?" I asked.

"I do," she replied.

"I don't like the job, so I am looking at the 'Want ads'; something more suitable might come up." The time was short and I had to go back to my job. I hated leaving the cosy, warm atmosphere of Mam's kitchen. Arriving at Abby Town, Mr O'Keeffe and the two children were waiting for me. They were happy to see me back and I was glad to see them too. I settled back into working.

Shortly after my visit home, Aunt Mary wrote to tell me she had got a very good job working in the kitchen of the Agricultural College in Athenry, County Galway. She had accommodation in the college, but cycled home on her day off to see my mother. I was very happy for her.

1950 - AGE SEVETEEN

I was now three years doing housework and nothing was changing for me. I did knit myself a jumper and continued visiting the library and selecting books to read. Mrs O'Keeffe showed me how to break down the hard words to get their pronunciation. Christmas was coming around again and I would be going home to Ballybrit for my four days off in the New Year. I was starting to feel the need of a change, but how? And where?

Aunt Mary was on her New Year's break from the College in Athenry and spending it at Mother's. I stepped off the bus in Galway and walked to Ballybrit. I was thankful it wasn't raining but the cold wind was cutting through me. Going in the hall, I stopped at the kitchen door and listened to Mother, Aunt Mary and my sister Mary talking. I ease the door open and peep in. My sister says: "Maggie is here!" I get the usual big welcome and seasonal greetings. Mother pulls a chair near to the range, and I am glad to sit down. Tea and cake is handed to me. Mother says to Aunt Mary: "Tell Maggie your news." "What news is that?" I asked.

"I got the job as cook in the Agricultural College."

"That is wonderful Mary; it must be hard work cooking for all the young farmers."

"Its plain cooking, the college matron is a great help, and I have a kitchen helper."

"I'm so happy for you Mary." The conversation changed to how I was getting on in O'Keeffe's. As I was getting older and wiser, I knew I needed to better myself. Aunty was appalled at the amount of work I did in a day for a small monthly wage with very little free time. "Would you like a waitress job? There is a vacancy in the college."

"I would love that!" I almost shouted.

"I will put a word in for you, you will need to write to the matron of the college and tell her you're interested in the job."

"I will write straight away," I said.

"When you go back, you will need to give notice to Mrs O'Keeffe."

"I will. Thank you so much Aunty."

1951 - TAKING A BIG STEP

I worked for, and obeyed Mrs O'Keeffe for three years. Now at seventeen years of age I was going to make a change in my life; it was a very big step. One morning after a sleepless night, with all my courage in both hands, I said to myself, 'here goes'. When Mrs O'Keeffe's back was turned to me, I bluttered out, "Mrs O'O' O'Keeffe, I'm leaving!"

"What, Margaret?" It was a shock to her. A bigger shock to me; I had taken the first step in giving my notice, and there was no going back.

"Have you got another job, Margaret?" A hard question; how should I answer? Yes or no? Best to tell the truth.

"I have, Mam."

"Where, Margaret?"

"In the Agricultural College, Athenry."

"Oh! When did you apply?"

"When I was home for holidays."

"How do you know they will keep it for you?"

Answering quickly, with a dry mouth, I said, "My, my Aunt Mary is the cook there; she said they would keep it for me."

"You must give a months' notice here, you know."

Another shock; I was sure I could leave at the end of the week. I felt my knees going weak. "All right Margaret, get on with your work. I will talk to you about this later."

SHE DID TALK TO ME

And at length, I only half-listened. She reminded me of how she had taught me everything when I came to work for her. That I had known nothing about housekeeping. I felt like saying, I was only fourteen.

"The children love you, and of course you love them, they are getting older and you won't have as much work with them, and of course Mr O'Keeffe and I trust you. We were just saying that you were due a pay rise." She paused. "Well, think about what you are about to do; you have a month." There was no more said; she knew I had my mind made up.

PACKING UP TO LEAVE

At night, when the house was quiet, I would parcel up some of my clothes, then when I got a chance in the morning I would go to the post office and post them home. On the morning I was leaving, I made breakfast for the children before they left for school. I had to brace myself to say goodbye to Aideen and Terry. They asked, "Will you be here when we come home after school?"

I said, "I won't." I could see tears coming in Aideen's eyes. Mr O'Keeffe shook my hand as he was going out the door to his office. Hugging baby Mary gave me a twinge of sadness, but I kept strong. Mrs O'Keeffe said goodbye to me at the door and wished me luck; she also had tears in her eyes.

I turned away quickly and went out the gate with my heavy case. I was lonely for the three children, especially baby Mary. I had been showing her how to walk. Walking home from Galway, I was almost dead from carrying the suitcase. Sitting in the kitchen, I said, "Mother, I have taken a stand!"

"You have," she agreed. "When you're rested, take a look in the room behind the fire." When I did I got a shock. "Are all those parcels mine?"

"They are," said Mam, "Look at what it cost to send them. I'm sure half the clothes in them boxes could go in the rag bin."

"I'm sure you are right, Mam. What will I do now?"

"Empty the boxes and put what you don't want into a bag and put it out in the shed. They will come in handy when the painting season starts."

I had a few days at home before starting my new job. I called to see my friend Maureen Feerick to tell her about my new job. She was happy for me, "I'm helping Mam here at home," she said, "I can't get a job."

"Keep trying," I encouraged her. "We will meet up when I come for my holidays."

"We will," she said, "and we might go to a dance in the Hanger in Salthill." "We will, Maureen," I agreed.

I WAS CURIOUS ABOUT MY DAD

"Mam, can I ask you something?"

"Sure you can," she said.

"What is wrong with our Dad?"

"Oh, that's what you want to know? I suppose I should have told you."

She sat down and proceeded to tell how. "During the war he was hit on the head with the butt of a gun one night by a Black and Tan (English Army). He was in hospital for a short time and got better. But it left a bad mark on his nerves, although he continued to work in the marble quarry. In the evening, he worked in his garden. We always had our own vegetables and potatoes. "He was a great worker, Maggie. Suddenly something would trigger him off and he would go for long walks. Then it started getting worse and he would need to get help in St. Bridget's Mental Hospital in Ballinasloe. After a few months, he would be fit to come home. As time went on these attacks came on more frequent and lasted longer, in the end he had to stay in St. Bridget's. When he would feel out of sorts he would tell me to go for the Guards. I would walk in as far as Eglington Street. The Gardaí knew me. A Garda would bring me out to the house in the car, he would have a letter of admittance, which I had to sign and your Dad would go out and sit into the car and wait for the Garda to take him to Ballinasloe for more treatment. And that's it Maggie; he felt safe in there. In time, we thought he would be well enough to stay home, but it never happened."

"I would love to visit him, Mam."

"His doctor advised us, unless he asked for us, that he was to be left alone." We both cried. I was glad I asked.

"Well, you know now," she said as she stood up to continue with her work.

A NEW BEGINNING

My new job working as a waitress in the Agricultural College was a big change from minding children. Having the company of girls my own age was fun. The cook's helper, Maureen Buckley, was from Tuam, County Galway. We became close friends and remained close for the rest of our lives. The year and a half working in the college was a great experience. I learned many new skills in cooking and cleaning. I had plenty of free time and a good weekly wage. I was able to give mother a little more money too. We could go to the pictures on a Sunday afternoon, and dress up in our American style to go dancing in Murphy's Hall. We got a treat from Mr Ruane to attend the Athenry Opera, the 'MIKADO'. It was a good life in the college.

1950 – Age seventeen Maureen Buckley and I in our aprons. Agric College, Athenry, Co Galway.

Me and Aunt Mary Hurley, college cook

1952 - EMIGRATION

Emigration was sweeping the country. And, so I too prepared to immigrate to the USA. I was sad to leave the college. My friend Maureen Buckley had left before me. Before parting, we swapped our American addresses saying we would meet over there. Then it was goodbye for a while. Aunt Mary was pleased I was going over to Aunt Margie, her and Mam's sister. "You will have someone to mind you in that strange country," they said. Back in those years, America seemed so far away, with days of travelling by ship on the ocean. I would be going to the lady who sent all the American parcels home to us. Most of the clothes that came would only fit my young sister Mary, as Aunt Margie's daughter Maureen was the same age as her. "The clothes that came were beautiful," I said to mother one day. "My sister must be the best dressed child in Ireland."

"You got a few nice outfits out of the parcels yourself, Maggie."

"I know I did, I'm not complaining."

MAKING PREPARATIONS

Before I left home, there was much preparing to be done with official papers for the American Consulate in Dublin. It was necessary to have a letter of permission from my parents and a character reference from the Garda and the Parish Priest, also the letter from my Aunt Margaret (Margie) Callaghan who lived in the Bronx, New York. She was sponsoring me out to America.

Aunty had posted a large envelope of information she had received from the American Embassy, on what I must do and what her responsibilities were when bringing a person into the United States. Reading it, was very daunting. However, I had everything ready for the Emigration Consulate and the two-day stay in Dublin and the questioning. I also had to be X-rayed in case there was a history of tuberculosis (T.B.) in the family and questioned if there was a history of insanity in the family.

Before I went to Dublin, mother advised me to explain about my father being in St. Bridgets Mental Hospital, Ballinasloe, in case that information might be in the character reference from the Garda. If I denied it, I could be in trouble. Yes, it was one of the questions that came up. Was there insanity in the family? Remembering my mothers' advice, I explained about my father. The consulate told me they would need a letter from my father's doctor in St Bridget's Hospital explaining the degree of his illness. Until they received that letter they would hold my visa. I was given my passport.

Returning home without the visa was devastating for me. I wrote immediately to the doctor in charge, explaining my situation. He promptly forwarded a good report on my father to the consulate and sent me a copy. I had my visa in less than a week. The date of sailing was the seventh of December, 1952. Miss Kay Fahy of Fahy's shipping travel agency, Bridge Street, Galway, was very helpful to me in booking my passage on the S.S. Franconia ship. She also got me a room in a convent in Dublin for the two nights stay, while I went through the rigors of tests in the American Embassy. She gave me instructions as to the woman I would meet in Dublin to take me to my appointed destinations. Miss Fahy also located a room in Cobh for me for the night before my departure.

She made sure all my papers were in a neat folder ready for when I disembarked in the USA.

SAYING MORE GOODBYES

Before leaving, I went to County Clare to say goodbye to Uncles Paddy, Jack and Jimmy. Jimmy said, "I will be up to Galway to see you before you leave." There was Uncle Paddy's wife, Anne, Cousins Pa Jo and Anna May Hurley, Grand Uncle Mick O'Mara and my dear girlfriend, Maureen O'Neill, together with her mother and brothers. Maureen gave me a gift of a tablecloth of Limerick's famous places. I kept it for fifty years, until it faded. I was very lonely leaving my many friends and family in County Clare for the second time in my life.

Saying goodbyes, Maureen O'Neill holding Sparky, her mother Mrs Ann O'Neill

FAREWELL TO FRIENDS OF THE TEAROOM

Mother reminded me to say goodbye to Mrs Lynskey, who ran a lovely little tearoom on Bridge Street. One was aware of its presence by the display on the window for everyone to see. A small round table with a tablecloth spread over it, and set for tea with pretty cups and saucers. What caught my eye was the unusual teapot. Mother, after her Saturday shopping would go there for her cup of tea and was glad of the sit down, while Mrs Lynskey served her with a pot of tea, homemade brown bread, butter and jam. Mrs Lynskey's daughter, Mrs Costello (Nora) also worked in the tearoom. It was a very busy place. "I am going to town Saturday, Maggie," said mother "and I would like you to come with me. After the shopping is done we will go as usual to Lynskey's tearoom for our tea. I have told them you are immigrating to the States; they would like to see you before you go." It was coming close to Christmas and the tearoom was very busy. We sat at a little table set daintily. I looked around admiring the little tables set with a

Lynskey's tea room.
Bridge Street. Galway City.
Opened pre 1900 -1966

Christmas atmosphere. Mrs Costello's little son John, about the age of four, was sitting on a stool looking at a picture book. Both Mrs Lynskey and Nora came to our table to say their goodbyes to me, wishing me the very best of luck. Nora whispered in my ear: "I have a little something for you." I watched as she reached up to a high shelf where they kept their homemade Christmas puddings. Nora brought down the smallest one, putting it into a brown paper bag, "This is a little going away gift for you Margaret, to have a tea with your friends before you leave." Mrs Lynskey winked her eye at me and whispered, "We don't sell them, but Nora wanted to give you one." I thanked her sincerely. I didn't expect her to give me one of her prized plum puddings. Mam said, "you are too good; I will bring your bowl back the next time I come in."

Apologising for hurrying away, "We cannot stop to talk, you can see how busy we are," Mam and I finished our tea; I had another hug from them. Nora called her son John, to shake hands with me. "She is off to America John." We shook hands and John went back to looking at his book. Outside the door I said, "Aren't they nice people?"

"The salt of the earth Maggie, the salt of the earth," said Mam. I felt like crying.

A LIVE WAKE

Mother held a party for me known as a 'live wake'. This was to give friends and relations a chance to come and say goodbye to the person emigrating. It was a sad occasion, for sailing across the sea was a strange and mighty mystery. It was a foreboding thought; the person leaving might never return home again. My mother played the gramophone. I sang 'A Mothers Love is a Blessing'. Uncle Jimmy sang an old I.R.A. song, 'The Three Flowers'. This was a song which named three patriots 'Men who died for Ireland'. The neighbours gave me little gifts of hankies, Holy medals; one woman gave me the Statue of the Child of Prague. After a lot of jokes about all the dollars I would be making, handshakes, kisses and hugs and the "God speed you, Maggie" were said, the neighbours left. We went to bed for a couple of hours, but the morning came too fast. My brother Eddie hired a hackney to take us to Cobh in County Cork. Uncle Jimmy, who had cycled from Limerick, put his bicycle into the boot of the hackney. We stopped at Limerick and went to Hogan's for tea and met Uncles Paddy and Jack. After more goodbyes, we were finally on our way.

DECEMBER DEPARTURE

On the seventh of December, and after saying goodbye to my mother, brothers and sister in Cobh, County Cork, my heart near broke. The full realisation hit me, I suddenly felt very alone in the world. No time for self-pity now. I had to hurry and find my accommodation. I was sharing a room with three girls who were also emigrating. Early Sunday morning, we embarked on the tender to take us out to the Franconia, a Cunard Liner. It was standing far out on the ocean. The sea was so rough; we were sitting in the tender for half the day, waiting for the sea to abate. Eventually a steward came handing out vouchers, telling us we would not be sailing today. We had to return to our accommodation until the next morning, we should be able to sail then. We were very hungry, having had nothing to eat from early morning. The landlady had hot tea and a big plate of ham sandwiches for us; we were so tired we went to bed after eating.

Next morning, Monday, we were called at four o'clock; we had tea and slices of white bread and butter. It was a nice calm morning, but terribly cold. This time the tender took us out to the ship. The sea was rough, and the waves were bouncing off the sides of the tender. It was very cold. There was no shelter on the tender. We eventually arrived at the ship. Climbing from the tender onto the Gang plank to enter the ship was a shaky experience. Finally, we were on board the Franconia, and some people cheered. A steward showed us to our cabins, a small dark poky little space with bunk beds, a wash hand basin and four pegs on the back of the door for our coats. I was asked if I would sleep in a top bunk. I said, "Sure." A Limerick girl slept in the one under me, a Mayo girl in the other bottom one. We never got to know who the fourth girl was. She was Irish, but kept to herself.

It took ten days to sail the long trip over the rough sea. I was sick the ten days. Many of us were new to sailing, and spent most of our time above deck, hanging over the rails trying to vomit. After five days sailing with the ship rocking from side to side, it finally stopped moving. We were ordered to stay below deck. I got a glance of the sea water rolling in across the deck. I guess I should have been afraid, but I wasn't, "Sure the sailors were there to save us," was my thought. At night, we went to the cabin and climbed into our bunks. One night, I won't ever forget it, was during the night the ship gave a terrible heave and keeled to one side, I hit my head off the cabin wall. If I had gone the other way I would have dropped to the ground and would surely have been hurt or killed. As we were near the dining room, we could hear glass breaking. When we had time to think and talk about it, we realised how dangerous the sea was. It was a frightening experience. At last, the ten days were over and with the stillness; I was able to put a few lines of a poem together.

ANGRY SEA

Staring, out across the mighty sea. Staring as far as the eye could see.
The ship cutting through the waters, leaving a trail of trashed up foam.
Exciting, to see, her cutting through, the calm and the blue.
Deeper and deeper as she sailed along.
While the odd gull soared, with an eerie song.
It was winter time we sailed the tide.
Soon the mighty one, showed her angry side.
As dark clouds, raced overhead.
We were trespassers on her foamy bed.
Breakers clawed the sides of our wooden home.
Creaking and moaning she battled away

Like driftwood bouncing on its way.
Dear God calm this wretch, that we may see another day.
For hours and days, it roared and roared.
Angry waves cut like a sword.
The sea is now our only world
As around the ship we are tossed and hurled.
What will be our fate? Will it e'er abate?
Ah! Stillness, a hush, the old ship heaves and groans.
All is well; once more she's ploughing the balmy foam.
While we gaze at the gentle swell.
And think, one day,'yes we will have a tale to tell.'

17TH DECEMBER, HAVING ARRIVED

At last, disembarking from the Franconia, we are in the USA. My mother's sister, Aunt Margie, her husband Dan and daughter Maureen Callaghan were at the docks to meet me. I recognised Aunt Margie immediately; she was the image of Aunt Mary. They had a great welcome for me; I was the first close relation Aunt Margie met since she emigrated from Queenstown, Cork about 1928/29. This was twenty-three years ago, the years of the Wall Street Crash.

A STRANGE NEW WORLD

Everything was so different. A three-roomed apartment was Aunt Margie's home at the top of a five-story apartment building on Archer Street, Bronx N.Y. It had beautiful furniture with rich pile carpets, couches, armchairs and gorgeous window drapes, and a television; 'movies in the house'! What a novelty. Everyone was going mad to watch the glamour and glitz of Queen Elizabeth being crowned Queen of England.

Another interesting issue, which I took little notice of at the time, was the election of a new President of America. Harry Truman's term of office was up and the constant discussion was who would replace him. Dwight Eisenhower was tipped and was elected November 1953. His wife Mamie, got my attention for her hair style, which was cut short, and she was also known for her bangs (fringe). The hair was brought over the forehead and cut short, then rolled under across the forehead. This hair style captured many ladies' attention, and everyone wanted to be in fashion with wearing the 'Mamie Eisenhower Bangs'. Mamie's dress code got my attention, especially her jackets. The sleeves always came to the elbows. Her suits were my preference though, pencil-slim skirt with a kick pleat at the back, the three-quarter jacket with wide raglan sleeves coming to the elbow. I bought a black wool suit of this style and toned it with long red gloves, matching hat, pocket book (purse) and shoes, a full replica of the White House First Lady. I would change to full matching accessories in colours pink, green, blue or whatever took my fancy (I was not to know then, in my care-free years, that in years to come, this black suit would be worn at a very special and sad funeral. Black accessories would take the place of the bright colours).

I had to get used to climbing the five flights of stairs to reach the apartment. Five apartments occupied each floor. The residents were Irish, German and Italian. Looking out the back windows, all I could see was concrete everywhere, the backs of high buildings, and iron railings. Not a green field anywhere. The smell of diesel hit my nose. Uncle Dan, who was Scotch, was a very nice, kind man, but I found it hard to understand his Scottish accent. He told me the railings were fire escapes. Often you could hear the lids of rubbish bins banging. I thought to myself, "I hate it here, I'll never stay." Aunty seemed to be reading my thoughts. "I felt like that too, when I came over, I was not going to stay. Look at me now, I'm here over twenty-five years and haven't gone back once. When my mother died I had no wish to return, for home was gone then." One day, I overheard Aunty talking to her daughter Maureen; I could hear her say, "I think Peggy would be a more suitable name for your cousin. Margaret is too long a name for such a petite little girl, let's call her Peggy." I liked the name Peggy, so the decision was made. I was now Peggy Abberton.

FIRST CHRISTMAS IN THE USA

My first Christmas was very different from home. The bringing of a fir tree into the apartment and covering it with sparkling decorations was strange to me (at home it was holly and ivy across the mantelpiece, Holy pictures and on the dresser). The crib with the Holy Family was very elaborate. Many gifts were wrapped in colourful paper and left under the tree. The names of the recipients were written on pretty cards and placed on each gift. There were lots of gifts for me.

In comparison to mother's Christmas dinner, which was goose with potato stuffing, vegetables, potatoes, homemade gravy and a mug of giblet soup, which were all home-made products including the goose. (Giblet soup was made from the goose's gizzard, liver, heart and the neck, with onions, barley and porridge oats added to this and boiled for hours. It was delicious), Christmas dinner in America was turkey with bread stuffing, potatoes, vegetables and what I thought was a bowl of jam. When I asked, "Why the jam?" Aunty laughed. "That is cranberry sauce; it's served with turkey; ye don't use it in Ireland?" "No, I never heard of it," I said. "We don't eat turkey; it is goose for Christmas dinner in Ireland." There were also Christmas crackers to pull, with a little toy inside.

My first Christmas was one that I should have enjoyed but I was very lonely. They understood how I felt. "Have a good cry," Aunty encouraged, "let the pent-up sadness flow out." And I did.

JANUARY 1953 - EMPLOYMENT

I got employment straight away as a waitress in a big house in Manhattan. The family's name was Cromwell. Bridget, the cook, was from Armagh and in her sixties. We had many reminiscences to share and got on well together. I wrote to my mother and told her the name of the family I was working for. In her next letter, she let me know she was not impressed.

"How did you get in with Cromwell? Didn't you learn the history of the tyrant Cromwell and what he did to Ireland?" I told Bridget about mother's feelings. Of course she laughed! "Write to her and tell her this family is far removed from Oliver." I did what she said, and thank goodness, I heard no more about Irish history.

ST. PATRICK'S DAY

Here I am in New York City, and hoping I will be let out to watch the St. Patrick's Day Parade. I said to Bridget, "I would love to see the Parade marching up the green line on Fifth Avenue."

"Tell Mrs Cromwell you would like to see it and she will give you the day off." The sun was shining, but a little cold; I stood on the sidewalk (footpath) as the parade marched past. It was a sight to behold. So many school bands dressed in their varied uniforms, cops, nurses, many colourful groups showing artistic displays of dancing, and school girls in pretty short skirts and frilly blouses, twirling batons. All the Irish counties displaying their county's name on magnificent banners, marching in step. I joined in behind the Galway banner and marched up Fifth Avenue. I was so proud and I only three months in the country.

That night, many counties held their County Ball. Aunt Margie and Dan joined with their friends, Felix and Molly McArielle from Armagh. I was taken with them to the Armagh Ball in the Manhattan Centre, dressed up in a pretty white dress and a green bolero. Everyone displayed the shamrock, pinned to their lapel. "What do you think, Peggy?" asked Aunt Margie.

"It's magnificent." I said. I couldn't get over the style of the gowns that the elite committee ladies wore as they stood with handsome men in tuxedos. Up in the balcony, families rented a booth/box. This was an enclosed space with table and chairs facing down on to the dance floor. People brought their own drink and snacks to the box. The night started with a greeting from the Master of Ceremonies. Before the music started for the nights dancing, the pipers in kilts marched around the hall playing old Irish tunes. Then the night started with plenty of dancing. We left the box and went down to the floor, where I got plenty of dances; it was a night of enjoyment.

CONNACHT TRIBUNE

Keeping me up with the news back home, mother would regularly post the Connacht Tribune to me, especially with news of my brother Eddie, having scored a goal or point for his team, the Castlegar Hurlers. Also, a photo of the opening of the new Briarhill School by Bishop Brown.

"Your old school is idle now," she wrote. There was the opening of the Marian Shrine Grotto in Athenry by Dr. Walsh, Archbishop of Tuam, County Galway, in 1952. Another time, a photo of the Castlegar GAA hurling club committee, of which Eddie was a member; it included Fr. J. O'Connor C.C. And not forgetting the one of the Ladies' Castlegar Camogie League, which showed seventeen ladies including my sister, Mary Abberton, and our brother Eddies' wife, Honor.

In one of the Tribunes mother sent was a picture of the Rosary Crusade in the Ballybrit racecourse. Thirty thousand followers came to hear the great Rosarian Priest, Fr. Patrick Peyton, he was delighted with such a turnout. It was proof that the Rosary was a strong prayer in Ireland. I would look forward to getting the Tribune neatly wrapped and left on the hall table among some letters; "Now for a good read tonight," I would say.

OUT IN THE COUNTRY

In the summer, we went out to the Cromwell Country Estate in Morris Town, New Jersey, away from the sweltering heat of the city. It was a beautiful, wild country area. Hundreds of birds were singing from early morning; at night, the crickets took over. I thought I was back in County Clare. Until the skunks gave of their warning stink, then you had to go indoors until it passed. They were beautiful creatures, black and white with a sweeping bushy tail up across their backs.

At night, I would look up at the moon and ask it, "If you are over Ballybrit now, tell Mam I'm doing well, goodnight moon." At that time of night, it would be daytime in Ballybrit. Getting a letter from Uncle Paddy's wife, Anne always meant a good read. I ran upstairs to my room wondering what news she had this time. Anne had lots of news, but the one piece that hit me was the death of my grand-uncle, Mick O'Mara, fourteen years after his twin sister, our granny died. He was eighty-six.

"Your Uncle Jimmy found him dead. He died as he lived Maggie, quietly in his bed," she wrote. I felt sad, thinking of my time living with him in his old house in Reniskamogue. I had to get back to my jobs quickly and forget about crying.

Mrs. Cromwell entertained with feasts for the Tennis Tournaments and Golf Matches; there was no end to it. When she would have more than fourteen guests, she would bring in outside help. They took some of the workload from Bridget and I.

We spent three months in the country. Bridget and I were glad to hear that Mr. and Mrs. Cromwell were taking a break and going to Maine, N.Y. for two weeks. There was no cooking to be done. Bridget took her chance and went to her brothers in the Bronx for two weeks. Their son, Rodger Cromwell and his wife were to stay in the house with me. They too decided to pack their cases and go to the city. As they were leaving, I asked, "Am I supposed to stay here by myself?"

"Peggy," said Rodger, "you have nothing to be afraid of here. If you need anything the caretaker and his wife are only up the lane." The caretaker's house was half a mile away. I was on my own and there was no television. I would be by myself for two weeks and no way to get to Mass on Sunday. I phoned Aunt Margie crying. "What's wrong Peggy?" she asked.

"Everyone is gone away for two weeks and I'm by myself."

"One minute Peggy," Aunt Margie always to my rescue. "I have a few days off from work and Maureen is on vacation from school, we will pack a bag and go out to you. We could do with a break out in the country away from the heat of the city."

"Will you be able to find your way? You will need to take a taxi from Morris town Station to this house."

"Don't you worry about us Peggy; we will be out to you tonight."

I was overjoyed when they arrived. Looking around, Aunty said, "what a lovely country place." I showed them to the guest bedroom; it had twin beds with pink satin bedspreads, white furniture and pink carpeting. "Peggy this is very posh" said Maureen, "I could get used to it." After having a meal, we sat outside in the cool, clear, country, refreshing air and listened to the noises of the night.

"It's a pity they don't have a TV, you would enjoy the movies," said Aunt Margie.

"They only use this house three months of the year, the rest of the time it lays idle, so they don't bother with television. Mrs Cromwell says it's a time waster. The caretaker looks after their property for nine months of the year."

"Isn't it great to have money," said Aunt Margie. During the day, we took long walks through old roads lined with briars.

"This is the kind of country place your mother came from, Maureen."

"Its beautiful Mam, why did you ever leave such a place?"

"In need of money, Maureen!"

She then told us of her first job in the United States which was working in a boarding house. There was no automatic appliance of any description; the laundry was done in a washtub left up on a stand. Sheets, all white, were soaked the night before in hot water with a couple of fistfuls of washing soda added.

"That was my first job on a Monday morning. I had to be up before six o'clock to get started and try to be finished by noon. Another girl helped me to put the sheets through a mangel/ wringer. From the constant washing of clothes, I lost the nails off my fingers. They weren't interested in my red raw hands. I had to leave or lose the use of my hands.

My next job was as a housekeeper and the lady was very nice, she said I didn't need to go near water until my fingers was healed. There was a lot of work to be done and my fingers healed, even though the nails took a year to grow back. I was doing well until the winter came, and on Christmas morning the street was covered from a heavy snow fall. The lady of the house told me to go out and sweep the footpath in front of the house. I turned to her and said,

"I didn't come to America to sweep the streets of New York on Christmas day." She took the brush from me and told me to get my bag and leave immediately. I walked the streets of New York that day until late evening. Everywhere I looked there was signs up, 'No Irish need apply', or 'No Catholic Irish need apply'. What was I to do? I had no money to pay my passage back home. I came to a house where I knew a Clare girl worked. I had $10 in my pocket, which was two weeks' pay. I knocked on the door, Teresa answered. 'Margie what happened to you?' I was collapsing with cold, hunger and disappointment. 'Can I come in?'

'You can, the people here are away for Christmas week, you can stay until they get back.' Teresa ran me a bath and gave me a meal. Teresa's bedroom was very small; she put me to bed in her tiny bed, where I slept until the next day. I helped her with the housework. I was still there when the family came back. I sat in Teresa's room until the coast was clear, then I would leave quietly. Teresa had a surprise for me. 'My boss wants to see you,' she said.

'Oh God,' I thought 'I am going to end up in jail, can it get any worse.'

The lady said, 'Teresa tells me you're looking for a job, we need a second worker here, so I am offering you the job.' I thanked her so much; I could not believe my ears. I worked in that house until I married the Scotch man, Dan Callaghan. I tell you this Peggy; the Irish got it hard when they came to America back in the early 1900's." The four days flew, we had a great time together, the taxi arrived and we waved goodbye. I am once more on my own, but not lonely or afraid.

EVERYONE IS COMING BACK

Bridget arrived back first and asked me how I got on. "I was fine Bridget, how was your holiday?"

"I had a nice time with my brother, but the heat of the city is killing." Mr & Mrs Cromwell arrived back. Mrs Cromwell came into the kitchen and asked Bridget to make up a meal. Bridget was looking in the fridge. "There's not much here, Rodger and his wife must have been eating a lot." I still said nothing about my visitors. Bridget made up a big egg omelette.

"This will have to do until we order some groceries." I'm thinking there is no one to tell them about my visitors, and I won't. Everything was going fine until I got a shock. Next day Bridget and I were sitting to our lunch. Mrs. Cromwell walked into the kitchen and asked, "Peggy, who was the visitors you had here?" I almost fell off the chair and Bridget's fork stopped halfway to her mouth. "My Aunt and Cousin," I answered.

"Why didn't you tell me?"

"I don't know."

"Why didn't you ask my permission Peggy?"

"I was on my own and afraid."

"You were afraid?"

"How could you be afraid when my son Rodger and his wife were here?"

"They left the day after Bridget left."

Mrs Cromwell stopped for a second, and then looking at Bridget she said, "I will have a word with him." Then she left the kitchen. Looking at me across the table Bridget said, "Eat your lunch Peggy."

"How did she find out Bridget?"

"Peggy, what do you think they pay a caretaker for?"

"Oh, I never thought of him."

IT'S BACK TO THE CITY

We are back to the city house again. The weather is still very hot. The big house had to be aired out before Mr. & Mrs. Cromwell's arrival. I had a lot of preparing to do. First, I had to strip the dustsheets off the furniture. Then, get busy setting the dining room table for six people. Next, go up the five flights to my room, which was on the top floor next to Bridget's, unpack and get into my uniform. I didn't ask which one to wear, but took it for granted I would be expected to wear the green one this evening. I got it right for once.

Mrs. Cromwell was back to throwing lavish parties; a lot of late night entertaining took place, with poker and bridge games, and high teas in the afternoon. The table had to be set with the appropriate tableware. I would ask, "Is it a tablecloth or mats for this evening, Mrs. Cromwell?" She would give me instructions on the outlay of the setting and the waitress uniform I was to wear. When very formal, I wore a black dress and white little bib; for informal parties, it was the green uniform, and always white starched cotton uniform for lunches. For general work, I wore grey.

There was no end to the washing-up of dishes. In those times, dishwashers weren't heard of. Bridget and I worked hard, but we didn't let it get in the way of a bit of free time. We would make time to go to see a good film together. We enjoyed 'Gentlemen prefer Blondes' with Marylin Monroe and Jane Russell. Another Sunday, we went to see 'The Robe.' This was on the death of Our Lord, and the main actors were Richard Burton, Victor Mature, Jean Simmons and Jay Robinson. We would go most Thursday evenings to the Novena of the Infant of Prague. In January of 1954, I was enrolled for life in the Confraternity of the Infant of Prague in the Church of our Lady of the Angels in Manhattan.

One day, I said to cook, "I'm going to look for another job. I'll not survive another year at this. I'm sure to lose my finger nails with all the washing of dishes."

"What do you mean, lose your finger nails?" said Bridget staring at me. I told her about my poor Aunt and how she lost her finger nails.

"Peggy, there is no comparison between these times and back in those years, long ago. Be sure to give in your notice and Mrs Cromwell will give you a good reference, Peggy."

"I will Bridget."

1954 - A JOB CHANGE

I found a nice job in the help wanted ads, where a young couple were looking for an Irish girl to take care of their two young sons.

I applied and got the job. The parents were a lovely young couple named Philip and Marggerie Von Stadea. They had two little sons and lived in a small house which was once a lodge on Mr Von Stade's parents' vast ranch estate. This was a country estate in Old Westbury, Long Island. I was very happy here, taking the boys for walks through country lanes. Philip was aged three and Bobby aged two. While working for this family, I was included in their vacation to Florida, travelling in the Pullman train. We had a large, comfortable cabin. At night, the beds were let down out of the wall, and this was done for us by a coloured steward. It was a twenty-two hour trip to Melbourne Beach. Mrs Von Stade and I slept in the top bunks and the two little boys slept in the bottom ones. We changed into our nightwear and climbed into the bunks. The rattle of the train rocked us to sleep.

In the morning, after breakfast we collected our bags and Bobby's stroller. Stepping onto the platform, I felt the heat. Waiting for us was Marggerie's parents. After they hugged and kissed, Marggerie introduced me to them and I felt very welcome. They took us to a small hotel. We were shown to our rooms. Marggerie and her sons slept in the same room; my room was adjacent to theirs. It was so small I could barely turn around; the ceiling was sloped at an angle across above me in such a way that I couldn't stand up. I consoled myself at the thought we would be there only two nights and then it was onto Miami to stay in a cottage by the sea. Just before we left the hotel, Marggerie looked into where I had been sleeping. She couldn't believe the hotelier would pass it off as a room, and complained at the desk and refused to pay for it. "Why didn't you tell me, Peggy? I would have told them to get you a proper room."

"It was only for two nights, I didn't mind," I said.

Before we left for Miami, we went to visit the second largest birdcage in the world. It was enclosed all around and over the top with a strong mesh wire, fencing it in, so the birds would not fly away. It took us a couple of hours to walk around it and admire the beautiful birds. Some were very big like the ostriches, which I had never seen before. The children's granddad explained about them, "They're not able to fly look at their big feet. A kick from one would kill a man," he told us. Even so, they were a wonderful sight to see.

The cottage in Miami was near the beach and I had a big bedroom to the front. At night, I could hear the calming roll of the waves.

It was strange to be out on the beach in our swimming togs in the month of January. As we were preparing to leave the beach, I saw a building with the word 'Black' on one end and 'White' on the other end in big print. In a loud voice over the sound of the waves, I asked, "What does it mean, black, white?" Marggerie hushed me up quickly. There was a bit of explaining to be done. "The black people are not allowed to mix or use the white people's toilets, restaurants, schools and a lot more, but they are allowed to work for the white people," said Marggerie. So now I knew. After lunch, it was time to leave and we would be travelling home on the overnight train again.

FIRST PLANE FLIGHT

Mrs Marggerie Von Stade was from St Louis, Missouri. Our next vacation was to her home. This time we travelled by plane. Flying to

St. Louis, Missouri was my first time to travel in a plane. I was trying not to show how scared I was. It was the summer time and very, very hot. As the plane landed, loud rolls of thunder could be heard; forked lighting streaked across the tarmac lasting only seconds, but it didn't seem to bother the people. Marggerie told me not to be afraid. "St. Louis gets many electric summer storms," she said.

We spent a month with her parents, in which time I rarely saw the two boys. Marggerie and her mother, their granny, took them every day visiting family. I babysat at night while the adults went out. Their granddad, who was a surgeon, was concerned about me, being Irish and not used to such strong sun and intense heat. One morning he gave me a ticket and said, "I'm taking you down to the cinema, it will be nice and cool in there. Have you ever heard of the film, 'Gone With the Wind'?" He asked. I was very shy, and just shook my head. "Its four hours long. I will drop you off and come back to pick you up, so wait by the door for me. You won't see the children until tonight."

I said, "Thank you, sir." It was nice and cool in the cinema. 'Gone with the Wind' was a fantastic movie, with the stars Clark Gable and Vivien Leigh.

The next treat I got from the granddad, on another hot day, was to an outdoor opera, 'The Mikado.' An umbrella was needed as protection from the sun. It was the same arrangement, dropping me off and picking me up. I was beginning to find my way and ventured out one day to travel in the street trams, a big experience for me.

They ran on tracks through the town with aerials gliding along overhead wires. One had to be quick when alighting in the middle of the street, as cars would be coming close to the tram, and the street was very wide to cross, you had to run fast. Incidentally, our grandfather, Michael Hurley RIP, Kilnacree, Six-Mile-Bridge County Clare, drove one of those tram cars when he immigrated to St. Louis, Missouri, many years ago. But being needed on the family farm, he returned home. I was thinking to myself, "Maybe he drove this one". Before flying back to New York, Mrs Von Stade and her mother were taking the boys shopping, and they asked me if I would like to come with them. I said,

"Yes please, I would like to buy a dress."

"You want to buy a St. Louis dress?" Said the granny with a smile. "You can be doing that while we shop for the boys." I had a great shopping day; I bought a lovely paisley pink and grey coloured dress buttoned down the front, which left me with very little money for the rest of the month. After shopping, we went for ice cream; this was the last treat. We packed to fly home the next day; I had had a wonderful time there. The weather was a bit cooler in New York, which was a welcome change.

FUTURE HUSBAND

I had weekends free and commuted from Westbury to N.Y. and spent the time with my Aunt. On Saturday nights, my girlfriend Maureen Buckley and I would meet up and head to the Tuxedo Ballroom, where we met Irish girls and lads our own age and had a good night's dancing.

It was at one of those dances I met a nice young County Monaghan man; his name was Michael Beggen from Scotstown.

After dating for a year, we got engaged for my twenty-first birthday on the 29th of September in 1954. I wore a black taffeta, off the shoulder dress. Aunt Margie put up a great party in her apartment and invited relations and friends. It was here we met each other's relations.

I met Michael's brother, Packie, wife Marie, his cousins John and Margaret McKenna, his aunts Mary McKenna and Margaret Connolly. Michael was introduced to Hugh and Harriet Callaghan, their son Eddie, in-laws of Aunt Margie. Michael was very handsome with blue eyes blond hair, and was dressed in white shirt and navy pants. I could not take my eyes off him. Aunty whispered something in his ear and he nodded his head. In the old-fashioned way, he walked across the room, went down on one knee in front of me, opened a little box, and inside was a lovely ring with a row of sparkling diamonds. With a very red face he said, "Peggy, will you marry me?" I put my arms around his neck and said, "I will." He put the lovely diamond ring on my finger, then we kissed and everyone clapped and wished us the very best of luck. I felt I was on top of the world. It was a wonderful evening with cake, drinks, birthday presents and good wishes for our future.

Our Engagement party in Aunt Margie Callaghans

1955 - OUR WEDDING

Eight months after our engagement, we started planning for our wedding. Aunty took me shopping to the Bowery for my wedding gown. (If you never heard of the Bowery, it is a place where people, mostly men, who have had very bad disappointments in their lives, end up drinking cheap wine; lying around all day on benches and doorsteps where no one pays them any heed. Some of the most respectable people could be found there who were down in their luck, they were known as down and outs.) As we passed through, Aunty told me not to be afraid. Some would whistle and others would say,

"Hi Irish."

A few blocks from there, we found a big selection of Italian wedding-gown stores, with choices no one could ever imagine. Aunty was very helpful in choosing my wedding gown and veil. After a lot of fitting on, we finally choose one with layers of tulle and underneath a full-length skirt, a wide v-shaped neckline and long sleeves. There was also a full-length veil held in place with a lovely tiara. On my wedding day, wearing my beautiful white gown and full-length veil flowing down my back, I felt like a princess on the arm of Dan Callahan, who cut a dash in his black tuxedo and bowtie. Walking me up the aisle, he kissed me and gave me over to Michael, who was looking very handsome in his black tuxedo and white bowtie. His brother, Packie, was best man and was also handsome in his tuxedo and black bowtie. My bridesmaid was Cousin Maureen, who wore a pale blue dress with accessories to match. We were married by Father Alexander, a nice Italian priest who blessed the wedding band, which matched the engagement ring. Michael placed it on my finger as I placed a gold band on his finger.

The priest pronounced us man and wife, then said to Michael, "You can kiss your bride." We were married on the 7th of May in 1955, in the presence of about eighty wedding guests. We headed to the local hall for the wedding reception. The music started and the new bride and groom danced the customary first dance, an old-time waltz, while everyone clapped. The guests then took to the floor.

Our Wedding, Mr and Mrs Michael Beggan after their marriage in St. Anthony's Church, Bronx, USA (07/05/1955)

Soon we were asked to sit at the tables; the welcome meal was on its way. Next, the best man, Packie Beggen stood up and made a little speech and welcomed the Galway Girl into the Beggen family. We cut the wedding cake, everyone had a slice and I had plenty to take home. Then there was the throwing of the bouquet and the lucky girl to catch it would be next to get married. We changed into our going away outfits. I wore a blue shoulder strapped dress with matching bolero jacket. Michael was in grey trousers and short-sleeved white shirt. We spent our two weeks honeymooning in the Katskil Mountains. During our time there, Michael was feeling sick, but we put it down to all the excitement.

"The first thing I am going to do when I go home is go to the doctor," Michael said.

"Good idea Michael," I agreed.

We received many useful gifts and dollars at our wedding. I wished my mother could have been at my wedding to see me. Michael had the same wish for his parents.

I have wonderful memories of our wedding day in the beautiful photos taken on the day. Recently, I have undone the wedding album and divided the photos between my two sons and my grandchildren.

OUR HOME ON TAYLOR AVENUE

Number 1443 Taylor Avenue, Bronx N.Y., was our first home; which was just one block from Aunt Margie's. When we came home from our honeymoon in the Katskills, Aunt Margie had placed a lovely vase of flowers on the kitchen table, a thoughtful welcome. We set to getting on with married life and going to our jobs each morning to pay off the bills. Michael worked in the Internal Revenue office in downtown Manhattan. Travelling on the subway every day, at times he would feel a bit sick but then it would pass off. When he came home after work he would sit for a while to rest, then he would feel like eating. I would have a grilled lamb chop, mashed potatoes and a vegetable.

"Don't cook vegetables for me anymore," he requested, "I think it's them that's making me sick." I agreed not to. He would sit for the evening in his cosy chair and watch TV. Then we would say the rosary and go to bed.

WAITRESS

After leaving Von Stade's to get married, I got work as a waitress in Longley's Restaurant, which was one block from St. Patrick's Cathedral where I got Mass on Sunday Mornings. The hours I worked started at seven a.m. to three p.m. five days a week. They were long tiring hours standing so long on my feet. An early rise at five thirty a.m. to be at the subway to get the six a.m. subway train at Parkchester to take me down town to 125th Street, change there then get the next train across to 5th Avenue. I worked for six months in Longley's, the money was very good. Michael thought it too much for me and said I should leave it. I left and stayed at home for a while visiting friends and having company in to tea.

SURGERY

August, three months after we got married, Michael was seriously sick. Doctor Galvin had to admit him to St. Elisabeth's Hospital in Lower Manhattan where he underwent serious surgery on his stomach.

He was three weeks in hospital with round-the-clock private nursing for the first week. It was a slow recovery for him. At home, it was a pleasure to see his appetite improving. Within three months he was back to work again in the Internal Revenue.

ELDERLY LADYS' COMPANION

One day I said to Michael that I was fed up being at home. "I'm going to look in the help wanted ads and see if I can get something suitable."

"Go ahead Peggy," said my husband. There was nothing suitable, so I tried an Employment Agency on Lexington Avenue, and was lucky to get a position as a personal companion to an elderly lady; Mrs Wade and her dog, a miniature poodle by the name of Mini. This was so much better, only one train to catch at nine a.m. for this job.

It was a very high-class, posh apartment building with a door man, whose job it was not to let anyone in the front entrance if they had a dog with them. I tried it often after walking Mini; she was so little I would hide her under my arm, but it didn't work. I was always sent to the servant's elevator at the back of the building. The pay was good and only six hours of work per day. I was there for a year, during which time Michael and I were saving to come back to Ireland for a holiday his health was much improved. Mrs Wade could not understand how we could afford the trip and be expecting a baby too. She was very good in giving me a travelling bag lined in red silk, also a black shawl for my mother. I kept my promise that I would come to visit her when I came back.

MY BROTHER EDDIE'S ANNOUNCEMENT

Just four months after our wedding, my brother Eddie wrote to tell me he was getting married to Honor Carrick in September. Mother found the whole thing a bit much. Two of us marrying in the same year; she would be losing two contributions towards the up-keep of the house. Our brother Paddy was working in England, and our sister Mary had started working in the Royal Tara China Factory in Mervue, two miles from home. I bought a beautiful, blue V-necked dress and accessories for Honor to wear for her wedding and mailed them to her. I wrote to mother and explained that as now I am married, I could only send her some dollars occasionally. It was a shock to her, for I sent her dollars monthly with my letter. She tried to understand and wrote and gave me her blessing, which I was grateful for.

1956 - IRISH HOLIDAY

In December, we booked our passage on the Marataine Liner for a three-month holiday in Ireland. People thought we were daft going for three months.

"Your jobs will be gone when you get back, and how will you afford the rent?" Were some of the discouraging questions! Aunt Margie stretched out her hands, saying, "Ignore them Peggy, go for it."

We went for it, and like a lot of chances I took in life; this was one I never regretted. The crossing was rough; I didn't get seasick too often, although I was now in my second month of pregnancy with our first baby. Michael's brother, Frank, and Mick Rooney, who had a taxi service in Scotstown, County Monaghan, came to Cobh to meet us. Our first destination was Michael's home in Scotstown.

Here I met Michael's mother, Susan, and two more of his brothers, Felix and Leo. Their father Pat had died in April of 1956; this was very upsetting for Michael, for the last time he seen his father was when they said goodbye when Michael emigrated in June 1952. Michael was the oldest of the family and was very close to his dad. There was a big gathering of family and neighbours in the Beggen house that night, and next day people were coming to sympathise with Michael on the death of his father. I went to bed early; I was tired and two months pregnant. I was lying facing the wall when he came to bed, and I heard him crying. I knew he was overcome with grief and all the visitors and sympathisers. I turned over and put my arms around him, "Cry it out Michael, I know you miss your dad." He eventually went to sleep. In the morning, he was thanking me for my understanding but asked me not to tell the family he was crying. I promised I wouldn't. "How do you feel now?" I asked.

"I'll feel better after I visit my father's grave today."

Michael had many relations all over County Monaghan and Beggen relations in County Armagh where his late father came from. Next day we hired out a Hillman car and this made travelling much easier.

CROSS-BORDER SEARCH

Having a car made it easier to get visiting the numerous relations and friends Michael wanted to see in his home county and in crossing the border. One important place he had a wish to visit was Armagh. We brought our wedding album home with us to show the wedding photos to our families. On our way across the Border into the North of Ireland, the Border Security stopped us to search the car. "Open the boot," was the stern order. "What is in that box?" the security officer asked.

"Our wedding album" answered my husband.

"Open it up," was the demand and we did as we were told. The album was searched, every page roughly turned. I was afraid they would destroy it. They then told us to be on our way after Michael had given them every detail of our visit. It brought home to us the seriousness of the situation in the troubled North. We met Michael's relations on his father's side, his aunts Susan Mc Convell and Sarah Beggen, and uncle Eddie Beggen. Aunt Susan asked me if Mike told me that he spent three years in a seminary collage studying for the Priesthood. "He did," I said, "but he didn't like the Latin and left."

"Did he tell you his brother Packie joined him there? I think my brother Pat Beggen (R.I.P.) thought he was going to have two priests in his family. It ended up when the two boys landed home one evening."

"What are you doing here?" their mother asked.

"It's too lonely there," said Packie, "so we left." I don't think my poor sister-in-law knew what to make of the two of them".

"Michael went to Westport, County Mayo to train as a hotel manager. And Packie turned to cobbling shoes until the smell of the leather made him sick. He then emigrated to the States".

"I know," I said, "and Michael did the same. He took up training as hotel manager in the Statlerr Hotel in Manhattan until his health started giving him trouble".

"Yes, that's true," agreed Susan. "But his dad thought he would stay home, being the oldest of the family and take over the farm. As you can see Peggy, it is a big well-equipped farm and a fine dwelling house with it and other properties too, like for instance the extra houses you see in Scotstown. But to his Dad's disappointment, Michael had no interest in farming."

I was listening to what she was telling me and as we were living in America, I wasn't too interested. I said,

"Michael says his brother Frank, who is over six foot tall, is the farmer in the family."

"He might be right Peggy," agreed his Aunt Susan.

Aunt Susan and I corresponded with letter writing for a long time after.

GALWAY

It was a pleasure travelling down the country to Galway in the Hillman. Our next destination was to my home place in Ballybrit, Galway. Here I introduced my husband to my mother, Bridget Abberton, to my brothers Eddie and Paddy, my sister Mary, and to Eddie's wife Honor, who was soon to have her first baby and lastly to my Aunt Mary Hurley. There was great excitement, everyone was overjoyed to meet Maggie's husband. We spent New Year's celebrating and meeting neighbours. My mother was happy to hear I was expecting a baby later in the year. "You and Eddy got married the same year and now ye are having yer first babies in the same year, how did ye manage to do that?"

"You would say that Mam," I said, we both laughed. Michael was delighted when Mam played the gramophone. Aunt Mary took him out on the floor to dance the stack-of-barley. There was a lot of fun as she tried teaching the dance to him. I said, "Mary, the only dance he knows is a waltz."

"Put a waltz on there for us Bee. Now, Micheal you lead." Michael was a bit shy and said,

"You're better able than me at leading, Mary." And so they danced around the floor like professionals.

We had roast goose for our New Year's Day dinner, cooked the way I remembered. Mother laid on a lovely meal for everyone. We had such a great time meeting the neighbours, with everyone delighted to meet the Monaghan man. Mother opened the bottle of Sandeman port in celebration of the New Year and our visit home.

1957 - COUNTY CLARE

Our next trip was to Kilnacree in County Clare, to see the relations and the house I was reared in. Uncle Paddy, his wife Anne, their two children Pa Jo and Anna May were there to welcome us. My husband loved it there; he also loved playing marbles with my young cousins Anna May and Pa Jo. The home-cured pig meat was cooked by Anne. "It's the best meal I ever got," said Michael. Anne, before boiling the cabbage, would chop it up on a wooden board outside the door as she was about to prepare a turnip. I brought out the camera on the quiet to take her photo, but just as I was about to snap, she ran inside the door and held the turnip out, "Now, take a photo of that." And I did, but no amount of coaxing would she let me take a photo of herself.

There was a visit to Uncle Jack and his wife Bridget's house, which was located in the windy-gap village. A big welcome awaited us here too. They had a big family; I had at least five young cousins to hug. Bridget took us into the parlour where she served us a lovely meal with home-cooked ham and brown soda bread. Every house we visited we got the homemade Christmas cake and everyone was fascinated with Michaels' Northern accent. We visited O'Mara's old house to meet my bachelor Uncle Jimmy; he gave us a big welcome and apologised in his own way about the state of the house.

"This is an ould house, so don't put any heed to the way things are in it. You are more used to the American style of things, Michael. Your wife there was reared here for a while. You are from Monaghan, it's near enough to the North," said Jimmy, and then he waded into his favourite topic, the I.R.A. and their bravery, and how he was the leader of his own platoon. He offered Michael some Guinness, "I'm sorry, I am a pioneer, but thanks," Michael said.

"I couldn't do without a pint of Guinness now and then," said Jim. I could see the relief in my husband's face when I stood up to leave. Uncle Jim could have talked all day about the I.R.A. "And where are ye off too now?" he asked.

"O'Neill's, Jimmy," I said, "and thanks for your welcome." As he shook hands with Michael, he said, "You will come back before you leave Clare."

"We will indeed," said Michael, looking at me with a grin that said it all. Then on to meet my girlfriend, Maureen O'Neill, her mother, father and her three brothers at their house. A lovely thatched cottage a long , distance in the dirt road. There was a deep slope down to the front door. It brought such happy memories of my childhood back to me. Mrs O'Neill brought Michael up close to the blazing, open turf fire, which was throwing out heat that no oil fire could match. Maureen's brother, Pa, took down the fiddle and played some tunes. Maureen was a lovely singer and sang a few songs; it was a great evening of music and singing. Tea was served with homemade bread, cake, jelly and custard, and Michael did well eating everything.

Maureen was overjoyed to hear I was expecting a baby. Her mother had tears in her eyes and shook the Holy water on me. The time was going too quickly, and we said our good byes and then it was back to Uncle Paddy's, where we were staying and another lovely blazing fire greeted us as we walked in from the cold night. I was glad to get into bed. I was now three months pregnant. Michael was complaining how he was feeling sick; we put it down to the variety of rich food he was eating. Of all the people Michael met, Uncle Jimmy was the one he remembered most, telling of his exploits in the I.R.A. Michael would tell the stories to his friends in Monaghan, to my embarrassment.

RETURNING TO GALWAY

Driving back to Galway, after a great week in Kilnacree, we stayed only a few days with mother and family and gave them plenty of news. "What did they think of your man?" asked mother.

"They loved his northern accent," I told her.

She played the gramophone again and more neighbours came in to meet my husband and dance some céili dances. Eddie and Honor were living in Mom's house until their house was ready in Mervue.

JANUARY 3RD 1957

There was great joy as Eddie and Honor became parents to a son. They asked Michael if he would be the baby's godfather. He said he would be delighted to stand for him! Honour's sister, Josephine was godmother and they named him Eammon. He was baptised in the Regional Hospital Chapel, which was customary in those years. We had a little toast in the hospital to the new baby.

BACK TO MONAGHAN

It was a long drive back to Scotstown. Michael would feel sick, we would make stops along the way at restaurants, where he could have a cup of tea and a slice of toast, after which he would feel better. "When I get back to Monaghan I will go and be seen by a doctor, he might give me something to ease the sickness."

I was relieved when we reached Monaghan and Michael went to a doctor he knew, and the doctor recommended some medicine that gave him relief. He advised Michael to cut back on the homemade soda bread. Following the docters advice he would feel a lot better. He laughed saying, "It's you who should be sick."

Another couple of weeks in Monaghan and then goodbyes were said. Michael cried fearing he would never see his mother alive again, and I did my best to console him. We paid for the hired car and a driver to drive us to Galway to say our last goodbyes to my family before heading to Cobh in Cork the next day.

Michael's brother, Leo, came with us to be company for the driver when they started on the long journey back to Monaghan.

BACK TO GALWAY

Back to Galway to say our last farewells to my family, and arriving at my mothers in Ballybrit, we found Mam looking very pleased.

"You're happy to see us, Mam."

"You have good news for us?"

"I have, come in and sit down until I tell you."

"Tell us quick, I can't wait to hear it."

"Soon after ye left, Eddie and Honor got a lovely two-bedroom bungalow in Mervue."

"That's wonderful news, a new baby and a new home."

"That's right Maggie, the best of luck to the three of them. Michael, your brother Leo and the driver can sleep in that room tonight."

"That will suit us just fine, Mrs Abberton," said Leo.

We were so sad to be leaving the next morning. The journey to Cork was long so we had to leave early after saying goodbyes to everyone. I was lonely leaving mother; she'd gone to a lot of trouble for us making sure we were comfortable in her small home, she made room for everyone.

We stopped in Limerick to have tea. The drive to Cork seemed very long. When we reached Cobh, we were ready for dinner. The driver was in a hurry to be on the road back to Monaghan, so we had one last goodbye to Michael's brother, Leo, and we wished each other safe travelling. We stayed overnight in Cobh. There was more luggage coming back to N.Y., with all the gifts we got, than we had coming to Ireland. Tired and happy after our three-month's holidays, indeed we were ready to embark on the Maritainea for the long sail back to N.Y.

It's the 29th of March, 1957 and we have arrived back safely in the USA. I'm five months pregnant, feeling great; but wishing I could say the same for my husband.

Taylor Avenue was a sight for sore eyes, we were glad to be home.

Once again, Aunty has a bunch of flowers on the table and this time she has the fridge filled! We were so happy to see her.

Early next morning Michael is off to see Doctor La Verdi, and I'm heading to Macy's to buy maternity clothes. I'm anxious about Michael. I went into a Church to pray for him and to give thanks for our wonderful holiday and safe journeys.

I hear the key in the door, and anxiety took a grip of me.

"What is your news?" I wondered. The look on his face was a happy one.

"What had the doctor to say?" I asked.

"He said it could be all the travelling, the change of food and maybe I'm a little worried about you, so he prescribed this bottle of medicine for my stomach. I'm to take a tablespoon of it before my meals everyday." I was so relieved to hear that.

JULY - A BABY BOY

The four months went by very fast, and on the 21st of July, we were at a movie in downtown Manhattan, when my waters broke. I said, "Michael we have to go."

"But the film is not over."

"My waters broke, hurry and get a taxi and we will go to Aunty Margie's." Telling her that we were at the movies, she asked, "What was the movie about?"

"It was a comedy with Buster Keaton. We were laughing quite a bit and my waters broke, but I'm not in labour."

"I will call the hospital," she said, and explain to them how you are feeling. The midwife said you are to go in right away. Another taxi and a return trip to Manhattan, but this time to St. Elizabeth's Hospital. A midwife met us at the door, where I explained my situation to her. The midwife told Michael and Aunt Margie to go home and she would phone Michael when he was a father. I watched them leave, and hoped this won't take too long. The midwife took me to the labour ward. "I'm not in labour," I said.

"I want you to get undressed and put on this hospital gown, I will be back in a few minutes," she said. I sat on the side of the bed and looked around. There were two electric fans standing in a corner and the clock on the wall was two hours slow. When the midwife returned, I told her that the clock was two hours slow. "That's for your benefit, when you are in labour you will try to figure out the time, now lie on your side and pull your knees up, I am giving you an enema to help start your labour."

The pains started very mild but got strong. My baby was no way near ready for birth, and the pains went on for hours. I was given an injection; it numbed the pain for a while. A coloured midwife came on duty. She said, "Today is the hottest day in the year".

I said, "I don't give a damn."

"Shee, shee, save your strength," she said gently, as she turned the two fans on me. No air conditioning in those days. "Oh never, never again," I bawled.

"You will be overjoyed when you hold the baby in your arms, and all the pain will be forgotten. I have the two fans blowing on you, now here is a little cold water to sip on."

"I will never have this baby."

"You will. I go off duty at eight o'clock in the morning and you will have your baby by then."

"What time is it now?"

"Six o'clock, honey."

"Oh God, two more hours of this agony," I thought. True to her word, our first son was born weighing 8lbs 4oz at five to eight on a Monday morning, the twenty second of July 1957, after 22 hours of labour in St. Elizabeth's Hospital, Manhattan N.Y. He had a head of black curls and I couldn't stop kissing his chubby red cheeks. I smiled at the midwife. It was a long one and such a big baby for a little mother and she kissed me on the cheek. She said she was going home to get her lot out to school. "You and baby are tired too."

"Please call my husband," I asked.

"The nurses will look after that for you and anything else you need, just ask them. You are going to breast feed your baby?"

"I am," I said, then she bent and kissed me on the cheek again. I never saw her after that (but I never forgot her).

Next morning, I was given my baby, I carried him to the nursing room and was shown how to hold him and give him my breast. He was a hungry baby; it gave me a warm feeling to be bonding with this little gift from God.

Michael was in great form being the proud father of a son. "What would you like to name him?" I asked.

"I think Michael," he smiled gazing at his adorable son.

I agreed, "But we will have to call you Mike from now on." He was happy with that.

Six days later we were on our way home and Aunt Margie, Dan and Maureen were there to meet us with a warm welcome. Margie was telling me how it was when she had Maureen. At home, life was easy as I was nursing, so there was no formula to be made up, no sterilizing of bottles. The job of washing diapers (nappies) was taken over by Aunt Margie and my good friend, Molly O'Neill. I was sore and unable to sit down. Aunty put two pillows under me making it easier to sit as I had a lot of stitches. I moaned and Aunt Margie asked me, "What do you expect? You had a big baby, God bless him."

Young Michael was baptised in the Church where we were married. Cousin Maureen Callaghan and Packie Beggen were his Godparents. Baby Michael was a good baby and growing fast.

BABY'S FIRST CHRISTMAS

It was a very happy Christmas; we were a family and it would be the best one I would enjoy for a long time. We had our Christmas tree with wrapped gifts underneath and the Holy crib on the sideboard. A small turkey and all the trimmings were on the table. "Dig in now, Mike." A plum budding with cream was the finishing touch. Santa brought plenty of Christmas gifts to baby Michael. On St. Stephens's day, Mike's brother Packie, Marie and their son Johnny came to visit, also other family members and friends. We in return paid our Christmas visits to them. Michael was home a week from work feeling sick, again we blamed the food. He returned to work and felt better for a few months.

1958 - ONE YEAR OLD

Our son Michael is one year old, and his dad and I are going to have a big birthday party for him in our apartment. We invited about thirty guests, some of whom were at our wedding. We enjoyed meeting up again, they loved little Michael and wanted to hold him, which he wasn't happy with. Aunts, uncles, plenty of cousins and friends came. One of Mike's relations, Jimmy Boylan, brought his accordion and played lots of traditional tunes for us. Dan Callaghan sang Scottish songs. Of course, we all sang 'Happy Birthday' to the big one-year old. His godmother, Maureen helped him to blow out the candle and then everyone got slices of the cake plus food and drink. It was a great party, Mike was in good form but I was tired. In America, back then an extra candle is put on the cake no matter what the birthday. On Michael's cake, even though he was only one, Cousin Maureen placed two candles.

One year old, Baby's first birthday with his proud parents, Mike and Peggy Beggen.

COUSIN MAUREEN'S PLANS

Aunt Margie and Dan Callaghan's only child, my cousin Maureen was making plans to get married to Henry (Hank) Doerr. The fuss was on choosing Maureen's wedding gown. A beautiful full lenth old English lenion a heart shaped tearia to hold her full lenth veil in place.The Matron of Honor (that was me), would have a dress of dusty pink knee length velvet the four bridesmaids had royal blue velvet dresses with crinoline underskirts to puff them out, which were all specially made. Fittings and measuring took a long time, but the dresses were beautiful when finished. We carried white muffs with a small corsage of flowers pinned to them and wore a simple white hair band. And of course, the mother of the bride was very elegant in a layered, chiffon, pale blue dress. This time Dan was walking his own beautiful daughter down the aisle of St. Anthony's Church. It was a beautiful wedding and we all enjoyed it; even Mike didn't feel sick. After a great day, Mr and Mrs Henry Doerr left in a shower of confetti on their honeymoon with plenty of good wishes. I wore the pink velvet dress to many an occasion. It began to fade and I made tablemats and cushion covers from the material, they were in use a long time.

1959 - AUNT MARGIE'S FIRST GRANDCHILD

Maureen and her husband Hank's first baby, was a little girl. I was very happy at the thought of being her godmother. Leading up to the christening, Mike was very sick and I worried about him. On the morning of the baby's christening I was ready to leave for the church, when Mike says, "You can't leave me." I was crushed; I knew he was nervous of being on his own and I couldn't argue with him, so I just sat on the side of the bed. What was Aunt Margie going to say to me; there was no way of reaching them to let them know that I couldn't be at the christening of their littlegranddaughter. There was no way I could phone as they would have already left the house.

Next day Aunty called to see me, she cried a lot. "I'm heartbroken you are not Katherine's godmother," she said.

When she had left, poor Mike called me into the room and took my hand; he didn't say anything. "I'm going to make a pot of tea, will you have some?" I asked, He nodded his head.

I thought they would never talk to me again. Eventually Maureen phoned asking me, "When are you going to come and see my baby?" I started to cry. "Look Peggy, don't cry, we understand. I would love if you were there, but I know how it is with you and Mike so sick."

I had a gift and a card for my new baby cousin. I was nervous as I rang Maureen's doorbell. "Come in Peggy," she said. I entered timidly. Aunt Margie said, "Come and look at this little girl; is she not the most beautiful baby you've ever seen? Here, hold her," she said with excitement. I sat down and held her on my lap. "Congratulations Aunty, on your first grandchild," I said. I handed the baby gift to Maureen and she was very thankful to me. "You are so good, Peggy, taking the time to buy the baby a present when you have so much trouble"

"It's the least I might do, Maureen," I said. There was nothing more said about the christening. Mike is once again on the mend and he is up and watching TV with his son, who is enjoying his favourite program, 'Lassie.'

MOTHER'S ARRIVAL

I invited my mother to the States for a month's holidays. She arrived in August, the hottest month of the summer. What was I thinking of, bringing her out in such heat? She flew out in a Boeing 707 plane; she had travelled by plane before ever I did. Her stay was to be a month, but she stayed for eight months and to my relief she loved the heat. She met her sister, Margie for the first time in thirty years; there was much rejoicing on the occasion. And thanks were given to me for making it possible.

Mother/Granny had great fun with her grandson Michael, who was now two years old. Not long after she arrived she told me she was getting a bad pain through her stomach occasionally and the sweat would pour out through her. "Oh dear," I said, "the next time it hits you let me know." Two months after Mam's arrival, I notice her sitting quietly on the couch and looking very pale. "Are you all right, Mam?" I asked.

"I have the pain." She was doubled over with it, and it lasted for half an hour, she then fell asleep from exhaustion. I told Aunt Margie that Mam was sick. She told me to make an appointment with my doctor for him to examine her. "It might be something simple; if she needs an operation you might have to foot the bill Peggy, she would not have insurance I'm sure." This is an extra worry on me, what with Mike getting sick and his medication being so expensive and missing work, we didn't have a lot of money.

"I'm sorry Peggy, don't worry. It won't come to that; just get her checked out." The doctor did check her, asking a lot of questions, taking blood and having her X-ray'd. "I will let you know the results in a couple of weeks," he said. They were the longest couple of weeks I ever endured.

Finally, back in the doctor's surgery the results were in.

"Mrs Abberton, the X-ray has shown a slight gloss on your liver; it is very minor, but will need treatment. I am giving you a prescription for a month supply of tablets and a diet sheet you must follow and no more white bread."

"What will I eat?" Mother asked, alarmed.

"Brown bread from now on plus your diet."

"How much is this costing Doctor la Verdi?" I asked.

"I will be sending you the bill," he answered.

I picked up the tablets on the way home for her to get started straight away. "They cost $100, is that a lot of money?" Mother asked. My husband and Aunt Margie were glad to hear it wasn't something more serious. Mother never got the pain again. Aunt Margie said, "You were cured in America, Bridget!"

DUSTING LOCKERS

There was a job going in the Internal Revenue building, dusting the tops of lockers and desks. It would be a two-hour job in the evenings and paid well. I applied and got the job. I said to Mam, "You will mind your little grandson for a half an hour in the evening after I leave, his dad will be home then. I will leave yer dinners ready." I knew by the look on her face she was thinking about this. "It's only for four evenings a week and the money is needed." She nodded her head.

On my first evening in the job, meeting the supervisor; she told me she was from Mayo. She handed me a few dust cloths, a long-handed feather duster and a small stepladder. I was shown the locker to keep my tools in. She then brought me to the offices. "What! Oh God!" There were acres of lockers, as far as the eye could see and all over five foot high. "Two hours," I thought, "I won't ever get them done in two hours." For the first week, a Polish woman showed me what to do. She was going at top speed, which I had to learn how to do, and I did.

CHRISTMAS IS APPROACHING

I had happy thoughts with two wages coming in. We could afford to spend a bit more on gifts and invite friends to celebrate mothers visit.

Early in December, I get a bill from Doctor La Verdi. "What is this for," I wondered. It is the bill for mothers' treatment. I had forgotten all about it and I had only two weeks to pay the $400 owed. "Well, there goe's the extra Christmas gifts and the visitors."

Mike is not well and in bed with a bad dose of shingles all over his body. Dr La Verde came to see him several times he would spray his body and give him a painkilling injection. I explained to the doctor that I would be unable to pay mothers' bill all at once; and now with doctor's house visits, the bills were mounting. "Pay what you can, when you can," he said. Looking at mother, he said, "You are looking well!" She thanked him. I had to give up the job of dusting the tops of lockers and stay home to look after Mike. I took a chance and went to collect my last pay packet. When I opened it, I expected to just find my one weeks' wages, but to my surprise the Christmas bonus was included. "Now," I thought, "I can pay the rent and the Con Edison bill (ESB). I won't have much left after". I got a few groceries and treats for little Michael.

Coming in the door, my son rushed to meet me. "Has he been a good boy?" I asked. Mam was looking a little stressed. I thought I must not leave her too often with them. Poor mother thought Mike was going to die. After suffering the pain of shingles for three hard weeks, it started to ease and the shingles were gone, but they left many deep scars on his back.

Mike's wages would be at his place of work it had to wait until he was fit enough to work and sign for them. No one could go outside, for the snow was coming down heavy. It reached two foot high. Mother was looking out the window; she had never seen so much snow.

I did my best to make it Christmassy for poor little Michael. I was glad we had shopped for Santa a few weeks earlier. I went to midnight mass; it was lovely and I wanted to cry all through it. I met Aunt Margie, Dan and Maureen, "We will see you after Christmas," she said. I had a lovely surprise waiting for me when I came home; Mike was sitting at the kitchen table having tea and a piece of cake with Mam. Michael was in bed, fast asleep. "How do you feel, Mike?" I asked.

"A little weak, but otherwise I'm good; I should be able to go back to work after the New Year."

"Not if the snow keeps falling like it is now," I said.

1960 - NEW YEAR'S DAY

At breakfast, we wished each other the very best of health and luck for the New Year. I didn't invite anyone to come to visit us as we would be staying at home too. Our good neighbours, Molly and Con O'Neill, who lived across the hall, called in to wish us a happy New Year. Another knock came on the door, and as I answered it I see that it is Aunt Margie, her husband Dan and Maureen. They made me happy with their visit. "Come on in." I said. They were glad to see Mike sitting in the kitchen, as were Dan's brother Hughie, his wife Harriet, Mike's brother Packie, his wife Marie and sons, Johnny and Kevin, who all called to wish us happy New Year. At the same time having a house full of visitors, I wondered how Mike would be, but there was no need to worry; he was handling all the chat without effort. They brought plenty of food and gifts, and presents for mother too, and cheering Mike up. Michael showed his toys to his cousins Johnny and Kevin; they were about his own age, four and two years. Mike's Aunt Mary and her son John McKenna arrived giving Mike big hugs and presents for everyone. Aunt Mary remarked, "You have a bit of colour back in your cheeks, Mike."

"It's all the excitement," he told her. The good news from outside was the snow was starting to melt.

After all the months of trouble we had, the visitors gave us a great uplift. When everyone had gone home, Mike was worn out, but in the best of form.

"I will go to bed now," he said.

"Did you enjoy New Years day, Mike?" I asked.

"The best I ever had," he said. Mam and I stayed up talking, while little Michael played with his new toys until he got tired. I tiptoed into the room to put him in his cot for it was well past his bed time. His dad was out for the count. Mam and I stayed up until the small hours of the morning watching old movies. She went to bed and I thought it better to sleep on the armchair rather than disturb Mike, who slept until noon the next day, waking up hungry.

I was so sure he would be too weak to get up but he got up and went into the bathroom and shaved. He looked well, but oh, he was very thin. Mam made him porridge, as I watched him eat it, I was thanking God.

AN APRIL WEDDING

My girlfriend, Maureen Buckley and her fiancé, Frank Farrell were planning their wedding. She invited me to be one of her four bridesmaids, which I was very happy to do. Her sister, Clare Burke would be her Matron of Honor. Clare wore a pale blue dress and the bridesmaids wore cream colour dresses with crinoline petticoats underneath to give the dress that puffed-out look. We wore a little veil on the top of our heads. Maureen was tall, elegant and looking like a model in her beautiful full-length lace-trimmed wedding gown, as she walked down the Church aisle on the arm of her brother-in-law, Mike Burke. Her husband to-be, Frank Farrell was looking smart in his tuxedo. It was an enjoyable day and one of my mother's highlights to be invited to an American wedding. I bought her a flowery dress and hat to match for the occasion; she looked lovely and enjoyed the fuss she was receiving. She was telling everyone that her holidays were coming to an end. "I have had eight enjoyable months and seeing my sister Margaret (Margie) after thirty years was a wish that finally came true."

MOTHER GOES HOME

There were tears in our eyes as mother was saying her goodbyes to us after eight months; we knew we would be missing each other. I know she will miss her sister Margie Callaghan the most. I was handing her a bag full of parting gifts saying, "Mam cheer up, here is a bag full of holiday reminders." She tried to smile. As she was leaving she said, "I have a lot to tell them back home." We remained at the airport until her plane took off. In a few short hours, she would be home in Galway. We missed her and Mike missed the crack he had with her. She had the best of times, especially with her sister Margie and grandson Michael.

A MORNING JOB

My neighbour and very good friend, Molly O'Neill called in for a visit. She had a cleaning job two mornings a week. She told me the lady she worked for has a sister who is looking for someone to do a few hours tidying her apartment one morning a week. "It would suit you, Peggy," she said.

"I couldn't Molly, I have little Michael."

"Here Peggy, this is the lady's phone number, you should call her."

"It won't be any good Molly."

"Go on, call her." So I did. The lady had a lovely gentle voice, and I explained my reason for calling.

"Come over to me and bring your son with you, and we will talk," she said.

"My goodness Molly, she wants me to go over to her apartment and bring my son," I exclaimed. It was only a twenty-minute walk to Parkchester with me wheeling Michael in his buggy. I rang her doorbell, at the same time thinking, "This is not going to work." Mrs Kazdin was a very warm person and gave Michael some candy; she was impressed when he said, "Ta, ta." She showed me around her beautiful apartment which had two bedrooms, a sitting/living room, breakfast room, kitchen and bathroom. "I would need you from nine to midday, just the three hours every Thursday, and I will make you a lunch."

I opened my mouth to say, "but," and before I had a chance to answer, Mrs Kazdin said, "I will mind little Michael while you do the cleaning and pay you on the day." We shook hands, I said, "I am so grateful to you Mrs Kazdin."

As time went on and Michael was getting older, she took him shopping and to the laundromat. She was so proud when people asked if he was her grandson. "I would love to tell them he is," she smiled, "but it will be a while before Irene, who was sixteen and Carolyn, fourteen, will make Oscar and I grandparents." When I had been working a year for her, she got very sick and was in hospital for two weeks. When she was allowed home, she needed me four days a week, so I would be finished at five in the evening and her husband, Oscar, would be home by then. He had a sense of humour and say, "I'm on the night shift." I brought Michael with me the four days, and Florence would read to him while he sat beside her in the bed. He would help with her tray and they would watch T.V. together, and when she went to sleep he did too.

Florence Kazdin and I first met in 1960; we are now sixty-six years close friends, and even though we are miles apart we still talk on the phone. She is ninety-six years young and in a residential home in Florida near her daughter Irene and her grand and great grandchildren. Her daughter, Carolyn dedicated much of her life in voluntary work for the poorest of the poor in Brazil. She is a walking saint. Florence's husband, Oscar, died thirty years ago, about 1985. They are Jewish people. Florence and I would talk about our religious beliefs, especially at Easter time, and found that there wasn't much of a difference between the religious beliefs. We prayed, we fasted, we went to Church, and they went to synagogue. As she said, in our own particular way, our religion is similar. Catholic boys and girls are confirmed; the Jewish boys have a bar mitzvah but not the girls.

Florence and I have had a wonderful relationship all through the years.

ATLANTIC CITY

It was May 1960, and we would celebrate our fifth wedding anniversary. Mike was on vacation, so we decided that the three of us would go to Atlantic City. Mike hired a limousine to take us. We packed our cases and put Michael's stroller (push chair) into the trunk of the limousine. I won't ever forget our trip, along the highway with the blue sky overhead and the sun beaming down. I felt rich with my husband and son beside me; I could have been anyone, even the richest movie star in Hollywood. Michael's excitement was contagious.

Mike had a good eye for nice accommodation; he found a lovely boarding house. As it was off-season, it was very reasonable for the two weeks. Our bedroom looked out on the Atlantic. We walked the prom and Michael had fun in the children's playground, riding in the bumper cars and on the hobby horses; everything was available to him. The landlady would babysit in the evenings, letting Mike and I out to enjoy the evenings' entertainments. On the last day of our vacation, she told us she wouldn't be able to mind Michael that night, as she had to go out. We had packing to do, and didn't mind. We thanked her for all the nights she did mind our son, free of charge, and for her kindness to us.

On the last morning as we came to breakfast, standing at Michael's place on the table, was a big red and grey dog. "Oh look," said Michael his eyes open as big as saucers. "Is this doggie for me?"

"Yes, it is," said the landlady, "I won it for you." We couldn't believe it. Smiling, she said, "I kept trying up to the last minute to win it; my number finally came up and I grabbed it."

"You are too good," said Mike and Michael ran and hugged her.

The limousine was waiting for us and we came home with a very happy Michael. It was a wonderful way to celebrate our fifth wedding anniversary.

UNCLE LEO

Mike's brother Leo, after immigrating to America from County Monaghan, came to live with us in Taylor Avenue, where he got a job working with Mike. During the year while Leo was living with us, Mike was sick many times, and it was a comfort to have Leo's company. He and Little Michael would play games together. He would take Michael for walks on a Sunday and buy ice-cream. When they came home, Michael would say, "Uncle Leo is the best uncle." Then the Sunday walks stopped. After Mass, Leo would say he was going visiting. I was thinking he may have being visiting his brother Patrick (Packie).

Mike had another thought, "I bet Leo has a girlfriend, but he is saying nothing yet."

1961 - WE ARE GIVEN THE NEWS

It's New Year and Leo tells us he is going to a party and won't be home tonight, "Where will you be staying Leo?"

"I'll be staying with friends in Brooklyn."

"Who do you know there?" I asked.

Mike answered for him, "His girlfriend of course; you're holding out on us Leo, tell us more." Leo blushed and sat down. "Her name is Josephine, and she is from Mayo."

"Well, the best of luck Leo be sure to bring her for a visit."

"I will Peggy," and then we wished each other a Happy New Year.

IT IS NOT GOING TO BE A GOOD YEAR

For Mike, his appetite was getting worse and he was spending more time in the hospital for tests. I made a suggestion, "We should go back to Ireland." He wouldn't hear of it. I asked, "Why?"

"The doctors here know my history; I would never survive in Ireland." Then I had a plan: a vacation in the Katskill Mountains, where we spent our honeymoon. He was delighted with that; "Just for a week," I said, "your son Michael is in his last year at kindergarten school."

Once again in the month of May, Mike hired the same limousine as we had when we went to Atlantic City. We set off on a beautiful May morning. (Anyone who didn't know us would say we had the world at our feet). Aunt Margie said, "It will be a nice break for Mike." The driver was a nice man who helped us with our bags. He had a quiet word with me. "It's only a little over a year since I last saw you," he said, "I don't like to say it; but your husband looks very frail."

"He hasn't been well for a long time." Looking at Mike from a distance he said, "Poor young man. I will be back to pick you up in a week."

Michael enjoyed his time, especially when we visited a field looking over the wall. We saw a pony grazing; when he saw us, he ambled over to the wall where Michael rubbed his nose. We would go most days to see the pony. Michael would pretend the pony was his; talking and rubbing the pony's nose was very exciting for my little son. "What name did you give your pony Michael?"

"Beauty," he replied, "just like Black Beauty on T.V." Mike would lie down until we returned. Michael would give his dad the news of how the pony let him rub his nose. The mountain air did Mike good but did nothing for his appetite. He could eat a dry mashed potato, tea and a plain cookie. I think he felt the week long as he didn't have the energy to keep in chat with the other guests.

The limousine arrived right on time. Michael took his Dad's hand as they walked slowly to it. "Will ye two get in quick," I said in a playful scolding tone; (I was trying to be light hearted). The driver put our bags in the trunk.

"Look daddy, wave to my pony, say goodbye to him," and the three of us did. Back home Mike perked up. "I think the break did you good Mike."

"It did," he answered, "and I feel hungry."

"I'll cook you a boiled egg and some toast."

"That will be nice."

"Uncle Leo is here," said Michael, "I'm going to tell him about my pony." There was a big long chat about the pony. I knew my husband was itching to hear more news about Josephine and if there was a wedding been planned. We got our answer. "There is, early next year," said Leo, "and I'm asking you to be my best man Mike."

"That is great news."

"You will be looking forward to that, Mike."

His face was all flushed up with the excitement at the thought of being best man for his brother.

WE ARE BACK TO ROUTINE

Michael was back to kindergarten and Mike went to work. As per normal, I would meet my friend, Margie McAndrew and we would go together to pick up her daughter Maureen and my Michael from kindergarten school. Walking home we would swap about and go to each other's house for the tea. On one occasion as we walked down the path to my house, I told her about a disturbing dream I had. I said, "In the dream, you and I were coming down the path with the two children and I saw Mike coming towards us, I said, 'Mike is home early, he must be sick again.'"

"It was only a dream Peggy, don't think about it," she said. Going in the door, I said, "You're right Marg." I gave the children some milk and cookies, and just as Margie and I were settling down at the table to have a chat while drinking our tea, the door opened and in walked Mike. "I don't feel well," he said, "I'm going to bed." I looked at Margie and said, "He is sick again."

Margie and Maureen left to go home. "I'll see you tomorrow," she said as they went out the door. I gave Mike some tea and his tablets. "Take a rest; you will be fine again when the tablets kick in."

"I'll have a sleep, and then get up," he said.

I HAVE NEWS

There is something I have to tell Mike, but how am I going to do it, for he will worry. That night, kneeling by the side of our bed, after we finished saying the rosary, I got a little courage. I spoke, "Mike; I have news for you."

Looking at me, he asked, "What kind of news?" It was over four years since Michael was born and this might come as a shock to him.

"Michael is going to get a little brother or sister." His mouth hung open. "It's a surprise, isn't it?"

"God, Peggy, that's great news, when are you due?"

"Next February, about the same time your brother Leo is getting married." "You're four months pregnant; you never said a word."

"I'm sorry, I was afraid you would worry."

"Let's get into bed; I want to hold you both," he laughed.

1962 - UNCLE LEO IS LEAVING

We are going to miss Leo. I'm apologising to him, saying, "I might not be able to go to your wedding, Leo."

"Bring the baby with you." We had a laugh at that. Michael is crying, saying, "I don't want Uncle Leo to leave."

"I'll tell you what I will do; I will bring Josephine here next week for a visit, would you like that, Michael?"

"I would, Uncle Leo." When my brother-in-law went to live in Brooklyn, our house felt empty. "Do you miss him, Mike?" I asked.

"I do," he said, "but the thought of the wedding and an increase coming in our family is distracting me." I don't know where to look. "There is so much excitement going on all at once," was his answer.

OUR VISITORS

We were looking forward to meeting Josephine. I told Mike my plan. "We will have a cold meal because I'm not able to do much cooking."

"The cold meal will be fine, Peggy."

"You can eat cold chicken and a plain boiled potato?"

"I can," he said.

Josephine was a beautiful, soft-spoken girl from County Mayo; she had a head of beautiful, black curly hair. I was so glad for Leo to meet someone so nice. When they arrived and after greetings, Michael took over by sitting on Josephine's knee or in between her and Leo. "Mike," said to Leo, "I think you have competition."

"I think so too," he agreed. We had an enjoyable time together, and I took a photo of them with Michael. He was at last happy. Forgetting about myself, I said, "You won't feel it until your big day is here, Leo." And quick enough from Leo, "But you might feel your big day, Peggy"

"Thanks for that, Leo."

BEST MAN AND A NEW BABY

Mike was proud being the best man for his brother Leo on his wedding day. I was in Westchester Hospital in the Bronx having our second son. Mike was excited that morning at four a.m., as he rushed me to the maternity in a taxi. This baby came in four hours and weighted 9lb 2oz on the 26th of February, 1962. Two lovely County Kerry midwives delivered him. Mike took a couple of days off to be with his son Michael, then, leaving him into Molly O'Neill, he got ready for the wedding. On the day of the wedding, Aunt Margie brought baby and I home from the hospital. Molly and Michael were at the door to greet us when we arrived. "I have the kettle boiling for ye" she said.

Margie thanked her, "It's needed; I have never felt such a cold day." Michael was reaching up to try and see his baby brother, so I bent down, and when he saw the little sleeping baby, he wanted to hold and kiss him.

"We will put him into his bassinet and let him sleep as he is very tired," I explained to him.

"Thanks for getting me a baby brother, Mom."

"You are welcome, sweetheart."

When Mike came home after the wedding, his son Michael ran to meet him shouting, "Daddy, Daddy, I have a baby brother." It was big news.

Mike looked well in his tuxedo. He filled us in on the lovely wedding and enjoyable day he had. We named our baby Leo, after his Uncle Leo and like his brother, he was baptised in St. Anthony's Church. My sister, Mary was his godmother by proxy as she was in Ireland, and Aunt Margie stood in for her and Uncle Leo was godfather. It was a happy day, but being February it was very cold.

Back in Taylor Avenue, it was cosy and warm in the apartment. While I nursed baby Leo, Aunt Margie, Maureen and Mike's Aunt Mary got busy with setting out the tea and sandwiches. Unlike when Michael was born, when Aunt Margie and Molly O'Neill took turns washing the diapers (nappies), this time I took advantage of the diaper service. For three months, a large bundle of diapers and two white buckets with lids was delivered to me, one bucket for the wet diapers and one for the soiled ones, which of course must be rinsed clean before dropping them into the bucket. Every two days fresh ones were left and the two full buckets were taken away. Once a month you paid $27; it was a service well worth the price.

Bestman and new baby son Leo, Mike celebrating two occasions on the same day.

MY BROTHER PADDY

I sponsored my brother, Paddy Abberton out to the States and he would be living with us. The apartment was too small for three adults, a small boy and a baby. I was prepared to make the most of it for a couple of months, until Paddy got a job and his own place.

I finally secured a job for Paddy, as caretaker in the local St. Anthony's Church. Mike was upset at this as he felt, because of his health problems, that I should have told him first about the job. It was close to home and he could avoid using the subway. I was upset too, I was thinking of having Paddy out of the apartment and in his own place. I said to him, that Mike was more entitled to that job than he was. He surprised me by saying that there was a vacancy for another caretaker. Mike was glad to hear this, he was lucky in getting the job. But the change was short-lived for he became very sick and was unable to work.

MY HUSBAND PASSES AWAY

Mike was getting worse with his sickness; he had constant diarrhoea, loss of appetite and weight. The tablets the doctors recommended, which were a wonder drug, were not helping him. The Friday before he passed away, (I won't ever forget), he was in great form. He got dressed up and went to a card game in St. Anthony's hall, and had a good time.

The next two days he was very sick and I could not get a doctor to come to him on the weekend. Westchester Hospital wouldn't admit him without a doctor's letter. It was Monday morning, and my good friend Molly O'Neill was with me when Dr. La Verde came. Michael, aged five, looked up at the doctor and asked him, "Is God going to take my daddy?" Doctor La Verde told Molly to take the little boy out of here, he then told me to go into the kitchen and boil the kettle to make Mike a cup of tea. As the kettle was boiling, the doctor came into the kitchen. I asked if Mike was all right; his answer was, "Only a miracle now." There were tears in his eyes and I knew God had taken Mike, like his son Michael said.

The doctor held me a while, as I was unable to cry, then he sent me to my friend, Molly, whose apartment was on the same floor as ours. Molly phoned for the priest in St. Anthony's, and he came and anointed Mike. I was worried because he was dead, but the kind priest assured me the soul remains with the body for three hours after death. That was a consolation for me. I don't know how I had the strength. I had a number of phone calls to make one to Margie McAndrew.

"I've been waiting to hear from you Peggy, that dream you told me about, I told John about it. He said, 'it is very close to the grain, the time is near, Peggy has had a premonition.' "

I said, "Margie, I had forgotten about that dream." Then we were both crying. "We will see you soon Peggy." After the phone calls, I went into a daze.

My brother Paddy came in from work. I called Mike's brother Leo to tell him that Mike had passed away. He thought I was making a joke but as I was crying, he started to cry and said he would tell the family.

Doctor La Verde called the cops as in the case of a sudden death of a young person.

"The cops must come and take the body for examination." I couldn't bear to see him being carried away like that. Mike was only thirty-five and I was now a young widow of twenty-eight years of age with two little sons, one age five and a baby of nine months.

Aunt Margie came with me to the hospital morgue to claim the body. The undertakers came and took him to the funeral parlour where he was embalmed and laid out in the suit he wore to the card game, two days before he passed away.

HIS FUNERAL

I had a lot to do for the funeral of my beloved young husband of only seven and a half happily-married years. This was not a job I was prepared for. But many were the hands that helped. I had to try, in the best sensitive way I could to explain to Michael that his daddy was now in heaven. My little boy wrapped his little arms around me and cried; I held him until I could talk to him and tell him he had a brother to play with. It was equally as hard to find the words to write the few lines home to tell mother that poor Mike had passed away. There were no phones available in Ballybrit back in those years.

My brother Paddy met some people he knew from Castlegar in the pub he drank in, in Foredoom. I was in a daze through it all, but from the names signed in the memorial book I recognised many from home: Hosty, Molloy, Ryan and O'Brien. Some of my friends were saying that Michael being only five years old was too young to attend his father's funeral. I was introduced to a very nice girl, by my friend Margie McAndrew. The girls name was Jeannie Paton, none other than the niece of Fr. Paton, the Rosary Crusader. She said she would love to take care of Michael for the day. I was glad to see Michael taking to Jeannie and holding her hand. I was lost for words to thank her; I knew he would be fine with her. Mr and Mrs McBennet, who lived across the hall from us, took care of baby Leo for that sad day.

Michael John Beggen died in his apartment at 1443 Taylor Ave., Bronx, N.Y. on the 19th November 1962, age 35 and is buried in St. Raymond's Cemetery, Bronx, N.Y. U.S.A.

Michael was from Scotstown, County Monaghan.

FIRST CHRISTMAS

This is our first Christmas without Mike (R.I.P.). Kind people gave us so many presents, donations, cards of sympathy, invitations to meals. Everyone was wonderful but nothing would or could take the ache away.

We had our Christmas dinner in McAndrew's; Margie and John were our good friends. Their daughter Maureen was the same age as our

Michael and Johnny a year older than Leo. (As time went on we drifted apart.)

1963 - MOUNT SINAI HOSPITAL

Many of my friends were advising me to find out exactly what the nature of Mikes illness was. I went to the Mount Sinai Hospital where Mike had undergone some tests. During the many years of tests Mike had endured in at least two hospitals, we had never been told the reason why he was constantly sick. On his death certificate was written, 'He died from double pneumonia,' but that had come on in the end.

After much waiting and answering questions (I was young and very timid), eventually I was told they would send out Michael's medical report to Dr. La Verdi. It finally arrived; there was a lot of detail within the report, but the answer to my question was Michael had a shrinking liver and possibly born with it. As he was getting older it was shrinking more and the only cure was a transplant, but this procedure was in the experimental stages and would not be completed for at least the next twenty years.

I was at last, satisfied and could tell his family the full cause of his long sad suffering.

GOING BACK TO IRELAND

Aunt Margie encouraged me to go back home to Ireland, and I took her advice. It took four months to get ready. Before leaving I had a headstone erected on my husband Michael John Beggen's grave. Shamrocks and a Celtic cross engraved on it with the necessary details, it stands in St Raimonds Graveyard, Bronx, N.Y. Next were the funeral expenses, which was already taken care of as Mike, 'rest his soul', had paid up his Union dues to the end of the year, so the Union paid the funeral costs, as was the case with sudden death of a young person. I had to show the death certificate at every stage of the organising, including my returning home to Ireland, and bringing my two sons out of America, but it was what I expected. The authorities I had to deal with apologised for the trouble they were causing me.

LEO'S FIRST BIRTHDAY

During the packing for leaving, Leo turned one year old on the 26th of February, 1963. Most things were packed and the apartment was in a mess.

"I won't be able to have a party for little Leo," I said to Aunt Margie.

"Don't worry," she said, "come up to my place and we will get a cake and invite a few friends in." This we did and Leo had a great time, and was running around. "He is good on the legs," said Marie Beggan. I told her how sad I felt when he started walking at ten months, because I couldn't tell his Dad. His brother was fourteen months when he took his first steps. Leo was having a great time being the centre of attention on his birthday.

AMERICAN LINER

I got the children's names on my passport and booked our passage on the 'S.S. America.' The shipping agent booked an elegant stateroom for us. On the 26th of April in 1963, we were to sail from the USA. Next was to continue the job of packing the trunks; and large cardboard boxes. Michael's tricycle, which his dad had bought for him, was secured in a wooden crate. Another piece of packing was the greeting cards Mike had given to me during our time together. Birthday, Valentine's, Easter, Christmas, wedding anniversary, Mother's day cards, I have them all wrapped up and tied with a ribbon. After over fifty years, I still have them.

Margie McAndrew helped me with the packing. I gave notice to the landlord and paid the last rent. Aunt Margie would mind the children during these busy times. My brother Paddy had moved to a family by the name of Dean who gave him accommodation.

It was a sad occasion for Mike's brother Felix, who had just arrived in the States the day before we left. He came to our apartment, which was empty of furniture. He stood against the wall crying; he was never to see his brother Mike alive again. My heart ached for him. Our luggage was already on the ship. Some of our furniture, I sold or gave to friends. The complete set of rosebud china, I gave to Uncle Leo. The sitting room Persian carpet, I sold to a couple; they would've paid me whatever price I asked. I wasn't sure how much to charge, but I knew I got its worth.

FAREWELL WEDDING DRESS

I left to the very last the packing of my wedding gown and veil. The two boys were with my dear friend Molly watching TV. The cardboard box was on the floor in the empty bedroom. Taking the beautiful white gown off its hanger, I kissed it laying it down on the floor; I wrapped it in several layers of white tissue paper then placed it inside the box. I proceeded to do the same with the veil and the white satin shoes. I had an image of the next person who would wear it and walk up the Church aisle to the altar, a young novice to make her vows as a bride of our lord. The Sisters of Charity came to collect the precious parcel, and they were very thankful to me as many young girls who wished to join their Order came from under privileged families and the donations of wedding gowns for the day of their special occasion was very welcome. The two Sisters in grey hugged me and said, "God will reward you for this." In my mind, I thought he already has, with my sons. "Now that we have met you, we have the very novice in mind who will wear it and she will pray for you and the boys at her profession." This made me happy knowing where it was going. Sell it!? That I could never do. Crossing the hall to Molly's apartment, I felt relieved. "Well Peggy, you will need some tea after that."

"I'm fine Molly. I thought I would be crying my heart out but I wasn't."

"God has blessed you with strength," said Molly.

BOARDING THE S.S. AMERICAN

Aunt Margie and Dan Callaghan brought the three of us in a yellow cab to the ship. I counted it among the rest of my loneliest days in my life. Aunt Margie in her grief voiced out loud, "I met you coming Peggy, and now I'm seeing you going." Mikes brothers Packie, Leo and Felix, Mike's aunts Mary McKenna and Margaret Connolly, his cousins John and Peggy McKenna, my girlfriends Maureen Farrell, Margie McAndrew, my good and loyal next-door neighbour, Molly O'Neill and some other neighbours came to the ship to bid us, 'Bon Voyage'. Our first-class cabin was full of family and friends. Someone ordered drinks, it may have been Packie. The goodbyes were over too soon. The ship's steward was going around ringing a bell shouting, "All non-passengers leave the ship in five." Oh God, it was a terrible feeling. Michael was fascinated with the cabin and the portholes. Baby Leo slept through all the farewells. Our luggage was in our cabin.

We did some unpacking; Michael wanted to play with his dinky cars. There was plenty of space on the fabulous red-carpeted cabin floor. I had a little chat with Michael before we headed to one of the state rooms. "Now my pet, you don't need to tell people about your daddy having gone to heaven, they might ask you too many questions."

"I won't, Mummy."

"Good boy." We found a nice small state room to sit in; a group of people were sitting in a circle, where a priest was with them. In no time, my son made his way to them. The priest asked him his name and Michael asked him his name. Michael came running to me and baby Leo, "Mam, Fr O'Reilly said for you to come and sit with them." I was going to object until I saw the group making room for me, so I joined in with them. One lady took Leo from me and sat him on her lap, I appreciated her help. The next day we joined them without invitation. Fr. O'Reilly sat next to me. In the course of our chat he remarked what a lovely chatty son I had, I agreed. Then he surprised me by saying, "You have had a tragedy recently in your life?" I blushed and nodded my head. I asked him had my son been talking about his dad?

"Indeed, he told all about him going to heaven, it's good for the little boy to talk about your loss."

"Thank you, Father." Thinking to myself, I was not thinking of the impact the death had on my young son, so I was glad he talked about it to Fr. O'Reilly. "You will be alright, your sons look well fed and dressed and so do you. I would say you are comfortable."

"I am Father, thank God."

"But you feel sorry for yourself, which is understandable, for you lost a good man."

"Only the best Father."

"Tomorrow I want you to meet a young mother with two small children. I would like you to listen to her story."

"I will, Father," I said.

MEETING THE YOUNG MOTHER

I will call her Mary and her little son and daughter. She was Irish and so was her husband. This was Mary's story: after the little girl was born, the father abandoned them and gave them no money. The landlord was asking for the rent of the apartment, and she didn't have it. The neighbours gave her food for herself and the children and some clothes and the parish priest gave her the rent money for a while, but then it stopped. "One neighbour encouraged me" said Mary, "to go talk to my husband's sister, and tell her the situation I was in, so I picked up the courage and travelled to her house, and knocked on her door. She looked at me and asked, "What is wrong Mary?"

I told her, "Your brother has left me and the children destitute; I am going to be turned out on the street. I have no money to pay rent or buy food; my neighbours are giving me food and clothes." She took a long time to answer me. I didn't know what I was going to hear her say. She was my only and last hope. "I don't have much money for you; my husband and I have two school-going children and a high monthly rent to pay. You and the children will have to go back to Ireland."

I cried, "I have no money at all, we had some savings in the bank, but he took the bank book."

"Do you know where he is living?" She asked.

"I don't," I said.

"Did he say why he was leaving you?"

"He did; he has a new woman and she is very good to him."

"The B------d!" Shouted his sister. "I will pay a month's rent and I will pay a one-way passage for you back to Ireland. Write and tell your family back home the way things are with you. You will have to pack."

I told her I had nothing to pack, so she gave me two big paper bags and said, "Put what you have into them. I will see you when I have things paid for you. I know I will never get the money back. I feel I must take care of my niece and nephew." I tried to thank her but she wouldn't listen to me. I went back to my neighbour who was minding the children and told her what happened.

My good neighbour said, "I will explain to the rest of the people helping you, we will take it in turns to feed you and the children until you leave; we don't have much ourselves."

"She was a Jewish lady and I will never be able to thank her enough."

"Oh Mary," I said as I held her tight, and I thought, "I was badly off." Next day I met Fr. O'Reilly, a Cavan man.

"Well, she told you of her plight?"

I said, "I want to cry for them."

"I want one more favour from you. You have a state cabin and I'm sure the latest in a shower?"

"Yes, Father, I said, "I have."

"The night before we disembark in Cobh, I want you to tell her to come to your cabin and take showers, and if you have any clothes that will fit her son dress him in a change of clothes. As you see, she has nothing only a few rags in them paper bags."

Everything went as the priest said. I was so proud as I looked at her little son looking so nice dressed in a pants and jumper of Michael's. The poor thing, she was so grateful to me. We hugged and said goodbye. I thought how hard a country America is to live in if you don't have the dollar or a family; it was an education for me. For months, I thought about her. I am sure she was in need of psychiatric treatment when she landed in Ireland. I prayed for her family to be kind to her and her children. All of this because of my five and a half year-old son Michael, disobeying me. I hope I was a help to the poor young mother and children. Our luggage was taken away the evening before we disembarked in Cobh. It was only a five-day trip in this beautiful liner. But so much had taken place. We were lucky we didn't get seasick.

ARRIVING IN COBH

Meeting us at Cobh was my brother Eddie, my sister Mary and Jimmy Nally. There were hugs and tears. Jimmy's large white van was packed to the roof taking us and our luggage back to Galway. Eddie had Michael on his lap crammed next to Mary in the back seat and I held Leo with me in the front. How was I surviving the whole thing? My nerves were at breaking point. Out of the blue without warning, I would get fits of the shakes and think I was going to die, they would last from two to five minutes. When they started first, about two months after my husband passing away, I went to Dr. La Verdi and told him I had this awful feeling hitting me on and off. He prescribed tablets. I thought they would clear it away, but they made me worse. I would go about in a daze and almost forget the baby, only for my son Michael reminding me when the baby would be crying. Then one day I realised what they were doing to me. It must have been God who alerted me, for I immediately decided not to take any more of them. I used my inner strength and prayer to work through the demon, and after two years it eased off. I lived in constant fear something would happen to me (and then what about my precious sons?). You watched over us, Mike.

Sitting quietly in the van, I got several bouts of the shakes as Jimmy drove the van nice and steady with the heavy load back to Galway. I tried to concentrate on all I could see, the cattle, green fields, men working in the fields, etc. Regardless, I would get an attack of the shakes. On one occasion, I wanted to jump out of the moving van.

Stopping in limerick, we had tea. Eddie and I switched seats and Michael liked this as now he could look out the front window but, tired out, he fell asleep. Mary took Leo from me and I fell asleep.

MOTHER WAITING AT THE DOOR

We arrived safely at Ballybrit; Mam with outstretched arms hugged and held me tightly to her chest. "Wish-a God look down on you, Maggie," she wept, and then looking at Michael she asked, "Do you remember me?"

"I do, Granny," he said. There were more hugs and kisses and Mam thought she could take Leo in her arms from Mary but nothing doing! He let out an unmerciful roar. "That's it, he is hungry. Come in. Honor has put a big fry up on the table for ye." Mam was pushing us ahead of her. Michael and his cousin Eammon made great friends. Eammon's brother James was younger and a little shy.

HUNGRY

Everyone ate plenty of rashers, sausages, puddings, black and white and eggs with homemade brown bread. My two sons didn't like the milk. I knew this would happen. "They won't like the food here," I said to Mam. Michael wasn't too bad but Leo turned up his nose at everything even though he was starving. I boiled a potato for him and mashed it up dry and he ate it up and was in great form after.

Eddie, Jimmy and Mary had a hard job trying to get the heavy luggage out of the van and bring it in the front door, and finally into the small room. The wooden crate with Michael's tricycle was left outside. He wanted it opened straight away to show Eammon what his daddy bought him. Jimmy opened the crate to take out the tricycle, but discovered it was broken; the front handle bars and front wheel had separated away from the rest of it. Michael cried, "I won't be able to ride it now."

Jimmy consoling him said, "I'll take it and fix it back together." In a couple of days it was back as good as new. Michael was a happy boy.

Mam brought me into the bed room behind the fire to show me how she had fixed it up for us. I thanked her. It was nice and cosy. Michael and I would sleep together and Leo slept in his Cousin James' cot. It was a small room but the best she had. I still had a box of presents to open. I had bought a red suit for Mary; the jacket had a black fur collar, a flecked coat with a wide collar, a sweater each for Mam and Honor, a shirt for Eddie and Jimmy, and T-shirts for Eammon and James. Everyone was happy with their gifts saying, "Maggie you had enough to do besides shopping for us."

"I'm glad you like them." I was very pleased with Mary's red suit and in guessing her size. It fitted her perfectly.

I AM BACK IN GALWAY

Back in Galway where now I would be raising my two sons Michael (six) and Leo (one year old). We lived for about a year with my mother in Ballybrit. The weather was very wet and I was unable to take Michael to school in Briarhill. He was missing a lot of days because I couldn't let him get wet as he was subject to getting tonsillitis. Doctor Michael O'Flaherty would come to the house and prescribe penicillin for him and tell me to keep him warm. One day I was sitting at the end of the kitchen table. Mam sitting by the fire looking at me. "Maggie," she says, "are you ever going to smile or laugh again?"

I didn't have an answer, and a few days later when something funny happened, I tried to laugh and a strange noise came from my throat. It scared me. In time my laugh came back. I discovered the deep sorrow was easing away. Mam asked, "Did you realise you weren't smiling or laughing for months?"

I said, "I did but I wasn't able to do either. Thank God I am now. Mam," I said, "I'm going to buy a car or Michael will never be able to go to school."

"Are you joking?" She laughed; "sure you're not able to drive."

"I'll have to learn," I said with a laugh. During our stay with Mam my brother Eddie came to visit me often and talk to my two sons. I told him about my idea of buying a car. "Buy a small one," he advised.

SCOTSTOWN

I had to go and visit the Beggens in Scotstown, County Monaghan. The boy's Uncle Frank and family wanted to meet their brother's two sons.

"I'll come with you," my sister Mary offered. We packed a couple of cases and got the Derry bus to Monaghan town. It was a long journey with at least two changes of buses. When we arrived at the Beggen family home in Scotstown, Uncle Frank and his wife Rose were there to meet us with open arms. I could see the tears in Frank's eyes as he looked at his little nephews. It was a sad meeting. They brought us into their warm kitchen. Frank introduced their daughter Susan who was about the age of two. Their son Brendan was a baby. "These are your cousins, Michael," said Frank, "shake hands."

The children stood looking at each other. Susan was looking at Michael from behind her dad. It was an emotional time for me as I was remembering back to the time I was in Scotstown and the marvellous three months holiday Mike (R.I. P.) and I enjoyed. His mother, God rest her, was living at the time.

We spent two nice weeks in Scotstown. Many callers came to sympathise with me and to meet Mike's two sons. I was glad I made the trip for Frank to meet his brother Mike's children. When we were leaving, my brother-in-law had some kind words to say. "Peggy if you ever meet someone you would like to marry, feel free to marry him. We won't mind and I'm speaking for all of us. You are a very young, attractive widow."

"Oh thank you Frank, but marrying again is far from my mind. My thanks to you and Rose for everything."

It was a long journey back to Galway but now it was done and I could relax.

HIRING A CARAVAN

After our trip to Scotstown, County Monaghan, and our welcome visit to the Beggen family, it was time to have a holiday in County Clare. I hired out a caravan. Mary's friend Veronica Heneghan hitched it to her car and we headed to Uncle Paddy Hurley's. Not to Kilnacree this time, but to their new residence in Moygala, Six-Mile-Bridge. We parked in their front lawn. Mother and Mary came with us. Veronica and mother spent one night and drove home next day; they would be back in two weeks to tow us back to Galway. It was a lovely, hot summer. I had a small pram for Leo. He was a year and a half old. Michael celebrated his sixth birthday while we were in Moygala. We walked miles up and down the mountain roads visiting family and friends. Aunt Mary was back living in the old house in Reinaskomoge with her brother Jimmy, until a senior's house was available in Six-Mile-Bridge. She gave us a big welcome.

"Well, Maggie do you remember the night long ago when we moved from Kilnacree to here?"

"I will never forget it," I said.

"Ah times change Maggie, sure look at you now a young widow at 28. You'll marry again?"

"Never, Mary," I said.

"Ah, a stor, we never know what is laid out for us." moaned Aunty with a faraway look in her tear-stained eyes. When so many sympathisers hugged me in this way, Michael would stand by my side looking at the ground.

"What is my little man thinking?" I would wonder to myself.

Our next two-mile walk was to visit O'Neill's and my dear friend Maureen and her mother, and like everyone we visited, there was great sympathy pouring out for me, a widow so young with two young sons. They were delighted to have had met my late husband when we made the trip in 1956/57.

The long, bright summer evenings made walking the countryside extremely enjoyable. During the long walk back down the hill to Moygala, I would point out to Mary the road I had to walk to Six-Mile-Bridge school when I was only eight years old. She found it hard to believe. Mary would carry Leo when I gave Michael a ride in the pram.

Coming in view of the caravan, Michael would run to get into it. Uncle Paddy's wife Anne would have the table set for our tea in her kitchen; ham, hard-boiled eggs and home-made bread, we would be ready for it. She would have a lovely boiled potato kept for Leo. In between mouthfuls we would tell her of our day and the people we visited. She wouldn't let us do the washing up;

"Go to ye're beds," she would say with a laugh. As a farmer's wife she had plenty of farm work for doing. We slept in the caravan. In the morning, we woke up to the musical sound of cows being milked, the cock crowing, the dog barking as he helped to get the cows up to the field. It was magic. Soon the holiday was over and mother and Veronica were back to hook the caravan on to the car. We said our goodbyes and headed home. As I looked back I could see the ground where the caravan was parked; it was bare of grass! "I hope Uncle Paddy won't be mad, I have destroyed his lawn," I said.

"The grass will grow again." said my sister, comforting me.

PRESIDENT KENNEDY

June 1963, and Ireland is preparing for the visit of the American President. Galway is also very busy for John F. Kennedys' visit to Eyre Square. Michael was excited. "Will we get near enough to shake hands with the President, Mom?"

"There will be a lot of people there and the cops will allow only certain important people near him," I answered. We were near the Great Southern Hotel and couldn't see him but we could hear him. It was a beautiful summer's day and the cavalcade of cars and motorbikes added to the whole atmosphere. The corporation, in their robes, was led by the Mayor of Galway, Martin Divilly, in his chain of office. It was a pity we could not get nearer to the platform for my son to shake the President's hand.

FIRST CHRISTMAS IN GALWAY

This was Michael's first Christmas away from the home he knew in America. He was very worried that Santa Claus wouldn't find him in a different country. I reminded him of the letter he wrote to Santa and how he put his new address on it and Santa knows where all little boys live. He was still not too sure until the day I took him and his brother to Glynn's in Shop Street. Here in this shop there were all kinds of toys sold, but the main attraction that day was Santa Claus. I paid the six shillings for the two Santa gifts. Going upstairs to Santa's Cave, I got some doubtful looks from my six year-old son. We had to queue for a while and when it was Michael's turn to sit on Santa's knee, he made such a rush he almost knocked poor old Santa off his chair. They had a long chat and he got his little bag from Santa and was the happiest boy in the world.

I was happy too. Leo was not two years old yet, and when it came to his turn and he saw the man in the white beard, he began to cry. Santa laughed and handed me a little bag for him. It was the greatest day of the festive season for Michael; Santa now knew him and where he lived.

Christmas morning and arriving home after early Mass in Castlegar, there was great excitement in my mother's kitchen. There was no Christmas tree but plenty of presents placed around the fire place and Santa remembered everyone. Mother did the cooking of the goose and all that went with it; my sister made the trifle the night before. My job was setting the table. We sat around with the big red candle glowing in the centre, our plates laden with food and Michael was happy. It was a beautiful Christmas day.

1964 - A MINI MINOR CAR

I bought a green Mini Minor Car H I M 192 in Paddy O'Flaherty's garage in Galway for £400. After three driving lessons I took over. "Now," I said to Michael, "you won't miss any more days from school." On Fridays I did my shopping in Cameron's in Bohermore, and then drove to Shop Street, parked the mini outside Lyndon's Bakery shop, and took my two boys upstairs to the restaurant to find a table, while the waitress would bring a highchair for Leo and give the boys pages and colouring pencils. It was Friday and eating meat was forbidden, so I would order fish, potatoes and vegetables. Michael would ask for toast and a scrambled egg, and Leo would have a dish of mashed potatoes. On the way out I would stop at the bread counter and buy cupcakes/buns. The boys loved the cottage loaf. At home, mother made soda and treacle bread.

As there were few cars on the road in 1964, I was able to cope in a low gear until I'd get the courage to drive in the second one. This little car lasted over eight years until the floor started letting in the water from the road. I would place pieces of carpet on it to keep the boy's shoes dry.

MICHAEL GOES TO SCHOOL

It was a great adventure for Michael when he went to school in Briarhill. The kids were fascinated with his American accent and some would try to imitate him and make fun of him, but there was always a friend to back him up, especially with the Connolly's nearby (Later known as the Connolly Hurlers).

In the same year there was more news of President Kennedy; he was assassinated in November, one year after my husband Mike Beggen died. On the day he was killed, my son Michael was having his tonsils removed in Galvia Hospital (now Bon Secours). The nurses and patients were being very careful that Michael wouldn't hear the sad news as he was American and six years old, he might get upset. There was so much sadness around; everyone was in mourning.

NEWS OF ANOTHER ADDITION TO THE ABBERTON FAMILY

On one of Eddie's visits to mother's house, he told us Honor was expecting a baby sometime in August. "We will be praying for ye," said mother. When I heard that news, I would bring Leo with me to Honor's house every day and help her all I could. Michael went to school with the neighbour's kids and granny Abberton gave him his dinner in the evening; Eamon and James were in school also. Leo had fun playing with their toys. When Eddie came home from work in the evenings, I would go home to mother's and my two sons, and they would play until it was rosary time and then to bed. Start of the next day it was the same routine again. As time went on, I was taking Honor to the doctor for her check-ups. The time came and Honor gave birth to a baby girl in the Regional Hospital on the second of August. Eammon and James were happy they got a baby sister. Everyone was thankful that mother and baby were well.

One day, mother was bursting with news. "Maggie," she said, "you had better go down to Honor, she has news for you."

I got a feeling of anxiety; "What could be wrong?" I asked.

"You go down and you will find out."

"Come on boys, we have to go to Honor's." Of course they didn't mind; they would be playing with their cousins Eammon and James. Going in the door, I asked, "What is wrong, Honor?

"Nothing is wrong; we are having the Christening on Sunday, and would like you to stand as godmother for baby Ann?"

"Thanks," I said, "it will be my pleasure. I must shop for a nice present for my God-daughter."

Anthony Ryan's shop sold children's clothes for all sizes. I decided to buy a cuddly pink baby blanket for her. I showed it to Mother.

"Sure, Maggie it's lovely; you wouldn't get the like of it in America."

"Oh Mam," I said, "thanks."

LEGION OF MARY

My sister Mary and I joined the Castlegar Legion of Mary. The meetings were held weekly on Friday evenings in the old school. My two sons would stay with their granny. Driving down to the meeting in second gear, Mary would be telling me to pick up speed.

"I will, give me time." We had good laughs about my driving. There was a big group of people in attendance at the Legion of Mary meeting. I knew most of them from my time going to Briarhill School. The setting was very devout. A white cloth was spread on the table, a statue of Our Lady placed in the centre, a model of the "Vexillum Legionis" made with a staff resting on top of the world, attached to the staff a Miraculous Medal, and above Our Lady's head the words: "Legio Mariae." Over that there was a dove with wings spanned out, finishing with a circle, someone would place two small vases of flowers each side of Our Lady's statue.

The Spiritual Director opened the meetings with everyone sitting around the table reading the Legion prayers from the Tesseria. Instructions were given as to what charitable work we should do during the week. Some would do house visitation, others would visit the sick in hospital. I went with Mary Wall on hospital visitations. It was sad for many of the old people to have no one to visit them. They appreciated our visits and we would take them religious magazines. A summer outing was arranged. One of the sights to see was Ardnacrusha where the electricity was generated. It was a wonderful outing. I, of course was anxious to get back to my two sons and give my poor mother some peace. It was my last connection with the Legion of Mary, for afterwards we moved to a flat in the town.

Legion of Mary

TOO RICH

I applied for a corporation house in Mervue. A council surveyor came to mothers to take my details and measure the room the two children and I were sharing. Yes, I would be eligible for a cooperation house. He sat at the kitchen table to take down personal details from me, and when it came to the question of my monthly pension from the States, I gave him the details of my pension and the children's separate pension they would be in receipt of until they finished college; he looked at me, and immediately closed the book.

"What is wrong?" I asked.

Tapping me on the shoulder, he said, "Your American pension would keep six widows in this country." And with that he left.

Mam said, "Well Maggie, you are too rich."

RENTING A FLAT

With the return of my brother Paddy from America, I moved out from mothers and rented a furnished flat in Munster Avenue, Galway, from Silke & Company. The entrance to the flat was down a laneway at the side of the building. I thought it very safe and convenient to park the mini at the door. We had to climb a stairs to the three rooms, a bed room, bathroom and kitchen-cum-living room. The man who handed me the keys showed me the shower switch. He said nothing as to how the water was heated. After moving into the flat, I tried to get hot water but it never heated. I wasn't told I must put money in the meter for this purpose. Search as I might, I couldn't see how the flat was heated. It was the month of August and the weather was warm and the schoolchildren were still on their holidays. I was thinking to myself that when Michael goes back to school I will need to get the two of them up early and dressed and then drive over three miles out the road to Briarhill School, then drive back again in the evening to pick him up. I thought, "This is not a good move." My sister Mary came to stay with us a couple of nights' she would leave her bicycle in the hall ready for the morning to take her to work.

Early one morning as she was leaving, I could hear her opening the door then she let out a shout. "Maggie, come down quick! Your car is destroyed."

Taking one look at my new Mini Minor, I almost fainted. Part of the roof was bashed in, two windscreens were broken, and the back seat was soaked in Guinness. A man came down the lane to tell me the guards caught four young lads vandalising the car. They had stolen full siphons out of McNamara's shop and banged in the roof. "It's a new car, I have it only four months," I said.

The man advised me to go back to where I bought it and tell them what happened. I told Paddy O'Flaherty of O'Flaherty's Motors what happened. They took the mini and fixed it as good as new, but could not get the smell of Guinness out of it. I asked how much it cost. They told me if vandalism occurs in the town, the Corporation pays the cost. I was very thankful to them. A week later, a little thatched cottage became vacant in Ballyloughane.

LIVING IN A THATCHED COTTAGE

I rented the thatched cottage in Ballyloughane for the boys and myself from Maureen Nolan and her niece Nora. I had already bought a quarter acre of land in Ballybane from Mickey Coyne, in order to have a house built to my liking.

Fr. Jack O'Connor gave me the name of a builder; Sean Usher. I spoke to Sean and we agreed on a price of £4000 to build a two-story house designed by engineer John/Sonny Coyne. Sean said he would get the men to start right away. We lived nine months in the cottage until our house was built. While living there, I held lots of parties for the boys. For Michael's 7th birthday, I collected as many children in the Mini Minor from Ballybrit as it would hold, Corcorans, Flahertys, Connollys and O'Connors, and brought them to Michael's party. It was July and beautiful weather. They played outdoors and ate lots of goodies and chunks of cake. The time flew and soon it was time to gather them all up and take them home. They were nice, mannerly children and all thanked Mrs Beggen. I met Lucy Glynn in Nolan's one evening; she was very friendly and invited me to visit herself and her husband John.

"You would be welcome any time," she said. They lived close by.

The evening I called to see them, I brought Leo with me. John and Lucy had five children and I had a lovely evening with them. Michael was playing with a boy he made friends with from next door. As I was leaving, Lucy suggested we go out to a dance some Sunday night. "I would really love that," I said. As soon as I had a babysitter arranged to stay with my boys, I would let them know. A girl I went to school with, Maureen Egan was willing to oblige. I got ready and picked up Lucy and John for a night of old-time dancing in the Lebane Hall. We had an enjoyable night and I said I wouldn't mind going again. John said,

"Why not? There are some nice farmers out there." Lucy and I laughed.

"I think he wants you to marry a farmer," Lucy said.

"She could do worse."

"I know I could John, thanks anyway." Soon Halloween was with us, so a Halloween party was in preparation. I did the same thing again, gathering the Ballybrit children in the Mini Minor. This was a great party, with pin-the-tail-on-the-donkey, snap apple, and dunking for an apple in a basin of water, blind-folded. There was a prize for winners in spite of the cheating. Returning the kids back home again to their parents, they all once again thanked Mrs Beggen.

Years later, having put Ballyloughane to the back of my mind, I met Joe Connolly of "Connolly Hurlers."

"I will never forget the great parties you put on in the cottage, Mrs Beggen," he said. "I enjoyed that Halloween, one the best."

I couldn't believe my ears. "Joe," I said, "imagine you still remember that time and it's so long ago."

"I do," he said. It was so good to hear.

SEWING MACHINE

In 1964 as I was walking down Shop Street, I decided to go into the Singer Sewing Machine Shop. There and then, I bought a sewing machine. It had an electric motor on its side and a floor pedal. It was a big challenge for me. I had never used one. I spent hours trying to work out how to thread the bobbin and set the needle into its place; it was more complicated than I expected.

I was looking forward to making my own curtains and drapes, to have them ready for when we moved into our new house. It was in constant daily use. I also challenged myself at trying to make a summer dress for myself. I discovered this was not easy. I had to learn how to follow a pattern. But I mastered that too. I was proud of the flowery summer dress I made myself.

OCTOBER

It was a cold wintry night and as we lived near the sea, it made it all the colder. I was getting the two boys ready for bed in front of the warm open fire, when I heard a knock on the door. I wondered, "Who could be calling at this hour?"

I opened the door a little and peeped into the dark. "Who is it?" I asked. The person that answered was someone I would never have thought of in a million years. It was my brother-in-law Leo Beggen, all the way from Brooklyn.

"Leo," I said, "what are you doing here?" While welcoming him in at the same time. "Come in out of the cold," I said. He made straight for the warm fire and to hug his two nephews. He explained his sudden visit. His old Aunt Margaret had died in Scotstown. "I'm home for the funeral; Mick Rooney came to pick me up. It's a long drive from Shannon to Monaghan." I shook hands with Mick. Michael kept them entertained while I prepared the tea for them.

"Would ye like a sandwich?" I asked.

"A couple of slices of bread and butter will do nicely," Leo answered. "What a nice old house you are living in."

I said, "Yes, but in another few months we will be moving into the one I'm having built."

"You are great Peggy, and the two boys are getting big."

"How did you find us Leo?"

"It wasn't easy but Mick knows his way around Galway."

"Thank you so much for calling on us; will ye stay the night?"

"We won't. The funeral is tomorrow; as it is, they are holding it over for us."

"I think I will go too, I knew poor old Aunt Margaret so well, she was your mother's sister."

"There is only Aunt Mary left and she is already in Scotstown, she flew in yesterday to Dublin."

"I will go, I'll get ready early in the morning and head off up to the funeral too." "Why did you come by Shannon airport, Leo?"

"As I was coming I thought I would call to see you and the boys."

"You are very kind, Leo."

"We will go now; it's a long road. Thanks for the tea. Sure, we might see you tomorrow." I wished them a safe journey.

Early morning, I dragged the two boys out of bed, we ate a light breakfast and dressed up warm. I packed some food for the long journey and put pillows and a blanket in the back seat of the Mini and snuggled the two boys down. I locked the door and shook the Holy water on us before heading out on this long journey. We made two stops, the first one after two hours of driving and the boys were ready to eat. I was ready myself for a hot mug of tea. God bless the inventor of flasks. We arrived safely in Scotstown and the boys were fine. Their Uncle Frank and his wife Rose welcomed us. I was glad to see Aunt Mary Mc Kenna who was crying after her sister. "I'm the only one of the three left," she sobbed.

Many people were coming and going, paying their respects to the Beggens. We enjoyed a lovely hot lunch and the heat of the blazing open fire in the parlour. The guest bedroom was off the parlour where Mike, R.I.P. and I slept when we were home eight years ago on our three-month holiday. Happy times back then. Michael and Leo slept upstairs. Their Uncle Frank had a bed for them. I slept in the guestroom with about five more in the one bed. We had a laugh, two at the bottom and three at the top. Urbalshany Church was full for the funeral of Margaret Connolly. She was well-known to the people of Scotstown even though she spent many years in America; it was her wish to come home to die in her village of Scotstown.

The time came for us to hit the long road home and I was glad to have met up with the boys' Uncle Leo. "I hope we will meet soon again, Peggy."

"We will, please God." I filled the tank of petrol and got the boys into the car after many hugs from their Uncles and grand Aunt Mary. We headed out on the road. The weather was so cold, I was afraid it would freeze before we were home. Stopping in Athlone for a meal and a short rest broke the journey for us.

Wake up boys, we are home." They stretched and yawned, then hit the cold. "Hurry boys, help me bring in some of the things out of the car. I will get the fire lit." We kept our coats on and with the welcome heat from the blazing open fire and hot soup we soon warmed up.

CELEBRATING CHRISTMAS

It was fun in the cottage for Michael; he would look up the chimney of the open fireplace to see that Santa had plenty of space to come down. "I can see the sky," he would say. It is bedtime and with two hot water bottles to warm the bed on the very cold nights, the three of us slept together in the one double bed. Tomorrow was Christmas day and we had to be up in time for Mass and to visit the crib, come home and finish opening the presents. We would be going to Uncle Eddie's for dinner. Early morning, Michael was up and out in the kitchen. He let out a shout. "What is it, Michael?" I asked.

"Come quickly, Mam until you see what Santa brought me! Look Mammy, a bicycle." There was great excitement. "Will you teach me how to ride it, Mam?"

"I will Michael, but not today. Let's see what Leo got." He got a train set.

"Can we play with it?"

"After Mass; right now we must get dressed and have breakfast."

"What did you get, Mam?"

"Let me see, Oh! A bathrobe, just what I wanted. It's a lovely warm one too."

The boys had a lovely time playing with Eammon and James as they tell each other what they got from Santa. Selection boxes were great gifts then, with a variety of sweets. Eddie and Honor gave my lads one each.

"Don't open them until you're at home," said Honor.

Michael said, "Thanks for the gifts." A tin of USA biscuits, colouring books, and pencils were our gifts to the family. The dinner of goose and trimmings was tasty with custard and jelly for the sweet. Honor had made a nice Christmas cake. I felt the emptiness of not having my husband Mike, but watching my sons playing games of Ludo with their cousins, I knew they were happy. It was time to leave for home. We didn't like leaving the warm kitchen and going out in the freezing cold night.

We thanked Eddie and Honor for a lovely dinner and went back to the cottage. The three of us settled into the one bed together again. I asked what they would like to do the next day.

"Teach me how to ride my bike," said Michael.

"We will wait until the weather warms up, son. How about we make our Christmas visit to Granny Abberton's tomorrow?"

"I would love that," said Michael, "and bring her a Christmas present." Granny was happy to see us and hear all about what Santa brought down the chimney; to Michael a bicycle, and a train set to Leo. Then she gave the boys biscuits and lemonade and cut a big slice of her Christmas cake for me, at the same time pouring a glass of Sandeman port wine for the two of us. It was a good Christmas.

1965 - FELL FROM HER BIKE

Mother had the dinner ready and was waiting for Mary to come in for her lunch. We sat at the table looking out the window watching for my sister to come cycling up the mile of a road, as she did every day at lunchtime from her job in the Royal Tara China Factory, Mervue. Mother was a bit anxious as she was late that day. Then we saw her coming, walking and wheeling her bicycle.

"She must have got a puncture," I said and I went to help her.

"What is wrong, Mary?" I asked.

"I fell off the bike."

"Go into the house and I will put the bike away."

"You had better take her to the hospital; that arm is broken," said Mam

"I will be alright; I'll go tomorrow," said Mary.

"You should go now," mother encouraged, "get into Maggie's car and she will take you to the hospital. That arm needs to be seen to."

At the Regional Hospital in Galway, Mary was taken for an X-ray and a doctor came to talk to me.

"Your sister has a bad break at her elbow. She needs an operation and possibly the support of a pin or two. I started to cry. "Will she have the use of her arm?" I asked.

"She will. We are keeping her in for a few days, go and talk to her. She may need a few things."

I found the ward she was in. Poor Mary was feeling miserable. "You will be alright, Mary. What do you need brought in and I will get them?"

"Call into the factory on your way home and let them know what happened to me."

This I did and the girl in the office was very sympathetic to hear that Mary Abberton had, had an accident.

Mary was allowed home after a few days. She had lots of visitors, especially Veronica Heneghan and Jimmy Nally.

The six weeks passed and it was time for the plastercast to come off. On the way to the hospital, Mary and I were rejoicing at the thought of her arm being free from the cumbersome cast. Sitting in the out patients waiting room, I began to worry if something had gone wrong. As I was so long waiting. Then the nurse came and told me, "Your sister fainted after the cast was removed, don't be worried this happens to some patients. I will have her up to you in five minutes."

At last we are on our way home. "Do you feel sick, Mary?"

"Not now. I did when the cast was taken off, my arm felt so weak. I won't be going back to work for a few weeks. I need physiotherapy to help straighten my arm."

Mother was glad to see Mary home and so were my two sons.

A SAD MOMENT

One of my saddest moments was when my son Michael made his First Holy Communion. I wished his daddy was there to see him looking smart in his brown pinstriped suit, white shirt, red tie; rosette with his First Holy Communion medal pinned to it, white socks, and brown shoes. How proud and sad I was all at the same time. Granny Abberton and my sister Mary attended the Mass in Castlegar church and of course his brother Leo added to the celebration for Michael. Afterwards we went to the G.B.C. restaurant for a little treat.

OUR OWN HOME

In June, we moved from the cottage in Ballyloughane to our own home in Ballybane which was getting the last finishing touches. But before we left we had to say our goodbyes to Lucy, John Glynn and the family. Lucy knew I liked to attend the Patrician Musical Society Concert (P.M.S) when it would be performing in the Town Hall Theatre. She suggested we would arrange to go the next time. I said, "For sure, Lucy." We said our goodbyes to Maureen and Nora Nolan who had been so good to us and promising to keep in touch. I packed our few items up on Paddy McDermott's ass and cart and left with a feeling of happiness and loneliness. Michael was very excited about the ass and asked me to get one for him. He promised he would give Leo a ride on the donkey's back. I said love we have a car. We were on our way to our new two-storey, eight-room home with a quarter-acre of ground that in time would be growing a variety of vegetables. On settling into our new home, I felt something was missing.

At dinner-time one day, I said to the boys we need to give our home a name. Lots of suggestions were made and finally we decided on ""Rock Dale"." It kept that name for forty years.

B&B

Having painted and furnished the house, I started the business of Bed and Breakfast. The last week of July was the week of the Ballybrit Races and I was ready to receive paying guests. It was very exciting and it helped me put the loss of my husband to the back of my mind for a while. The first year my sister Mary helped me during the busy two days. The holiday season lasted to the middle of September. I enjoyed this venture. The season of B&B started again in Easter week, and eased of for a few weeks before getting into full swing from June to September with foreign visitors, mostly German. The house was paying for itself. The first few years was hard going, as the property rates encrested each year and we didn't have running water, as the tank would be empty in the dry, hot summer time. We had to buy water. The amount we would get delivered was about a hundred gallons, as the delivery tank would only hold about that amount. Like the farmers, we prayed for the rain to come.

CONCERT

I called to see Lucy to remind her that P.M.S. were putting on a concert in the Town Hall Theatre for Christmas. "Thank you for reminding me; my son Liam will join us. Do you have a babysitter?"

"Yes, Maureen Egan is staying with the boys for me." I picked Lucy and Liam up and we headed for a night at the theatre. There were some wonderful singers but the one that stands out in my mind was Gerry Glynn of Glynn's shop. He had a wonderful voice. It was a beautiful way to start the Christmas season. I left Lucy and her son Liam home and then took Maureen home. The boys were cuddled up fast asleep in their beds.

HISTORY

History was repeating itself. Like my mother changing me from Briarhill School to the Convent of Mercy in the town in 1946, I was taking Michael from Briarhill School to send him to St. Patrick's School, also in the town, in 1965. The difference was I had to walk the three miles. Nineteen years later, I have a car and Michael doesn't need to do the three-mile walk. It was at this time, aged nine, Michael took up learning to play the piano. The next step was to buy one for him. It was a second-hand Steinway, recommended by his teacher, Mrs Bucan. I bought it in Rafferty's, paying £180 for it. Michael loved playing the piano, and he passed his grades with excellent marks each year. He also played the piano accordion. He was learning Irish dancing in the Peggy Carty School of Dancing and winning many medals and trophies. One very precious medal was the Connacht champion silver medal award. He won it in a feis, dancing a heavy jig. When Michael and Mary Moran were getting married in 1981, I was hoping he would take the piano with him. He said, "No Mam, Mary has a small organ and it will do the two of us." The piano was lying idle for a few years. I decided to sell it for what I paid for it. Having it tuned first, I asked the man tuning it, how much I should sell it for?

"It's a Steinway, the best piano made; you should get £300." I thanked him for his advice and paid him his fee of £9. I did not believe I would get such a price for it, as it was well over twenty years old. I advertised it in the Connacht Tribune and was successful in getting £300 for it without question from a person who I'm sure knew its value.

EDDIE MAKES A SUGGESTION

During one of my brother Eddie's many visits to mother's house to talk to Michael and Leo. He made a suggestion saying, "Now you have a car Maggie, would you like to come up to Ballinasloe to see our father?" It took me a while to comprehend what he said. "I don't know," I answered. He explained that when he would be playing hurling matches in Ballinasloe, Dad would come to watch him. Then, after the match they would have a chat. Dad would sometimes ask for me. "The last time we were talking, I told him that your husband died. he said to tell you to come up to visit him."

I agreed to go saying, "I would love to meet him. But he is a long time in St Bridget's."

"That makes no difference," he assured me. Eddie called St. Bridget's Hospital and set up a day for the visit.

AT AGE THIRTY-TWO

At age 32 to be meeting my father for the first time made me both nervous and excited. On that exciting day, I brought my two sons to meet their Granddad Abberton. Eddie, his wife Honor, and their two sons Eammon and James also came. Eddie walked in first and said, "Dad, this is Margaret." We looked at each other for a while, then he reached out his hand and said, "You're welcome."

"Thank you, Dad." The word 'dad' was out of my mouth before I knew it.

"Tell me who the boys are." Eammon and James were introduced first. "They're our lads," said Eddie, "this is my wife Honor."

"So these are the yanks," said Dad with a smile as he looked at my boys. "Lovely boys," he said in a half-whisper. The introductions over, Dad said, "Sit into the table. I have the tea and cake ready for ye, with lemonade and biscuits for the boys." He had his own private quarters. Dad was quite tall, about six foot; he was dressed in a grey jacket and pants, a striped shirt, and wore a peaked cap. Smiling at me, he said, "Tell me, what it was like living in America and about your life there." We talked for a long time and I told him about my husband Michael passing away so young. He was sorry to hear he died before his sons grew up, adding, "That's life. You had to emigrate," he said, then laughed.

He was a lovely singer; and sang 'I'll take you home again Kathleen' while we clapped. "Now, Michael and Eammon, you boys sing us a song."

They sang a school song. As we were leaving he invited us to come again soon. It was to me a great day meeting my father.

At the start of this story I mentioned our father and mother getting married. As you read through you will have noticed I have not mentioned him. He was a person I didn't remember, as I was only two years old when I was taken to my grandmothers in County Clare. Early in my story, I explained how I asked my mother about my dad, and she told me the circumstances of his illness and why he was in a psychiatric hospital getting treatment. Being so long in what he felt was a safe place, and being used to a certain routine; he had no desire to leave.

DAD SHOWS US HIS GARDEN

We went again to visit dad. This time he brought us out to see his garden of potatoes and vegetables. "This is my kitchen garden. I grow lettuce and everything for salads, and I have some rhubarb growing here too. The hospital chef comes out and gathers what he needs." Dad gave Eddie some advice on gardening and he told us how he liked to exercise the doctor's hounds by taking them for walks in the evenings. He and Eddie's conversations were mostly on hurling matches, while I served up the tea and biscuits. This time, I had a cake for him. "Did you make it yourself?" he asked.

I felt embarrassed saying, "No."

"Next time you come, bring me one you made yourself. I'll give this to the staff unless the boys want it." They didn't, preferring the biscuits. I asked dad what kind of cake I should make for him. "Plain homemade brown bread," was his answer. When we were leaving he said, "Come soon again."

"We will," we promised, as we waved good bye. Driving home, Eddie would tell me how dad would come to the wall and watch the hurling matches. Eddie took great satisfaction out of these meetings and the discussion on how he played the match. In years to come I would think how privileged they were to have those times together. Dad took a great interest in everything Eddie did, especially the sport he loved, hurling, He would watch him lifting the sliotar (ball) off the ground onto the hurley, then the different poses he would take to strike it either high or low. He played the match with gusto and celebrated, win or lose. He had a liking for the drink on the weekends, like many of his comrades. I often felt he drank to fill the absences of his father. But the meetings at the hospital wall and knowing his Dad had watched him playing the match gave him satisfaction.

He was the oldest of our family and as a very young lad, the only bread winner our mother had.

MARY'S WEDDING

My sister Mary Abberton was making plans to get married. Herself and Jimmy Nally had set the date. I would be her bridesmaid, Harry Nally was best man, and my son Michael and his cousin Eammon were pageboys. Among the invitations were ones for Aunt Mary Hurley, Anne Hurley, Uncle Paddy's wife and my friend Maureen O'Neill. I drove to County Clare the day before the wedding to pick them up in my Mini Minor. Maureen stayed with me, a great treat for the two of us, and Aunt Mary and Anne stayed with mother. My sister made a beautiful bride in her long, white wedding gown and veil, as she walked down the aisle of St. Columba's Church, Castlegar on the arm of her brother Eddie. Coming behind her were the two pageboys Eammon and Michael, and I was behind them wearing a full-length blue dress and matching hat. Maureen Nolan (owner of the cottage I was renting) took care of baby Leo for the day.

GOING TO A WEDDING

Going to a wedding is the making of another, or so the song says. I did not believe in such things.

At Jimmy and Mary's reception in the Banba Hotel, Salthill we were all chatting and admiring the handsome couple. It was then I met Paddy Dowling. He was a friend of Jimmy Nallys. In the course of our conversation we disclosed some of our past to each other which held a resemblance. He suggested we meet up again sometime. Paddy was the first man I took a liking to since my husband Michael's passing; it was the same for Paddy. I was the first love of his life after his wife Rita passed away. Mary and Jimmy went on their honeymoon to Monaghan to friends of mine, Frank and Nelly Kelly. I told them to be sure and come to my house when they came back. "I'll have a little party for ye, it will be just the family." I also invited Paddy Dowling. It was a lovely get-together and the first party I held in "Rock Dale" on the 21st February. I didn't know it was Paddy's birthday until he said, "Guess whose birthday it is today?"

I said, "Don't tell us it's yours, Paddy! All right everyone, let's sing Happy Birthday to Paddy."

"Oh," said my good sister, "the party is not for us Jimmy, it's for Paddy." I was explaining that I didn't know it was Paddy's birthday until he told us just now, so we are having two celebrations. Paddy felt uncomfortable. "I shouldn't have said anything," he apologised.

"If I had known I would have a baked you a birthday cake, Paddy."

"I'm getting a bit old for birthday cakes," laughed Paddy. It was soon time for everyone to say goodnight. Paddy and I sat a while chatting. Before he left, Paddy asked if he could take my phone number and said he would call me some time, giving me a peck on the cheek. Then he walked home to Bohermore. I wondered when the sometime would be.

A BARBER

Paddy was a barber in Grant's, Eyre Square, Galway. He and his son Eugene lived in Bohermore. His young daughter Geraldine lived with her late mother's sister Mary, also in Bohermore. Paddy was the oldest of his family and went to Cavan where his mother's father, granddad Brennan, owned a barber shop. Here he learned how to shave with the cut-throat razor, by coating balloons with shaving foam and then shaving it, until he eventually stopped bursting the balloons. He would tell how he could not remember the many balloons he destroyed; there were bags filled with the burst remains. When he finally stopped bursting balloons, he was allowed to shave a man's face. His granddad said, "A steady hand now, Paddy." He was at last qualified. Paddy's mother, Mary Brennan Dowling, passed away in the 1950's leaving his father Michael/ Mick Dowling to rear seven very young children. In the course of time his dad met a gentle Connemara lady, Bridget Murray, who worked for a priest in Monasterevin, County Kildare. Mick and Bridget married and had four children; three daughters and a son. Bridget was now a mother to eleven children and she was a kind and caring person. Paddy came to Galway from Monasterevin and worked in Healey's Barbers in Dominick St. He eventually went to Grant's in Eyre Square where he remained as a barber for many years.

1966 - DATING

After a few weeks, Paddy did phone me for a chat. He invited me to a musical in Seapoint. I said, "Yes, but I would first need to get someone to stay with the boys."

"There is a nice girl working in Grant's ladies hairdressing. Her name is Theresa Cummins. I'll ask her for you," said Paddy, "if you like."

"Thank you, I would like to meet her," I said.

Theresa lived close by in Mervue and came to visit me one evening. She was indeed a lovely girl and my two sons took to her straight away. It was a very enjoyable concert and Seapoint was packed. At the end of the evening we agreed to meet again. Sundays became our dating days. Paddy would bring his son Eugene to "Rock Dale". After dinner, we would go for long drives out to Connemara in the Mini Minor, bringing the three boys with us. Geraldine was only one year old and would stay with her Aunt Mary. It was a happy time getting to know each other, with the boys in the back seat of the Mini

Minor playing guessing games. They got on well together but on the occasions that a row erupted, the threat of stopping the car and leaving them on the side of the road soon brought peace. I made a suggestion to Paddy for him to learn to drive the car.

"Would on my half days suit you to give me a few lessons?"

"It would," I said, "but won't it take you away from your gardening?"

"How about Sundays?"

"That would be better," he agreed. The driving lessons took place up around the Digital factory grounds. It was quiet there on Sundays.

After a few lessons, Paddy was soon able to take the wheel on his own, and it suited me for when doing long journeys we could take turns driving. He had to pass a driving test to get his driver's licence and was lucky first time.

MANY WERE THE TRIPS

Many were the trips we made in the Mini Minor to Monasterevin at Easter time when spring was in the air and the two of us sharing the driving. Paddy loved to drive up the country at this time of the year and admire the budding of the trees, the golden daffodils growing along the side of the road. He would stop the car to let the boys out to watch the young lambs running and leaping into the air, a joy to see. We visited his father Mick and stepmother Bridget, his sisters Lily and Alice, his twin brothers Mick and Jim, Tom and Lar, and their wives and families, his half-sisters Teresa, Julia and Ann and half-brother John. This was the time of the year he knew there would be a get-together of all the Dowling Clan. Everyone talking at the same time, so much chatter in their soft midland accents. When the weekend was over, on Easter Monday we would back a couple of horses in the Irish Grand National. After a big dinner and having heard all the latest, we would gather up the children, before leaving for home. We would give Bridget our tickets in the hopes she would have a winner. Home at last, tired and happy. Paddy was well pleased with the visit to his old home.

ANOTHER GRANDCHILD

Granny Abberton is very happy to hear her daughter Mary has given birth to a little son; that made it five grandsons for her, and a Godchild for me. Seamus Nally came into the world with a lovely head of black curls; his dad Jimmy was proud to have a son to carry on the name Nally. He was my first Godchild; his uncle Harry Nally was Godfather.

1967 - VISITING OUR DAD

Eddie and I made our next visit to see dad on our own this time. "You are just in time for tea," said dad. I left my home-made bread down on the table.

"So you remembered to make the bread for me," he said.

"I hope you like it, dad."

"Cut a slice for me and I'll soon tell you." After buttering it and taking a bite, he said, "Well you're well able to make soda bread, Margaret." I was pleased, and as everything was going well, I decided I would tell him my news.

"I have met a widower, Dad."

"Have you, indeed? You intend to marry again then?"

I said, "Yes."

"You're as well off; you're still young and the boys can do with a father."

Then he and Eddie got on with their usual chat about the hurling. As we were leaving he said, "Next time you come, bring your man."

"I will," I answered.

PADDY A GARDENER

Paddy proved to be a great gardener. Working as a barber, his hours were long: nine a.m. to nine p.m. Thursday was his half-day and he would come to work in the garden, preparing the soil for planting potatoes and a variety of vegetables. After a few hours work, he would put away his spade, fork and wheelbarrow into the shed, wash his hands, change the boots and have a cup of tea. Then he'd go to pick up his son Eugene from school. On Sundays, Michael and Leo would be watching for Eugene, it was when Paddy and I had our dates. I would have dinner ready for everyone when they arrived; after dinner we would go for our usual Sunday drive in the Mini Minor out the country, mostly Connemara direction. The boys loved these spins.

NOSTALGIC DAY

It was a nostalgic day when my very dear friends, Molly and Con O'Neill came to visit me from my old address, 1443 Taylor Ave., Bronx, N.Y. They were indeed my good friends during my late husband Michael's (R.I.P.) illness. I was overjoyed to see them. We shed some tears as we reminisced about the past. Their daughter Kay had just got married to a Sligo man and they were on their way to meet his family. Molly and Con admired my house saying, "You did the right thing to come back to Galway." They were in awe of Michael and Leo. "They are young men now, Peggy," bringing me back to the memory of the name "Peggy" my Aunt Margie had decided on so long ago. We had the tea and the boys joined us, Molly asked Michael if he remembered her. "I do remember you and Mr O'Neill too," he said and Molly laughed.

"Mister! You haven't forgotten your respect for your elders; call him Con, Michael."

"I was often in your apartment, Mrs O'Neill." Molly smiled at this, but I knew she was again close to tears. After the tea and hugs we had to say our goodbyes and promised to continue our corresponding which we did. Until the day my heart nearly broke when I got Kay's letter telling me the sad news that her mother had died (Con had passed away some years before Molly).

"Mom had been sick for some time, Peggy so it wasn't sudden," she wrote.

I cried and all I could think was, "God rest you Molly, you were a friend in a million."

WE ARE PLANNING

Paddy and I had been seeing each other for two years. It was time to talk about getting married. The boys were getting on well, and Geraldine had come to live with me. We told the children our plans and explained to them that they would have a Daddy and a Mammy and we would be all living in "Rock Dale" together. They looked at each other and then back at us. Michael had the first questions, "Are we going to be brothers and sister?" We had plenty of questions to answer, like, "Which bedroom will we be sleeping in?" and, "Can the three of us sleep in the same room?" The questions went on and on.

Paddy had to tell Eugene, who was eight years old, that they would be giving up their house in Bohermore and coming to live in Ballybane. We understood Eugene would be a little upset but we assured him he could go back to see his aunts any time he liked. He was fine, knowing he had that freedom.

OUR SECOND MARRIAGES

Canon Hyland united Paddy Dowling and I, Margaret Beggen, in Holy Matrimony in St. Columba's Church, Castlegar. On the 2nd of December 1967, I took the name Dowling; this time my sister Mary was my bridesmaid. She wore a blue check suit. I wore a blue wool jacket and skirt, a navy-blue jumper, and a matching hat. These were all purchased in Nester's Galway (In those times it wasn't considered proper to dress in white for a second marriage, even though I was a widow and only age 33). Paddy looked dapper in a dark grey suit and blue tie. Although he was only thirty-five, his hair was prematurely grey. It was winter time so I dressed Geraldine in a grey wool dress, white angora bonnet, blue check coat, long white tights and black patent leather shoes. She looked like a little doll. Our three handsome boys I dressed in grey short pants and the Bainín jumpers I knitted for them. Paddy's brother Jim was best man. My brother Eddie walked me down the aisle of St. Coloumba's Church, Castlegar. We only invited a few to the wedding; Paddy's father Mick, and wife Bridget, his brother Jim, sister Julia and brother John from Monasterevin. I was happy my mother was there to see me getting married this time, and to wish me good luck in person. The Canon joined with our small group in "Rock Dale" for the wedding breakfast; it was nice and intimate. We explained to our families the reason for only having a few family members; money was scarce and we didn't go on a honeymoon. After getting married, I had to undertake a task and write a letter informing the American Social Security office I had remarried so I would not be entitled to my American pension. It was then stopped; a big loss to me.

Our second Marriage, Signing the book witnessed by Cannon J. Hyland

GOING TO ST. PATRICK'S SCHOOL

I explained to my step-son Eugene that it won't be like when he lived in Bohermore.

"There you had only about a ten-minute run through the town to get to St. Patrick's School, now you have a twenty-minute walk to Mervue to get the bus with Michael."

"I don't mind that, Mom," said Eugene.

"When it is raining, I will drive you both to school," I told him. Paddy had bought a Honda Fifty bike to take him to and from work, leaving the use of the car to me. Leo was going to Scoil Isiegan/Infants School near Cemetery Cross. The next year, he too would be going on the bus to St. Patrick's School and Geraldine would be starting to attend the Mervue School. Until then she would be at home playing with her dolls.

1968 - VISITING DAD

On my next visit to my father, I brought my husband Paddy, his son Eugene, and my son Leo. Michael stayed with his friends.

As Dad shook hands with Paddy he was quick to say, "You are not a Galway man?"

"No, I'm from Kildare," said Paddy. "I'm a barber in Grant's in Eyre Square for the past fifteen years." Dad was in a good mood and easing up his cap, he showed his bald head saying, "You won't get any business from me!"

They both laughed. (It was the first time I seen the deep dent on the side of my dad's skull, and I gave a little shiver). Dad was looking at Eugene and asked, "Who is this handsome red head?"

"That's Paddy's son Eugene," I said.

"I was a redhead in my young days too!" Then he reached out his hand to shake hands with Eugene, who got shy and went behind his dad. It was time for tea, cake, biscuits and lemonade. No one was shy when it came to enjoying the treats.

When we were leaving, Dad invited us to come again soon. On the way home, I told Paddy how I seen the dent on Dad's head when he lifted his cap. I explained how Mam had told me the Black and Tans (English soldiers) had ambushed him one night and left him almost dead on the side of the road. A neighbour found him and brought him to hospital. Even though these nasty incidents had happened years ago, at times they could be very vivid in Dad's memory. This caused him a lot of suffering and nervous breakdowns, depriving our Mother of her husband and us of our father.

I was glad of that visit and came home happy but at the same time I was thinking of what he said about being a redhead. Now I know where my sister Mary got her red hair, she inherited it from dad. Mary was like me, shy about meeting him for the first time. She planned on coming with us on our next visit. But Dad passed away before she got the opportunity.

1969 - ANOTHER FAMILY WEDDING

There's news of another wedding in the family. Our brother Patrick/Paddy Abberton will be marrying Teresa Doyle from County Clare. They are busy making plans, setting the date for early in the New Year.

"I hope I'll be able to attend this wedding," I said to my husband Paddy. "It will be near my time to have this baby which is due in March, and I'm getting bigger and bigger."

I was able to make the trip to Knocknageeha, County Clare for their marriage and back to O'Sulllivan's Hotel in Gort for the meal. It was a lovely celebration and Mother had now attended all four of her children's weddings. Alleluia.

ST. PATRICK'S DAY

I was overdue by two weeks, so to have this baby I took a couple of spoons of castor oil. It was horrible; I undressed and took a hot bath. Drying myself I decided to wear my best nightie and be prepared. I lay down on the bed for an hour and prayed that labour pains would soon start. Paddy brought me tea. I say to him, "All is still quiet." Just at ten p.m. the first pain hit me. "Paddy," I called, "help me down the stairs and pick up my bag, it's at the door. We need to get to the hospital." The midwife brought me into the labour ward where another mother was lying on her bed. "You can go home Paddy."

I didn't need to say it twice. The midwife said she would be back in a while. "Are you long in?" I asked the mother who was lying on her bed.

"I'm here since yesterday and they can't get me started."

"Oh, you poor thing," I sympathised. My pains were coming every few minutes. I wanted to moan out loud, but with the other expectant mother in the ward, I was afraid it would upset her. The midwife examined me, then left again and came back with a trolley, I was sure it was for the other mother. "Ease yourself onto the trolley," the midwife said.

"Me?" I said.

"Yes," said the midwife.

"But I'm only after coming in," I protested.

"If you don't hurry you will have that baby in the bed." I did as I was told and just reached the delivery ward in time.

We were blessed with the birth of a baby daughter! Born at 11:55 p.m. in the Regional Hospital, Galway, on the night of the 17th of March; she weighed 8lbs. Her dad Paddy was happy for me to have a little girl. He had a son and daughter and I had two sons. Margery was a lovely quiet baby.

Her first week home she had a slight cough that was worrying me. I told the doctor. He said if it persisted, to take her to the hospital. I did as he said and she was admitted back in. Next day when I went to see her, I was told I could take her home. The doctor on duty gave me a prescription to get her a cough bottle. I was concerned to find her in a cot inside an open window and the misty March rain blowing in on her. I asked a nurse why my baby was lying in her cot inside an open window and she apologised. I didn't know what to make of it. I brought my baby home; she was only two weeks old. I laid her on the single bed beside ours. I kept saying to her dad, "She doesn't look well." I sat watching her all night, I couldn't get a drop of water into her little mouth or medication, neither could I wake her up. I called Doctor O'Flaherty who came out straight away. He examined her and said, "You have to take her straight back to hospital. I will let them know this baby is coming in with pneumonia."

The doctors were apologising. It was worrying to look at the little one in an incubator and her little chest panting up and down; her dad and I stayed until we were told to go home and get rest, as it was well after midnight. I almost had a nervous breakdown. I was given a couple of little tablets to help me relax.

We were assured a nurse would stay with her all night to keep her monitored. Next morning, the nurse who was with her for the night told me that at five a.m. my baby had passed the crisis. I was let hold her for a few minutes. A doctor came and brought me into his office, where he took a statement from me and again apologised. He told me a nurse had baptised my baby the day I brought her in. They didn't tell me, it would've added to my anxiety.

"Thank you, I am grateful to you."

"The good news is you can bring her home in a few days." Then smiling, he said you can have a big Christening for her."

"That I will do," I said. Geraldine, now age five, was very upset for her little sister to get so sick. I tried consoling her and bought her a big teddy bear; the boys were worried too. When at last I was allowed to bring her home, they had a big welcome home for their baby sister. I kept her very close to me and thank God, she thrived. We named her Margery Ita. She was baptised in St. Columba's Church, Castlegar. Her godparents were Jimmy Nally and Alice Dowling. "Rock Dale" was now a busy house. The three boys attended St. Patrick's School in the town, going by bus from Mervue. Geraldine went to Mervue School, as did Margery in due time.

LADIES CLUB

In September, I joined the Renmore-Mervue Ladies Club. It helped me take a break from the house. The club was held every Tuesday night in the hall beneath the Mervue church. At least seventy women attended this active club. My favourite times were the visits to the library in an adjoining room. On craft evening, I would attend and learn new skills. Lil Pearse taught me how to crochet; I learned to make ponchos and caps through crochet. On the social evening, I felt like an outsider; I could not connect or as they say today, bond with any group. I would sit beside women but there was no conversation with me. Most of the women came from various parts of the town and would group together for chatting.

Years after I would have discussions with others who would have times like me, even though they never attended a club, and would be advised to mix with people by joining a club. But joining a club didn't work for me. Was it because I was so long in the States, and had nothing in common with the people at home, or was it the sudden loss of my young husband that was responsible for me losing my confidence? I will never know.

Fr. Ned Kelly was appointed Parish Priest of the Holy Family Church, Mervue, by the Bishop of Galway. His job was to organise events to help in paying off the debt on the Holy Family Church. Some club members suggested we put a musical together and I got very involved. We put a lot of energy into choosing songs and picking the title, "The Gypsy and His Lady." I had a big part in it as a gypsy woman, with Kate Carr as my husband. It was a great success and the proceeds went to help pay of the church debt. I was greatly disappointed in being left out of the credits by the woman I helped in structuring the show. I have learned since then of the many people being let down in all walks of life by the people they trust, and the way some people can take credit for another's hard effort. I also wrote a poem commemorating the Club.

At an A.G.M, I was proposed as Public Relations Officer. I enjoyed taking part as P.R.O. It gave me back a little confidence. I also enjoyed the summer outings. I remember the boat cruise up the Shannon with Cepta Byrne and Tom Mulhair playing their accordions and singing. It was a ladies club but Tom was invited to play music with Cepta on the Cruise; this added fun to the outing.

1970 - OUR NIGHTS OUT

Whenever I mention a concert or a popular singer coming to town that I would like to see, my son Michael would offer to babysit so that Paddy and I could have a night out. There were big promises made for everyone to go to bed when Michael told them. I would be a bit anxious in case the boys would have a fight. Paddy would tell me to stop worrying."You are going to spoil our night out," he said.

"Alright, I won't worry," I would half-agree. We enjoyed the beautiful old-time singing of Brendan O'Dowda in the Leisureland hall, Salthill, which was packed. "All is quiet on the western front," said Paddy going in the door. Michael came down the stairs to ask if we enjoyed the night.

"We sure did," we told him, "was everyone good for you?"

"They were, Mom."

We thanked Michael, and after a peep into the rooms where everyone was asleep, we went to bed. "I told you, you had nothing to worry about," said Paddy as he settled down to sleep,

"Well, you're not a mother," I said to a snoring Paddy.

With increases in the family there weren't very many nights out for Paddy and I together. One night in particular I can recall, Michael overheard Paddy saying he heard Joseph Locke was coming to Leisureland, Salthill and that he would like to go and hear him sing. Paddy's favourite song was, "Hear My Song, Violetta." Michael said, "Why don't you go, I will mind the house. I'm free tonight." We decided to go with warnings and promises to the younger ones to obey their brother Michael; they promised they would be good. Television was a good distraction. Arriving at Leisureland, we found the hall was already full with people. I said, "You are not Joseph's only fan."

"It looks that way," he said. We made our way to get as near as possible to the front row. As Joseph walked out on the stage, there was loud clapping and the same thing after each song. Joseph sang some wonderful songs in his golden voice. "You enjoyed that Paddy?"

"I did," he said, "did you?"

"Yes," I said. On the way home, I looked at my watch. "It's after one a.m. The family will be well into a deep sleep by now," I said.

Drawing near the house we could see all the lights were on. "Don't tell me they are having a party."

"Don't say anything until we hear what is going on," advised Paddy. As we opened the front door Michael came to meet us. "Why is everyone up? Is one of you sick?"

"No, but there was a terrible storm, did you hear the thunder? It was right on top of the house and the lightning was flashing and lighting up everywhere for about twenty minutes, the rain was hitting the windows. It was frightening." "With the singing and clapping we never heard a thing, Michael," I said, "what time did the storm start?"

"About twelve o'clock."

"Were you scared, Michael?"

"I was a bit; Geraldine was very frightened and crying, the baby didn't wake up at all."

"Good baby Margery," I said peeping into the cot at her. "I am so sorry Michael," I said hugging him.

"It is alright Mom; you weren't to know a thunderstorm was to happen. When it stopped, Leo made tea and we finished off the cake. We decided not to go to bed until you came home." I could picture many a thing happening, but never a thunderstorm.

"We are very sorry," said Paddy.

"You poor children. Thunder and lightning can be very frightening."

We said a decade of the rosary in thanksgiving that everyone was alright. Michael and Geraldine went to bed happy, Mam and Dad were home. Leo stayed to help with washing up the cups with Paddy.

I said, "We won't be going out again for a while; poor things must have been very frightened."

"I agree," said their dad.

PADDY WAS A FEATHERWEIGHT

Paddy was a boxer in his young years and won many competitions with the Galway Boxing club. In 1947, he won the County Junior featherweight title. He gave up boxing to look after his wife Rita who had poor health and to mind their young son Eugene. Paddy also took leave of absence from work for a time. When his son Eugene was five years old, Rita gave birth to a baby girl. They named her Geraldine. Soon after her birth, Rita passed away. One of her sisters took care of baby Geraldine. Eugene went to school, giving Paddy the opportunity to go back to work barbering.

AFTER WE WERE MARRIED

Paddy's talent at boxing came in handy on wet days, when he would spar with the three lads around the kitchen, tiring them out; they enjoyed this game. He would be invited to the local parishes to give some boxing training to young lads. He took up badminton and played in the Columban Hall on Sea Road. Paddy was a good badminton player and entered many matches that were played in a wide selection of country villages.

1970 - CABARET

Peggy Carty was preparing her dance troupe to perform in Cabarets in Ryan's Hotel, Dublin Road, to raise some money towards their trip to the Isle of Man, where they would be competing against other groups, including Galway's Twin City, Lorient. She gave me instructions to make three sets of fishermen outfits for my three boys, plus a fourth one for another boy. Four pairs of tweed pants and four waistcoats to match! The tweed was expensive but I managed to scrimp and scrape together enough to buy three yards of it for my three lads. I had to wait until our little toddler Margery was gone to sleep at night, before taking out the singer sewing machine and starting work at measuring, cutting and sewing, until three in the morning. I got them finished in good time, plus the extra one for John Shaughnessy; his mother paid for the material for his one. John and Eugene were the same size; making measuring easy. I was bothered in case fussy Peggy would find fault with them. I would not be happy to remake them. But she was satisfied with my tailoring, as she said.

On the nights the Cabaret would be on, I watched with pride when my boys were dancing in their tweed outfits, wearing Bainín jumpers and crochet caps that I had made for them. The day finally came for Michael and Eugene to be ready and meet their friends at the boat to set sail for the Isle of Man to take part in the traditional dancing competitions. Leo was too young to go, but he wasn't disappointed. Peggy's troupe was very successful in winning many medals and trophies. I was glad to see the boys back safe after their tiring long week dancing.

Michael was now thirteen and he was happy to be part of the Isle- of-Man experience. He wanted to finish with the dancing and try something else. He begged of me to let him leave.

"You will have to tell Peggy," I said.

"Will you tell her for me, Mom?" I phoned Peggy to tell her of Michael's decision and she asked to talk to him. I handed him the phone, and he was looking at me with pleading eyes. Peggy explained that she needed him for one more performance for the parents' night.

"I will see if I can talk him around." I did, with a promise of it being the last time. I was sad as my lad had started making his own choices. His choice was the game of badminton with his step-dad Paddy.

1971 - NEWS FROM BALLINASLOE

Mother received a letter from Dad's doctor, letting her know her husband Edward Abberton had suffered a serious stroke and was bedridden. Mam said to me, "You and Eddie should go to see him."

The two of us went to see how Dad was. It was sad to see him lying in bed and struggling to speak, which agitated him when he couldn't make himself understood; he only had the use of his hands. He was age 82. The nurse told us we could leave at any time.

"He will be just go back to sleep, we will let you know when the time comes." We both kissed him and left (it was our first time to kiss our dad, it was a thing he wouldn't do). Eddie and I drove home in silence.

MAKING A FIRST COMMUNION DRESS

Geraldine was preparing for her First Holy Communion. Money was tight and First Communion dresses were dear. I bought some satin material and lace and taking out the sewing machine, I set to work making a First Holy Communion dress with a matching satin sleeveless bolero. "Try it on Geraldine until we see how it fits." It was perfect.

"Mam, I will need a veil."

"You will, and white socks, shoes, gloves, a rosary beads and prayer book; we will buy them on Saturday."

The morning of her First Communion, I dressed her for this very special day in her life. Geraldine looked like an angel in her homemade First Communion dress, the veil over her lovely, long red hair and wearing her medal around her neck on a silver chain. I also made an outfit for myself; a pink floral skirt, navy blouse with pink floral sleeves matching the skirt, and a navy-blue, full-length sleeveless coat in a crepe material. I knew her dad was sad that her mother wasn't there to see her pretty little girl making her First Holy Communion.

It was a beautiful day for taking Geraldine's photo. We usually had a roast lamb dinner on Easter Sunday. Instead, I thought it would be a nice treat to have it for Geraldine's First Communion day, with jelly and custard for the sweet. She called to the neighbours to show her dress and was given the traditional First Communion money to put in her little satin purse. She had fun counting it. I said, "Geraldine, you are a rich little girl."

Geraldine's First Communion

CONFIRMATION

In the same year, 1971, Michael made his Confirmation in St. Patrick's Church. Michael and his classmates looked very smart in their school uniforms. They wore a black blazer with school crest and grey pants, white shirt and school tie. The white rosette and medal, a symbol of the Holy Spirit, was pinned to the lapel of their blazers. As I watched them walk to the altar to be confirmed by Doctor Brown, Bishop of Galway, I was thinking back to twenty-seven years ago when I kissed the ring of the same Bishop who confirmed me with a slap on the cheek. We celebrated Michael's big day with a dinner of roast chicken, roast potatoes and the usual vegetables, all Michael's favourite. Granny Abberton joined us in the celebration. She was making sure Michael understood he was now a full Christian. Michael liked to tease his Granny by hiding her purse or taking the hatpin out of her hat. "You are a terrible rascal, Michael," she'd say. The two of them would have a good laugh together.

1972 - PADDY'S INJURY

Paddy was playing a badminton match in Craughwell and he thought he sprained his ankle. An X-ray in Merlin Park Hospital showed it was far more serious than a sprain; it revealed that he had hardening of the arteries and needed a major operation to bypass the affected area in his right leg. Blood clots were attaching to the inside of the artery preventing the blood from flowing freely through the artery, causing him constant pain. Mr Galvin, the Surgeon who would perform the operation, told Paddy it was a six-hour job and he, Mr Galvin, would need a free day to do it. "You will need to wait a few months; in the meantime I will prescribe strong painkillers for you." Mr Galvin advised Paddy, who was a heavy smoker, to give up the cigarettes, and he would live pain-free for many years.

OUR SECOND DAUGHTER

Blessed with a second daughter, born on the 25th of July 1972, in the Regional Hospital Galway, weighing 7lbs 9oz. After three days, I arrived home with our new addition to the family. My son Michael, who was now age fifteen, was looking at the baby in deep thought. "Mom," he said, "when she is fifteen, I will be thirty, can you believe that?" Looking at this tall, young lad standing beside me, I said, "No I can't; I just could not imagine it."

USA VISITORS

It was the week of the Galway Races. The news that members of the late Mike Beggen's family were home from America, in Scotstown, County Monaghan, and would be coming to Ballybane, Galway to see us in two days time, set me in a flap. I said to the boys, "I will need everyone's help." They did their best. The baby was quiet; she slept most of the busy time.

It was a treat to see my late husband Mike's brother, Packie, his wife Marie, and their five children. Packie was an editor of the New York Times. He worked hard to secure a job with them. Their brother

Frank the farmer lived in the home place in Scotstown and arrived with four of his children; their Aunt Mary McKenna from the States and her friend Evelyn McWilliams also came. They hired out a minibus and driver to bring the fourteen of them from Scotstown to Ballybane.

Our house was bursting with excitement on that wonderful day. I cooked a big pan of lamb chops and onions and Paddy filled the pots with new potatoes and vegetables from his garden. The boys set two tables in the sitting room; adding our family of seven made it twenty-one people sitting down to dinner. The Beggens brought a variety of cakes and buns; Aunt Mary brought a big box of chocolate sweets and the children had a feast with them. Baby Caroline was only two weeks old. I knew I would be flat out for weeks after all the excitement, but it would be worth it. It was a beautiful day and the children spent the time outside playing. "They will sleep on the way home," said Frank, laughing. We had lots to talk about, and my two brothers-in-law complemented me on the good catch I made in Paddy Dowling. "We have to hand it to you, Peggy," said Frank, "you had a fine house built for your family too. It's a shame about our brother Mike. He went so quick, his health was not the best." I explained about Paddy's wife who was in poor health and died young too, after their daughter Geraldine was born.

"Ye have a lot in common," observed Aunt Mary. Frank's wife Rose was expecting their sixth child so she and their oldest daughter Susan could not make the long trip. It was a wonderful day; I was glad they met my husband Paddy and his son Eugene and daughter Geraldine. "You're going to be very tired," said Packie's wife Marie.

"I know, but it will be worth it, having seen so many of the Beggen family."

"We are glad to have seen you too and Mike's two sons; they have grown tall, especially Michael, God bless them; and now you have two little daughters."

"I have Marie and you got a little girl too Marie, to keep your four boys in their place."

"I did," she said, "its lovely having a little girl for dressing up."

It was late in the evening when they started out on the long journey back to County Monaghan. The parting and goodbyes lasted a long time; finally, after many hugs and kisses we said our final farewells. I felt very happy to have seen them. "When will something like this happen again?" I said to my husband.

"Well, we don't know," was all he could say.

CHRISTENING

I gave myself a month to recuperate before planning baby Caroline Marie's christening. At the christening in the Holy Family Church, Mervue, we joined six little boys for this important occasion. Seven mothers stood around the baptismal font holding lighted candles, while the godparents took up their place behind us. Fr. Delaine performed the baptism. Paddy's brother Tom and wife Nancy Dowling came from Shannon Co.Clare to be Caroline's Godparents. After the Christening we went to Ryan's Hotel for dinner. It was my first time to attend one of my own children's christening.

Somewhere along the way, the church was changing some of her rules. The 'Churching of the mother' after the birth of a baby had ceased too; this was a blessing the Mother received while she knelt at the alter rails on her first Sunday to Mass. When the priests gave her this blessing, it was called 'Churching the Mother.' We were told an old wives tale that it was to make her clean.

MY TEETH

Paddy would remind me about seeing to my teeth; the top ones were gone bad and two of the front ones had a big gap between them. I went to the dentist in the Shantalla Clinic. "There are a few extractions to be done," he said.

"I have only a few teeth in the top," I protested.

"Yes," said the dentist, "but there is no way of saving them." I suffered with the pulling of the four front ones. "You have another four at the back that need to come out in two weeks time." My front gums pained me all night. I dreaded the thought of the next four extractions, which weren't as bad. I felt funny without my top teeth, and I had to wait six months before being fitted for dentures. The Castlegar Hurling Club Social was to be in another month. "How am I going to go to it without my teeth?

My husband's advice: "If you keep your mouth shut, no one will know the difference."

"How am I going to eat with my mouth shut?"

He laughed out loud, "Sure, you can't chew anyway."

"You are a help," I told him. I was able to have the soup, mashed potato and the custard and jelly.

The social was enjoyable and I got plenty of dances both from Paddy and my brother Eddie. They were both good at waltzing; as for any other dance, well, I had to sit them out.

SLEEPLESS NIGHTS

As time went on, baby Caroline began to have restless nights; she slept very little. This went on until she was two years old. Her daddy was very patient with her. I couldn't be asking him to get up at night with her; he had to go to work. Her brothers would play with her for a while on Saturdays, giving me a chance to catch up with some work. When Caroline was two years old, a child specialist was recommended to assess her. Our first and only visit to the child specialist was a visit I won't forget. Caroline had a look on her face like she didn't trust this man. He was gentle with her. "Sit her on the floor he said," which I did. "Now," he said, "Caroline, I am going to give you some blocks to play with." He put a square frame with round and square holes on the floor beside her, then he threw some blocks next to it. He fitted a square block into a matching hole. "There," he said, "you try doing that, my little one." After a little effort she fitted all the blocks into their matching holes. "Well," said the child specialist, "she has amazed me. There are children who need less sleep than others and you are blessed with one of them, it won't harm her, but it will exhaust you."

"How long will she be like this?" I asked, "she only sleeps three hours out of twenty-four. Can you give her something to slow her down?"

"No, she is a perfectly healthy child. Go to your doctor and he will give you something to help you sleep."

I picked up my bundle of joy saying, "I will give her to the first gypsy woman I meet." He laughed and wished me luck. With so many sleepless nights and comfort eating, I went from ten stone to almost fourteen. Thankfully she did settle down. And I, with my neighbour Jean Folan joined the Uni-Slim classes in the Burrenmount Hotel, Salthill. In nine months, I lost four stone. Taking out the sewing machine, I made myself some new outfits and cut down some of the old to fit me. At last I was happy with my figure and restful nights.

1973 - JANUARY

The long-awaited call came from Mr Galvin telling Paddy that he was now available to operate on his leg.

Paddy was happy about this, but quite nervous. "Don't worry," I told him, "this time next week it will be all over."

"I might be all over too," he said with a laugh. Blood tests were taken. Paddy received the news that due to his blood clotting, he would not be allowed to donate blood any more. Paddy was a recipient of a Silver Pelican, so his hopes of receiving a gold one were dashed.

The operation took almost the full day. We thanked God it was over and a success. After three weeks stay in hospital, Paddy was allowed to come home, but looking quite shook. He had to practise walking everyday to keep the blood circulating through the leg. The boys helped him to make the effort; gradually he was able to walk further and further without pain. By May, he was ready to go back to barbering again.

CUB SCOUTS

Cub Scouts meetings were held on Friday evenings in the hall under the Mervue Church. Leo asked me if I would take him down to the hall, telling me he would like to become a Cub Scout. Entering the hall, we were met with a big troop of young active boys between the ages of eight and eleven. I could see Leo's eyes lighting up. When the Scout Master had a chance from the busy activities he came to welcome us. I introduced Leo saying, "He wants to join."

"He is very welcome; we have a big troop of Cub Scouts. Leo, you are welcome to join us. I am Scout Master Tim Molloy. There are two of us working with this big troop and we also have young Cub leaders training to help. Tim was very welcoming and shook hands with us saying, "I will see you next Friday Leo, I will get a list of what you need as a Cub". Tim Molly from Renmore worked with the Connacht Tribune and regularly put articles on Scouting in the Connacht Sentinel.

Leo was very excited about his new adventure. I was so proud to see him in vestured as a Cub Scout, looking smart in his Cub Scout uniform. It was the greatest day of Leo's life and he looked forward to all the challenges.

AUGUST

Word came from Ballinasloe that Edward Abberton, our dad, had passed away age 84. It was a sad time for us, his family. We dressed him in his grey suit and picked out his coffin. He was waked in the Hospital Morgue. His remains were brought in a motor hearse to St Michael's Church, Ballinasloe. The priest said kindly words befitting the life of our dad. It pleased us to see so many of our neighbours from Ballybrit attending his funeral, and walking behind the hearse to his burial place in the graveyard across from St. Michael's Church.

At home, we consoled Mother who was crying. As she said, "It's all over for him now, may he rest in peace, amen." She later had a headstone placed on his grave.

FIRST COUSIN'S PROFESSION

An invitation came from our first cousin Anna May Hurley of Moygala, Kilmurry, Six-Mile-Bridge, County Clare to her Profession on the fifteenth of August, 1973, in the Church of St Finnucans, Six-Mile-Bridge. Anna May is the daughter of Patrick/Paddy and Anne Hurley and sister to Pa Jo and to Margie. I was looking forward to this special event, but our daughter Caroline was only thirteen months old so I didn't think I could go.

"Of course you can," said my son Michael, "Leo and I will mind her."

I wasn't sure; still we would be gone only a few hours. I had to get a dress for this occasion. Sad to say I had gained so much weight, I found it hard to get one to fit. Eventually I squeezed into a size eighteen.

Paddy and I felt safe leaving the baby in the care of her brothers and her sisters Geraldine and Margery. This was the first time a blessed occasion like this would be performed in St. Finnucane's church. Anna May took the name Sister Margaret Mary as she was being accepted into the Religious Order of the Blessed Sacrament Sisters. Her Provincial and many sisters of the order were present with her family members and friends. She was kept busy shaking hands and posing for photos. It was such a happy day for her immediate family. Sister Margaret also had a feast laid on in the Queens Hotel, Ennis for everyone. Paddy and I regretted leaving early and we shook hands with her and her parents and excused ourselves, for we had to get back to the baby. We were very thankful to the boys for giving us the chance to attend this holy event.

First cousin profession, Sister Margaret Hurley on the day of her Profession, seated with her aunts Mary Hurley and Bridget Abberton, standing is her father Patrick Hurley, Uncles Jack and James Hurley.

DECEMBER - CLARE TRIP

The weather had turned cold, but there was no frost. I was longing for a trip to County Clare to visit Uncle Paddy Hurley, Anne and family. My husband thought the weather was a bit too cold. "I would love a day away and it will do us good," I said.

"OK," agreed Paddy. "I will cover the car engine for the night; it might help to keep it from freezing." Because the Mini was hard to start in the mornings, Paddy would take out the spark plugs and warm them on the range; it helped sometimes (it was a handy way of getting many a car started back in those years).

I told the children to get up early in the morning and dress warm for the trip to Clare, and they didn't need telling twice. Caroline was just a year and a half old and I wrapped a warm blanket around her. Margery, four, Geraldine, nine, and Leo, eleven were in the back seat; I gave them a rug to wrap themselves in. Michael and Eugene were staying home. They didn't mind; they knew there was no room in the Mini Minor. We set off with a home-made Christmas cake for Annie, some food for ourselves and bottles of milk for the baby. As always, we got a great welcome.

"You're making your Christmas call," said Anne.

"We are, but we won't stay long in case it starts to freeze." The kettle was always hopping on the range in their house. Anne set the table with her home-made bread, butter and jam. Then she went to the parlour and returned with a glass of whiskey for Paddy and a small port wine for me. We laughed, saying we will be too drunk to go home. Season's greetings were wished to everyone as the children sipped lemonade. I put out sandwiches for everyone.

"You needn't have brought all that food Maggie, there's plenty here."

"I don't expect you to feed us when we drop in on you like this, Anne."

"You're welcome any time!"

"Thank you, Anne." She was admiring our family.

"Well, they are growing fast," she remarked, "and sure herself is keeping up with them."

"She is Anne, but I wish she would sleep at night."

"Ah! Indeed, some babies are like that, they won't sleep and no one knows the reason why." said Anne, consoling me.

Uncle Paddy and his son Pa Jo came in from milking the cows. They were up to their knees in wellington boots. Pa Jo set down the buckets of milk he was carrying, and shook hands with everyone. Caroline turned her head away. "Shake hands with your cousin, Caroline," I coaxed but she shook her head. There was lots of chat and very soon it was time to leave. I gave Anne the Christmas cake. "I hope it's alright, Anne."

"You needn't have done that at all, Maggie."

"It's nothing, I said," thanks for your lovely welcome."

Waving goodbye we were soon on the road home. Coming into Newmarket-on-Fergus, I got the smell of burning. "Pull in near that paper shop, Paddy and take a look at the engine." Stopping the car, he slowly lifted the bonnet to see what was wrong. He let out a shout. "What is it?" I shouted back.

I forgot to take off the old coat I covered the engine with last night. "Oh! Jesus, Mary and Joseph! Everyone out of the car before it goes up in fire," I yelled. I went into the shop and explained our dilemma to the girl who was serving a customer. "We will need several bottles of water to get us home to Galway."

"I will see what I can do," she said.

"Never mind your bottles of water." said the man she was serving. In my panicking state I hadn't noticed him. Looking at him, I said, "Oh! My God, you're the accountant from Hynes Building and Supplier's in Galway; I used to pay my bills to you when I was having my house built."

"Lock up your car and leave it until the morning and get someone to bring you down for it," said Pat Heir, "Climb into the back seat of mine and I will get you home."

"There are six of us," I blurted out.

"Ye will fit", he said, without batting an eye. It was a big car, but there were four of them in the front; Himself, his wife and two children. I didn't know if I should say thanks or apologise; "You're alright, sit in," she said. There were six of us in the back seat and four of them making it ten people. He drove home very slowly; he was being very careful. We wanted to give him some money. He refused it saying, "You will need it by the time you get your car fixed." In the house, poor Paddy was in a state. We were all tired and I was praying Caroline wouldn't wake up while I was putting her down in her cot. Geraldine and Margery went quietly to bed. Leo stayed up to make tea for us. Michael and Eugene were wondering if the Mini would ever go again. "Don't say too much, your dad he is in a bad way; to think he forgot to remove the coat off the engine." The sight of the bed was never more welcoming.

Early next morning Paddy called a man he knew to ask him if he would drive him to Newmarket-on-Fergus to get the car, explaining where it was. The man said, "I will pick you up in half an hour."

I gathered what money I could find, to give to Paddy in the hopes the Mini could be fixed.

Caroline slept until seven a.m. "You sweet child." I kissed her, and as I picked her up she was indeed in need of changing and feeding. It was late in the evening when Paddy arrived back driving the Mini. "Tell me how you got on," I asked.

"They didn't have far to tow it, the garage was near to the paper shop. The mechanic couldn't understand how we drove all the way to Clare without the coat catching fire from the heat of the engine. The biggest delay we had was waiting for a part.

"Did I give you enough money to pay for the damage?"

"You did, here is what is left."

"Why didn't you give it to the man who took you all the way to Newmarket-on-Fergus to get the car?"

"He wouldn't take anything, but I owe him haircuts for the rest of my life."

TRADING IN THE MINI

The Mini Minor was letting in water up through the floor. I would put pieces of old carpet on the floor to keep the lads' shoes dry. It was time to change it. I was a bit lonely at the thought of parting with 'HIM 192,' my very first car (I was very glad I learned how to drive in 1964). The last long journey we did in the Mini Minor was to my father's funeral. It had served and suffered us well for nine years. We went back to O'Flaherty's garage to trade in the Mini for a Morris Minor, a more modern and dearer car. The price was £1000, less £200 on the trade-in. The colour was a chocolate brown this time, AZ 52 was the registration. The sales man said he hoped I would knock as many miles out of this one as I had done with the little Mini. There would be a lot of travelling done in this car too, ferrying the children to dancing and music classes, football training and, as Michael had taken up badminton, Paddy would drive him to the matches, and then of course, the school runs.

REGIONAL COLLEGE

Michael loved sport, especially badminton. He was proud of the many trophies he won playing this game. I reminded him of the numerous dancing medals and plaques he had won. He was attending the Regional College, studying accountancy. The college was a twenty-minute walk from our house.

Michael, from a very young age, suffered from allergy attacks; it was the reason I sent him to dancing classes, in the hopes the exercise would strengthen his lungs and chest. During the pollen season, he would have bouts of hay fever, with sneezing and itchy eyes. Through it all, he rarely missed days from school or college. Here in Ireland, I discovered many children suffer from allergies; the older people blamed it on the dampness.

EUGENE'S CONFIRMATION

Another Confirmation, this time it was Paddy's son, Eugene. He was also in the St. Patrick's school uniform; black blazer and grey pants and wearing the symbol of the Holy Spirit pinned to his blazer. He was also confirmed in St Patrick's Church by Dr Brown, Bishop of Galway. For Eugene's special treat, his late mothers' sisters took him for the day to treat him. Later on, I asked him if he was going to go to college. He said, no, that he would rather get a job.

1974 - DENTURES

At last I am being fitted for my top dentures. I had to leave them in my mouth for three nights. I found it hard to take them out. They were very uncomfortable. The dentist had to do a lot of filing down and replacing them back into my mouth. He told me, "It will take a while to get used to wearing them, buy some hard toffee sweets and stick one against the roof of your dentures; leave it until it melts away. Keep doing that and you will soon find you will get used to the dentures and forget you have false teeth." It did work.

A SCOUT

The investiture of a Scout, my son Leo. It was an organised event and quite military, and one Leo took very seriously. This was the life for a young lad; training in discipline and learning many outdoor skills, pitching tents, setting an outdoor fire to cook on, and clearing it away without leaving the sign of a fire. Leo was very proud of his uniform. I was in the habit of writing poetry to celebrate events. I wrote:

Staunch and True

A boy dressed in blue, proud no doubt, chest sticking out;
Today he became a full-fledged Scout, from now on, loyal and strong.
Honest, upright, true to his word, a worthy addition to the Galway 3rd.

The Galway third was very proud in their Scout Uniforms when they formed a Guard of Honour for the visit of Pope John Paul II in the Ballybrit Racecourse in September 1979. "*Young People of Ireland, I love you.*" Each of the scouts received a replica of the Pope's Coat of Arms in memory of his visit.

EUGENE RETURNS TO BOHERMORE

Eugene appeared very restless for some time. His dad was getting worried about him, and so was I. One evening he took Eugene one side and said to him, "If there is something bothering you, tell me about it?"

Eugene said, "I would like to go back and live in Bohermore with my aunts." Paddy gave his son a pep talk; "First you are only fifteen years old and still have to attend school, and don't forget your soccer training and matches; you can go back to your aunts, but I will miss you, son. When would you like to leave?" "Immediately," was the quick reply. Eugene had cheered up and I was glad to see the smile back on his face. His dad would miss him, for they would have many arguments about football and soccer matches. That evening they packed his clothes, books and his football posters into a bag. "Will you take the accordion, Eugene?" I asked.

"No," he said, "you are a good musician and love playing it." I tried to insist.

"I prefer soccer," he said. His dad drove him to his Aunt Kathleen's. When Paddy came home, I knew he had been crying. I said, "Paddy, Eugene is with his own now, and sure he can come here for visits when he likes."

"I told him that when I let him off in Bohermore," said his dad in a sorrowful tone.

"I'll make cocoa for everyone; you get the mugs, Paddy," I said.

MONASTEREVIN EASTER

Easter, and we are packing to pay a visit to Monastarevin, Paddy's home place, for a few days. We are taking the three girls and Leo, all six of us in the Morris Minor, plus the boot packed with changes of clothes and some Easter eggs for everyone. Caroline, only two, sat on Leo's lap in the front passenger seat. There was plenty of room for myself, with Geraldine and Margery in the back, until Caroline decided she wanted to join us; Leo didn't object. The Morris Minor was new and a very comfortable car to travel in.

There was a great welcome for Paddy and for all of us from Granddad Mick Dowling, as he was known by. Everyone was delighted to be meeting and greeting each other. "Where are Michael and Eugene?" was the question from them all.

"Eugene is with his aunts in Bohermore, and Michael is minding the house. He wanted to catch up on his studying too; anyway we wouldn't have enough room in the car," I explained. Bridget had a big dinner of turkey and all the trimmings ready for us. We were ready for it.

Paddy was happy to be in his old home and meeting his brothers and sisters and their families. Spending Easter together with the family was the highlight of the year for the Dowlings. Paddy enjoyed meeting the family to catch up on the news of the past year. My father-in-law asked me if I was ever at Bingo. I said, "No, I wouldn't know the first thing about it."

"We will take you with us tonight."

I said "Sorry, I can't go, little Caroline will kick up a fuss."

"Don't worry about her; there are plenty of babysitters here." I was happy to get away for a while.

We headed off to bingo. I was apprehensive, for I had never played the game.

I was soon shown how to cross off the numbers, which were called out rapidly. Someone would shout, "Check!"

"Why are they shouting check?" Poor Mick was trying to explain it to me. It was all going too fast for me. The hall was in Kildare town and packed with bingo players. "The people here must like this bingo game," I said.

"They are mad about it," said Mick, "some will go four times a week."

On the way home, I thanked him for bringing me.

"Did you enjoy it?" he asked.

"I did, Mick."

Arriving back to Bridget's warm kitchen, we found the kettle was boiling and cups were on the table, with slices of sweet cake cut for us.

"Oh Bridget," I said, "you do put yourself out!" I asked if I was missed.

"Indeed, you were not; Caroline went to bed with her Aunty Anne and was asleep in no time."

Next day, Easter Monday, we were ready for home. But, before leaving, we did the usual backing of a couple of horses in the Irish Grand National. When we were leaving, we gave our tickets to Bridget. "If any of them horses win, the winnings are yours," we said. We left the Easter eggs on the table for the young Dowlings, and said thanks a number of times.

We were sorry to leave so soon; I really enjoyed the break. I heard afterwards that my horse won, so Bridget got a couple of pounds.

BUILDING A CHALET

The Regional College was twenty minutes walk from our house. Many students were looking for accommodation. I had an idea to have a chalet purpose-built at the end of the garden. I had the idea with students in mind. It would have four separate bedrooms, with the students sharing the kitchen, sitting room and bathroom with shower. I set out making it comfortable with central heating and the necessary essentials for sleeping and cooking. Four lads came and took up residences.

Everything went well for four months and I was relaxing. Then, one morning I saw five extra people coming up the path with rucksacks. I didn't recognise them. In the evening, I challenged the four lads. "How long have ye had these boys here without telling me?"

"Ah, just a couple of weeks," they said. "We didn't think you would mind."

"I may not mind, but five free loaders? Well, I ask you! You don't need to pay rent this week, your deposit will cover you and I want you out this weekend and leave the place as you got it."

I wasn't very lucky with students; the girls proved no better than the lads. I said to Paddy, "I will advertise for workers instead." It was a much better choice. The men would come on Monday morning and go home Friday evening for the weekend. With so much building going on in the area, there was no shortage of lodgers.

STEEPLE JACKS

Early one morning, as I was getting the children ready for school, Leo coming down the stairs called to me, "Mam, there's two men at the door."

I answered it to two very tall men. One man reached out his hand and introduced himself. "I'm told you keep lodgers," he said. Looking at the two of them I wondered if I had beds long enough to suit them, replying, "Yes, I do."

"Do you serve meals?" Was his next question.

"Yes, I serve breakfast."

"What about lunch? He asked.

"I guess I could do that," I answered.

"There are five of us steeplejacks; we are building a mill over in Tom McDonough's yard on the Minna Road and this is nice and near, we would want breakfast at eight o'clock five mornings a week, and a full dinner at one o'clock four days a week, for six weeks, could you do that for us?"

"Yes, I could. As for your accommodation, I can keep two of you in the house and three in the chalet."

"I would like to see the rooms please."

"Follow me."

I showed him the three small rooms in the chalet; there was hot and cold water and a separate toilet, I then brought him into the house to show him one bed room with two single beds and the sitting room, explaining, "This is where you will be eating."

"That will do nicely, thank you," he said, "I need to know for the boss what you charge; he will be paying for the five of us, and you will get one cheque per week. I will be giving it to you myself on Friday mornings."

"Can you give me a little time and I will tot it up?" I wasn't sure what way to work out the cost. I went by what I charged on race week and handed him my price. He took a while looking at it and then said, "This will do; we will see you Monday morning."

It was hard going for the six weeks. I made a big saucepan of porridge each night for five nights ready for the mornings. Keeping the fire on in the range at night was a blessing as the bowls would be warm to ladle the porridge into. I would pass the bowls to Michael, who took them into the men. Michael helped before he went to school and Paddy before he went to work. Those five men I will never forget; they were over seven foot tall and ate big meals, but only the plainest of food.

After getting the first cheque, it was easier to plan the meals. Growing our own potatoes and vegetables was an asset. We had pots and pots of potatoes, cabbage and bacon, roast legs of lamb, big jugs of gravy and all the rest. Paddy's fingers were sore from peeling; "I won't be able to cut any hair today," he complained.

"It is only for six weeks, I reminded him.

I would let them know the night before what was for lunch the next day. Once I asked if they would like shepherd's pie. Two of them shouted, "No thanks," and one man asked if I had the mincemeat bought. I told him I had. He was very jolly and said, "I'm in charge of the menu this evening!"

Then he asked, "Would you guys like a couple of homemade beef burgers?" Everyone agreed on this lunch. I loved making burgers for my family; it was usually the Saturday lunch, with custard and rhubarb for desert, also tea with my home-made currant bread, which went down well with the men. I would do the baking at night when the family was in bed, except for Michael; he would be up some nights until four in the morning studying. We kept each other company even though we never spoke a word.

The six weeks was finally over and the last lunch served to the men. The man in charge who paid me came into the kitchen to thank me for looking after them, and to tell me they would be gone in the morning after breakfast. He then gave me the last cheque, I thanked him and said, "I will be missing this."

"And we will miss your meals, too." I felt good with that compliment.

"Last morning, Michael, to do your waiter's job. I will have money for you when you come from college; thanks for your help, son."

"You are very welcome, Mom." Paddy was upstairs in the bathroom getting ready for work. Margery and Caroline were holding their bowls for their porridge. Lifting the big saucepan to scrape out the last of it, I said to the girls, "You have been very good for the past six weeks; I am going to take you to town today when I pick Geraldine up from school." As I put a spoon of porridge into a bowel the saucepan twisted in my hand and I got the worst pain through my body. I fell to the floor.

"Margery, get Dad quick," I whispered. Paddy got a fright and helped me to sit up. "Start the car and get the girls into it," I said; he rushed them out the door, "Hurry girls, into the car!" Then he was rushing me to the hospital.

- *171* -

Oh, the pain; I couldn't tell where it was.

The doctor said I would need tests and X-rays done. I was in excruciating pain and couldn't tell them where it was. I wasn't given anything to ease the pain. Next morning, I was taken to theatre and put to sleep. When I woke up, I was back in the ward and a doctor was standing next my bed.

"What were you doing when you got the pain?" he asked.

"Spooning porridge out of a saucepan into a bowl."

"You gave yourself a massive Hiatus Hernia."

"What is that?" I asked, scared out of my mind. The doctor explained that it is where the lining of the stomach tears and the gut comes through. "Oh God, will I need an operation?"

"We don't think you will, but you need bed rest. I would advise you not to lift anything, not as much as a cup for a week or two. I will recommend strong pain killers for you. Your husband can take you home when he comes in; a nurse will give you an injection before you leave to ease the pain."

"Thank you very much, doctor."

As Paddy walked in the door. I said, "I'm allowed home."

"What did they say was wrong with you?" he asked.

I gave myself a massive hernia. What did you think happened to me, Paddy?" "The way you were working for the past six weeks, I was sure you had got a massive heart attack."

Relieved, I said, "Thank God it's not that."

"You had better mind yourself; no more big meals for big men. It happened on their last morning."

"How lucky is that? Leo and Geraldine are saying they are getting their summer holidays from school in a week's time; they will be a great help to this invalid."

MONASTEREVIN SIEGE

In October, Paddy has a wish to go to Monaterevin for a visit to see his dad. "Safe driving," I said as I shook the Holy Water on him.

"I will only stay a few days; spend a while with the ould man."

"Enjoy," I tell him. I dressed baby Caroline warm and put her into the pram, took Margery by the hand and walked down to Mervue School to meet Geraldine. It was cold but dry. "Your dad got a lovely day for travelling," I told the girls.

Sitting having our evening tea, I turned on the news. A siege was happening, in St. Evans Park, Monasterevin. I was in disbelief. The Dowling cousins lived in that area. Their father, being a fireman, was in possession of a phone. Geraldine asked, "What is going on, Mom?"

As we listened, it was getting worse. Eddie Gallagher and Marion Coyle, a member of the I.R.A., had kidnapped an industrialist, Tiede Herrema, at his home in Castletroy, a suburb of Limerick, and were holding him in a house in St. Evans Park.

"Why, Mom?" asked Geraldine. It was saying on the news that Rose Dougdale was Eddie Gallagher's girlfriend, and they had a baby and were in jail, because Rose stole a lot of expensive paintings from Russborough House. They would let Mr Herrema go free if Rose and the baby are released from prison.

I was in a state of worry as I phoned the Dowling Cousins without success; all phone lines were closed down for police work. On the news, it was saying that Mr Herrema was being held at gunpoint. When I heard that, I turned off the news as the girls were crying. I had no idea where Paddy was. It was about a week before I heard from my husband telling me that he went that very evening to visit his cousins in St. Evans Park.

"Shortly after I arrived, we looked out the front window there were police cars everywhere. The police were announcing for everyone to stay indoors and lock the doors."

"Were you scared, Paddy?"

"Everyone was a bit nervous, but the police kept reassuring us that everything was under control. I knew you would be worried about me but due to the lock down I couldn't phone you."

"Where are the bad people now, Dad? Geraldine asked.

"They are all in jail."

"Oh, thank goodness," she said as she clapped her hands. It was a relief to have Paddy home safe.

1975 - A HERNIA

Lifting a heavy cylinder of gas gave Paddy a hernia. He was in great pain. The doctor admitted him to hospital to have it operated on. Having to spend two weeks in hospital, Paddy was bewailing the amount of time he was out of work and this time it was his own fault.

"Now another month lying on my back."

"Take it easy; the month will fly," was the only consolation I could give him.

MOTHER'S FIRST BIRTHDAY PARTY

Our mother was born in the month of March, 1900 and now she was age seventy-five. I told the family I was giving Mother a surprise seventy fifth-birthday party in the chalet. All her family were to be invited for this special occasion. It would be the first time she ever had a birthday party given for her. My brothers and sister got into the mood of the special occasion and, with their families, they arrived at my house. Mother asked, "Why was all the family coming in?"

I said, "The chalet is finally built and I want everyone to see it. Everyone down to the chalet now," I said, as we walked down the path. I could hear Mam saying, "This must be a great place altogether." Then to her surprise, we all shouted, "Happy birthday Mother!" She was overcome when she saw the decorations, and then the cake.

"Is that for me?" she asked, "ye never told me anything about a party and I'm not even dressed for it."

"It's in your honour," I said. My sister Mary poured drinks and minerals, while Mother held the knife over the cake. "I won't cut it," she said, "it will spoil the look of it."

Still holding the knife in her hand, her grandchildren encouraged her to hurry on, that they were dying for a slice. We all sang 'Happy Birthday' again to her, as she kept wiping the tears away. The weather was fine, but a cold March wind was creeping in. I had the central heating on, making the chalet nice and warm. "It's warm in here," said Mother.

"Yes," I said, "I have the heat turned on in your honour."

"Everything in my honour today; I can't believe it."

"Are you happy, Mother?"

"Sure, I could be nothing else, only happy with a spread like this and my family around me."

"You deserve it, Mother," said her son Eddie. The children ran out to play. In our conversation, I explained my idea for having the chalet built. "Your birthday is the first party to be held here."

"Well, I hope it brings you good luck, Maggie."

"Thanks, Mam."

Going home, her arms were full of gifts as she tried to get into Paddy's car.

"It will take me all night to open this lot," she said with a laugh.

My poem, in honour of Mother.

OUR MOTHER

Everyone has a mother, but none just quite like mine.
She's not tall and slender, like the ones of modern time.
She's not a wearer of high heel shoes, or suits with jacket and pants.
She doesn't frequent the beauty parlour, or fashion a-la-France

She is rich in charm, she wears a mother's smile, her face is lined
with worry, from years of hardship and toil.
No automatic appliances did she possess,
Or handy transportation.
Baking, sewing, washing was an accepted challenge
and not a heavy Station.
She walked to Mass, she walked to shop.
With style, and quality.
Her big treat of the month, was the Sacred Heart Sodality.
Today we thank God you're alive to
Celebrate, your birthday "seventy five."

A DEATH

Almost a year after Paddy's visit to see his dad in Monasterevin, he got a phone call from his brother Mick to tell him their father had passed away suddenly. Bridget was taking their father a cup of tea in the morning before he would get up. She thought he was reading a book, instead he was dead. She got a terrible shock. Michael Dowling died at the age of sixty-nine on the twenty-fifth of March 1975. Paddy was all choked up. I consoled him by saying, "Thank God you saw him last year. You go to the funeral, Paddy. I can't go; the kids are in school. Be careful driving and give Bridget and all the family my condolences." We were saddened at this latest news; I told the children their granddad had passed away, that he was a kind man; and that we would remember him in our rosary tonight.

TULLA, COUNTY CLARE

My first cousin Anne Flower, who I had never met. I heard that herself and her husband George and their three young daughters had come home from Wales to live in County Clare, making their home in Tulla. It was the summer holidays and I felt it was a good time to go visit them. I said to Leo, "How would you, Geraldine, Margery and Caroline like to come to Clare tomorrow to meet a first cousin I have never met?"

"That would be great, Mam, I love going to Clare."

"So do I," agreed Geraldine. I had never been to Tulla, so it was going to be an experience driving through the mountainy road with so many green trees and the yellow of the furze bush growing in abundance; wild primroses growing along the side of the old bumpy road, with potholes every few yards.

We came to a part where I stopped the car. We were on a height looking across for miles at lush green fields below us. The occasional whitewashed farmhouse was dotted here and there with cattle grazing in the distance. I said, "Children, I hope you remember this view for the rest of your lives." Reaching the town of Tulla, we were looking for the number of Anne's house. I see a lady on the foot path and called to her, "Could you please tell me where the Birds live?"

She had a strong English accent, "Well, she says, as far as I know the birds live in trees; but you are looking for Flowers and I'm your cousin, Anne Flower." Leo was laughing in the back of the car and said, "Mam, you're stupid, you forgot your cousin's name."

I was not let forget that mistake in a hurry. Anne, a pretty person with her thick blond hair piled up on her head, her tall, handsome Welsh husband, with a mild-spoken gentle Welsh accent, welcomed us. They had three daughters; Clare, aged six years old, the same age as Margery, Irene, five, and Julie, four; a few months older than Caroline. It was a most unusual way for cousins to meet for the first time. It made no difference, as we got a warm welcome. The girls went away playing together as if they knew each other all their lives. Geraldine, eleven and Leo, thirteen, sat for a while in the kitchen. "You didn't expect us Anne, so here is some food; just a little salad, bread and cake. Plenty for everyone."

We had years of news to catch up on. I was telling her about Mike's death (R.I.P.), and then marrying a widower. We both had two children each and now we have two ourselves, six in all Anne." Anne met George in the hospital where they both worked as auxiliary nurses. They married in Wales and lived on there until, as Anne said, "I got lonely for my native County Clare; so here we are. This is a very old house. They are building new ones up the street. We have our name down for one."

When it came time to go home, the girls didn't want to part. "Now we know where ye are living, we will visit often and ye will be welcome to Ballybane." Leo and Geraldine returned from their walk up the street. On the way home, I asked them what they thought of Tulla. They both agreed it was a nice town with nice friendly people. "I wouldn't like to live here," says Leo.

"Why?" I asked.

"There's a lot of old, spooky empty houses," answered Geraldine. There was at the time a good many old, derelict buildings.

1976 - FIRST HOLY COMMUNION

Margery is getting ready to make her First Holy Communion. I am taking the little white dress and veil out of their box; it still looks like new. I was proud to dress her in it for her special occasion.

"Your Mammy made this dress for your sister Geraldine's First Communion five years ago, do you like it?"

"I do, Mam." I dressed her up in her pretty Communion outfit. She was looking around.

"Did you lose something, pet?" I asked.

"Where is my first Communion medal?" She asked in a worried tone.

"Here in its little box on the table." Putting it around her neck, "I asked are you happy now?"

"I am, Mam," she said. Her first Communion medal was most important to her. "We are ready," I said giving her a kiss on the cheek. During the morning, I wondered what was wrong; she was getting cross. Then I noticed she was scratching. "Oh dear," I said to her dad, "she has the chickenpox, I hope she will be all right for her first Communion; and not get sick."

All was going well until she was going up to the rails to receive; she was scratching her head and the veil was off to one side. This embarrassed her father; "Don't you understand? The poor child has chickenpox," I scolded him.

We promised ourselves we would have dinner in the Furbo Steak House; we thought we would give it a try. Michael was nineteen years old and he was intending to have his first glass of wine and drink a toast to Margery.

We ordered dinner for seven. It was a disaster; a tiny piece of chicken in the middle of the plate; vegetables were instant-cooked out of a packet, including the mashed potatoes. Margery was getting very feverish and sitting on my lap. The boys were complaining that they didn't get enough to eat. Paddy was raging. "I'm not paying for this instant stuff out of a packet." Caroline was the only one who was satisfied. At only aged four; the piece of chicken filled her. We left, and in all the upset I never asked Paddy if he had paid. At home, I undressed a sick little Communion girl and put her to bed. In the kitchen Paddy had a pot of spuds on the boil; Michael was scraping carrots and Eugene and Leo were busy setting the table. Geraldine and Caroline were watching Tom and Jerry on TV. "Now for a decent meal," said Paddy as he dished up the mashed potatoes with a fry of sausages and eggs.

GRANNY'S TREAT FOR MARGERY

Granny Abberton called to see me; she had something on her mind.

"I want to give Margery a little treat for her First Holy Communion."

"What kind of a treat, Mam?"

"I want you to come and we will have our photos taken in Farrell's Photo studio with Margery in her first Communion dress."

"Thanks, Mother, she will love that." I told Margery she was getting a big treat from her Granny; "What kind of a treat, Mam? She asked.

"She wants us all to get dressed up and you must wear your Communion dress." "Oh, that's great," said my excited daughter, clapping her hands.

We had a great day posing for the photographer; Mother in her lovely coat and matching hat, Geraldine in a pretty green dress setting off her red hair, Caroline in her chu-chu dress, and me, I wore a flowery dress. The pretty girl of the moment was dressed in her first Communion dress. All prettied up to be photographed. After the photos were taken, Granny had another surprise: inviting us to the G.B.C. for tea and cake. It was a wonderful day. That photo still hangs in my kitchen and whenever I feel sad, I look at it and it brings happiness to my heart.

Grannies treat for Margery

TULLOW, CO CARLOW

After leaving St. Patrick's Primary School, Leo decided he would go to the Christian Brother's Boarding School in Tullow, County Carlow. He got the idea after a visiting Brother came to St Pat's trying to recruit boys to join the Order of the Christian Brothers.

We drove to the town of Carlow, a place I was never in. The College was a fine old building with fields near it and plenty of cows. "Will you look at them Leo; you will have fresh milk and cream every day." We introduced ourselves to the head Brother, who in turn welcomed Leo.

"We expect a number of boys your age this evening; I am sure you will have a lot of fun." The Brother brought us into the dining room where a younger Brother served us tea and cake. Looking at Leo, he smiled and said, "You are joining us, Leo?"

"I am," said Leo. After tea and plenty of information on the College, we were shown to the boy's dormitory where there were about twenty beds, very low to the floor. I pointed this out to the young brother. He said, "For safety, you know young lads, how they like to jump on beds. If they fall, they are close to the floor and won't get hurt. Now," said the Brother, "choose a bed Leo, before more lads come in."

For the first couple of years, Leo shared with the young lads his age, spending a lot of time together studying, playing football, and of course, sleeping in the one big dormitory. When Leo came home on holidays, he would have stories to tell about the country boys. Graduating time came, and the boys were split up. The boys who remained on were given a single room/cell. Leo became very unhappy. The Brother in charge phoned to tell me Leo wanted to leave and go home. I asked if something had happened.

"Leo was very happy with you." The Brother replied that he didn't know.

I said, "Of course he can come home; I would like to speak to him."

When Leo came to the phone I said, "Leo, son, are you all right?"

"Can I come home, Mom?"

"You can, Leo," I said.

"I have no money for the bus."

"The Brother will give it to you and I will refund him. You come on home; I will meet you at the bus in Galway."

When I met my son at the bus, the first thing I asked him was, "Are you all right, Leo?"

"I am," he said, but he didn't look all right. At home, I made him tea and buttered some bread for him. "I don't want to go back there again, do I have to?"

"Of course not, Leo," I said. "I will send the Brother what I owe him."

Leo sat quietly for a while, then he began to play with Caroline; she got up and sat on his lap. I said, "Leo, were you lonely?"

"I hated in the single room, it was a big change and some of the lads I made friends with in the dormitory had left and gone home to work on the farm with their dads. I missed them."

"Do you want to continue your education?" I asked.

"I do; I want to graduate," he replied.

"Very good, Leo," I said. "I will speak to Fr. Willie Cummins as to what secondary school to send you to.

Fr. Willie recommended St. Mary's College, saying he went there himself. I thanked him for his help. Leo asked if we could go the next day. I agreed we could. Fr. McInerney was in the office when we arrived. We introduced ourselves and he welcomed us with a handshake. Leo told Fr. McInerney who he was and the reason he was here, explaining that he didn't want to continue staying in the boarding college in Tullow, Carlow. The priest was very understanding, agreeing that not everyone likes boarding schools.

He then introduced Leo to the College Principal who shook hands and welcomed him. Leo was happy and finished his education and graduated from St Mary's College, Galway. He then went on to Dublin to learn about the food business in H. Williams's supermarket.

1977 - GERMANY

Its summer time and the students are out from the Galway-Mayo Institute of Technology (GMIT) and looking for summer jobs. My son Michael is preparing to travel to Germany for a summer job. He was a tall, slim lad. With his rucksack packed he said, "Mom, I want to thank you for never leaving Leo and I on our own when we were small."

"Why would I ever do a thing like that?"

"When you met Paddy Dowling, I thought you would be out on dates at night with him. Instead your dates were always going out the country, driving on Sunday afternoons in the Mini Minor, taking my brother Leo and I with Paddy and his son Eugene. I loved the summertime; it was great having picnics in Connemara and Paddy/Dad kicking football with us.

"Michael, son," I asked, "what do you mean? Why would I ever leave you and Leo, and you only young children? You and Leo were, are my whole life. Be safe in Germany and don't bring home a fraulein to me."

We hugged and kissed. I sprinkled Holy water on him, and watched as he went out the gate. "God look after him," I whispered. It took me a while indulging myself in the lovely compliment my son paid me.

Three months later, Leo came with me as I drove to Dublin Airport to pick Michael up after his season working in the aluminium factory in Dusseldorf. This would be the first of three summers Michael would spend in Germany; two summers working and one summer touring.

At the airport, we scanned the passengers arriving. "I cannot see him, Leo, can you?" No sign yet. The trouble was, we didn't recognise the long-haired man, with a good bit of weight on, wearing knee-length shorts, striped t-shirt, opened-toed sandals and a big rucksack on his back. This wasn't the son who I said goodbye to three months ago. "Good God, Michael, we didn't recognise you!"

"I know I have put on a bit of weight; it was the German beer. It was very hot working in the factory and drinking water didn't quench the thirst," he explained, "so we drank German beer."

We arrived home. Paddy and the girls stood staring, "Who is that?" asked Margery; we laughed. Paddy had the tea ready, and Michael handed out little German gifts and drinks named Schnapps. They were small but strong. "I think I am in need of a haircut, Dad?"

"I think you are," Paddy agreed. Margery, aged seven, was very excited with the pair of German roller skates her brother brought her. I wasn't quite so happy.

"I hope you don't fall and break your head with them". No one was happy with my commments. I didn't have to worry; she was roller skating up and down the path in no time at all. I had a sip from a little bottle of Schnapps. I guess I drank it too fast, for in a while I was unable to stand up and I was talking rubbish.

AUNT MARY HURLEY

The woman who reared me passed away in a nursing home in Ennis, County Clare. When she retired as cook in the Agricultural College, Athenry, she returned to County Clare and lived in the old house in Reinaskomoge with her brother Jimmy, until an old person's house became available for her in Six-Mile-Bridge.

She was happy with this move, for now she was near the church and shops. She lived there with a lovely, black dog a local policeman gave her. "You can have him," he said, "I'm away all day; its late when I get home to feed him at night, so he is yours now." Aunty was very happy with this lovely, big dog, "Don't worry, he will get plenty of feed from me."

Mary lived there in comfort until her health failed. She was admitted to a nursing home in Ennis, where she died, she is now buried with her brother Jimmy in Ballysheen, Six-Mile-Bridge. My Uncle Paddy advised me, "As she reared you Maggie, it is your duty to look after her belongings." Which I did, including the big black dog.

She had very little in the way of possessions, and just about enough money put aside to cover the expenses of her funeral, and some Masses after her death, and the last of the rent, which I paid on returning the key to the housing authority in Ennis. I brought her dog and her few belongings home with me to Galway. Her little trunk I gave to mother, and her sewing machine to Honor Abberton; the rest I burned. The big black dog was family-friendly; he settled in straight away. Caroline named this addition to the family "Barky". How quick his tail could wag when he would see Paddy taking down the rifle, as man and his dog went hunting for rabbits. They usually caught two, and Barky got the praise for chasing them out of their burrows.

Paddy would set to work skinning, gutting, scalding and boiling them with onions and carrots. What a lovely meal they made with a big dish of boiled spuds. I told Paddy that when I was very young, my brother Eddie once told me he and his dog hunted rabbits for dinner and how I turned up my nose in disgust, saying I wouldn't eat rabbit, "And here I am, serving them up for dinner."

"People can change," he said. Barky lived to a ripe old age, and like all old friends it was sad to see him go.

1978 - CONVENT OF MERCY, SPIDDAL

Geraldine, after finishing in primary school, Mervue, told us she would like to attend the Convent of Mercy in Spiddal, Galway as a boarder. Her dad and I agreed, she was very smart and loved the Irish language. It would be expensive on us, but as I still did B&B I said we could afford the cost, and being a boarder, she could borrow some books from the library. There were some new clothes needed, and of course the navy uniform. She was very excited at the thought of attending an Irish secondary school and boarding in.

We would enjoy the twelve-mile drive out the country road to the convent in Spiddal, when collecting her on the Friday evenings, and again on the Sunday evenings when we would leave her back for another week. Her dad and I would take it in turns, and Margery and Caroline would join in for the spin and accompany Geraldine up to her little dormitory. The Mercy Sisters admired Geraldine. She was quick to learn. Her dad and I loved the Christmas parties the students prepared to entertain the parents; some of them would put on a play and act out the story in Irish. Geraldine would sit beside us and explain the story in English to us. Then came the time when she got more independent and would travel to and fro by bus to Spiddal. We appreciated this, and watched for her coming in the gate on the Friday evenings; it also meant she didn't need to go back until the Monday mornings, giving her a longer weekend.

The last school year, there was going to be a change. The principal called me to let me know the school holidays were starting and Geraldine would have a lot of heavy books to bring home; "I would be going out to collect her anyway," I said. The principal continued, "I know you want the best for Geraldine; she is a brilliant student," she paused for a second. "What is she going to tell me," I wondered?

"I have a feeling Mrs Dowling, that Geraldine would like to be at home."

"Oh," I said, "she likes it in the school."

"I know she does; but girls that age can have a change of heart. She can finish out her last year in the Mercy Convent in the town, and graduate from there."

"Thank you, Sister; I will have a talk with her." I didn't say anything to Geraldine the day I was bringing her home with all her books and clothes. When we arrived home, I put my arm around and asked, "What is the matter?"

"There is nothing the matter," she answered.

"Do you want to go back to Spiddal after the holidays?"

"No, I don't."

"Why Ger, did something happen?"

"No, the Principal said I could come home and graduate instead from the Convent of Mercy in town; I would like to do that."

"Very well, the next thing we must do is go to town and visit the Convent of Mercy and talk to the Principal and get you on the roll for next September." "Thanks, Mom," she said.

MERCY CONVENT, GALWAY

We were shown into the Principal's office. A welcoming nun shook hands with us. Geraldine explained that she would like to do her final year and graduate from the Convent of Mercy in the town. The Principal asked her a few questions and was pleased with her answers. "I will need to call Spiddal and get the update on exactly where you are so we can put you into that grade. Come back to me in two hours."

"Thank you, Sister, we will," I said, "Come on Ger, we will have something to eat, I am starving." I knew Geraldine was not happy about what the outcome of this phone call might bring. I assured her it would be alright.

We knocked gently on the office door, "Come in," said the principal. As she sat behind her desk, she began, "Sit there in front of me. I have been speaking to your former Principal and she tells me you area brilliant student. I want you to fill in this form and your mother will sign it. It's just a formality, Mrs Dowling, to say you are giving Geraldine permission to make this change. I will add you to the roll book for September." On leaving we thanked the Principal for her cooperation.

It is September and Geraldine needs a navy skirt; "You have grown a bit during the summer; we will shop Saturday for whatever you need." I am sure you will need a new supply of books too."

"I think I have the most of them, Mom."

"That is good."

Her first day, and I'm worrying how she will get on.

"How was your first day, Ger? I was worrying about you. How did you find the change?"

"It was fine; I got on a lot better than I thought I would. But it is only the first day."

"Did you see the Principal?"

"I didn't, she was busy with all the new girls starting today. I was the only senior student already on the roll book; there was no need for me to queue." I was relieved with that news.

I was glad to be at her graduation from the Mercy Convent. After Mass, the graduates received their certificates. I was proud to see Geraldine receiving her honours certificate. For her graduation she wore a pretty cream skirt, blouse and jacket, high-heel shoes and a pair of nylon stockings that wouldn't stay up. I did the old-fashioned thing, making a pair of elastic garters. She told me that before the night was over, "she binned the nylons." It gave us a good laugh.

During the summer holidays, Geraldine secured herself a very good position in the Regional Hospital, Galway, typing up thesis for a doctor. She went on to attend the Regional College, Donegal, having a wish to learn languages and travel, but her college grant wouldn't cover the cost. Her father wasn't well and with two other daughters to support, it wasn't possible for us to pay for such a high standard of education. She travelled to France and Germany and worked as an au pair while still studying, and returned as usual home for her holidays.

MORRIS MINOR

The new car was very comfortable and would be doing its fair share of family duty. I said to Paddy, "You will be careful when you and Jimmy go out to Ballyglunin. Don't drink and drive."

"I won't he," promised, "Jimmy and I take it in turns. I can have a drink when he does the driving. Jimmy can have his drink when I do the driving."

"Do you have many men for haircuts in Ballyglunin?" I asked.

"It depends, three or four most times."

"Do they wait until you cut their hair before starting the game of cards?"

"Most of the time they like to get the hair cut first, and be done with it. I can then relax to play my game."

MY HUSBAND CONTINUED SMOKING

My husband continued to smoke the merciless cigarettes, regardless of the doctor's warnings, and the pain he was suffering the constant pain in his left leg. We are trying to prepare for the celebration of Christmas. I invited my mother and Paddy's son Eugene to Christmas dinner.

We set the table in front of a roaring fire in the sitting room, which Michael had set early in the morning for the comfort of our Christmas dinner. Everyone helped to get the dinner on the table. Margery and Caroline set the chairs around the table. We sat Mother at the head of the table and Paddy sat by the fire. The roast turkey was carved, and full platters and dishes were placed on the red tablecloth, with the Christmas candle lighting in the centre. A blazing fire, Christmas tree, Christmas gifts wrapped and left under the tree, not forgetting the crib with baby Jesus placed in it by the youngest member of the family on Christmas Eve.

It was upsetting to see Paddy in so much pain. We were all trying to be cheerful, including Paddy himself. Mother would bless herself and say a prayer to baby Jesus in the crib, "Take Paddy's pain away." The circus was shown on T.V and I was glad the children were distracted with it. Paddy wasn't able to eat dinner. I told Marg to go up and turn on Dad's electric blanket; "He will be going to bed soon." Before he left the room, he wished everyone a happy Christmas and apologised for having to leave the family gathering. I helped him upstairs to bed and made him a hot toddy (warm whisky) he soon fell asleep. When it was time for Mother to go home, I knew she was relived; Eugene went back to his aunts in Bohermore. And I lost myself in the washing up of the dishes. Leo offered to help. I said, "No thank you, son; this is my relaxing time. Go back to the sitting room and watch the circus."

1979 - SECOND OPERATION

Paddy was admitted for the bypass to his leg; another six-hour operation. After the operation, he was in a lot of pain and unable to walk. I knew he wouldn't be able to climb the stairs. Before he came home, I turned the dining room into a bedroom for him. As I was bringing him home, I told him about his new sleeping arrangement. "Where will you sleep?" he asked.

"Upstairs in our bed room," I said.

"You won't be able to hear me if I need you."

"I'm a light sleeper," I assured him.

He got a big welcome home from the family. Margery was busy showing him his new bedroom, saying, "I wish I could sleep down here. Look, Dad, you have a bedside lamp for reading." He settled down and thanked me for my efforts.

THE LITTLE ONE'S FIRST COMMUNION

The Holy Communion dress is probably getting its last chance at doing its duty. I am preparing it for Caroline to wear on her First Communion day. Taking it out of the box, I hang it out, to air the smell of mothballs out of it. I compliment myself on being like the Victorians; everything they wore was handed down through the generations and made over to fit the next one, even to this present day, that is why they have money. I'm not a Victorian and neither do I have money; my reason for economising, was because of necessity.

Caroline looked like a little angel as she joined her hands at the altar to receive Our Lord. Admiring the little dress, I thought it looks as good as the day Geraldine wore it fifteen years ago. We had the usual celebratory dinner in "Rock Dale" and were happy to have Granny

Abberton with us. Caroline showed her first Communion medal to her Granny. "It's lovely," she said, at the same time putting a pound note into her hand.

"That's too much, Mother," I said, "say 'thank you' to Granny." She thanked her with a kiss on the cheek. Mam looked at me and asked, "Will this be the last of them for you now?"

"Mam, what are you thinking?" We laughed. "To answer your question, it is."

THE END OF PADDY'S CAREER AS A BARBER

During the course of our conversation one day, we talked over what Paddy might do now he was getting stronger. In a sad tone he said, "My career as a barber is over."

Trying to give him courage, I said, "Don't say that, Paddy."

"It's over. I will give in my notice to Luke Grant; he can get someone to replace me." I went into the kitchen and cried, saying to myself, "You're only forty-six Paddy, are you going to give up?"

As he was getting stronger, he got an idea we will clear out the spare room off the hall. "I will set up a barber shop in it," he said. Although he was still in some pain, he was persevering on.

"Thank God," I said to myself, "you are not giving up."

His friend, Mikey Ward called to see him and told him about a job that was going; driving a security van. Paddy applied and was given the job. He had very little walking to do. That same year, he announced, "It's the end of badminton and the boxing too. But I have the card playing," he consoled himself. He and Jimmy Nally would drive to Ballyglunin, Jimmy's old home place, on Saturday nights. Paddy would be home in time to watch 'Match of the Day'. I would be in bed and hear himself and the boys in the sitting room discussing the winners and the losers.

DRIVING THE VAN

Driving the Securicor van was fine for a few months, until Paddy's legs began to give him some pain. He was assigned to doing security mostly in the local factories, like Digital and ThermoKing. His job was to check the gates and then key in the times to a clock. The work was easy but his legs were causing him great pain. He continued for as long as he could; in the end, he had to resign.

SCOUTING AND GUIDING

Lord Robert Baden Powell, the founder of the Boy Scout Movement in 1907, was an English army general. He had seen that his training in the army could be of service to young boys, in learning to be of service to their country through fun and games. His wife, Lady Olive Baden Powell was not to be outdone; she saw potential in this movement for young girls too. After much opposition and advice from her husband, that such training would be too strenuous for young girls, Lady Baden Powell won out and formed the Girl Guide movement in 1918. Scouting and Girl Guide movements became popular throughout the free world.

GIRL GUIDE MOVEMENT

The Girl Guide Movement was also very popular in Ireland. In the 1970's, a group of mothers got together in Mervue/Ballybane, Galway and attended many training sessions in preparation to open Brownie Packs and Girl Guide Units in their areas. This took some time, as there was much to learn and many trips made to the Irish Girl Guides (IGG) headquarters in Dublin. Trainees had to pass tests to qualify and be responsible leaders in order to organise and set up such units in their localities.

The younger girls were called Brownies, and ranged in age's seven to eleven; Guides were eleven to fourteen. Any girl who wished to continue after that, trained as a Ranger or Young Leader. The instigator for IGG units to be set up in Mervue was Mrs Eileen

Carrick, who in time became Area Commissioner of IGG. I qualified to open a Brownie pack of twenty-seven little girls in Mervue. Leaders for younger groups would have the names of birds; owls were considered the most suitable. I was Brown Owl and Joan Mc McCormack was Tawny Owl.

The Leaders wore a pale blue shirt, navy skirt and neckerchiefs to match their units. The Guides' uniform was a blue dress, brown leather belt, and a woggle to keep her neckerchief in place, also a blue beret, navy socks and black shoes. The Girl Guides were divided into four patrols, with six to a Patrol, and four Patrols in each Guide unit.

Each unit had a Patrol leader (PL). She was privileged to wear a lanyard, a white cord worn around her neck, with a whistle attached which she blew to summon her Patrol's to order. Brownies wore the blue uniform; a yellow cravat, navy socks, black shoes and a blue wool cap. IGG was very sought-after in our district and many mothers were very keen to learn the art of becoming an IGG Leader.

IGG District and Area Commissioners Eileen Carrick and Jane Thornbull

MICHAEL'S NEWS

My son Michael had exciting news for me. "Mom," he says, "I have met a nice girl from Ballinrobe, County Mayo."

"That is wonderful news, Michael," I said hugging him, "when can I meet her?" "Would you set an extra place at the table on Christmas day?"

"You have invited her to Christmas dinner?"

"I have Mom, and would you mind if she stayed a few days?"

"That is wonderful, Michael; she will be more than welcome. But you know our house, it is always up in a heap."

"Thanks, Mom, don't worry about the house."

Christmas Eve, Michael and his lovely girlfriend arrived. "This is Mary Moran, Mom."

"I am very pleased to meet you, Mary, you are very welcome. I hope you can put up with the chaos here."

"Don't fuss Mom on my account" she said, as we hugged each other. We were all happy to meet her. There were eight in our family including me and my husband Paddy; now we had Mary to make it nine. The house was warm, with a fire in the kitchen range and another in the sitting room that heated the bedrooms. Christmas Eve, we all went to midnight mass. The singing of the choir in the Holy Family Church, Mervue gave us a warm Christmas spirit.

It was tea, drinks, and cake when we came home. I said to Michael, "I hope Mary is comfortable?"

"Will you stop worrying, Mom?"

Christmas morning, the excitement in the sitting room was catching, and Mary was fitting in, everyone grabbing his and her gifts from under the tree and tearing off the colourful wrapping paper. "Oh look," said Margery, "a gift with Mary Moran's name on it."

"How did Santa know you were here?"

"Santa knows everything. He knew to bring me a pair of slippers," said a happy Mary, "I forgot to bring a pair with me." On the quiet, she gave me a hug; I think she was the happiest of all. Even though it is years ago since that Christmas, Mary still talks about her unexpected Christmas gift. And still calls me Mom.

It was a most enjoyable Christmas for us all. Everyone stuffed with plenty of turkey, trimmings and Christmas pudding with cream and custard. Apart from the entertaining Christmas programs on TV, there was plenty of boardgames played late into the night. Come the morning and everything was going back to routine. While saying goodbye to Mary, I told my son Michael to be sure to bring her often; "I will," he promised with a smile.

SPARE ROOM

We converted the spare room into a barber shop for Paddy, complete with a swivel barber chair. He had many clients, mostly doctors and priests, and of course the neighbours.

It was a little money coming in. Trying to get proper people to rent the chalet was giving me a lot of trouble. I could not cope with the drunks and trouble-makers while rearing a family of six. I closed it down, and got a job in the Regional Hospital, Galway working with Bride Molloy, who pulled the heavy shop trolley around to the wards for the patients to buy what they needed. By the time we reached the fifth floor, it would be empty. So back down to the basement to collect the smaller trolley. It was laden down with female and baby necessities to be taken across to the maternity hospital and sell to the mothers. Back again to the basement to load both trolleys for the next morning. The job was from 8.30 a.m to 1 p.m. Happy to get home. Paddy would have the lunch ready.

A FIRST TRIP HOME AFTER FIFTY YEARS

It was July and our Aunt Margie Callaghan came back to Ireland for the first time in fifty years. I drove to Shannon to meet her finding her in the airport sitting on a bench gazing out the window. Putting my arms around her I said, "Welcome home, Aunt Margie."

"Oh! Peggy it's you, is it? I am home. I can tell by how green the grass is." She enjoyed the drive to Galway looking at fields, sheep and cattle, but above all she admired the houses. "Ireland has come on since my time; it's a different country now." I brought her to my house where we were joined by Geraldine, Margery and Caroline for lunch. The girls were excited to meet her.

Paddy arrived to join us. He reached out his hand and said, "I have heard so much about you Margie, I feel I know you already."

"I have the same to say about you," said Aunt Margie, as they both shook hands. It was a very emotional time when Michael and Leo arrived in. Aunt Margie stood with outstretched arms. "Michael and Leo, are you the same two boys I said goodbye to when you were boarding the S.S. American to come home to Ireland? After the death of ye're poor father. How long ago is it?"

"About sixteen years Aunty," said Michael, "I was six years old then, and now I'm twenty-two and planning on getting married next year."

"Well, good for you; who is the lucky girl?"

"A Mayo girl, Mary Moran."

"You were very little boys when I last saw you." She looked him up and down. "Are you six foot tall, Michael?"

"Not quite, Aunty."

"And you Leo, you were only a baby. You don't remember your dad? Do you Leo?"

"No, Aunty."

"How about you, Michael, have you any memories of your Dad?"

"I have flashbacks of him and I remember what he looked like."

"Well, you both have grown into two handsome young men. Your Mother has made a fine home for you all. And now you have a step-dad and two sisters and a stepsister and stepbrother."

"Sit to the table," I ordered, "and eat." It was a wonderful moment; I was so glad my Aunt Margie was at last in my home. It was getting on in the evening and the arrangement was that Aunt Margie would be staying the week with her sister Bridget Abberton, my mother. But first there was news. Margie's late husband, Dan Callaghan's brother Hughie, his wife Harriet and three of their adult grandchildren, a cousin Tommy Callaghan and his wife were coming. That was seven Callaghans coming from the States and would be arriving for the

Galway Races in Ballybrit. I asked Aunty where they would be staying for the week.

"Oh, I'm sure they have booked a hotel," she replied. I gave them your phone number. They will call you when they arrive in Galway. Tommy is hiring out a minibus for the two weeks."

Mother was impatiently waiting; "I thought you were never going to come," she said. They hugged and kissed. I drove back to the family.

"Well, did you remember Aunt Margie, Michael?" I asked.

"Not at first," he said, "but I did when she spoke."

In our family, there was as much of a welcome for Aunt Margie as there was for the coming of the Pope, who came to Ireland on the twenty-ninth of September that same year. I remember because he arrived on my birthday. Aunty stayed for the week with her sister in Ballybrit, a joyful time for the two of them. It was twenty years since Mother was in N.Y. They had a lot of catching up to do.

First trip home. Aunt Margie Callaghan, first visit home form the States in fifty years. Me with my mother Bridget Abberton, Geraldine, Margery and Caroline Dowling with Barky, the dog.

CALLAGHANS' ARRIVAL

It was the second day of the Races when I got the phone call in the morning from Tommy Callaghan looking for directions to my house. After giving them to him, I drove to Mothers to collect Aunt Margie. "I won't be long, Bee," she said.

The Callaghans were not prepared for the traffic and it was at least an hour before they got to my house. Margie helped me to prepare a salad tea for them as we grew our own lettuce, scallions and radishes, weadded hard-boiled eggs and plenty of sliced ham. And having bought a coleslaw maker, I showed Margie how to work it. She took over and made a big bowl of coleslaw from the freshly-cut cabbage adding plenty of salad cream with my home made bread.It was a feast.

I was so very happy in meeting Hughie and Harriet. They were so good to me when I lived in the Bronx. "Oh, Peggy, what a house you have; you are a smart lady and your boys have grown," said Harriet in her very Kerry accent. It was the first time I met her grandchildren. The oldest, Colm, was about Michael's age. The two girls were beautiful with long hair down their backs. "Come on in," I said, "you are all so welcome." The cousin Tommy and his wife were very Scotch with strong Scottish accents; a lovely couple.

They were glad of the meal, But in a big hurry to get to the Races, they would not believe me when I told them if they hadn't booked in somewhere for the week's stay, they would be out of luck, for everywhere would be booked up. It would be the same thing for a meal. They didn't believe me. They left their luggage into the garage and hurried off.

The girls were doing the washing up Aunty was going to help them. I said, "Margie, I think we will have to make up some beds; they won't get anywhere to stay for the week." I told Geraldine to set the dining room table for dinner for seven people. "I will, of course," she replied.

Margie and I prepared six single beds, and the double bed for Tommy and his wife; everyone else could choose what ever bed they wanted. Margie was concerned as to where my family would sleep. We had a double pull-out couch in the sitting room and a blow-up mattress, the spare room off the hall was converted to a bed room for the week. We will be alright for the few nights Margie," I assured her. Aunt Margie was amazed at all the big rooms there was in the house. "A far cry from the little apartment in Taylor Avenue," she remarked.

Margie stayed on to help me. I was feeling guilty she was gone so long from mother, who would be annoyed at me. We cooked up a big dinner of potatoes, vegetables and a pan of chops. We had no running water and what we had was running low. I told my family they would need to go down the field to do their business; the girls didn't like that.

It was very late in the evening when the phone call came. Tommy was in a state of nerves and everyone was hungry. He asked me to cut some bread and butter and make some tea and they would sleep for the night in the minibus.

When they finally came in the door, the women were running for the toilet. "Go easy on the flushing, and don't run the taps; we are running out of water," I told them. Leo showed them to the dining room. Harriet asked, "Is this set for us?"

"Sit down," I said, and they gladly did! "And we made up beds for you too; Margie will show you where ye will be sleeping." It had gone very late and I knew Mother was about to kill me.

"I will tell her the dilemma the Callaghans got into," said Aunty.

The outcome of the whole saga was that they stayed the week, and paid me generously for my trouble. As they were leaving, Tommy turned to me and in a whisper said, "You saved my skin, Peggy. I was supposed to book accommodation before we left the States; but I thought I would have plenty of time when we arrived. We could not believe how popular the Galway Races is." Aunt Margie was staying for another week; everyone else was going to tour the country and would be back to collect her at the week end to head to Dublin and then on to Scotland.

AUNT MARGIE SEES HER HOME COUNTY

It was a day in which all the family wanted to travel to Six-Mile-Bridge, County Clare. Leo, Geraldine and Margery travelled with Michael in his car. Paddy drove the Vanette, and Aunt Margie, Mother, Caroline and I went in it. We arrived in Six-Mile-Bridge. As prearranged, we went to a pub. There, we met Margie's three brothers, Jimmy, Jack and Paddy Hurley. They were so happy to have lived to see this day and meet their sister Margaret/Margie after an absence of fifty years, since the time she emigrated from Kilnacree, County Clare to America. There was sadness as their sister Mary and brother Mick had passed on. The three brothers each wanted to be the first to buy their sister a drink; all she wanted was a strong cup of coffee.

The next stop was to Uncle Paddy's house where Margie would be staying for the next week. She was looking forward to meeting her sister-in-law, Anne, and her two nieces, Sister Margaret Hurley and Margie, Margie's husband Brendan Sheeran, and her nephew Pa Jo. Paddy's brother Tom Dowling also arrived. I would be staying in Shannon with Tom and his wife Nancy, and make the trip to Moygala each day to pick up Margie and take her to the places of her childhood. I had brought a birthday cake with me and Caroline celebrated her seventh birthday in Hurley's. After that, the family went home in Michael's car. I think the most pleasurable part of the stay was when Uncle Paddy took us to where their mother and father were buried in Broadford. We visited Margie's old school in Oatfield and the Chapel of St. Vincent De Paul where she made her First Communion (and where years later I made mine).

Another day it was Kilnacree, to where her old home used to be. "It was here I was born and reared," she said shedding some tears at the thought of the past. The little, old thatched cottage had long since fallen down. She saw the stream, the fields and the spring well where she often drew water from in her youth. I got the feeling that she didn't enjoy the memory as much as she thought she would. There were big changes. As for me, I was exhausted from all the driving around.

We next visited Bunratty Castle. Here she treated her brother Paddy to a Guinness. It was good to have him with us as they could reminisce back to when they were young. On the way home we stopped at O'Mara's, where her brother Jimmy was living. Her stay in Moygala was fast coming to an end. The morning she was leaving, she was so happy to have made this memorable trip. She said, "I thought it would never happen." She was so thankful to her brother Paddy and his wife Anne and for their warm hospitality after so many years.

Its last goodbyes and we are on our way back to Galway. I was getting a bad pain in my left hip. Back home, and after a good night's rest, I felt much better. My dear Aunt Margie had to pack and be ready when the Callaghans would pick her up from Mother's and drive to Dublin. It was then on to Scotland where her late husband Dan came from. I was ready for a good rest. My husband said, "Margaret, you pushed yourself too much." I knew he was right. What could I do? Aunt Margie was very good to me in America, I was glad I had the opportunity to repay her.

1979 – SEPTEMBER, POPE'S VISIT

This was the year Pope John Paul II came to Ireland and visited Ballybrit. Leo was still a member of the Boy Scouts and his troupe had the privilege of doing a guard of honour for his Holiness in the Ballybrit Racecourse. They received a certificate of the visit with a picture of the Papal Keys. A great honour. "I will frame it for you, Leo," I said.

A FLEETING GLANCE

It was a fleeting glance at a future Saint. For the thousands of people who gathered in the Ballybrit Racecourse, on the thirtieth of September 1979, little did we know we were having the privilege of seeing in person (even though it was a fleeting glance, as he was speeding by in the open-top Pope Mobile) a future canonised Saint. I have the happy feeling that his first step on Irish soil was on my forty-sixth birthday, the twenty-ninth of September 1979.

1980 - NEED FOR A PLAYSCHOOL

The years of agriculture in Ballybane were coming to an end; the area was in development for industry and house-building for young families. An estate, Castle Park, was developed in 1978, and many young families were removed from the waiting list and into their own home's.

Talking with Paddy, I said, "There is a need for a playschool in Ballybane and the chalet would be suitable for a playschool." I explained my idea of starting one and he fully agreed. It would be a lot easier than accommodating young students or workers. "I will give my notice to Michael Convey and tell him I won't be working with the hospital shop trolleys any more." Paddy set to work making a sign and displaying it on the corner of the garage, ""Rock Dale" Playschool". I said, "Paddy, you're a genius."

"ROCK DALE" PLAYSCHOOL

"Rock Dale" Playschool opened in September, it was an exciting time. I had to have the inside redesigned by opening two of the four bedrooms into one, making a large playroom, while a third room held the seesaw, sandbox and a reader's corner; the fourth was used as a washroom with a dolly's bath on a stand. This was where the little girls washed dolls and their clothes, then hung them out to dry, weather permitting, and of course we needed a low toilet. Four parents enrolled their little ones. Through word of mouth, that four grew in number to thirty little ones, of between two and four years of age (plus a waiting list).

With such a big number, I employed a mother and asked voluntary mothers to help. These mothers were willing; it was a wonderful time helping the children at play. Mrs Barbara Ward, Margaret Gunning, Teresa O'Connell, Rita McDonagh, Kathleen Cooke, and many more (forgive me if I forgot your name) were among my helpers. The hours were from 9.30 a.m. to 1 p.m. four mornings a week.

As time went on, I was saving a little money. This I was putting aside to furnish the school with proper playschool equipment. Paddy and I eventually went shopping and we selected various pieces. We bought two each of the following; (one for inside and one for outdoors), slides, sandbox, seesaw, rocking boat, then a selection of little chairs and tables specially made for indoors. Outside we fenced off a part of the garden, making it into a playground. A gift from Micky Ward of Clareview of two old-fashioned desks was added. The children would hurry to get sitting on them, about five or six would fit on one at the same time. The official opening was a big morning by Fr. Willie Cummins, C.C. of Mervue. church He was happy to oblige by saying a Mass and blessing the school. He sprinkled holy water and blessed the rooms and the playground.

"ROCK DALE" PLAYSCHOOL IS NOW OFFICIALLY OPEN

It was a busy school from September to June. We closed in June for summer holidays, with Mass said out in the playground. Every Christmas I would have a volunteer disguised as Santa. For example, Tom Portal, Paddy Dowling, and on one occasion we had Kathleen Cooke to pass toys in blue and pink bags to good boys and girls.

"Rock Dale" play school is now officially open. The Play School decorated appropriately with flowers by my daughter Caroline seen in front with her daughter Caroline.

BROWNIES

Having completed my training as a Guide leader, I realized the chalet would make a perfect meeting-place. Mervue had many helpers and leaders. So I passed my Brownie pack over to two Mervue leaders. I opened a Brownie Pack in Ballybane. This got off to a great start. I was the Brown Owl. I then needed a Tawny Owl. Teresa O'Connell volunteered; she did her Guiders training and gained her Guiders pin from the Area Commissioner, Eileen Carrick. It was important that every volunteer do leader's training and sit a test before being officially recognised as a qualified leader.

BROWNIES ENROLMENT

Having attended at least six weekly meetings and carried out her duties as a Brownie, Brown Owl would be helping her to prepare for enrolment. This was a big occasion with an invitation to parents to witness the formal enrolling of their little girl as a member of Irish Girl Guides. Each little Brownie would stand in front of the pack and answer the Area Guide Commissioner's question,

"Do you know the Brownie Motto?"

"I do, a Brownie does her best to help others and do a good turn every day." Then the Brownie pin in the shape of a Sprite would be pinned to her tie, she would shake hands with the left hand, saluting, with two fingers touching her cap, with the right hand. Each Brownie would go through this ceremony to gain her Brownie pin. Then of course everyone celebrated with a party. The increase of little girls wanting to join Brownies was amazing. A list was drawn up. Each pack could have no more than twenty-seven Brownies with two leaders, a Brown Owl and a Tawny Owl. Before long, the chalet was catering to four Brownie packs, each pack having two leaders.

DANCING CLASSES

The three boys learned Irish dancing at the Peggy Carty School of Dancing. Michael and Eugene were Connacht Champion dancers three years in succession. Michael received a Connacht silver medal, and Eugene a Connacht leather belt that had to be returned in a year in exchange for a plaque. Eugene learned the button accordion and he also played soccerl. Michael learned to play the piano; his teacherMrs Bucan who was very pleased with him. He passed all his piano exams. As he got older, instead of step-dancing, he took up the game of badminton. He was sportsman of the year in Offaly where he and his wife with their two sons lived for a time.

Leo learned to play the piano; he played clarinet in St Patrick's School brass band. Leo joined the Mervue Cub Scouts and went from Cubs to Scouts, and then became a Scout leader. He was eventually commissioned as Scout Master. Geraldine spent a while learning piano, but she gave it up when she went to the Convent of Mercy boarding school in Spiddal. She was a bright girl and learned many languages. Margery and Caroline were strong in Brownies and Girl Guides. Margery played the accordion and Caroline played tinwhistle. They were both successful in winning trophies at Fleadh's.

1980/81 - A COMHALTAS CEOLTÓIRÍ BRANCH

I opened a branch of Comhaltas Ceoltóirí na h-Éireann, and set up a music class in the hall beneath the Church in Mervue. The teacher was Tom Mulhair. Tom could teach a variety of musical instruments. The class increased from ten to sixty-five children in a couple of years. Although Tom was on in years, he was a master at his job. The children ranged in ages from six to fourteen years. There was no nonsense taken. The children came to learn, and practise their pieces at home; their parents saw to that. The more traditional music they learned, the keener they became.

An American friend of Paddy's told him that he had the makings of a hundred clothes horses; the trouble was they had to be assembled and he wasn't going to do that. The whole bundle was left into our garage. I set to work; it took me weeks to make fifty. I called on our treasurer Bernie Folan and told her about the clothes horses. "What are you going to do with over fifty clothes horses?" She asked.

"We could sell them through the Parishes of Mervue and Renmore and use the money to tog out the children in band uniforms."

"Who will we get to sell them?" she wanted to know.

"You and I of course," I said. The two of us laughed at the idea.

"We will," she agreed, "but we need to tell the committee members, Maura Walsh and Marie Fahy." They agreed that it was a great way to get the children into uniforms.

We started selling and laughed as we made our sales pitch at the doors. It was a great success. With the help of the parents ideas on colours and style; we decided on black skirts for girls, trimmed with green braid and white blouses, and green stripes stitched to the legs of the boys' black pants and white shirts, and green waistcoats for all. Our tailor was Michael Holleran and our dressmaker was May Naughton; two people from the Parish.

The children were now in band uniforms. We were proud to see them lead the community games onto the field while they kept time playing marching tunes. They played for an all-Irish Mass in the Mervue Church on St.Patricks day to the delight of everyone. The classes lasted almost nine years until Tom, their teacher, got sick and resigned. During the nine years they competed in many Fleadhs, both at home and away and always won a number of medals and trophys. We gave our group the name 'Naoimh Seamus'. The children's parents were delighted to see how their children were getting involved and learning traditional music and taking part in competitions. We also decided we should hold a Céilí for the parents.

Naomh Seamus Branch of Comhaltas Ceoltoiri Eireann accompanies the Mayor of Galway, Councillor Bridie O'Flaherty, 1980. In the background, Jean O'Brien, Maura Walsh, Bernie Folan, their teacher the late Tom Mulhair, Margaret Dowling, Chairperson and Con O'Donovan.

CÉILÍ

I contacted the Kilfenora Céilí Band, and asked them to play for a Céilí night in the Mervue community hall, Galway. Their response, "We would be glad to play for ye." The hall under the Mervue Church never witnessed such a crowd or such brilliant music. The night was a wonderful success, as anyone can imagine when it was the Kilfenora Céilí band playing. Friends of Paddy's from Connemara, that he met during his years at barbering, always brought him a bottle of poteen at Christmas time. He brought a few bottles to the Céilí and many a man had a swig/drink of it, making them all the merrier.

CAROLINE ON CALL

Anything her father needed, Caroline would do her best to help in getting it for him. Like the buying of the paper and cigarettes at the local shop (there were no restrictions on the sale of cigarettes them years). Paddy also loved reading. On Saturday mornings, Caroline and her friend Shirley McEntee would go into Galway to the County library and pick out three detective books for him. He would settle down to a good read and always rewarded Caroline with a few shillings for herself and Shirley. Thanking him, they would then run to the shop to buy sweets. He was still suffering some pain in the left leg. I advised him to tell his doctor at his next visit about the pain. "I did as you said and he has put me on a stronger painkilling tablet; I have to take one three times a day with my meals. I didn't think he could prescribe a stronger tablet than I am already taking."

"They should help you then, Paddy" I said.

CARD PLAYING

My brother-in-law Jimmy Nally and Paddy would drive out to Ballyglunin on Saturday nights to play cards. One Saturday night after leaving Jimmy home, Paddy, on his way back, didn't see a big rock on the road and hit it; the Morris Minor turned upside down on the road. Some people came along and pulled him out of the car and turned it right way up; they then drove him home in the car. No one was hurt, but the passenger door was badly damaged and cost a lot to be fixed, and still it didn't close properly. I was very upset. "You told me you wouldn't drink when you drove to Ballyglunin," I yelled at him, "well that's the end of it now; you are not driving to Ballyglunin anymore."

A RED OPEL CADET

I decided to trade in the Morris Minor. After seeing a lovely red car in J.J. Fleming's garage, Tuam Road, I enquired about it. The salesman told me it was an Opel Cadet and was only two years old. He then opened the door saying, "Sit in, and I will give you a run in it." I fell in love with it; the smell of the leathers and the red colour; oh! It was a beauty.

"I think I will take it! Providing you give me a good trade in on the Morris Minor?" The salesman agreed and told me he would fix up the insurance and road tax for me.

I was very apprehensive about letting Paddy drive this car too far. It worried me since Paddy had had the accident with the Morris Minor. Remembering how upset I was at the time, I set to writing a little note to Jimmy telling him Paddy would not be driving to Ballyglunin any more. If an accident happened, Paddy might be the cause of it, and the onus would be on me as the car was in my name. Paddy sulked for a bit but got over it. I had peace of mind for a few months. Until one day he came to tell me that Jimmy's father and a few men in Ballyglunin wanted their haircut. So, I gave in, providing Jimmy drove the car.

Then I asked for a promise that the night he, Paddy, would drive, that he wouldn't drink, and it wasn't fair for Jimmy to do the driving each time. As Paddy made the promise of not drinking while driving, I relented.

MUSIC CLASS – ENTER-CLASS COMPETITION

This would open new ground for the music class; it meant the musicians would have to get down to very serious practice. It also meant the committee would take on a new responsibility. The number of children under the different ages and taking part in the various categories had to be counted; adjudicates needed to be allocated. The entrance fees were to be decided on. It was suggested the date to hold the competitions would be the sixth of January; this was unanimously agreed on. Then the buying of trophies had to be undertaken.

BUYING THE TROPHIES

The children were constantly rehearsing for this serious inter-class competitions which was to be held on the 6th January 1981. Their parents would be attending this great occasion. I was very excited and nervous, for this was a big undertaking. Bernie Folan, our treasurer, and I, headed off to Richard Quinn's Trophy shop in Lower Dominick Street, together with the chequebook and the list of trophies, cups, medals and plaques to be purchased for the competitors, in their various ages and categories. Richard Quinn kindly donated a silver cup, as did the C.C. Father Willie Cummins of Mervue.

I was very tired after the shopping. Margery, Caroline and I went to bed early. The boxes of trophies were already in the kitchen for the next morning.

Our bedroom was over the sitting room, so I could hear the boys talking about the match of the day. I listened for the key in the door when Paddy would come home and enquire how the match was going. It didn't happen. The boys came up to bed and looked into my room to say goodnight. "Dad's not home, is he?" I asked. "He should be in soon, Mom," said Michael.

I turned over in the bed, and waited for the phone to ring.

1981 – 6th JANUARY

The phone call came at two o'clock in the morning from the Regional Hospital, Galway. It was Jimmy's brother Michael Nally's voice telling me there was a bad accident in Ballyglunin. I said that I knew something like this would happen. He assured me they were both fine, but my car was a write-off. I didn't mind about the car at the time, so long as they were all right. Leo was standing in the hall looking at me; "What's up?" he asked.

"There has been an accident, Leo; the two men are in hospital. Get your coat Leo, and we will go down to see your Aunt Mary; maybe she hasn't heard yet." It was a beautiful January morning at two a.m. with the moon shining bright. When Mary saw us at the door she said, "Has there been an accident?"

"Yes," I said, "but according to Jimmy's brother they are both in hospital and are ok. Were you not in bed?" I asked.

"No," she said, "I was restless. And tomorrow we are holding the first Ceoltas inter-class competitions. But don't worry, my Seamus and Michael will be there."

"I'll go to the hospital in the morning to see Jimmy and Paddy; I'll call you and tell you how they are," she said.

"You and Leo go on home now; you have a big day ahead of you tomorrow,".

"Thanks Mary," I said, "I will see you at some time during the day."

We left but I could not shake the awful feeling I had that it was a bad accident.

COMHALTAS COMPETITIONS

Next morning, it was an early start to the community hall, with the doors opening at nine a.m. Having no car, I hired a taxi to take Margery with her accordion and Caroline and myself, and all the heavy boxes of trophies to the Mervue Hall, to get everything set up for the children to register. The treasurer, Bernie Folan, took the remainder of the entry fees. The children were coming in by the dozen; there were sixty-five children ranging in ages from six to fourteen years. Parents were helping by putting out the chairs, getting the stage ready and setting a table and three chairs in place for the adjudicators. Pat Murry from Oranmore and the Fahys from Balinakill were adjudicating. It was a hectic morning.

At last everything was ready, and the children were lined up to perform. But there was no sign of my two nephews Seamus and Michael Nally. I told Bernie about the accident. I said, "I'm quite sure it was a bad one." She put her arm

Fr Willie Cummines presents his cup to over all winner Geraldine Coyne.

around me.

"They will be here," she said, "you'll see."

The competition was a success; the children won cups, medals and plaques for music, singing, recitations, and drama, and I was happy it went so well. By seven in the evening it was over and the adjudicators complimented the children and their parents, and especially their teacher, Tom Mulhair; also the committee who worked so hard to organise such a big event. The committee included Bernie Folan, Maura Walsh and Marie Fahy.

As their manager, I had to go up on the stage to take a bow; I tried to thank everyone, my voice got lost in the applause. Due to the circumstances, it was the hardest part of the whole program for me.

I was so glad it was over. I told the person who was leaving my two daughters and I home about the accident. He said that he had heard about it on the radio, but no names were mentioned. I didn't hear any news from my sister Mary.

I was so tired, I couldn't face going up to the hospital. I phoned to find out how they were. I was told my husband was not in any danger, they wouldn't divulge any information about Jimmy only just that he was resting. I was glad to know they were alive.

AFTERMATH

The aftermath of the accident was horrendous. I got up early next morning and got myself ready for what ever the day might bring. I called Leo before I left to tell him to mind Margery and Caroline until I came home. "I'll try not to be long," I told him. On reaching the hospital I could feel the anger rising up inside me. "I must not feel this way going in," I reprimanded myself.

I went to see my husband Paddy first.

"What happened?" I asked.

"I'm not sure," he answered, "but a car came towards me and hit the side of our car. Jimmy almost went through the windscreen, I pulled him out of it; the next thing I knew I was here in hospital. Jimmy's brother Michael was here and told me he was all right. How did you find out?" he asked.

"Micheal Nally phoned me at two in the morning. Leo and I went to tell my sister Mary, as she would not have known. I'm going to see Jimmy now," I said. There was a shock for me. Splinters from the windscreen went into Jimmy eyes. He told me he was going to be moved to a special hospital in Cork where a specialist would remove the splinters. Jimmy told me it would cost a lot of money but the car insurance would cover the cost and that I wasn't to worry that I would lose my house, "Nothing like that will happen," he said. I came away feeling numb.

When I reached home I told my sons the awfulness of what happened. They put their arms around me. "It's not your fault, Mom," they said. I think to myself, "Will this upset bring back the panic's I used to get after Michael and Leo's father died?"

"They hadn't put their seat belts on," my dear sons were trying to console me. I brought Paddy home from the hospital in a taxi. Because of his legs' operations, he was not able to walk very far. It was costing a fortune, hiring taxis for him, and I let him know in no uncertain terms.

My son Michael reprimanded me for being so angry with him.

"He knows what has happened, and it wasn't his fault entirely I'm sure, Mom."

My next task was to visit my sister Mary. She was also very upset.

I had lived in fear every Saturday night when Paddy took the car, that if there was an accident it would cost me, as the car was in my name. And now it has happened and worse than I ever predicted. Walking home, I knew that this accident had affected our two families physically, financially, mentally and personally.

PLAYSCHOOL

Working with the little children kept me sane; Reading little stories to them, and playing games, talking to their parents who came to collect them up after their morning playschool session. It all helped and I knew with God's help that I would get through this crisis.

MOTHER PASSED AWAY

For some time, our mother had not been well; she was getting weaker and her appetite was poor. I wrote to her brother Paddy Hurley in County Clare letting him know his sister Bridget was not well. Shortly after, two of her brothers, Paddy and Jack, and nephew Michael Hurley came to see her. I was glad of their visit as it cheered her up. If she understood the reason for their visit she never let on. Her grandson Michael Beggen was making plans to get married in April to Mary Moran from Ballinrobe. He was on his last visit to see his granny as she lay sick in bed at her home in Ballybrit. He said, "You know, Granny, you must get well and come to our wedding. I want you in the photos."

"I would, Michael," she said in a weak voice, "if I could get up out of this bed." The next day, I called the ambulance to take her to hospital. While the doctor examined her, I stood beside her and she reached for my hand. I could see the large swelling in her stomach. The doctor took me one side. "She has ovarian cancer, we will need to operate to relieve the pressure," he said.

As she was being prepared for her operation she asked, "What date are ye going to operate on me?" They told her the fifth of March.

"Don't operate that day; it's my birthday," she said, "I don't want to die on my birthday."

"That's fine with us; we will leave it for another few days."

She smiled and turned her head away. On the day of her operation, the four of us, Eddie, myself, Paddy and Mary walked beside the stretcher carrying her to the theatre, where a porter took and wheeled the stretcher towards the theatre door. He said to us, "Kiss her now. You may as well go home, we will take care of her." We left; each one with theirown thoughts of our dear mother.

A few days after her operation, our mother passed away in the Regional Hospital at the age of eighty-one. She was waked in the Hospital Morgue. Her funeral was well attended. Fr. O'Connor celebrated her funeral Mass in St. Columba's Church, Castlegar. He spoke many kind words, telling of how well he knew Mrs. Abberton who always wore a smile. She passed away peacefully on the eleventh of March. Again, the four of us walked, this time behind the hearse. We cried, her grandchildren cried, and many people shed a tear for the friend they knew many years. She is buried in the new cemetery in Bohermore.

IN DIRE NEED OF A CAR

I was unable to afford the price of a good car. Jimmy Nally told me to go to the Renault used-car showroom in Bohermore. His brother Michael was salesman there and he would sell me one at a reasonable price. Michael showed me an Austin Marina. It was very big and I didn't like it, but it was all I could afford at £300. I had to take out a Credit Union loan for it. The lovely red Opel Cadet was towed to the scrap yard and what I was paid for it went on towing it away.

APRIL WEDDING

In our family, my oldest son Michael will be marring Mary Moran in St. Mary's Church, Ballinrobe. It was a glorious Easter Monday morning, 20th April 1981. What a beautiful day for a beautiful bride, who was looking radiant in her white wedding gown and veil and carrying a red bouquet of flowers, as she walked down the aisle on the arm of her father Paddy Moran. Michael was handsome in his tuxedo waiting for her at the altar, his brother Leo, best man, also looking dapper in his tuxedo and holding the wedding rings. The bridesmaid Maura O'Malley was in pale pink and the two flowergirls

Margery and Caroline Dowling were in pretty, pink floating dresses made for them by Mary.

The bride's mother Jane was in a navy and white trimmed suit. I wore a cream blouse and skirt and a light pink sleeveless waistcoat. Other members of our family attending were my husband Paddy and his son Eugene, dressed in their tuxedos, and Paddy's daughter Geraldine in a navy blouse and tartan skirt. Michael and Mary's wedding day gave us a lift after the past months of trouble and sadness. Listening to the prayers of the faithful being read, it was touching to hear Michael's late father and Granny Abberton's names mentioned. I thought, "They are here at your wedding too, Michael." It was a fantastic day. The reception was held in the Heneghan Hotel, Headford, County Galway. The happy couple enjoyed their honeymoon touring Scotland.

MOTHER'S HEADSTONE

It was some time later that I went to visit mother's grave. I was surprised to find a headstone erected on her grave in the shape of a white book. I called on my sister Mary to ask her who put it there. She said, "I did."

"Why didn't you tell me?" I asked.

"I wanted to do it myself," was her answer.

A few years later, the book was removed and a larger headstone was erected in its place. As I knelt to say my few prayers, I smiled to myself saying, "I hope you are not being disturbed, Mother, with the switching of headstones above you. R.I.P. dear mother."

PLAYSCHOOL SUMMER HOLIDAYS

It's June, and the playschool children are looking forward to their holidays. I did the usual with the help of Barbara Ward, , and my daughter Margery. Volentary helpers. We set up an altar for the Mass out in the playground and two children placed small vases of wild flowers on it, and two more brought water for the priest to wash his fingers. It was all in preparation for Fr. Marrinner to celebrate Mass. The sun was shining down on us. I held the usual presentation of certificates for the little leaving certs, who would be going on to the big school. It was all done very nice. Each year at the closing, a little one would present me with a bell, but it was the party that would get the most attention, the goodies and drinks. Bye, bye, until September, for the little ones returning.

IN ALL WALKS OF LIFE

Sadness crosses your path; and for me, playing, reading, doing little drama acts to entertain their parents was always a joy, wiping tears, opening lunch boxs, it was a big part of playschool life. Looking at the carefree little ones, I never expected to hear the sad news of anyone of them being called by God in their young teenage lives. It hit hard to learn of Michael Mullins, Lee Fleming and Gary Harte at a young age,and at separate times, were called to heaven It was heart breaking, I often pictured them at play in my playschool. I won't ever forget them.

CAMP BALLYLANDERS

Mervue Guides and the Ballybane Galway Brownies were in full swing preparing for their summer camp holiday. The two units would be joining up for an exciting time. We were lucky having beautiful weather for this particular holiday, to spend two weeks at the top of a mountain in Ballylanders, County Tipperary. In what was once a little country cottage was extended into a holiday resource centre for IGG, by Mrs. Pat Snow, Irish Girl Guide Leader.

As the Brownies were underage for outdoor camping, they would be sleeping in the cottage, accompanied by their leaders, Brownie Camp Organizer/District Commissioner, Jane Thornbull, and Brown Owl, Margaret Dowling. The Girl Guides would be pitching their tents in the outdoor grounds under the supervision of their Captain, Eileen

Carrick, erecting tent poles and tents, outdoor toilets and a fire shelter, while Lieutenant Chris Curley and Brown Owl Bernie Higgins were busy preparing an outdoor fire and the food. All this equipment was delivered in a van by a good neighbour, Joe Folan, who would return to take it all back to Galway again in two weeks time; we were so grateful to him.

Our contingent hired a minibus to bring the Leaders, Guides and Brownies on this journey. The Brownies had only their personal items to bring. When everyone was settled in, Captain Eileen Carrick invited us all to gather around the Guide campfire for campfire singing. The Brownies loved this part of the camp holiday. Another occasion was going up a hill in the dark of night with their lighted torches. This adventure would be sussed out by the leaders during the day. After that walk, there would be cups of warm soup for everyone; it was so exciting eating outdoors in the dawn of a summer's morning.

For Sunday Mass, two young leaders were sent to the priest's house to find out the mass time. When they told him how many Guides and Brownies were in the group, he said, "That's a big group of people; I don't think you will fit in our little chapel with our parishioners. Tell your leaders I will be up to celebrate Mass at your campsite." We were very happy with such an offer. It was a beautiful morning to have Mass said outdoors and the priest joining us for breakfast.

There were lots of fun and games every day. The heat was getting to be too much for the Brownies. Jane and I decided to buy a hose to cool them down. I had an idea; I took a hammer and a nail and punched holes here and there through the hose, so when we turned on the water it came spraying out everywhere and the children were running and jumping through it. We were praying for rain in the hopes the weather would cool down.

One night, everyone decided to go to bed early we were exausted after the heat of the day; There would be no camp fire singing. There were "Ahs" and "Ohs" and "That's not fair." We assembled into a horseshoe form and sang 'Gone the sun, gone the day all is well, safely rest, good night'. Everyone settled into their beds for a good night's sleep. Little did we think that a bad storm was brewing overhead.

It was about three in the morning when Jane and I heard Eileen, her leaders, and Guides coming into the cottage. The storm that no one predicted was so bad it blew down the tents, the lightning was flashing and thunder rolling; it was frightening and we were glad everyone was indoors. Next morning, the weather was calm again. Two young leaders went to the village to get the milk. The villagers asked, "Are ye all safe up there?"

They said, "We are."

"That's good; because three of the cattle in the next field were hit by lightning and killed during the night. We were very worried about ye," said the man in the shop, "we don't get bad storms like that one too often." When the girls came back with the milk and told us about the cattle, we all prayed our thanksgiving that we were safe.

The morning of leaving was a big clean up and Pat Snow came to see us and collect the keys. We were hurrying the clean-up, and have the Guides' equipment packed for Joe Folan when he came to collect it in his van. The minibus was right on time too. We thanked Pat Snow for letting us have the use of the cottage and grounds. We were glad to get home safely and to see the parents collecting their Guides and Brownies with hugs and kisses. It was an unforgettable experience.

LEO GOES TO DUBLIN

Leo was going to Dublin to begin his training as a delicatessen supervisor in H. William's supermarket. Leo was a stranger in Dublin; he knew no-one. After mass one Sunday, he asked the priest where the nearest Scouts den was.

"You are right beside it," said the priest, pointing to a hut behind the church. Leo made many friends through Scouting. He had good experiences being involved in the Mervue Scouts and was a Scout Leader. It paid off well for him, as he was commissioned Assistant

Scout Master of the 165th Dublin Scout Troup. And very soon, he brought his young Scout Troop with three of their Scout Leaders to Galway, and joined up with Des Murry and the Mervue Scouts.

The 165th Dublin Scout Troop spent a week camping out near Ballyloughane. The weather was very bad, raining every day. It was August and my playschool was available. Leo took advantage of it and stacked up the little chairs and tables to make sleeping space for the Scouts. His fifteen Scouts had dry shelter for the second week, and with the central heating, their sleeping bags dried out fast. The Scout Leaders took turns sleeping in the playroom. Each one came before leaving to thank me for giving them dry shelter. As a Girl Guide Leader, I felt it was my duty. Checking the playschool, I found everything put back as they found it, and some little thank-you notes left for me. During their stay in Ballybane, they attended Mass in the John Paul Centre joined by the Ballybane Beavers, Ballybane IGG and Mervue Scouts, with a great big gathering afterwards with their leaders for a photograph.

JULY - USA

I was planning to visit the States. Originally, it was to be Paddy and I who were to go, but due to the car accident Paddy had to attend court in July.

So I prepared Margery and Caroline for the trip. At ages twelve and nine respectively, they were ecstatic about going to America. "Where are we going first, Mom?" Was one of many questions. I said we would be going to our very good friends Clare and Mike Burke and their son Michael and daughter Mary- Ann in Long Island for two weeks, and then we will go to the Bronx N.Y. to visit Aunt Margie.

Leo drove us in the Marina to Shannon airport. We had a nice flight. Coming nearer to landing at Kennedy airport, we began to feel the intense heat. "Now," I said, "girls, enjoy the heat for the next month."

Clare and her daughter Mary Ann were at the airport to meet us, it was very exciting. Drawing near to their house, I could see their new abode was a smart ranch house; a big change from the city apartment. "Wow," I said, "Clare, this is some place!"

Her husband Mike greeted us saying, "After you unpack, come out to the barbeque; the food should be ready by then."

We got settled into the newly decorated basement, which was like a house within a house. Mary Ann asked if we'd brought bathing togs, of course we did! "Well, put them on!" she said. The girls togged out ready for the pool, where they almost lived for the next two weeks, splashing with Mary Ann and her brother Michael.

THE BRONX

Soon we were packing again to go visit Aunt Margie. This was a much different story. There was no big back garden or swimming pool, for Margie lived in a three-room apartment. The girls had to sleep together in a pull-out couch. Aunt Margie's big welcome soon made up for the disappointment. I explained to the girls that it was here I came when I first came to the States in 1952.

Margery wanted to know if I liked the place. I told her that I loved Aunt Margie's apartment, but that I hated America, although in time I got used to it.

This was my first trip back in eighteen years. There was a big change in the Bronx. I could see changes everywhere and not for the better. The buildings were boarded up; there was crime, drugs, stores had bars on the windows, and many of the neighbours had moved to the country. My cousin Maureen, her husband Henry, and their three daughters had moved to a new house in Westbury, Long Island. Aunty Margie was one of the very few white people left in her neighbourhood. "It can't be safe for you here," I said, "why dont you move out to Maureen?"

"She wants me to, but I'm sixty years living here, and there are still a few of the old friends left. I have told her she will take me out of here in the casket (coffin)."

Aunt Margie took us on the subway train. Looking out the train window before it went underground was unbelievable; the Bronx was in a shambles.

"My good God Margie, what has happened?" I asked.

"People don't care any more," she answered. The train was speeding along, then all at once we were underground and every nationality had crowded on to it; you could feel their eyes on the very white people. We kept Margery and Caroline close between us; I knew they were afraid. We changed at 125th Street for a train to Manhattan; that was different.

SIGHTSEEING IN MANHATTAN

Now it was on to Rockaway Centre and St Patrick's Cathedral and the Empire State Building. On a hop-on, hop-off, open-top double-decker bus, we had a great view of New York City, the Big Apple. After our lunch of hot dogs from the venders, with sodas and great big ice-creams, we went to another part of the Bronx to visit Mike's Aunt, Mary McKenna, and there we met her daughter Peggy Connelly, her husband Mark, and her brother John McKenna. We had a lovely visit with them. Aunt Mary was saying she would have to move soon; it was too dangerous living on her own there. She gave us a lovely meal of bacon, cabbage and spuds; the smell brought us back to Ireland.

Aunt Margie was near to tears, and of course we had the big dish of strawberry ice cream. Margery called me to the toilet, "Mom, are we going back to Aunt Margie's in that train again? I'm scared."

"We might get a taxi," I said. John said he would be leaving soon, "If I leave my car parked too long on the street, it will be gone when I go for it." He offered to take us back to Aunt Margie's apartment, we could not thank him enough. John was married and living with his wife Jackie and family in New Jersey. But as he worked in the city, he took of a few hours to come to his mother's and have dinner with us. I was glad in meeting everyone after so many years.

COUSIN MAUREEN

The girls were having a great time with their grand-aunt. "I will be coming with you to cousin Maureen's," she said. Before Maureen came to pick us up, there was another treat in store. The lady I worked for before my husband Mike died, Florence Kazden, came to take the three of us to lunch. Florence and I were so happy to be meeting up; she was still the same lovely, welcoming lady. She gave the girls a choice of what restaurant they would like. Margery said she would like to try a Russian one; so Florence in her big air-conditioned Pontiac car, took us down town to Manhattan to a Russian restaurant. It was a beautiful place and the waitresses wore short black skirts, black nylons, and a white blouse with long wide sleeves, with tiny red pinny (apron) and a red bow in their hair. They served American food as well as Russian. It was a real treat.

(Florence and I have remained friends for years. She is a Jewish lady. I did a bit of house cleaning for her when Michael was two years old, and she would mind him while I was doing the work. We are now friends for over fifty-five years; she is aged ninety-seven now and in a care home in Florida. I call her on the phone and we have a chat rembering back to the times when we were young).

We said our goodbyes to Florence and thanked her for the lovely treat. She handed the girls a present each. "You are far too good," I said.

"The next time you hear from me, Peggy, Oscar and I will be living in Florida; he is retired now. The summers are much nicer there than here in New York." Then she drove away.

Florence's sister,
Florence in flounce dress.

"I can see you are having a good vacation, Peggy," said Maureen, greeting us with open arms. I can't explain what a treat it was for me to see my cousin again. Then she helped her mother into the car. "I have your luggage in the trunk of the car, Peggy. I couldn't leave the car unattended. You can see where it is parked?" There was danger lurking everywhere, eyes staring at my two little daughters; it was frightening. A few short years ago people could walk this same street at any time of the day or night, without any fear.

"It is hard to believe, Peggy. You must be glad you made the choice to return to the old country," said my dear aunt.

"I am glad, but you helped me to make that choice, I will be forever grateful to you," I answered.

We were out in the country once more where the air was nice and fresh, even though it was hot. This was my first meeting with Maureen and Henry since I left in March 1963. She had three daughters. I had seen Kathy and Jenny when they were babies. Kathy is now twenty-two, and a nurse, Jenny is nineteen and still in college, and Christian is fifteen.

"Your daughters are beautiful, Maureen. God Bless them," I said.

"So are yours, Peggy. Kathy has a boyfriend, Joe Maloney; he is a fireman, you will meet him this evening."

"Your house is lovely, Maureen."

"It's big, but not as big as yours. Mam was telling me when she came back after her Irish trip that you had a big house built for yourself and the boys. She admired you for your courage. Going back to her old county of Clare and meeting her three brothers and sister two years ago was something she didn't think would ever happen. She had the time of her life, Peggy."

"It was a great occasion for the five of them; they are well on in years, Maureen. You know my mother died in March of this year. I'm so happy for the time the sisters had together. We will be spending a week here in Westbury with Maureen and family.

On our night out, Maureen introduced us to some of her friends, who were lady cops like herself. Her husband Henry was a butcher; he would bring home big steaks in the evening and grill them. "There's nothing like a good piece of a porterhouse steak for dinner," he would say. Christine would take Margery and Caroline to the local swimming pool, but of course it wasn't like Burke's private one. They would stay only a short time as it was public, and young lads would jump in and splash around roughly.

Our time in cousin Maureen's went fast. We are again on the move and say goodbye to Aunt Margie, Maureen and her daughters; her husband had left for work early in the morning. We were on the train back to Claire and Mike Burke's. Arriving at the house, the first thing the girls did was change and head for the pool. Mike and Claire had invited family members to a barbeque. Claire's sister Maureen, who worked with me in the agricultural college in Athenry, came with her two daughters and son. We had a lot to catch up on; talking mostly about our time working in the college. It was lovely to reminisce. Mike was a great barbeque chef; we enjoyed the rolls and burgers, hot dogs and the salads that went with them. It was the last big meal we had together, for our holiday was over and Claire would be driving us to the airport next morning to fly back to Ireland, so our last goodbyes were said to Claire.

SHANNON AIRPORT

It was a lovely sight that met our eyes, flying in over Shannon and looking down on the green fields. Paddy was waiting for us. We were glad to see each other. Paddy remarked on the girls' good tan, especially Margery, who was as brown as a berry. It was good to be home again after a wonderful vacation.

It was now back down to work. My first job was to prepare the playschool for the next month when new little pupils would be starting off. Also, the Brownies and Girl Guide meetings would be starting up. Paddy had something to tell me. "I had to go to Tuam for the court case, Michael came with me. Because I was driving the car the night of the accident, the Judge put all the blame over on me and fined me."

"What about the car that hit you?"

"There was nothing said about it."

"What does that mean for us?" I asked.

"It means our car insurance will have to cover Jimmy Nally's expenses."

I was speechless each year for five years when I went to pay the car insurance; it was getting dearer and dearer. I had lost my no-claims bonus.

ACTIVITIES

When all the activities started up, I was keeping my mind focused on them. The playschool kept me occupied. This time we were rehearsing a little fun play we were going to put on for the parents, indeed the children invented most of it themselves. They looked forward each morning to acting out their little parts. After the morning school session was over and the children gone home, I was happy to head to the kitchen where Paddy would have a good fire on in the range and a lunch ready, and no doubt a cake of bread in the oven. He was a first-class baker. I used to tell him, 'you should have been a baker instead of a barber'. He was at all times trying to keep occupied and be helpful.

Standing up digging in the garden was putting pressure on his legs, so he invented a low stool to sit on, and with a short-handle spade and fork he worked away. Seeing him planting potatoes and vegetables, I had to admire him. Poochy was always at his side. His clients came for haircuts and for this job he sat upon a higher stool and managed well.

SEPTEMBER - MY OPERATION

I needed to see the doctor, for I was in trouble with a prolapse and unable to urinate properly for some time, and my tummy was all bloated up. After my visit to the doctor, he said, "I am sending you to the gynaecologist straight away." At the Regional Hospital, I was examined by a lady doctor; she told me to come in the next Sunday evening before six o'clock and I would have the hysterectomy operation the next morning. When I went home I told Paddy I was being admitted almost right away. He said, "That was fast."

"It was," I agreed, "you have only Margery and Caroline to mind, you have nothing to worry about."

"We will do fine," he assured me.

Sunday evening came and Paddy took me to the Regional Hospital. I told him to go straight home to the girls and not to visit me until Tuesday.

"All right," he promised, as he kissed me on the cheek, "good luck and don't worry about anything." The doctor told me I would have no stitches, for they were performing a suction on my type of prolapse. I was glad to hear that; it meant it was a small operation. As I thought.

The nurse looking after me took me to a ward where there were three patients; two were sleeping. The third one was awake and ready for chat. She questioned me about my operation. I was feeling good telling her of the simple procedure for my operation. She was able to tell me how it would be done. "They just deaden your lower part, you won't feel it, but you will hear everything they will be doing." I was almost in tears with fear. The nurse came with a little tablet for me, "Take this, it will help you to relax. We will be around later to take your bloods."

The tablet did relax me, but the fear of hearing everything the doctor would be doing worried me. Six a.m. and I got another tablet; that really did the job of relaxing me. I was wheeled into theatre. And when I came around the nurse said, "Margaret, your husband is here."

I took one look at Paddy and said, "I told you not to come until Tuesday."

He laughed and said, "It is Tuesday. You woke up yesterday for a short time, you have had a big operation so you have been let rest."

"Sorry," I whispered; he gave me a kiss and said, "I will see you tomorrow."

HIT BY LIGHTNING

The next time Paddy came to visit me he looked very shook. I asked, Are you not well, Paddy?"

"I got hit by lightning."

"How did that happen?" I asked. (When I had the house built in the sixties, there was no such thing as city water piped out to Ballybane; a concrete storage tank to hold rain water with a galvanised roof was built just outside the kitchen window. Inside the window was the kitchen sink). Paddy described what happened; he was washing vegetables for the dinner, and a flash of lightning struck the galvanised roof and hit the sink, and then struck him and sent him back across the kitchen floor, where he hit off the wall. "Michael was just coming in the hallway and heard the loud bang. He ran into the kitchen and looked at me, I was stunned. I asked him to help me stand; this he did, I was shaking all over. Michael was looking very concerned. "I'll call 999," he said.

"No, don't," I said, "I'm alright; make me some tea and put plenty of sugar in it."

"What a thing to happen to you, Paddy." I was choked up, "you could have died."

"Look," he said, showing me his belt-buckle where there was a big dent in it, "that's where the streak of lightning struck, the buckle saved my life; I'm fine now, don't worry about me. As soon as I go home I will call a plumber and have the sink moved to a side wall in the kitchen."

"What an experience you had."

"Worse could have happened, it could have been one of the children."

THINKING OF A BROWNIE CONCERT

While in hospital, I was trying to think up a little musical play for the Brownies to put on for parents' evening. I was trying to put together something around a popular song. The Brownies were fond of singing *"Oh! Lord It's so hard to be humble."* As I was being helped to the toilet, I saw an open press with grey cardboards in the shape of hats. I asked the nurse what they were for. "They are bedpan liners," she answered. "They're out of date now, we have more modern ones a white paper lining to fit on the bedpan they are much better."

"Could I have a few of the card board ones?" I asked, without thinking.

"What?" said the nurse, "why would you want them?" I explained how I was planning a little musical with the Brownies, and they would make perfect cowboy hats.

"How many would you want?"

"About twenty-five." They were in sealed bags; she took one down and gave it to me. "Thank you very much, nurse. I can give it to my husband to take home with him this evening when he comes in." She helped me to the toilet. I knew she was in a hurry to go somewhere to have a good laugh.

A TERRIBLE THIRST

I was in good form and glad to be home after my operation, everyone making a fuss. But all I wanted was to go to bed. For the next three days, I had a terrible thirst. Paddy called the doctor who said I had a high temperature. "I have given her an injection of penicillin; if there is no improvement in the next two days, take her to hospital." All night and the next day, the thirst was getting worse. I was drinking bottle after bottle of soda water, Cidona, and lemonade. Nothing would quench the thirst. "Get me to hospital quick, Paddy."

"We're on our way," he said.

"Why are you here, Margaret?" The nurse asked. "You're not due in for six weeks."

"Thirst nurse, I am going mad with thirst." I was taken into a cubicle and told to lie on a stretcher. The curtain was pulled around. The doctor told me to lie down and bend up my knees, then with a small torch, he looked up my vagina. I don't know for how long he was pulling out wad after wad of cotton wool from my insides. Looking at me, he said, "You poor girl; they forgot to remove the packing. You will be all right now, you are healing well." And that was the end of that. When I told that story to friends, they laughed out loud. I guess it was and' wasn't funny.

HALLOWEEN PARTY

It was Halloween and my first time out after the operation. The Brownies would be having their party, and all dressed up in scary costumes. Without telling anyone, I dressed as a witch and arrived at their meeting, and began running around with my arms stretched out and making funny noises. Some Brownies were afraid. Even the leaders didn't know me. I pulled off the mask and the Brownies began to scream. "It's Brown Owl," said Eileen Carrick, "Your legs are so thin I couldn't tell who you were." I was so glad to be involved again.

PLANING THE CONCERT

I explained my idea to Tawny Owl/Joan Mc Cormack; of course, she laughed when she saw what was going to be cowboy hats. She remarked that they were too wide for the children's heads. We set to work lining the insides with a thick, spongy material, then decorating them with colourful crepe paper; around the rim of each hat we stuck strips of colourful fur.

On the night of the concert, the parents waited in anticipation to see their Brownie daughters' performance. There was step-dancing, some solo songs of the little ones' choice, and a tinwhistle duet. Next it was *"Oh! Lord it's so hard to be humble"*. The lead singer cowgirl had her own proper fringed outfit, hat and knee-high boots. She strutted onto the stage singing a verse of the song. It was then the chorus group appeared in flowery dresses, and looking perfect wearing their impressive cowboy hats, singing the chorus, *"Oh Lord it's so hard to be humble."* They performed well and sang a number of songs, to the delight of their parents. (Joan and I could not look at each other knowing what the hats were made up of; we were holding in the laughing). It was a lovely evening, and ended with a party for everyone. I made sure I brought home the hat creations.

1982 - AFTER SHOCK OF THE HYSTERECTOMY

The New Year started for me at three o'clock in the morning when I awoke with the bed soaking in sweat. I hadn't been feeling well and had already moved into the single bed in our bedroom; we called it sickbay for the children. When they would be sick I would bring them into it. "Dear God," I thought. "Night sweats, how long will this last?" I asked myself. I was in and out of bed drying myself several times a night for the next few months, changing my nightwear and changing sheets. As sudden as they came, they left just as sudden. But I was left with hot flushes. Menopause, change of life, middle years, middle age spread, night sweats, hot flushes, name it what you like; I had it all. It was the end of the monthlies for me, and the saving on S.T.s. (Sanitary towels).

The hot flushes lasted for years; they would flare up occasionally and were very uncomfortable and embarrassing, my face would go pure red. One morning in the playschool, I was trying to ignore a hot flush; I knew my face was red. One little boy didn't ignore it. "Look, look, teachers face is red. She is shy," said the little rascal. A little girl put her arm around me and whispered, "Don't be shy." I was shy many times for the next number of years.

FEBRUARY - BABY MICHAEL

The best news ever, I am a grandmother. Michael's wife Mary gave birth on the twenty-first of February to a son in the Regional Hospital, Galway. I am so excited; I can't wait to hold my first grandchild, a little boy. I wonder if they will christen him 'Michael the third'. Granny Moran had a grandson already by her oldest daughter. We were looking forward to his Christening in Ballinrobe Church. His Uncle Leo was godfather and Mary's best friend Maura O'Malley, godmother. Holding this baby, I didn't want to give him back; another Michael in the family, and like his granddad who I named "Mike," his dad is now "Mike."

Summertime and Mike and Mary are coming for a visit to "Rock Dale". The family are waiting with anticipation to give a big welcome for this special visitor. Sure enough, everyone wanted all at once to hold baby Michael, "Granny here, I'm first." At just six months old, he was enjoying all the attention, Paddy had a turn to hold and hug baby Michael. It was a lovely day for taking photographs.

BALLYBANE GUIDE UNIT

The years were passing quickly; some Ballybane Brownies had reached Girl Guide age of eleven years old. A Guide Company was needed. So we formed a Guide Company starting with six Brownies to pass up to Guides; another big occasion where the Brownie would be enrolled as a Girl Guide. Some footsteps were cut out of cardboard and placed on the floor. A few Guides came with their Captain/Commissioner, Eileen Carrick who would enrol the Brownie as a Guide. The Brownie would walk on the footsteps from her brownie pack to the Commissioner to exchange her tie for a triangular neckerchief, held in place with a leather woggle matching her leather belt making the same promise. "I will do my best and do a good turn every day."

Six Brownies were enrolled: Caroline Dowling, Alice Higgins, Lorna Folan, Jean Cooley, Denise Belton and Lorraine Powell. Jean Cooley was chosen for Patrol Leader and received a white Lanyard with a whistle attached. Jean's next duty was to attend a Patrol Leader's training with many more from deferent IGG units. I handed over the Brownie pack to Teresa O'Connell, Brown Owl (who was once my playschool helper), Joan Carr, Tawny Owl, who had just completed her Guide training, and received her leader's pin the same day as I was enrolled as a Girl Guide captain after another session of training. Maura Kelly also finished training and was enrolled as Girl Guide Lieutenant. We were very pleased as we now had an official Ballybane Girl Guide Company.

ST. PATRICK'S DAY PARADE

The excitement of St. Patrick's Day parade was already upon us. The notes went home to the parents advising them to dress their Brownie/Guide warm with jumpers under their uniforms. It was a very cold day; like all St. Patrick Days, we were thankful it was not raining.

Brown Owl, Teresa O'Connell and Tawny Owl, Joan Carr, met us with their Brownies and our Girl Guide Company. Together we would join up with other Leaders and their Guides and Brownies in the wide-open grounds of St. Mary's College and stand at our specified number while the wind whirled around us as we waited to get the order to move off.

Hundreds of blue-uniformed children marched very proudly with their leaders up the town of Galway to Eyre Square, carrying the Irish Girl Guide Banner held high proudly as it displayed the Trefoil Logo. As each Unit/Pack disbanded, their leaders would wait with them, sheltering in doorways until their parents collected them (In those years, St. Patricks Day was an all-out National Holiday so there was nowhere open to give the children a treat).

The warmth of the kitchen hit my daughters and I as we walked in the door, and we were glad we had participated in yet another St. Patrick's Day parade successfully.

DISAPPOINTING NEWS

It came as a disappointing shock to us when the Regional Commissioner of Irish Girl Guides, Jane Tornbull, sent a copy of a letter she received from the Organising Committee of the Junior Chamber of Commerce. It read that, "As the St Patrick's Day parade is increasing in numbers; the parade is getting longer, so we are asking you to decrease the number of Girl Guides taking part in the Parade. There are far too many in the colour blue parading up the town. We suggest the leaders to select two or three Girl Guides from each unit as representative. We appreciate your efforts in the past and we hope you will take this in the manner it is sent. Yours etc."

GALWAY IGG

Leaders held a meeting to discus this issue. It was agreed unanimously that we could not favour one Brownie/Girl Guide above another. So we all pulled out. We then had the task of telling our Brownies/Girl Guides. We received many disappointing looks. Then send an explanatory note to the parents. It was a hassle, "not our doing."

DECEMBER - CHRISTMAS CAKES

We had a Christmas cake making and decorating competition between eight of the Ballybane Girl Guides. I asked Elizabeth Curran if she would give the Ballybane Guides a lesson in the art of Christmas cake making; she said she would be glad to give an evening class. A bakers badge would be earned in this challenge and an award for best turned-out cake. It was a frosty cold evening so I had the heat on in the chalet, it was nice and warm. I drove the two miles from my house to collect Elizabeth from her home near Móinín na gCiseach Cross. Elizabeth had her list of instructions and some baking utensils with her.

She sat into the front seat of the car and placed her equipment on her lap. The road was frosty, traffic moving very slowly. I was driving very slow and well over on my own side of the road. The next thing I knew the front of the Marina was down on the road, giving us a big shock, some cars stopped and men going home from work came to help. They pushed my car up on the grass. No one was hurt. "What happened?" I asked one man who tried to get a look underneath the car. "It looks like the axle has broken in two, you're lucky the night that's in it, if ye were travelling at normal speed a serious accident would have happened." He asked if we had far to go? I said about a mile. He offered to leave us to our destination; we were very grateful to him. Carrying the cake-making equipment into the chalet, Elizabeth told the Guides to get their ingredients ready and follow her instructions. We carried on with the job at hand keeping hushed about our breakdown. When finished, the Guides took their cakes home with instructions from Elizabeth on how they were to bake them. She would see them in a month's time to ice the cakes. I called for a taxi to take Elizabeth home. Paddy wasn't aware of this latest dilemma that had taken place concerning a car. Entering the kitchen, he asked in a cheerful voice, "Well, how did the cake making go?" I said, "Very well." Then I told him about our disaster with the rubbish car.

We are again without a car. I am going to speak to the Renault Dealers in Bohermore and ask if that piece of scrap was in a bad crash. I did make my complaint but without satisfaction; I said I couldn't afford another car. Next day I had the broken-down car towed to my front yard, where it remained for months.

Christmas week and the Guides arrived with the cakes for icing and judging. This time Elizabeth got a seat up. She demonstrated the way to ice their cakes and they got busy. Next, she showed them the best way to display their cake for judging, then a number was placed on each cake. Looking them over she said, "Well done, Guides."

While Monica O'Leary did the judging of the cakes, we waited in another playroom. When Monica called, "Ready!" everyone walked timidly into the room. She gave great praise to everyone on their beautiful cakes, but one cake in particular stood out. Marie Fahey of Castle Park was the winner, and received a plaque. After clapping for Marie, each Guide was a recipient of a baker's badge. Elizabeth and Judge Monica were thanked with a little gift, and everyone went home happy with their iced cakes for Christmas. I congratulated Elizabeth on her expertise and called a taxi to take her home; this expense would be included in the Ballybane Guide expenses, with receipts to show.

MICHAEL'S SUCCESS

Michael calls to see me. "Good news, Mom."

"Great Mike, let me hear it."

"Mary and I just had our photo taken in the college."

"Why?" I ask.

"I have been awarded a National Diploma in Business Studies (Accountancy), the only one picked from my class. My name will be inscribed on a medal and attached to a large shield and kept in the college. What do you think of that, Mom?"

"I am so proud of you, son; let us have a drink to your success."

"I have the shield here to show you."

"That is magnificent, son; do you get to keep the shield?"

Michael's Success

"Only for a few months; it has to stay in the college. Buy the local paper this weekend and you will see our photo on it." I did buy it, and I was a very proud mother.

1983 - BALLYBANE MUMMERS

It was the season of the Mummers' festivities in Ballyfae, County Galway. Sean Keane, Ballybane was getting a group together to take part. Sean asked me if I would take the part as the Bean a Tí (woman of the house), for the competition; I said I would give it a go. I would be the hard-working farmer's wife of Eamon Carr, Fear an Tí (man of the house). My daughter Margery wore a gingham apron with old fashioned ribbon in her hair, she played the accordion. Daughter Caroline was in a tartan skirt, and an old jumper, with a ribbon in her hair, playing the tinwhistle. They were also our two daughters in the act.

The rehearsals were held in the "Rock Dale" playschool. Other musicians were the piper Pat Broderick, and his wife Anne Marie playing the bodhrán, Sean Nashion on violin, Louise Walsh playing the piano accordion, Jim Cotter on the tinwhistle, singer Noel Spellman, and two dancers, Martina and Geraldine Heneghan. The scene was set. On stage, the music, singing and dancing were the main part of our group. The Bean and Fear an Tí had a couple of lines to say.

My entrance line was delivered after the evening's milking, carrying in a bucket of milk. "That cow gives a fair drop of milk." My lazy husband answered, "That's good; I'm going down to the pub for an hour." As he is about to go out the door we hear music. He shouts, "Be-dad, it's the mummers coming up the road." Then the music, singing and dancing takes over. It was a great experience, especially for the young people. There were many groups taking part from around the County; each group had an individual winner, our individual winner was Pat Broderick, the piper. It was early morning by the time we all boarded the bus for home. My head was in a spin, for I had left Paddy into hospital the day before. He wouldn't hear of me pulling out. "The girls will be disappointed if you do."

"What about you?" I asked.

"I will be fine, it is only a small operation; getting a few varicose veins removed from my legs, and I will be home in a couple of days."

I felt so guilty leaving him, but like he said the girls would be disappointed and so would the group. All went well and Sean Keane was happy that Pat Broderick the piper was a winner for the Ballybane Mummers.

THE JOY OF GUIDING

The Girl Guides was a big distraction in my life. Their weekly meetings were held in the chalet. There were many outdoor challenges. Trips to the local woods to learn the art of outdoor cooking, light a fire, and then cook on it. Each Guide brought her own spud, peeled and wrapped in tin foil, also a peeled split banana, with a square of chocolate placed in the slit, and wrapped in tinfoil. A tasty meal would be cooked on burning wood. Usually, six Guides would take part and compete three against three. The first group's fire to light and first food cooked properly would earn an outdoor cook badge. Ballybane Guides trained how to pitch a tent in my back garden and how to roll a bedding roll. We had our own big Icelandic tent and storage tea-chests to go on camp holidays.

DEATHS IN CO. CLARE

When I heard of a death in the Hurley Family, I was sure it was the oldest brother Uncle Jimmy. But nothing could have prepared me for the sudden death of my Uncle Paddy; he was the youngest of the family and the uncle I lived with, the one who taught me songs. It was sad news to get so early in the year, the month of February. His death was sudden and peaceful in his home in Moygala, Six-Mile-Bridge.

Driving to Six-Mile-Bridge, I wondered how I would react to seeing him laid out in his coffin; I managed with God's help, through the tears. Everyone was in shock. Because of his sudden passing, his was a big funeral. It was hard to think he wouldn't be there to greet us on our visits to Moygala anymore. Shortly after, that I got word of Uncle Jack Hurley's death; I was very sick and unable to travel to his funeral, so I was very saddened about this turn of events. Two brothers gone in a couple of months of each other.

We didn't have a car anyway. We had borrowed one to go to my Uncle Paddy's funeral.

Uncle Paddy Hurley on bicycle

"ROCK DALE"

The house finally gets its exterior painted, and being a two-storey house, it was going to be an expensive job. I had saved some money from my playschool job, but I wondered would it be enough? A man who came occasionally to Paddy for a haircut said he was a painter, and would look at the house and give us a price; if we were happy with that he would do the job for us.

One thing led to another, and as he did his calculations, he informed us that in two of the top back windows, the wood was going rotten. "I will putty as best I can and paint them; you might get six months out of them." There were eight large, wooden windows and four smaller ones to be painted, and of course all the old paint sanded off. Plus, he would powerhose the house, and as I wanted to change the colour from white to a pale green, he would give it two coats of the best brand, Weather Shield paint. He would let us know the price in a couple of days. I could hardly sleep worrying about the cost of such a big job. "Power-hosing, two rotting windows, and two coats of the best paint. We won't be able to afford such a big job," I grumbled.

"Wait and see," said Paddy as he sat back in his chair to read his book.

His price was £190 pounds. I drew a breath (I had £100). My next question was "How long will it take you?"

"If the weather keeps fine I should have it done in two weeks. The windows will be the slowest part of the job." I breathed a sigh of relief. Every penny from the playschool for the next two weeks would be scrimped and saved for this job.

We were happy to have the paint job well done, and the house now looked new again. Two windows needed replacing; we would keep saving as best we can, to get them replaced before the winter.

1984 - WITHOUT A CAR

We were six months without a car, it was hard going. As our three sons had moved on, I had empty bedrooms. I took in three lodgers, one a driver for Claddagh Minerals and two who worked in the Digital Factory. It wasn't something I had planned on. They were no trouble staying only four days of the week, then going home for the weekends.

At the end of the chalet was an extension we never put to use. Paddy took a look at it. He asked our neighbour Joe Folan, a plumber, to fit a bathroom into the smallest room. A hot press and a water tank was also needed. Then an electrician was also required. Anytime a small improvement is made it develops into a bigger job than anticipated; well, better get it done right anyway. When that part of the job was completed, Paddy said he was going to clean up the two rooms and paint them. I was feeling guilty for agreeing with him to take on the cleaning job.

"That kind of work will cause pain in your legs."

"It will pass the time for me and anyway there is only a little kitchen, one bedroom, and the hall to make presentable."

"And the four small windows and door," I reminded him. He set to work and for three weeks I rarely saw him. When he was finished the job, he invited me to inspect his effort. I said, "Paddy, I wouldn't mind moving into it myself. How are the legs feeling?"

"No different than if I was sitting down all day."

We advertised it, and two Murphy brothers from Dunmore rented it; we were quite pleased with them. The bedroom had a three-quarter bed and a single bed, a chest of drawers, and a small wardrobe.

"Just perfect for us," they said.

FINALLY WE RISE

to the price of a small car, with the help of a Credit Union loan. Now we could go places again and do proper shopping.

Paddy had an interest in politics and was able to go to the monthly meetings of the Castlegar/Briarhill branch of Fine Gael, a short drive to their meeting place in McHugh's Pub, Tuam Road. He was elected Chairman of the branch.

It was six months since the two Murphy brothers had moved into the chalet when I saw a third man coming up the path. I said to Paddy, "I won't say anything until Brendan comes to pay the rent on Friday evening."

As he knocked on the back door, I said, "Hello, Brendan."

"Mrs Dowling, is it alright if our brother Tom moves in with us? He works in Thermo King with Ollie. I think the place is too small for three and there is only the small gas cooker, they will eat in the factory canteen. I cook my dinner all in one in a pressure cooker," said Brendan.

"You are well equipped, Brendan; where do you work?"

"I work for the County Council."

"If you are happy that the three of you will be comfortable, I will charge Tom the same rent as the two of you."

"Thanks Mrs Dowling, we will pay you for last week too, as he was staying here."

Paddy sitting in the kitchen was listening to the conversation; "It seems they are three brothers and it's a little more rent. It has worked out for them, and us."

DECEMBER CHOIR

St. Brigid's Choir, Ballybane, was founded in 1984. The founder members were Sister Mary Threadgold, Sister Leila, Mary Brenan, Patricia/Pat Folan, Christina Kilkelly, Maureen Stack, Tom Talbot and Paddy Dowling. This first meeting took place in 197 Castle Park. Practise took place in the John Paul Centre where Sunday Mass was celebrated by Fr. Willie Cummins. It was the first public experience these seven people had, in the John Paul Centre. Fr. Willie gave them his blessing. For the next three years these same seven people were senior choir singers at the Sunday ten o'clock Mass. Meanwhile, a new Ballybane church was being built.

PLAYSCHOOL SUPERVISORS TRAINING

As playschools were on the increase, supervisors were advised to participate in a nine-month course of comprehensive and detailed training in the University College Galway. This course was the first to be run in the West of Ireland and was organised by the extra-mural Department in association with Irish preschool playgroups.

Patricia McAvoy, the course co-ordinator, stressed the importance of training for playgroup supervisors. Lectures were given by specialists in the fields of child psychology, and learning through play, the natural way young children learn social skills without pressure. The course also included visits; the play school trainees were asked to visit each other's playschools. I had a large spacious play school, and a fenced-in playground with some playschool furniture and a sandpit with buckets and spades. I employed one mother and had two voluntary mothers. My times were nine-thirty to one p.m, four mornings a week.

The nine months felt long, but were well worth the time spent, for we learned for our own benefit too. A test was set for the end of the course. Receiving the certificates, the twenty-six of us felt we had achieved a lot, and adding to that, the compliments we received from Seamus O'Grady, secretary of the extra-mural Department made it worth our while. It ended with a relaxing time over a nice meal for everyone.

Play School Supervisors Training. I'm front row in dark jacket with broch.

1985 - FINE GAEL SOCIAL

There was a time the Fine Gael Party was not recognised; if you weren't Fianna Fail you were nobody. When my husband became chairman of the Castlegar/Briarhill Branch of Fine Gael, my mother almost disowned me.

"Is that who you will be voting for now?" she asked. I made no answer. There was a very special night holding a Fine Gael social in the Sacrecour hotel. It was well attended, for the guest of honour was Taoiseach Garret Fitzgerald. One lady said to me, "Remember the years during election time when we would hardly hold up our heads as we went to cast our vote. Thank God for this change at last." I fully agreed with her. Who would believe there were so many supporters of Fine Gael in this area? It was a night to remember, with Garret making speeches and commenting on the great turnout. Paddy was especially pleased as he got speaking to the Taoiseach personally.

BUYING A VANETTE

We were passing a car sales show room one day, when I saw a lovely red Vanette. "Look Paddy," I said, "let's take a look at that Vanette."

"What do we want to look at it for?" he asked. We looked at it and the salesman let me drive it around the car park, then he described all the conveniences,

"You're high up, it's easy to see out, the back seat can be made down into a double bed, and two front seats laid back for comfort." It had everything and was considered to be the best family car on the market. The insurance was not much more than an ordinary car. "How much?" I asked.

"£3000, with £300 of on your trade-in." I looked at Paddy;

"Don't look at me, you have your mind made up already," was his retort. With everything set to go we could pick it up next day. On the way home he asked, "Why do you want a Vanette?"

"I can take the Guides and Brownies on outings in it."

"Very convenient; I shouldn't have asked, I knew the Guides would be involved in it," moaned poor Paddy. "Have you the money?"

"I have some but I can get a loan from the Credit Union; I haven't borrowed in a long time."

GREAT SOUTHERN HOTEL

A friend of Paddy's, Micky Ward, on one of his visits to the house, told Paddy that the Galway Great Southern Hotel was advertising for a security man, and maybe he should apply for an interview.

"I wouldn't have a hope in hell," was Paddy's reply.

"But try anyway," encouraged Micky.

"How was the interview?" I asked when he came home.

"It would be a nice little number," he laughed.

"Would it be a night job?"

"No, mostly day work, watching out for suspicious characters. I don't think I have a chance, there was up to seventy people applying for it, retired gardaí, army men and some elderly men; more agile than me."

A week went by and he had given up on the cushy job. Then a phone call came and he was asked to go see the manager who wanted to talk to him. I thought he would get a stroke from the excitement. Paddy was lucky in getting the job; it was, as he said a cushy number. During his time there, I had the privilege of using the Great Southern Hotel's swimming pool. I was allowed to bring my friends Mrs O'Meara and Margaret Keeney to the pool. Good swimmers, myself and three other ladies, struggled, but we had a good time splashing around in the warm pool.

I also had another advantage because of Paddy being employed there. I was allowed to have my playschool Christmas parties in a private room, free of charge. The childrens' parents made sure to get them there in time. My helper Rita McDonagh and some parents brought lots of goodies. I would have already passed on Santa's parcels to Santa Claus. Kathleen Cooke dressed in Red Santa Suit, cap and white beard. Arriving, ringing a bell, there were loud screams and the odd little one crying. Blue bags for boys and pink for the girls, Santa handed out to each one, while the parents stood around having tea and cake. Then the tidy-up. The parents thanked Rita and me as they left with their children for home happy.

FIRST AID TRAINING

Being involved with the IGG, it was imperative to be able to administer First Aid. I joined with my daughter Margery and attended a First Aid course, learning the skills needed to save a life. This course was run by the Order of Malta, Mervue. Lieutenant Margaret Mullgannon was our instructor. There were many details to learn; we wrote everything down for questions and answers. The resuscitation on the dummy on the floor was cause for a lot of laughter, but we had to get serious to earn our marks, getting every detail right was important to qualify for the certificate. After the nine weeks of intense training, Margery and I were very proud to be among twenty recipients of First Aid Certificates from Dr. P. O'Conghaile, Medical Officer, and Captain Nevin Breen. Of course, we ended with tea and biscuits, and feeling privilege at knowing we were going away with this knowledge for safety to children in our care.

BEAVERS

Paddy had a new ambition, after spending a holiday in Dublin with Leo where he got plenty of information on Scouting, said he could open Beavers for the boys age five to seven in Ballybane. I said, "Would you be able to handle such active young lads?".

"I know where I can get two young lads as Beaver helpers," said Paddy confidently. "Liam Concannon and Brian Scanlon, they are about eighteen, a good age to be Beaver leaders."

Paddy and his two young leaders, having had a few months of training for their Wood badge, were now ready to open up their Beaver lodge, getting off to a flying start with their Beavers. Their meetings were held in the chalet/playschool on Saturday mornings. The Beavers were well turned out dressed in grey jumpers, navy pants, and yellow neckerchief, for their investiture by Scout leader Des Murray. Fr. Paddy Heneghan gave twelve young Beavers his blessing. Their parents were very pleased to see their young sons receiving such a great honour in the John Paul Centre. Beaver leader Paddy and his Beaver helper Liam Concannon also received their Scout pins. There were some exciting days ahead.

LARCH HILL OUTING

The trip to Larch Hill for the National Beaver day outing. It was a beautiful sunny Saturday. We travelled with a full bus of Beavers and leaders. Arriving at Larch Hill, it was a fascinating sight to see so many yellow neckerchiefs meeting our eyes everywhere we looked. There were Beavers from all over Ireland. Liam and Brian supervised the Ballybane Beavers, making sure they were involved in the games. Sausages and rolls were dished up and each hungry Beaver had his dish ready as he took his place in line for his meal. Ice-cream and drinks followed. More games were played. Too soon the day was coming to a close. All Beavers stood to attention as they recited the Beaver Prayer loud and clear. Everyone was tired and happy going home. Paddy was very grateful to his two Beaver helpers for their day's work.

Another exciting day was coming up in the Portumna Woods, County Galway.

NATIONAL SCOUTS JAMBOREE

For the National Scouts Jamboree, over one thousand Scouts camped for over two weeks in very inclement weather. Beaver Leader Paddy brought six little Beavers on visitor's day, but as it was wet and stormy (the ground was muck to our ankles), we stayed just a short time. Paddy's legs felt the cold and he was in pain and glad to be heading home. The six little Beavers had an enjoyable spin in the Vanette, although they didn't get to see much of the Scout Jamboree. Paddy dropped his Beavers safely home. It was summer time without summer weather. The heat of the kitchen was welcome as we walked in. After a hot cup of tea and having taken his tablets, Paddy was happy "to hit the hay" as he said, in the comfort of his electric blanket.

BEAVERS QUIZ COMPETITION

Paddy Dowling, as Ballybane Beaver leader, introduced the Beaver Quiz Competitions. Thank you to the many Beaver Lodges that took part in this challenge. Sorry to say, Paddy's Ballybane Beavers were unlucky in never winning the perpetual trophy (After Paddy passed away, it was named the Paddy Dowling Perpetual Beaver Trophy, thanks in kind to Scout Leader Kevin McCafferty, Renmore).

BUILDING FUND

John Cleary, Ronny Ward, Patricia/Pat Folan, Ann Pratt, Paddy Dowling, and also Fr Paddy Heneghan met in the "Rock Dale" playschool to set up a building fund committee. It was envisaged that a community hall was needed in the fast-developing Ballybane area. Fr. Paddy announced at the Sunday Mass that he would like to see as many as possible at a parish meeting to be held in Flannery's Hotel. The date was arranged and a large crowd of the local people attended this meeting. It was proposed that a director's committee be formed. Paddy Dowling was proposed as Chairman of the directors, John Cleary Secretary, and they accepted. Next a proposal for Chairman of the building fund. As there were no takers, it was proposed Paddy Dowling as Chairman, he accepted. Pat Folan as Secretary, Treasurer, Padraic Conroy and Brian Mahon and Mary Madden as P.R.O.s. All were in agreement.

I wasn't that happy for Paddy to be chairperson of two departments, but was assured he would only be opening the meetings. It was now up to everyone to find a way to raise funds. Margaret Dowling immediately got the ball rolling with a very successful bonny baby and toddler competition. There was an entrance fee per child competing. The overall winner of the day would receive £100; this was donated by Mattie Walsh of the Farm House, Ballybane Village. Richard Quinn donated the Cup for the winning baby. There were many prizes for 2nd and 3rd places in the various ages. Margaret's effort raised over £500 for the days work.

LORD AND LADY BADEN POWELL

The 22nd of February was Annual Thinking Day worldwide of Scouting and Guiding, and it was the founders, Lord Robert and Lady Olive Baden Powell, combined birthdays. The Scouting and Guiding Foundation were celebrating seventy-five years. Galway Scouting and Guiding leaders with their Troops, Units and Packs, were coming together to help in the celebrating of this wonderful occasion and holding Ecumenical prayers in St. Nicolas' Collegiate church. But first, a Lord and Lady Baden Powell must be found.

Bernie Higgins was chosen as Lady Baden Powell and Paddy Dowling as Lord Baden Powell, and dressed in the costume of the period of the former leaders' uniforms. They were perfectly suited. After prayers and the taking up of the annual donations from each unit, the donations were passed on to help and promote Scouting and Guiding in the poorer countries. All groups formed in a procession and marched to Salthill. It was lovely to see Guides and Brownies in their colour blue, in step with Scouts, Cubs and Beavers, all with their individual banners sporting the Scouting and Guiding trefoil. I had the Vanette ready and was called to take Paddy home as his legs were in a lot of pain. I helped him into the house. I warmed up the bed with the electric blanket and made a hot whiskey for him then helped him up to bed. It wasn't long until he warmed and went to sleep. I was worried about him being so cold.

ANOTHER DEATH

In County Clare, our Uncle James/Jimmy Hurley passed away; he was eighty-nine years old. In his young days, during the time of the struggles in Ireland, he had enlisted in the I.R.A. and was captain of a platoon. In the winter evenings at the story-telling around the open turf fire, his contribution would be the times men like him hid in the trenches in the cold and wet weather. He bragged as to how he ran with Eamon De Valera through the trenches. There was one sad occasion he told about how the Black and Tans came in a surprise attack on the family home in Kilnacree, and pulled him out of the bed, amid the screams of his terrified mother, as she begged them to leave her son alone. They dragged him out of her clutches down the old road, while two of the Tans kept his mother in the house; she did not see what happened to him. He was tied to the back of the lorry and dragged along a stretch of the road, but the rope broke loose. He was lying on the road until some neighbour found him.

When he came around, he was in hospital. He hadn't a tooth in his head; he thought that at some time he got the butt of a gun into his mouth. As a little girl, I heard him tell that story numerous times. Other times he would sing rebel songs; his favourite was 'The Three Flowers'. I once saw him proudly wearing his I.R.A. medal attached to his watch chaine. He was the last of the four Hurley brothers to pass away. His brother Mick died in the 1960's, leaving his wife and two children; a son and daughter (Mick-Joe and Bonnie). They were about the only first cousins of the Hurley family I hadn't met as they went to England. They were never forgotten, but without their address we could not locate them.

1986 - THE LAST OF THE CONFIRMATIONS

Caroline is the last for Confirmation in our family. She will be making it in Mervue Holy Family Church wearing her school uniform; all nice and convenient. She wanted a change for the Confirmation meal which would be in "Rock Dale". It would be easier on her Dad. Meanwhile, he was hatching a secret idea. He'd heard of a place out the country where they sold pedigree Pomeranian dogs, and he thought of buying one for Caroline, a gift for her confirmation. All the family went for the drive to where they were sold. I was complaining all the way, "We can't afford such an expensive dog. Them type of dogs are harder to mind than a child."

"Leave it to me," said Paddy. I was told by everyone in the Vanette to stay quiet. We arrived at the house where we were meant to buy the dog. There were some very cute pups. I pointed to one, "I like that one," I said. The owner told us they were all sold except one, a soft fluffy little pup; everyone loved her. I too fell in love with the little fistful of fur. Paddy got the papers of the dame and the dog (the parents). She had her injections got and would only need a booster shot in six months. The little Pomeranian was handed over to Paddy who handed the £70 to the lady selling the tiny little dog; everyone was happy with this new addition to the family.

"Where did you get all that money, Paddy?"

"Ha ha," he laughed, "you don't know everything about me."

"Good for you, Dad," said Leo from the back seat, and the little dog licked his face. It was a toss up between the two sisters what to name the little dog; no matter what name one gave her, the other one didn't agree with it. I scolded the two of them, "If there are any more arguments over that dog, she is going back." It was quiet after that. The playschool door was open one morning and the little dog ran in. "Look," said a little girl, "a Poochy dog." I told my daughters that "Poochy" was now the dog's name.

CAMP BALLYFINN

We were getting prepared for Camp Ballyfinn. I was pleased that I had shown our Guides how to pitch a tent. Caroline was very busy creating a large banner. We stretched a large sheet, then doubled it lengthways a few times, cut away the excess, washed and starched it, and left it to dry. She painted the Trefoil emblem and the name 'Ballybane Guides' on it. Grainne Clone, the camp organiser (C.O), was very impressed with it.

We were proud of Caroline's banner on the day the Units were displaying theirs. Our Guides travelled on the bus with other Guides to the campsite. I took all our camping equipment in the Vanette. Tents had to be pitched and Guider Bernie Higgins was showing how to erect the latrines (toilets). The young leaders Margery Dowling and Sarah Scanlon were erecting the structure for the outdoor fire. Everything went well; we were lucky having a fine day when we arrived on the open campsite.

We were not so lucky the next day, the rain and the wind howled around us, while the Guides were snug wearing their wet weather-gear sitting in the tents. The two young leaders Margery and Sarah were unidentifiable in outdoor weather gear, and asked for four guides to volunteer to help them erect the shelter over the fire, but no one was willing to leave the comfort of the tent. As their captain, I made the decision for four capable Guides to assist, Alice Higgins, Jean Cooley, Shirley McEntee and Lorna Folan. A little moaning took place. "Come on," says Jean, "let's get this done." It was challenging, battling against the wind and rain, but they succeeded in erecting the fire shelter. "You four Guides will be commended for that," I promised. Then a shout from Margery, "What about the two young Leaders? We did most of the work."

"Don't worry, ye won't be forgotten." Groups gathered firewood and lit a fire for campfire sing-along, all wrapped in their decorated Guide blankets singing loud and clear. *'Campfires burning, camp fires burning, draw near, draw near.'*

I knew coming home; I would have a lighter load, for the tea chests were empty of food. My two daughters and Sarah travelled home with me. I was grateful to Rita McDonagh for calling in occasionally to see Paddy while we were away. He was happy to see us home after our week in the great outdoors, even though we stank of smoke.

*Camp Ballyfinn
Caroline shows her
hand made banner to
her daughter Caroline*

IT IS ALMOST CHRISTMAS

I have a feeling Paddy is putting on an act of feeling well. There are only four this year for Christmas dinner. It's Christmas Eve and Paddy has decided to go to bed early. I said to the girls, we will go to Midnight Mass. It was a real cold winter's night. The heat of the Holy Family Church, Mervue was a comfort and the Mass and carol singing warmed our hearts. After Mass, we visited the crib to pray to baby Jesus. On Christmas day, I was glad Paddy joined us for the Christmas dinner, it was good to see him up. He was telling us about his next idea for the Beavers.

1987 - RENMORE PANTO

Paddy is filling me in on his idea. "Joe McCarty, Renmore, was telling me about the Renmore Pantomime and he asked if I was taking the Beavers to see 'Humpty Dumpty'; Joe said he would make sure to book a place for them." "When is it on, Paddy?" I asked.

"Sixth January."

"You would need to get the money in. I'll call some of the parents tomorrow; they can pass the word and bring the money down to me."

It all went well; with everyone in uniform, the Vanette filled with Beavers. Rita McDonough went along with them as a parent helper. When he came home I asked, "How did it go for them?"

"They had a great time," said Paddy. I then remarked how handsome he looked in his Scout uniform (little did I know it would be the last time he would wear it at a Beaver occasion).

It was with great sadness we heard our friends the Coakleys lost their baby daughter on the sixth of January, the night of the Panto. "I'm going to that funeral," said Paddy.

"Dress warm, Paddy."

"I will," he said.

"And don't stand too long by the grave."

"I will only attend the Mass." When he came home the first thing he asked me, was, "Were you ever at a Mass of the Angels?"

I said, "No."

"It is beautiful but very sad." He had tears in his eye's for the family of their little baby girl.

"You're upset, Paddy; why don't you sit down and create some more of your Sea Shell crafts, make more Cornelian Ladies, or try some new inventions for the next 'Young Ireland' exhibitions, they liked what you showed at the last one."

"I don't feel well; I'm going upstairs to bed."

"You're not able for the stairs, why don't you sleep in your bed in the dining room."

"Thanks Margaret, but I'd rather be upstairs near you; if anyone is looking for a haircut tell them I won't be doing it any more." I was going down stairs after helping him to bed, when I heard him let out a moan. I ran back, "Are you in pain, Paddy?"

"I have a headache," he answered.

"I'll give you a painkiller."

"Thanks Mam."

PADDY PASSES AWAY

The twelfth of January and its freezing cold; the ground was covered with frost. Paddy stayed all day in bed. "The best thing for you, dear," I said. Margery, Caroline and I said a few prayers for Dad before going to bed. Paddy asked, "Are you asleep, Margaret?"

"No," I said.

"I'm very sick," he said. I got a basin for him to vomit into. He lay back on the pillows and went to sleep; in a few minutes, he was awake again. "I'm getting up," he said, "I'll go downstairs and make myself a hot whiskey. You go back to bed, I can manage myself." I was very tired and fell asleep.

A tap on my shoulder awoke me. "Oh Paddy," I said, "Sorry, I must have fallen asleep."

"I'm very sick, Margaret."

"You poor man, sit up in the bed." I held the basin while he threw up, and he went to sleep. I went downstairs and got dressed, then sat in the kitchen saying the Rosary. Through all his sleepless nights I had never done this before. I heard him call me, "Ring for Doctor O'Flaherty."

This I did, and the doctor said, "Get him to the hospital as fast as you can; I will let them know you are bringing him in." It was three o'clock in the morning; Caroline was standing at the top of the stairs. "Help your dad to get dressed, while I start the Vanette." I turned on the heat to melt the frost off the windscreen. We helped him into the back seat. At the door, she turned to me and asked, "Is Dad dying?"

"Of course not," I tried to assure her; "hurry up to your warm bed."

The roads were so white I wasn't sure of where I was, and in spite of his pain Paddy guided me. By the time we reached the hospital, he was no longer able to bear the pain. I ran into the hospital, "My husband is in bad pain." The hospital Porter asked, "Are you the aneurysm?"

"Yes," I said; I didn't know what he meant. In quick time, they had Paddy into a cubicle and a doctor came and gave him an injection. His eyes rolled to heaven. I asked, "What was in the injection?"

"A double morphine; the pain is gone now, we will take him for an X-ray." I was told to wait where I was, but instead I went for a walk around the hospital. On my return, Paddy was in a ward. I approached his bed, "Go home," he said with a wave of his hand, "go home to the girls." I kissed him and told him I loved him; he bowed his head, and as I walked away a warm loving feeling came over me.

I was hurrying home to get Margery up for her job in Singers and Caroline out to school. I had enough time to drive them to their destinations; it was very cold and a real winter's morning, adding to my sorrowful mood. I was trying to assure my daughters their dad would be alright. Sadness was hovering around me.

I opened the playschool. As the mothers and children were coming in, I said to each mother, "Paddy is in hospital; he is very sick." No one answered but they lingered on a while, then the last two mothers waited to help. I said, "Thank you," to them. A half-hour later a little boy said, 'there's a knock at the door'. When I opened, it a Garda was standing there. "Mrs Dowling, you are needed at the hospital; your husband is not well."

"Thank you, officer; I will go straight away." As luck had it, Mrs McCullach was late with her little son. "Is something wrong Margaret? I just met a Garda going out?"

"Paddy is very sick in hospital," I said, "I have to go there now."

"My husband has the car," she said, "and is at the gate; get your coat and we will take you." I was so grateful to her and the two mothers who stayed to mind the children. On the way, we picked up Margery from Singers.

PADDY AT REST

Margery and I went to find her dad. First a doctor and a nurse brought us into a small office where tea and biscuits were laid out; after a minute the doctor spoke with his head down. "Mr Dowling passed away a short while ago." Margery began to cry; I tried to cry but instead my nose started bleeding. I got up to leave, but the nurse sat me down and put cotton wool up my nose. We were given cups of tea. I eventually asked, "Where is my husband?"

"Just across the corridor, I will take you to him," said the nurse, "stay for as long as you like with him." My daughter Margery was a great support. Paddy looked so relaxed; the feeling came to us that he was happy now; we held his arm which was still warm and said a prayer. I said, "Marg, we must get Caroline from school before she hears from someone that her dad has passed away."

On the way out, I was told to take a phone call, it was Paddy's son Eugene,

"Is it true Dad has died?"

"It is Eugene, about an hour ago." The poor lad started to cry. I said, "Eugene, his pain is over him now." We collected Caroline from school; I didn't need to tell her, she knew by our faces. "Dad is gone, isn't he?"

"He is, love," I said. At home, I went first to the playschool; the mothers had taken home their children and had locked up. I couldn't bring myself to go into the house; instead I went to my dear friends Pat and Martin Folan's house. "We know," said Pat, "you don't need to say anything." She gave me a brandy; it numbed me. My next-door neighbour Nora Concannon came and put her arms around me. "I'll miss my barber," she said. This made me laugh.

HELP FROM A GOOD NEIGHBOUR

My daughter Margery, with the help of our good neighbour Geraldine Joyce, set to work. First, they picked out a grave next to baby Coakley's grave, where only the week before Paddy had attended her funeral. They then went to choose a coffin. Someone drove me to Connelly's undertakers where they took the information for the papers, etc. and made the necessary arrangements for the funeral.

Paddy was laid out in his Scout uniform and waked in the hospital morgue. The first people to the morgue were the Murphy brothers, even though they had moved out from the chalet the year before. It touched my heart to see them. I couldn't bring Paddy's remains home. We had burst pipes, no heat in the house and the pathway to the front door was like a sheet of glass. His family managed to drive through the fog from Kildare, his sister Alice came from England, brother Tom from Shannon. And some of my cousins travelled from County Clare. The bad weather made travelling difficult. His daughter Geraldine was unable to make the journey from France in time for the funeral; due to the bad weather, her flight was delayed.

Paddy would have been proud of the large turnout in the Holy Family Church, Mervue. His remains were met by Fr. Tom Tarpy P.P., and Fr Marrinner was chief celebrant in the absence of Fr. Paddy Heneghan. Concelebrants were Fr. Willie Cummins, Ennistymon, Fr. John O'Shea, St. Augustine's, and the regional Chaplain of the C.B.S.I.

Fr. Marrinner spoke highly of Paddy, who was for a long time in poor health but gave his voluntary services in every area of the parish that he could. Soloists were Sister Mary and Nancy Flynn. Alan Carrick played a slow air on the clarinet. Paddy's coffin was draped in the Flag of the Catholic Boy Scouts of Ireland (C.B.S.I.); there was no need for pallbearers to carry his coffin. My sons, Michael and Leo linked me as we walked behind the many men who placed their hands under his Coffin and passed it from one group of men to another group, from the altar to the hearse. Men had tears in their eyes. It is one of the sweetest but saddest moments that still stand out in my memory.

Myself and my family followed in a car behind the hearse, which made its way up the Ballybane Road to pass by "Rock Dale" where Paddy lived with his wife and children for over nineteen years, then on down to the New Cemetery, Bohermore. A guard of honour was formed by the Ballybane Beavers in uniform, 3rd Galway Mervue Scouts, Ballybane and Mervue I.G.G. Members of the Castlegar Fine Gale Branch, Members of the Ballybane choir of which he was a founder member, the Ballybane Residents and members of the building fund, at the Church and again at the graveside. The walk to the cemetery was led by his son Eugene, joined by Scout leaders. After the last blessing at the grave, the flag of the C.B.S.I. was taken from over his coffin folded, and presented to me, Paddy's wife Margaret Dowling, by the Mervue Scout Master Des Murry.

After the burial, all family members came back to a cold house except for a small gas fire. Leo had brought a deep fat fryer, oil and plenty of chicken drumsticks from Dublin; he made sure there was plenty of hot food and tea for the families to eat, sustaining the ones who would be travelling the long journeys back home to Kildare and Clare. We were sorry Paddy's daughter Geraldine missed so much of her father's funeral. When she finally arrived, she was very cold and hungry but after a good feed of Leo's deep fat fried chicken and hot tea she warmed up. Leo took her to visit her father's grave; it was a sad and heartbreaking experience for her.

Patrick/Paddy Thomas Dowling passed away on the 13th January 1987 at the age of fifty-seven, in the Regional Hospital Galway, and is buried in the New Cemetery, Bohermore, Galway. Paddy was from Monasterevin, County Kildare.

GETTING ON WITH LIFE

Getting on with life was hard. We got the water back through the help of our good neighbour Joe Folan the plumber. I was finally able to light a fire in the range to warm up the cold house. Margery and Caroline were finding the house very empty and lonely; even our little dog Poochy was missing her pal in the garden. Michael had returned to Tullamore to his wife Mary, who was expecting their second baby in a few weeks, Leo returned to Dublin, Eugene was married and living in Bohermore and Geraldine went back to France. The house felt so empty.

Fr. Paddy returned and called to visit us; he was very apologetic not to be here to officiate at his good friends' funeral. He told me how bad the weather was down the country where he was staying, everyone was snowed in.

I said, "Don't worry about that, but you were missed." Then we talked about Paddy for some time; now it was down to me. "You will keep the playschool up and running," he encouraged. "It is what Paddy would want; keep it open. It will be good for you too. The children and their parents would be upset if you were to close at this time." Only for his encouragement I think I would have closed that very day. Fr. Paddy came to visit the playschool a number of times and watched the children in action and to laugh with them.

The children missed Paddy's (R.I.P.) visits to the playschool when he would bring me my tea and sweets for them. At prayer time, we always offered one for Paddy Dowling.

CONTINUING WITH THE BEAVERS

Beaver Leader Liam Concannon kept the Beavers up and running for a year in the memory of Paddy; there was no second helper coming forward to support him. Liam had to resign as he was working; I was very grateful to him but sad to see the end of the Ballybane Beavers.

A SECOND GRANDSON

It's March and the Beggen family are coming from Tullamore to show the newest addition to their family, baby Gary. I was waiting in anticipation for this day. "Let me hold him, my second Grandson." He was a chubby little fellow and a month old. "Now," said his mother, "you see why I couldn't come to Paddy's funeral."

"You had a good reason, Mary it would have been a risk to travel but you are all here now and the dinner is ready, after we can go see the grave." Grandson Michael had a question to ask. Although Paddy wasn't his grandad, Michael called him Granddad. "Why did Grandad Dowling die?"

"He was very sick, love."

"Will I see him anymore?"

"No love, he is in heaven." Michael put his head down on his Mother's lap and smothered a cry. Margery and Caroline were covering baby Gary with kisses.

As the family was leaving they said, "See you at the Christening in Ballinrobe." "We are looking forward to it, safe home now."

MARGERY GRADUATES

Margery returned to Moneenageisha School from her job in Singer's to graduate. There was much preparing to finalise, but top of her list was the making of her graduation dress. She chose a beautiful deep-blue satin material and some white trimming. Mary Beggen was on hand to help with the difficult parts. Margery was a picture in her blue dress and her dark hair framing her pretty face, as she received her diploma on her graduation day. I thought, "If only her dad could see her." She decided to return to Singer's to work now she was finished school. "If it's what you want to do, Marg," I said.

SON MIKE HAS SOMETHING TO TELL

It is June and Mike and family are on another visit to "Rock Dale". I can't believe how big baby Gary is, and he only four months. Again, we make a big fuss of him. Michael runs outside to play with the dog, Caroline follows him. "Dinner is ready, sit into the table. I'm sure you are all hungry after your journey."

I always took pride in my Sunday dinner of roast leg of lamb, roast potatoes and plenty of vegetables, and the jelly and custard fruit trifle for the sweet. When we were finished our dinner, everyone went out. Mike and I sat a while talking at the table. "I have something to tell you, Mom."

"Go ahead, tell," I said. After a pause he said, "We are all going to America to live there, it is hard to get work here and save to buy a house." Then he stopped talking. I felt he was waiting for my reaction to his news.

"Well, Mike," I said, "the very best of luck and God's Blessings to you, Mary, and the two boys."

"Thanks Mom, it was easier than I thought it would be to tell you."

"Why do you say that, Mike?"

"Well, with Paddy so recently passed away I thought you might think it a bit sudden myself and the family to be pulling up roots."

"My prayers are with you and your family, son."

"Thanks, Mother."

"When are ye leaving?"

"I will be going in a month's time, and Mary and the two boys will come out later when I have a place got for them."

"Ye won't have any trouble since ye are both American citizens."

"We have a lot to do yet, the house is sold but some furniture still has to go. Mary will stay with her parents in Ballinrobe for the last couple of months; they will call on you before they leave."

"I will miss you; I always had a feeling you would eventually go back to where you were born." After they left to go home, I did my usual private crying.

"Mary told us they are going to America," said Margery, "is that why you're crying, Mom?"

"It is," I said.

"Mary said we can come to visit them any time."

"And we will too," I assured my two daughters.

MIKE'S FIRST JOB

After arriving in N.Y., Mike's first job was in Wall Street for an insurance company as an accountant. After a short time, he moved on to cost accounting for Brooks Brother's (Shirts). His responsibility was in their factory in Patterson, New Jersey. In the meantime, Mike found an apartment in Brooklyn and had it ready for his wife and their two sons when they arrived two months later. He continued commuting to N.J. for a few years while trying to secure a job nearer to home.

FAMILY ALL TOGETHER

Mary and her two little sons came to say their goodbyes. As we chat over tea I asked, "Has Mike a place got for you?"

"He has; he says it is small but it will do for a while."

"It will, Mary. It is going to be a big change from looking over the wall at the cows."

Grandson Michael says, "I will miss going up the lake in Grandad Morans boat."

"I know," I say, trying to comfort him, "but in time you will be back to enjoy a boating trip up the lake again with granddad." As we say our goodbyes, the only one not shedding a tear is baby Gary, who is only nine months old.

Mike phones to let me know they are all well and very happy now that the family is all together again in their apartment in Brooklyn. Mike is working for a company called Labda, an electric company in N.Y. as a cost accountant doing inventory; this job entails travelling to Mexico, Arizona and Texas. He is still looking for a job nearer home. "I will say a prayer you get one soon."

"You will need to say two prayers," he laughs, as he hangs up the phone. I am happy now they are together safe.

ISLE-OF-MAN GUIDE CAMP

Ballybane Irish Girl Guide (IGG) and leaders took a camp holiday in the Isle of Man. Outdoor camping has a lot of advantages; as well as sleeping in tents weather permitting, on real warm nights we would sleep in our sleeping bags under the stars. This was a very exciting adventure. The main highlight was the T. T. Motorbike Races. We asked why bags of sand were laid along the sides of walls; we were told they were protection for the bikers in case they lost control and hit the wall. We were so lucky, for our camp site was just behind the wall next to the road, where early in the morning the TT Bikers would practice their speed. We never saw anything like the speed they travelled and, staying up all night watching for them to speed past, we would all shout, "Hooray!"

There was great excitement on meeting the West Sussex Girl Guide Leader, Brenda Heald and her husband Tony. Brenda was there in search of a sister Guide Company to join with them in their upcoming international camp holiday. I volunteered the Ballybane Guide Company, taking them up on their offer. It would be a coming together with many international overseas Scout and Guide Companys. There was great excitement going up Snivel in a train; it was as if we were rising above the clouds. When we arrived, there was a lovely café where everyone availed of a snack. Going back down to ground level was exciting, for the Guides thought we are going to topple over, but there was no danger of that happening.

It was a wonderful camp holiday and as always no one wanted to leave, but leave we must, and happy to return home to our families. Our task now was to inform our Regional Commissioner Jane Turnbull and area Commissioner Eileen Carrick of the exciting news of twinning with the West Sussex Guides for an International Camp experience. Explaining how we met the leaders who gave us the invitation, Jane and Eileen were delighted we were so adventurous, and wished us happy camping, as they filled out and signed necessary forms for our international overseas camp holiday.

Me and my daughter Margery

LEO HAS A SURPRISE

Calling me on the phone, Leo has a big surprise. "Hi Mom, I have a surprise for you. We are coming down to spend a week with you."

"Great," I said. "Who is 'we'?" I ask.

"Joe and me, where will we sleep?"

"Ye can sleep in the room where the twin beds are."

"You mean in the same room?"

"Of course, why do you ask?"

"Because Joe is my girlfriend."

"Oh! Why didn't you say that first?"

"I'll prepare Caroline's room for her. I'm looking forward to seeing you both.

Josephine, or Joey as she was better known by, was a lovely girl with beautiful thick black curly hair and a Dublin accent. "I was born in Antrim," she told me, "but the family moved to Dublin to get away from the troubles in the North. Mam was a hairdresser and set up a hairdressing salon in Dublin and Dad a mechanic."

I appreciated their company as the house was quiet after Paddy passing away. We had a lovely week together. I took them sightseeing to Aillwee Caves and the Cliffs of Moher. It was an amazing sight to see the waves from a distance rising high up over the cliffs; on the way home, we had lunch in a place named 'Durty Nellie's' in Bunratty. Leo enjoyed driving the Vanette. Having the two of them visiting was good company for Margery and Caroline, although Poochy didn't think so. I told them about my plans of taking the Girl Guides to the Scout and Guide International camp in West Sussex.

"It is good you're keeping busy, Mom."

"It keeps my mind occupied, Leo." As I left them to the train station, we hugged and I said, "I hope we will soon meet again."

"We will," they said.

BALLYBANE'S NEW CHURCH

The fifteenth of August 1987, Bishop Eamonn Casey opened and dedicated the new Ballybane church, naming it St. Bridget's. Fr Paddy Heneghan C.C. concelebrated the Mass to a packed congregation. It was a beautiful church in the shape of a pyramid. Inside, the beautiful altar, ambo and tabernacle base were of Galway limestone, the Stations of the Cross were by the artist Vicki Crowley, and St Bridget's cross was placed above the front entrance. On the day of this great occasion, Ballybane Girl Guides formed a guard of honour from the priest's residence to the church door. The St. Bridget's choir was well-represented with the addition of new members, tutored by the choir leader Pat Folan for this auspicious occasion. Sadly, Paddy Dowling, one of the founding members, had passed away the previous January. It was sad for me and his family who missed him. He was also missed by the choir members.

1988 – APRIL, MY VISIT TO HAYWARD'S HEATH

I received an invitation in March from Brenda Heald to come and meet the other leaders and see the site where the event would take place, before our Guide Company would join with the Eleventh Haywards Heath Company (E.H.H.C.). I accepted the four-day invitation. I flew from Carnmore Airport to Dublin and then on to Gatwick, where Brenda met me and had a big welcome for me, and told me I would be their house guest. "That is kind of you, Brenda." Her home was comfortable and welcoming. Brenda's husband Tony had lunch ready. We set to work straightaway discussing the plans for camping; it would go on for one week and then our Guides would get homed hospitably with her Guides. It was all very exciting. I could hardly wait for the Ballybane Guides to be here. On my first day; there was a garden Fete. I bought some items, next there were sports and I joined in throwing rings and a game of miniature golf. The money was going to pay costs for Brenda's Guides; the weather was beautiful, so it was high tea outdoors served by the E.H.H.C. That evening I attended a Guide meeting run similar to our own meetings.

Next day, I met Brenda's helpers, Sue Perkins, Lisa and Rosie, and we all went to see the campsite and the spot where our Guides would join the E H.H.C Guides. The site itself was huge; it had to be, it would be catering to over twenty-eight countries and over five thousand people.

After that, we returned to Brenda's house for lunch, then a rest to prepare for an evening's dancing. Brenda and I had a little time alone together.

It gave me a chance to talk of how my husband had recently passed away. She was deeply touched to hear he had died so young. I felt better having told her.

Departure for home came soon. Margery and Caroline were glad to see me back; they were both working; Margery in Singer's and Caroline in Standard Printers.

PREPARATIONS WENT INTO ACTION

Having informed the Regional Girl Guide Commissioner Jane Thornbull, and Area Commissioner Eileen Carrick, of our plans to join with the West Sussex Guides for their International Camp, all documentation was then signed and forwarded to Dublin IGG headquarters. We got permission, granted from IGG headquarters and advice on how to apply for International Grant Aid.

Next step was the cost for the ten days and to apply for the International Grant Aid from the Educational Youth Affairs in Dublin. They sent me a form to fill out and I forwarded it to the National Headquarters of IGG. All was cleared and we received a cheque for £500. Next to apply to the V.E.C. Galway Local Youth Service Board, from whom we received £300. Brenda let us know the cost to each leader and Guide; it would be £20 sterling per person and had to be forwarded three months in advance. The next £35 sterling would include food and the camp; total £55, everything else was covered. The cost of travel by train and boat was £45 per head which would come from the V.E.C. grant aid. Next, we sent notes to the parents telling them of this upcoming event and invited them to a meeting. Five Ballybane parents agreed to fill up the necessary forms of permission and send them back to us with the deposit.

Preparations followed; proper rucksacks, to hold rain wear, underwear, sleep wear, receptacles to eat and drink from (all plastic), bedding roll, ground sheet, mini torch for midnight march, pencil, copybook and scrapbook. Uniforms had to be inspected and would be worn travelling. An Irish dance routine went into practice with a homemade invention. Traditional costumes were made by the Guides; long green skirt with shamrocks, a yellow cotton shawl and white blouse.

Five Guides from our unit plus seven from other units around Galway, twelve in all, made up our unit plus three leaders. Me, Guide Captain, Maura Kelly, Guide Lieutenant, and one mother Joan Powell. Guides, Valery Molloy and Louise Moran took charge of inventing an Irish dance routine for the entertainment night. We were very proud of their effort.

The date was fast approaching and all was going well to set off on the train from Ceannt Station, Galway to Dublin, where we changed trains for Wexford, then change and get the boat from Rosslare to Fishguard, then a train for the final trip to Hayward's Heath. I phoned Brenda, letting her know we had arrived; she in turn let the parents of her Guides know they would transport us to Ardingly. It was a relief to have arrived after our long journey; no one complained although they were tired and hungry.

We were taken to our camp where our Guides shared tents with Brenda's Guides. The leaders shared separated tents pitched close to the Guides. The name of our sub camp was Mole camp. Our neighbouring camp hosted Japanese Guides; one of their Leaders spoke good English. The Guides settled down and after a lovely meal, they soon forgot their tiring travel.

Brenda and her Guides were glad we had arrived in time for the opening ceremony.

ENTERTAINMENT AND ACTIVITIES

Host leaders took charge of our Guides with their own Guides.

More than sixty coaches came every day to take the Guides to various outings, sightseeing and activities. Abseiling, rock climbing, basketball, bowling, a tour of St Paul's, Westminster Cathedral, Kew Gardens and the changing of the guard at Buckingham Palace. They also got to visit Olive House, Chief Girl Guide Centre, where they bought Guide gifts to bring back to their friends. Craft-making was onsite, including kite-making, corn dollies, leatherwork, where they got to make a leather belt, and much, much, more.

Maura, Joan and I helped the leaders to prepare the meals each evening for the hungry Guides when they returned from a busy day. Then it was the Leaders' turn to be taken sightseeing. The couch was big and comfortable. We travelled with a mixture of nationalities. My company was the Japanese Leader; we had a lot to swap in our experiences of Guiding. My favourite part of the sightseeing was the Kew Gardens, where the pond-lily leaves were so big they would hold five people standing on one leaf; my second favourite was the retiring field for the Queen's old horses; here they could live out the last years of their lives in comfort. We were very hungry arriving back to camp. We passed in our plates and got them back with a small triangle of food in the centre; I said to, "Maura and Joan, if this is all we are getting we will starve." We ate it and loved it and felt full. I asked Brenda what it was. "Its quiche, did you ever have it before?"

I said, "No."

"It's a great filler and has everything in it."

She was right about it being filling; we were then served cake and tea, so no one starved.

It is coming to the closing of the Camp Holiday. All Guides are asked to get ready to perform their party piece. It was a spectacular evening with each unit putting on their best. Our Guides did us proud, someone had an accordion and played a reel as they danced with their long skirts flowing around their ankles. My favourite was the

Swedish Unit's dance, while Maura picked the lively Scotch sword dance, and Joan's choice was eastern, the Japanese display with song and the waving off fans.

The midnight March was held on the last night of our stay. There was a grand display of the many colourful international uniforms as they carried their units' flags parading around this massive stretch of campsite, holding lighted torches, sparkling out like stars in the dark; each unit marching in alphabetical order, while behind them walked their leaders. It was early morning before it came to an end, with all units standing to attention, this time holding their national flag as we recited the closing prayers. We were crying as we realised this was the last night. Well, almost the last, there was still the three nights of home hospitality.

Each unit cleared up their own campsite; this left just the dropping off the tents by the leaders and the removal of garbage bins.

Entertainment and Activities leading the group Vallery Molly and Louise Moran.

LEAVING TO GO HOME

As we prepared to gather our Guides from home hospitality and friends to leave for home, we could hardly pry them away from their new-found friends. Addresses were exchanged and more hugs had to be done; a pleasing sight for us. Now we are retracing our trip back home; everyone slept.

Maura, Joan and I were happy our Guides were safe. I couldn't have better helpers than Maura and Joan. Once more, I hear the welcome back from my daughters and plenty of tail-wagging from Poochy. As I picked her up she licked my face all over. "I promise that I won't be going away again for a long while"

"You had better not," echoed my daughters as Poochy agreed with a little yap.

LEO'S WEDDING PLANS

Leo and Joey are planning their wedding. Josephine O'Connell was born in Antrim but the family moved to Dublin when the children were young. So their wedding will take place in Dublin. Leo phones to invite us to meet Joey's family. I said to Leo, "I am just in the door from the U.K. And this invitation is coming at a good time; I can do with a break. The three of us will go up by train for the weekend and sneak Poochy on with us."

I was looking forward to meeting Joey's parents. They were very welcoming and lovely people. Joey had three sisters and two brothers; their house was quite big and situated on Old Cabra Road, Sandymount a quiet area on the outskirts of Dublin. Leo and Joey met where they worked in H. William's supermarket. "Are you looking forward to their wedding?" Asked Joey's dad, Pat.

"I am indeed," I replied.

"We are sending out the invitations this week," explained Joey. They were in sympathy with me and my two daughters on the death of Paddy. "I wish you could have met him," I said.

"We will be meeting in a month's time for their wedding," said Joey's mother as we hugged goodbye at the train. Sitting in the train going home, I said, "Now girls, you will have to decide on what outfits you will wear for your brother's big day."

"You're the mother of the groom, Mom, what will you be wearing?"

"I have an idea, but I will tell you when we are at home."

RACE WEEK

It is a busy time with the B&B. "We can do with the extra money," I said to the girls, "your brother Leo's wedding is only a month away. I won't need to buy an outfit. I have a nice white two-piece with the pale blue flowers Pat Folan gave me, and I will borrow her navy hat. I am giving them money and some presents from us for their wedding gifts. Have you decided yet what you are going to wear, Margery?"

"I borrowed this beautiful dress from a friend; you know I have to save for my own wedding now."

"Wise move, Marg. How about you, Caroline?"

"I can't get anything nice to fit me; my friend Shirley is lending me one of her dresses that is too small for her."

"Well, my goodness, we are all wearing something borrowed."

"Mom," said Margery, "it's the bride who wears something borrowed."

"I know, I know," and we laughed.

Michael and his family will be coming back from America for the big day. Michael of course, is best man for his brother, Joey's sister Madeleine is to be her bridesmaid. I just can't wait for their big day.

A VERY WET DAY

As Mike and Mary's wedding day was a glorious, warm, sunshine day, Leo and Joey's day was the opposite; the rain poured down all day, but it did not dampen the spirits of Leo and Joey or their wedding party. Their Mass was beautifully celebrated by Joey's first cousin, Fr. John Quinn, in the Church of the Holy Family. Joey made a pretty bride as she walked up the Church aisle in her exquisite white gown and long veil, on the arm of her proud Dad. Leo looked handsome in his black tuxedo and bowtie waiting for his bride-to-be, wearing a big smile for her. Mike, the best man, also proud in a black tuxedo and bowtie, his son Michael, the page-boy, in a white shirt, navy pants and red tie, holding the rings. Joey's sister Madeline, bridesmaid, in a pretty blue dress, standing next to her.

I missed Leo's father, who was now dead twenty-six years. I was so happy his uncle Frank Beggen and wife Rose, with their son Brendan and his wife, came to the wedding from Scotstown, County Monaghan and met Leo and his brother Mike. They hadn't met since 1963, when I took them as young little boys to Scotstown, after their dad had passed away. It was a great reunion for them, plus meeting Leo's wife and Mike's wife and family.

After the wedding ceremony was over and photos were taken, we were escorted to a couch by members of the O'Connell family, with umbrellas sheltering us from the downpour and again as we entered Wyeth's Hotel.

We had a beautiful meal. Best man Mike gave a lovely speech; then we toasted the happy couple. There was good music for plenty of dancing as we watched the bride and groom dance the first dance around the floor.

The bride afterwards threw her bouquet for some excited single girl to catch it with joyful screams of, "I'm going to be the next bride." The bride and groom departed for their honeymoon in Spain.

Next morning, my two daughters and I headed home on the train with my two brothers Eddie and Paddy Abberton, and their wives Honor and Teresa.

THE YEAR IS NOT OVER

The year is not over before I receive two more surprises. Leo phones to let me know that H. Williams is going to be sold, and he and Joey will be out of work. "Leo, I'm sorry to hear that news; what do you intend to do?"

"I'm looking into going back to America. As Joey is not an American citizen, we have some paper work to do, she has to have an AIDS test - she is so embarrassed, poor girl. Did you ever hear of such red tape?"

"It was bad in my time too, Leo. Lung X-rays, I had to show a doctor's letter proving there was no insanity in our family, so don't feel too bad Leo." We have a few things to do, it will be a while before we are ready to leave," he told me.

ENGAGEMENT

Margery was out with her boyfriend John Ruffley for an evening. In the morning, she shows me her left hand. Pointing to her finger, she asks me,

"Do you like my engagement ring, Mom?"

"You're not engaged," I say disbelievingly.

"I am, John asked me to marry him and I said yes."

"Margery, you are only nineteen, you are way too young; you have no money." "I'm working and I will save up."

"I don't know; I still think you are too young. Why don't you wait and see a bit of the world first?"

"John is in the army and has good money, Mom, and next month he is taking me to Cyprus."

I tell Caroline about Margery's plans. "Oh," she says, "I will be a bridesmaid," as she danced around the floor.

"Stop it Caroline, I'm not happy about this; she is too young."

"She will be fine as Mrs Ruffley, Mom."

"I guess you are right."

INVITATION

Early in the year, I send an invitation to the West Sussex leaders and Guides to come to Ballybane, Galway, Ireland, for a camp holiday.

The leaders were delighted to have the chance to come and see Ireland, and were glad to have at least six months to prepare their Guides for this adventure. I first consulted with our Regional Girl

Guide Commissioner Jane Thornbull and Area Commissioner Eileen Carrick; they each signed the consent form that I needed to send away to Guide headquarters in Dublin. A reply came promptly and agreed it was an educational thing to do. Having received the Chief Guide's blessing, I was free to apply to the Galway Corporation for permission to hold an International Girl Guide camp in their field, which was just over the wall at the end of my garden. This was granted and it would be free of charge. We also informed our Guides that the West Sussex Guides had taken us up on our invitation to come to Galway. They were thrilled to think they would be meeting again.

LEO AND JOEY

are almost ready for their departure to the USA but Leo hasn't yet booked their flight. "When is Margery getting married?" Leo asks, "She has asked me to give her away; I need to know soon for I must book our flight."

"Well, I don't know," I answered him sharply, "ask her yourself."

Margery was busy setting the date for May and informed Leo she was sending out her wedding invitations now. I remind her not to forget her father's sisters and brothers in Kildare, and to let Leo know her wedding date. "He has plans too." I contacted Leo to tell him that when he would be booking their flight to the States, to book for Caroline and I too, adding, "I need a holiday. And the change will do Caroline good. She is not taking the death of her dad too well." Margery sets her wedding plans in motion.

I ask my niece Brid Abberton to type up the wedding prayers. She types away on Fr. Paddy's typewriter; he has left it with me while he is away for the weekend. "Are you inviting many guests to your wedding?" I ask Margery. She says that John has a lot of brothers and sisters, and there are their spouses too; "There will be eighty at least." Margery takes me to Roche's to shop for the mother of the bride dress. "It has to be special, Mom. I'm your first daughter to be getting married."

"Well, here we are; will this dress with green background, dotted with pink flowers and flounce be suitable?"

"Fit it on, Mom."

"Well, what do you think?"

"It is perfect for you." Now I have my dress got, a hat is next. I choose a white, wide-brimed one, trimmed with a little green band. Caroline, as Margery's bridesmaid, is wearing a pretty salmon colour dress, with a bouquet of matching flowers in her hair. I was pleased to have made the bride and the bridesmaid's flower bouquets. John's best man was his friend, John Sweeney.

1989 - WEDDING MORNING

What a beautiful day. My daughter Margery made a beautiful bride wearing a flowing white gown, with a white flower wreath around her dark hair. Looking a picture, she walked up the aisle of St Bridget's Church on the arm of her brother Leo. John, her husband-to-be, waiting for her, looked well in his dark suit (again, nostalgia sets in for me. I'm remembering her father Paddy (RIP). And what he might say. "You are young Margery, only twenty years old, your whole life ahead of you. I hope you will both be happy").

The family were happy to welcome Paddy's sister Lily and her husband Paddy Storan, Paddy's three brothers and their wives arriving from County Kildare to see their niece getting married. Fr. Paddy Heneghan said a lovely Mass and remembered her Dad. Best man John Sweeney passed over the weddings rings as the priest gave the happy couple his blessing, and pronounced them husband and wife. The guests clapped, and so did the locals who came to see the pretty local girl getting wed on the fifth of May 1989. After photographs, we left for the reception. Leo looking at me asked, "Why you are crying, Mom?" I couldn't answer him.

"I know," he said, "you are missing her Dad." More photos were taken at the hotel. The bell rang for everyone to be seated for the reception meal, Fr. Paddy said grace, then everyone sat to a sumptuous meal of turkey and ham, vegetables, and all you wanted to eat. The best man was called to say a few words so John Sweeney stood up and wished the groom and his beautiful bride a long, happy and healthy life together; he then called for everyone to stand and toast the happy couple. Fr. Paddy had some well-wishing words to offer too, he then said grace after meals before leaving.

The music started and the bride and groom did the customary first dance. Then a photo of the bride and groom cutting the cake, a slice for the guests and the last tea. The time had come for them to leave one more job. Margery had to throw her bouquet. The single girls screamed as some lucky one caught it. It was time to change into the going away outfits. They left to spend their honeymoon in Killarney.

Relaxing at home, Leo said, "The day went off well!"

"It did, thank God," I agreed. "They are going to live in the small chalet at the end of the garden. I will have it ready for them when they come back. They know it is small, but it will be nice and cosy with central heating, until they get a bigger place. They can mind Poochy while we are in the States."

You are very good to them, Mother."

"Ach; it will give them a start, Leo."

"Joey and I will go back to Dublin tomorrow; we have a lot to do for next month's departure.

"I'm glad you are both here for another night. Caroline and I are going to really feel the house empty now."

CLOSING THE PLAYSCHOOL

I'm not feeling well. I miss the help I was getting from my husband Paddy. The lighting of the fire in the range, the cooking of meals, the bread he made, the cups of tea he brought down to the playschool and sweets to the children. I was feeling tired and getting cross with the little ones.

After a lot of prayer and thought, I made my mind up that I would close the playschool. I explained how I felt to Fr. Paddy and he agreed with me. "you know how you feel yourself, you have kept it going for two years after his passing and that can't have been easy."

"I have you to thank for the encouragement you gave me, for I felt like closing down the week he died. I would like you to say the closing Mass and maybe you will explain the reason to the parents."

"I will indeed, Margaret," he said. I was very grateful to him.

PLAYSCHOOL'S LAST MASS

Writing the last note to the parents inviting them to the playschool Mass, I included that I had something important to tell them. Giving the notes to the little children was heartbreaking, but I needed to do it. Some mothers thought I would be opening a second session in the afternoon, another said, "She is putting up the price."

On the morning of the Mass, Fr. Paddy welcomed parents and children, saying this is a very special Mass. As he continued with the Mass, I was afraid I would be crying before he made the announcement. I will never forget the way he started to explain. "There comes a time in everyone's life when they know they must step back, Margaret will be doing that. She has asked me to tell you that she feels unable to give you this delicate message herself. She is closing Rockdale Playschool this morning. She is sad to have to do it, but the care of Paddy (R.I.P.) and his death has caught up with her."

I could see tears in the parent's eyes, and I could hold back the tears no longer. There were tears in Fr. Paddy's eyes too. Our closing party was very silent. Each year at the summer closing, some little child would give me a bell, and this morning I received the last one; it was Galway Crystal. I have nine little bells in memory of my happy years as a playschool supervisor/teacher. Before they left, I explained how I had hoped that Rita McDonagh would carry on the playschool, for she had worked with me for so long and had a loving way with children, but she didn't want full responsibility. I understood, it is a big undertaking. She and I worked well together, and I also thanked sincerely the many voluntary mothers who would pitch in when needed.

IT IS HARD TO TRY

and understand or calculate, even predict, what is going to come one's way in life, good and not so good. I say to Caroline, "I am glad we will be going to visit Michael and family with Leo and Joey."

"I'm so glad you thought of it, Mom," she said.

"I closed the playschool this morning."

"For keeps is it, Mom?"

"Yes, it was a hard thing to do."

"You had to do it, Mam."

"I had, Caroline. And now I am going to get the house ready for race week and for a few grandparents who are coming with the West Sussex's Guides and Leaders; I will give the use of the house to them. The old way of running a B&B is changing and for the better. Now ensuites are requested by the visitors. Well, I'm not going to make changes in this house, it would be too costly. What are you doing today, Caroline?"

"I'm going to town with Shirley McEntee and Caroline Green, can I have some money?"

"Depends how much you want."

"Oh Mom, don't be making it hard to get." We laughed.

"Are the three of you doing the usual? Dressing all in black?"

"We are; and don't call us the three witches."

"You know Caroline I am only joking with you."

LEO AND JOEY ARE READY

Leo phones asking me to drive to Dublin. He has some items to be brought to Galway from his apartment. The paperwork was done and they were finally ready for their departure for America. I set off early in the morning. Driving the Vanette was so nice; I was high up and could admire the scenery ahead of me. I was enjoying this drive, especially because the time was coming when I would have to sell this beautiful vehicle; the insurance had increased double in the past four years since I bought it.

As I arrived in Sandymount, Joey's mother came out to give me one of her tight hugs. "Peggy, you are great to drive all the way up from Galway."

"It was no trouble at all."

"Come in, the tea is ready."

"Thanks, Madeleine." Leo and Joey had lived with her parents after getting married. Now they were on the move and their luggage was waiting in the hall plus extras.

"In a few days, they will be saying their goodbyes, Peggy."

"Yes, I agree."

Before they left, Joey's parents held a farewell party for them. It was a great night of music and song. Some of the retired singers from the Radio Eireann Orchestra came to play violins and flutes, and sang some great songs. Joey gave a beautiful rendition of Patsy Cline, as she sang, *'I go out walking in the moon light'*.

Joey was very lonely leaving her Mam and Dad, and siblings, but most especially her Mam. I knew exactly how she felt. Leo filled the Vanette with their suitcases, some pieces of furniture and the big music table he wanted me to have. It remained in my garage until I gave it away. Leo drove the Vanette to "Rock Dale" and unloaded it. The next trip would be to Shannon Airport.

1989 - PACKING

Margery and her husband John were settled into the chalet. Caroline and I had our packing finished. It was handy loading the cases into the Vanette; easier than struggling on the bus. "I will see you in about two weeks, Mrs Ruffley."

"Oh, you are so funny, Mom."

"Mind little Poochy for me."

"I will," she smiled. Leo, driving us to Shannon, explained the Vanette would be parked in the long-stay parking area at the airport; he gave Caroline instructions to take note of the area. I had to be convinced the Vanette would be safe parked for two weeks at the airport. With passports stamped and luggage checked in, we were ready to board the plane for departure to Kennedy airport. In about five hours time we would be landing there.

ARRIVING

At Kennedy airport, my son Mike met us and the weather was getting very hot. On our way to Mick's where he lived in Brooklyn, he was explaining that his apartment was not very big. "Caroline and I will be staying just two weeks, Mike, and we will stay some of the time with Aunt Margie, so you will only have Leo and Joey to put up with." We had a laugh.

I was overjoyed to see Mary and my two grandsons, Michael and Gary again. In the small apartment as Mike said, it was plenty big enough for the four of them. With the invasion of four people and a heap of suitcases, it was crammed a bit, but no one complained; there was so much to talk about. My most pressing thought was a phonecall to my Aunt Margie. After our greeting, she had the news that her granddaughter, Jeanney Doerr, was getting married in a few days. "I would like you to be at the wedding. I will phone Jeanney right now and tell her you are here, I know all the arrangements are made, but I am sure they can fit one more in," said my dear aunt. I told Mike about his second cousin's wedding. "I hope they can fit you in, it would be lovely for you Mom," said Mike enthusiastically, "don't mind about us."

The phone call came; "You are included, Peggy," said Aunt Margie. "You can get to the Bronx by subway and your cousin Maureen will pick the two of us up from my place and we will stay with them in Westbury. We will be all together going to the church, to see my granddaughter getting married," said Aunty with pride.

1989 - AMERICAN WEDDING

"Its a few years now since you were at a wedding in this country, Peggy."

"It is Margie, The last one was in 1961, Michael (R.I.P.) and I went to his best friend Paddy McCabe and Marie's wedding. It makes me sad to think of it. Poor Mike was very sick and could eat nothing; we left after the toast to the bride and groom. Thinking back, it's hard to believe the effort he had to make to attend the McCabe wedding."

"Weddings here have changed since then, Peggy. Now it's a big food eating and drinking reception, before you go in for the dinner at all."

The marriage ceremony was lovely with a Mass. Jennie a pretty Bride in her white gown and a wreath of white flowers around her blond hair, walked up the aisle on the arm of her father Henry Doerr. Her husband, John Roch and his groomsmen wore grey suits, Jennie's sister Kathy, was maid of honour and was a picture in a royal blue dress and a simple matching blue hat. Mother of the bride, Maureen Doerr, was wearing a beautiful light-green, figure-hugging dress trimmed with lace, grandmother of the bride, Margie Callaghan, wore a blue dress with a sprinkle of white flowers, and I was wearing a pale green dress, one of my Aunt Margie's.

It was a wonderful coincidence that I was in the States and having the chance to attend this wedding and meeting many friends and relations from my time when I lived there. It was pleasant staying at cousin Maureen's house for a couple of days but once again goodbyes must be said.

Aunty and I went back to her apartment in the Bronx; the hot weather was stifling. "We will go to the cinema and take in a movie, it will be cool there." We walked to Parkchester to the little cinema where my late husband Michael Beggen and I saw some great movies. One that I remember was, *'Three Coins in a Fountain'*.

"Is it making you sad to be here?" asked my considerate aunt.

"Just memories, Marg. Let us go in out of the heat." The *'Big Sleep'* was playing with two great actors, Humphrey Bogart and Lauren Bacall. "I love these oldies," I said.

"So do I, they show a lot of them in this cinema." The hot temperature had cooled down when we came out on to the street. We had a meal and Aunty had a glass of beer; my drink was a glass of iced tea. Next day Aunty walked me to St. Laurence Avenue to get the downtown subway train. It was goodbyes again. I hated leaving my dear Aunt. "Don't worry about me, I will sit in the park a while; who knows I might meet some ould one like myself." We laughed as we parted.

Our stay in Brooklyn with the Beggen families was short. As I was leaving, my thoughts were with Joey. Saying goodbye, I knew she was feeling lonely, telling her as I hugged her, "When you are in your own apartment and fixing it to your liking, you will feel better."

"I know," she said, "you will pray for us?"

"I will, Joey."

Caroline and I were chatting on the plane home; our conversation was mostly about Joey. "Will she settle down?"

"She will, Mam," she assured me, "when she is in a place of her own."

Touching down in Shannon, beautiful weather greeted us. Picking up our cases we made our way to the car park. "There," said Caroline, "the Vanette is quite safe." It was good to be home with the welcome, wagging tail of Poochy. I sat looking out the kitchen window, as Caroline was diving into her luggage, pulling out all the new things she brought home with her.

My thoughts were going back to 1963, when I returned home to rear my sons in Galway. How fast the years flew. Now my sons are grown up, married with children of their own, and have returned to the land of their birth. Man proposes and God disposes.

1989 – American Wedding
Me on the left and Aunt Margie in spotted dress.

RACE WEEK

I was getting the house ready for the busy race week without the hassle of preparing for B&B guests. Only Caroline and myself were living in the house now. She helped me to tidy the bedrooms and make up the beds for the three elderly couples who would be coming from West Sussex with the Girl Guides and their leaders. The weather was mild and I hoped the rain would stay off.

IT WAS NOW TIME

It was now time to send notes to our guide's parents, to let them know that the West Sussex Guides and their leaders would be joining us in Ballybane for a week camping and a few days of home hospitality. It was holiday season, so not all of our guides could take up the offer, and were apologising to have to miss it. Eight were available to participate in this event.

Everything came together nicely; we had help from their fathers in pitching the tents, cutting the sod for the campfire and erecting the

Guides Arrival

portable toilets. We received a substantial grant from the Vocational Educational Community (VEC) for this international effort, which provided us with enough money to have security present on the site, especially in our absence during the day. Three sets of grandparents came to see Ireland; as they said, grabbing the chance of an Irish holiday. I offered them the use of my house free of charge, and they could not thank me enough; they would be away touring the country until late evening. Again, I would be blessed with the help of Maura Kelly, Joan Powell plus another mother joined us, Bernie Molloy. Knowing everything would be safe in the capable hands of Micky Ward while we were away from the campsite, I could relax.

1989 - GUIDES ARRIVAL

West Sussex Hayward's Heath leaders were Brenda Heald and Sue Perkins; Brenda's husband Tony came wearing his Scout uniform, ten Guides; eight

Ballybane Guides and two leaders and two helpful mothers. Twenty-five people made up the Ballybane camp. I settled the grandparents into "Rock Dale", explaining the grant aid would cover their stay in the house. They were not prepared for such hospitality so thankful were they, in contrast to our contingent travelling to West Sussex. We travelled by surface to and fro, for hours to our destinations. The West Sussex Guides came to Ireland by air with a little travelling by train and bus. Their parents paid for their travel expenses; what an easy way to travel!

The weather was in our favour throughout the ten days. On their arrival, our Guides had a big welcome for them, and carried their rucksacks down the path at the back of our house, then out over the wall and right on to the campsite, where we had soup and a variety of sandwiches prepared for the hungry travellers. When everyone was fed, unpacked and had explored the area, we all sat down on the grass to discuss the week ahead. We handed each a list of the week's activities and discussed them; they were looking forward to so much excitement.

They would have a day to shop in Galway, a day at the Galway Races, a boat Trip to the Aran Islands, a morning cook-out in Unchlines wood, evening craft work, an early rise for a bus trip to Connemara, sight-seeing and a picnic, Mass in Mervue Church, for those who wished to go, and then back to campsite. Then, pick up lunches for a day's hiking in Merlin Park Woods, an evening campfire and a big pot of stew, then a sing-song.

On their last night, we had prepared an Irish night of entertainment in the John Paul Centre with English and Irish Guides and families invited. An early rise and we broke camp, and a couple of fathers came, as did Mickey Ward who did security for the week at the campsite. Guider Monica O'Leary came to help take down the tents and portable toilets. Mattie Kelly dug the pits to dispose of the toilet and food waste. Then, little gift tokens were passed between each of the Guides. Home hospitality was arranged. Brenda and Tony stayed with me, Sue went home with Maura Kelly; each guide had a guest for two nights and everyone happy. It was all over too soon; saying goodbyes at the train was sad, but promises were made to write.

AGRICULTURAL DOG SHOW

There is an Agricultural Show coming up in Corandulla. I'm going to enter Poochy in the small dog section. I set to dog grooming; first it's a bath, which Poochy hates, she barks her head off. I shampoo and rub, then rinse, next I blow dry. She hates the noise of the hairdrier. Now for the nice part, brush and comb. Her fur is beautiful and her tail is like a squirrel's, up over her back, the tip of it at the base of her neck. She holds her little head back to meet it. I give her some treats; she is tired and sleeps a long while in her favourite chair.

Next day, I am dressed up in a flowery dress with straw hat and sunglasses. I head to Corrandulla Agricultural Show. I enter her in the small dog competition, walking her around the ring, holding her lead as she trots beside me with her head held high, while I hold her number. There are many small dogs, beautiful little things. It's judging time. "Wow!" She gets second prize, a plaque. I give her a drink of water and hug and hug her.

Every time I hear of an Agricultural Show coming up, I prepare my model for entering; she's sure to win a plaque or a rosette. Then, I had to stop entering her, as one of her hips had come out of the hock and it needed replacing. Very soon, the second one came out. I had to take her to the animal hospital in Dublin, where she was looked after very well for the next few days. I would call on the phone enquiring about her. She came through the double operation well. Coming home was a joyful time for both of us; she looked so funny with both hips shaved. We had to mind her carefully for a few weeks. Our little pompous pedigree Pomeranian's days of strutting her stuff in the parade rings was over. She did well winning in the Athenry, Salthill, Clarenbridge, and Claregalway shows, and her first one in Corandulla.

COMMUNITY CENTRE

At last, Ballybane Community centre is finally up and running. The activities taking place in "Rock Dale" playschool will be moving to the new centre. Irish Girl Guides, Brownie pack and Ann Cameron's dancing class; there will be plenty of space for them in the new hall. I will be resigning from IGG after over fifteen years as Brown Owl and Girl Guide Captain. Maura Kelly as lieutenant will also step down. We are preparing the Guides for the move to the community centre.

There is going to be a day of celebration for the Guides who have worked diligently to receive many badges; and one hard-working Guide will receive her silver cords. Their parents were very proud of their Girl Guide daughter's achievements.

There was a treat for the parents also, with a sumptuous party for all.

The evening concluded with the taking over of the Ballybane IGG by their new Captain Elizabeth Curran.

CASTLEGAR HURLING CLUB

The many achievements of the Castlegar Hurlers will be forever remembered through the efforts of our brother Eddie Abberton, who compiled a book of treasured information on senior, junior, minor and U-21 hurlers collected by himself with the help of the Connacht Tribune. Having completed his comprehensive treasure, Eddie passed it on to John Francis King, Bookbinders, for the finishing touches. Many past hurlers were present in the Castlegar complex on the evening of the book showing, including John Molloy, Paddy Egan and John F. King who presented the book back to Eddie.

1990 - IN SEARCH OF A NEW HOME

Mike and his wife Mary with their two sons have resided in Brooklyn for the past three years, and they are looking for a house. They were at last successful in buying one in Long Island. "It's a lovely house, Mam, and the boys have their own rooms."

"I have some work to do on it, Mam" said Mike, "In the meantime, I'm still employed by Lambda Electronics N.Y., as a cost accountant doing inventory audits, and travelling to states like Mexico, Arizona, and Texas. I'm hoping to find something in the same line of work nearer to home and without the constant travelling."

I said, "I will keep praying something suitable will come your way."

THE VANETTE SOLD

A young man bought the Vanette for his job as a painter; he needed an enclosed vehicle to carry his paints and ladders. I was glad to see it was going to be useful for this young man.

It is time to buy a car and get a headstone erected on my husband Patrick/Paddy Dowling's grave. With some of the money from the sale of the Vanette, I can at last afford it. Getting used to driving a car again took a while; I felt so low down I thought I was sitting on the road, but in time I got used to it.

CAROLINE'S GRADUATION

Daughter Caroline is preparing to graduate from Moneenageisha School and has asks me to make her graduation dress. I plan to make an off-the-shoulder one. She chooses black taffeta material. After buying the material and pattern, I took out the sewing machine, then prepared by spreading the material on the table then pinned the pattern to it, cutting according to the instructions, I set to work on a style I never tried before.

Finding the making of an off-the-shoulder dress was challenging. I needed to buy stays/bones to insert into slots made on the insides of the material to keep the dress up on the bust; a stiffing was also stitched under a fold of the material, then a black cotton petticoat sewn to the underneath of the skirt. I sewed twenty-five close-set black buttones down the back and made loops for each one, last of all a black taffeta bustle and a muslin bow.

After many fittings and rippings, the masterpiece was complete and Caroline was pleased, with just a few grumbles at all the fittings and rippings. I was very proud to see her walking up the aisle of St Patrick's Church after the Mass to receive her certificate from the school principal, Mr Mahon. Then the fun began, and the graduation party headed to Twiggy's in Salthill where they celebrated. On another occasion, they held a get-together in the Oranmore Lodge. After all the excitement, it was time to settle down and get a job, which she did with a handy one close to home, working in Standard Printers.

1990 - CHOIR OUTING

Every year since the St. Bridget's Choir was founded in 1984, choir leader, Pat Folan organised outings. This year, it was to Westport, County Mayo. It was a beautiful summer's day. Our first stop was at Our Lady's Shrine in Knock, where we got Mass. Then, some sightseeing. There was lots of singing on the bus, the singer would go up to the microphone to be heard down the bus; of course I was one of the singers. One lady seeing me asked Pat, "Who was the person who went up to sing in her bare feet?" Pat said, "I will introduce you to her; ye have something in common." That was when Mary Sugru and I first met and became good friends, as we had buried our husbands about the same time.

We arrived at Westport Hotel very hungry. While we waited for a table, we visited the toilets. On this day, I had an extra bag with me. In a toilet, I changed into a long flowery skirt, a black shawl, a straw hat and a scarf to tie over the hat. I then watched for the coast to be clear; when I went to go into the dining room, a security man stopped me, "You are not allowed in there." I tried to persuade him that I was with the Galway group.

"If you don't leave the premises, I will phone the Guards."

"But I'm telling you I'm with a group."

"Give me a name to prove it."

So I asked for Pat Folan, and Pat came to the door. The moment she saw me, she said, "Oh she is, she's with us alright." I was finally allowed in. I asked Pat not to pretend she knew me. I sat in at the table with the group, there was a lot of complaints and security was called again, Pat kept saying, "Sure it won't harm us to give a little bit of dinner to the poor ould woman." No one would start their soup until the old woman was removed. Pat said the Grace before Meals and started her soup.

Security was wise to what was going on, and were repeating, "The Guards will be here any minute." I, the old woman started to slurp my soup. Finally, Pat said, "Margaret you had better come clean." As I took off the hat, everyone fell around laughing then clapped me, for fooling them.

I stood up and asked, "Did any of you miss me?" They looked at each other, "God no, we are sorry we didn't."

"Well you're lucky, I was almost arrested at the door only I asked for Pat to come and identify me."

"Pat, you knew it was Margaret all the time?" Pat nodded her head. "Well, you are as bad as she is." It was a beautiful meal even if the soup was cold, and a great day's outing.

LEO PHONES

"Hi, Mother."

"Hi, son, it's nice to hear your voice. What is new, Leo?"

"Joey and I are coming home for a couple of weeks next month."

"So soon; you are only a year gone."

"Joey is missing her mother, so we decided to come for a week at her house and a week with you."

"That's great, Leo, I'm looking forward to seeing you both."

Telling Margery and Caroline that Leo and Joey would be home soon, well, it was like winning a million dollars to them. Arriving in Galway after their week in Dublin, I said, "Joey, love, you are missing Mother?"

"I am, I'm missing everyone. Leo thinks this trip home will settle me."

"It will, Joey."

"I understand how you feel; I missed my mother too when I emigrated, my dear Aunt Margie was tired of my crying and she threatened to send me back; that sorted me out. I soon got my act together."

"You will be more settled now after this stay. Tomorrow evening I am having a Mass said here in the house and all the relations are invited, you will like that."

"We will," said Leo.

"It will be great to see Uncle Paddy and Teresa, Eddy and Honor and your Aunt Mary and Jimmy Nally, and I am sure a few cousins will come too. Fr. Moran came and said the Mass; it was lovely and the evening sun was shining in on us through the kitchen window. I had a meal of roast beef, salad, potato salad, plenty of green vegetables, and for dessert it was a custard and jelly trifle. Leo said, "Mum, you still make the trifle, I'm looking forward to a big bowl of trifle."

"And you will get it son." After tea and my homemade apple tart, Fr. Moran gave everyone his blessing, shaking holy water on us. We were thankful to him for the lovely house Mass. As he was going out the door, he smiled and said, "Margaret, I don't think I will need to eat for a week."

The holiday was soon over and Leo was heading back to the USA with a much happier Joey.

BALLYBANE DOG SHOW

Here I go organising a dog show (non-pedigree) in aid of the Ballybane Community building fund. This was a big involvement. There was plenty of help from the committee. We had to decide what to charge and how many categories to have. We agreed on four; large dogs, medium size, small dogs and a novelty section. We'd have three prizes in each section with a couple extra for specials. Someone knew of two judges who would do the judging free of charge, as it was for the Community Hall.

Caroline reminded me that poor Poochy would miss out. I told her about the novelty section. I asked a mother of one of my playschool children if her daughter Sharon would wheel Poochy in her doll's pram dressed up in a bonnet and a cape for the Novelty section. Mrs Cheevers was only too willing.

It was a lovely day. I was compleminted on holding a non-pedigree dog show.

We had a large dog section, only one was entered, a Great Dane, so he trotted around the field with his owner on their own, first prize, of course. There were too many medium sizes dogs, so it was split into two sections with 1st, 2nd, and 3rd in each section; the same applied in the small dog section, each group received 1st, 2nd, and 3rd. The novelty section was real fun; there were dogs dressed as cowboys, Claddagh women, nurses, ones with coloured ribbon bows on top of their heads, all parading around the field. Sharon Cheevers pushed Poochy in her little doll's pram, dressed like a doll, around the field; we were very proud she got first prize in that section, the prize being a plaque with 'Ballybane Dog Show 1990' inscribed on it; it was the last time Poochy was in a dog show. The day was very enjoyable, but the takings after expenses were paid out were small, but it was still a help to the building fund. Poochy lived from 1986 to 2002; what a loss, I cried for days. Her many trophies and russets are boxed and in the attic.

FLOWER ARRANGING

I put my name down to learn the art of flower arranging with a lady who called her class 'Silver Hands' in Barna. I'm hopeful Valery Whittaker, another Guide leader would give me a seat, as she had joined the class too and would be passing by my house. She said it could work well. We could discuss notes on the way home.

The art of flower arranging was more complicated than I expected. First, we needed to know the names of a variety of flowers, colour scheme and length to cut them to make an attractive display; there was much to learn, for example, grey oases were for dried or silk flowers, green oases for fresh flowers.

First, soak the green oases in warm water. A table centre made easy. In a low bowl, place in the wet oases, arrange large fresh green leaves overlapping around the bowl edge, and in the centre, place one large flower like a sunflower. This arrangement won't block the diner's view of each other. My favourite class was learning to make wreaths; I excelled at this.

It wasn't long until I was making them at home. First, I started with a wire coat hanger and fresh moss but this method became too tedious. I found out where I could buy everything for flower and wreath-making in Dublin. It was like an Aladdin's Cave; everything was there; you could buy in bundles of whatever you needed and quite cheap. I packed plenty into three large black bags, got a taxi back to Connolly Station and packed the lot into the bus. Arriving back in Galway at the GMIT College, I just crossed the road to where I parked the car in the grounds of the Corrib Great Southern Hotel. I pushed the bags into the boot of the car and headed home. I had an enjoyable evening sorting out my treasures for wreath making and table centres.

It was October and I began making wreaths for graves, also Christmas table centres, with and without candles. For the three Saturdays before Christmas, I went to the Galway market to sell my creative wares. I was quite nervous at first, being careful not to park in the regular farmers' spaces who sold vegetables and eggs every Saturday. It was important to be there at five a.m. to get parked. I set up my stall next to an egg seller, I asked if I was in his way. "Not at all," he assured me. I had found my spot. Leaving my car locked like the rest of the stall holders, I went away to get a hot mug of coffee; it would be three hours before the real busy time of setting up stalls and selling would start.

I opened the boot of the car and placed a table next to it and got to work (my thoughts were on my mother. She sold her eggs every Saturday in this market and at Christmas time she would have oven-ready geese to sell). It gave me confidence when my neighbour bought a wreath from me; I in turn bought a dozen eggs from him.

Margery came to give me a break. I did very well my first go, and I made £200. I had to deduct the cost of materials but even so I had good profit. I had enough to prepare for the next Saturday. Then, another trip to Dublin and Aladdin's cave as I called it. Two bags this turn (back in the 1980's, there was no charge to set up a stall in the Galway Market).

For the next four years I prepared for my Christmas craft sale and I was now adding to my selection by making and selling Christmas stockings.

There was always help from my daughters, and Pat Folan would send her daughter Michelle and Simon Brady off on the bus at nine a.m. to be on time to help me with my sales. They were aged about ten and eleven, and of course I gave them pocket money. 1993 was my last year as an open market saleslady. On the three final Saturdays selling Christmas wreath and flower arrangements, I had a profit of £600. At last I could buy a new washing machine.

MY NEXT VENTURE

This was to learn the gift of making patchwork and quilting. I joined the Corrib Quilters. And, just like learning the flower arranging, this was also a challenge. Here the cloth was called fabric, not material. Helen Harddese, our American tutor referred to it as fabric, so from now on it was fabric we worked with. It came in different textures and it was important to know what textures to join together. Colours too; you could mix them, but it was important that they complimented each other. Helen gave the five of us students a choice, we could hand-stitch or machine stitch; I choose the latter. I was pleased I knew how to use a sewing machine.

The first lesson was to cut four squares of equal size and sew together to make a block, mine was neither square nor triangle. Helen turned it upside down, saying, "Your squares are equally-cut, but like all my beginners, you didn't sew the seams equal width, so rip it out and hand sew." I did as she said, I hand sewed. I needed her opinion again, she took a look at it, "Perfect," she said. "Now press back the seams open." I could then see what she meant. I had a perfect block. "Sew by hand, Margaret, until you are more experienced." This block was the first piece for my sampler quilt; there would be three repeats of the same block. I was proud of having made my first three blocks.

Next, it was another set of blocks, cut two different colours, two dark and two a lighter colour. I cut two pink and two a dark green, stitch together a pink and green, then stitch a green and a pink together. There, I have another square, so three of them and I have six blocks.

Helen had every sewing tool we needed on her sewing tables. The next three blocks were not as easy. "Using a triangle template, cut four triangles; make sure you draw the lines equally." I continued with a dark and light green colour. Thank goodness there was a break for lunch; we brought a sandwich. Helen made tea and had cake for us. It was a social time and we got to know each other. I was the only real beginner; two of the students were quilting their finished work. I took a look at it and decided I would never be able to do quilting. Two were making cushion covers. Then back to work, sew the triangles, first pin two together, start from the narrow point and stitch it up to the wider part of the corresponding piece; continue until all four are stitched together. I had to rip a few times, with all four joined together, a point to a straight edge and so on, it was at last another square. Press them, my first one complete, two more to do. I would have another three. Time is almost up.

Helen gave instructions to the others. "Now, Margaret, I will give you instructions on making a St. Bridget's cross; she gave me the fabric and instructions to take home with me and to make one sample. "I will see you next Saturday, ten a.m. to three p.m.

I was struggling with this lesson; I thought to wait for Helen's help before I could finish the St. Bridget's cross. I persevered and got it finished, packed it into my quilter's rag bag, which was beginning to fill. "How is this, Helen?" I asked. She was pleased with it. I dreaded the thought of making two more. Helen gave me help with the tricky part; this was the centre of the cross. The next was a star. A template wasn't needed for this project; it was a pattern, first tracing it on to the paper from a pattern in a book; next trace it onto the fabric with all five points properly shaped. Having the three made, Helen suggested I had enough done for my sample quilt. She asked if I wanted to stitch the squares together and then stitch them onto fabric or space them out all over it. "I would like to space them," I said.

"You will need to buy about two yards of cotton fabric."

I thought I would be done then, but it didn't stop there; I also needed wading for backing and then lining to finish it off; an old sheet would do for the lining. Helen had a sample to show me how it was done. "Place the fabric right-side down on your sitting room floor, place the padding/batting (which she sold; it would be the right texture), fit it on top of the fabric, then every few inches, stitch the batting to the fabric like this," showing me how on the sample, "take your needle to the front with a few short stitches, bring it through to the back, and knot it on the batting. Continue on until it is secure, check it occasionally to make sure it isn't buckling, then lay the old sheet for lining on top, cut to fit and sew from the centre to each corner, hem the edges of the lining and fabric together turned in neatly."

When she was done explaining to me I thought, "Oh! What did I start this for?" Next of course was the nice part. Place and pin my blocks where I want to sew them. Before that was done, the edges of each block must be neatly pressed in. I grew to love this quilting craft and attended the class for a few years. My daughter Caroline loved my sample quilt on her bed. When I look at it now after over twenty years of use, a bit frayed and faded, it reminds me of myself. A bit frayed and faded.

The women of America have many quilters' Guilds throughout the country. The names of blocks or even whole quilts would come from the area they were made in, and many would carry family names or even an object a quilter looked at. Like 'Scrap Basket, snow flake,' this was done with the outer squares in dark colour and the centre one white; there would be dozens of these boxes all over the quilt. Many a daughter or granddaughter got a handmade quilt as a wedding gift. It is a beautiful pastime.

GOOD NEWS

Good news comes from daughter Margery and her husband John. "Well, it's good to see you," I say with 'Happy New Year hugs'. Margery is bursting with news. "Guess what, Mum?"

"Go on, tell me."

"You are going to be a grandmother again; we are expecting a baby in May." "God Bless ye," I say as we hug. "How are you feeling?"

"Great, I'm only having a little morning sickness. We are moving out of that flat and renting a house in Cook's Terrace, Bohermore."

"I'm glad you are; you will need the space when the baby comes. John, let me know when Margery is in to have the baby."

"I will," John promised. It was good to get so much nice news.

"Your baby is due in May, it might be born on your first wedding anniversary, and wouldn't that be a nice present." I am looking forward to this. I am going to look in my quilter's bag of scraps to make a cot quilt, use natural colours because we don't know if it will be a boy or a girl. Get started on the cutting and sewing.

A GRANDDAUGHTER

A granddaughter is born on the fifth of May. I have two grandsons and a granddaughter now; I feel like I'm the richest granny ever. Caroline is getting ready to be the baby's godmother and Jimmy Ruffley as godfather; such excitement. She was christened the beautiful name of Lisa Marie Ruffley in St Patrick's Church, Foster Street, Galway and everyone went back to Cook's Terrace, Bohermore for tea and cake while a good baby Lisa slept.

BRENDAN TOURS

Aunt Margie Callaghan at almost ninety years of age is touring Ireland with the Brendan Tour Company. She is accompanied by her daughter Maureen Doerr. On her list to visit are many relations in Galway and County Clare. I got in touch with my two brothers, Eddie and Paddy and my sister Mary to come to my house and bring their families. There would be a surprise for them.

They could barely believe their eyes when they saw their Aunt Margie and cousin Maureen sitting in the sitting room. It was hugs and kisses all-round. Margie was happy to meet some of the younger members of the family such as the grand nieces and nephews; she could not believe she had such a large extended family. It was a wonderful reunion. Making up four generations was, grandaunt Margie Callaghan, her daughter Maureen, her grandniece Margery Ruffley, and great grandniece, baby Lisa Ruffley. It was Aunt Margie's second trip to Ireland. On her first one, she met most of her siblings. This trip, she is the only one of them left, it is sad for her.

The next reunion was in Ryan's Hotel, County Limerick. Here she was introduced to many more of her extended close relations, many with the name Hurley, her own maiden name. "I'll never remember all your names," she said through tears. "I will remind you who they are," said her daughter Maureen. Margie was in such good form, it was predicted she would see her hundredth birthday. Everyone felt privileged of this occasion to have met their elderly aunt. There was plenty of chat as Margie tried to find out which of her brothers was the parent of which niece or nephew.

It was time to break up and the nieces and nephews with their own families left for home. Aunt Margie and cousin Maureen were staying in Ryan's Hotel for the last night of their tour, so I stayed with them. The next morning, Maureen was up early to get Mass before they departed for their home in the States. Margie and I stayed in the hotel having breakfast. It was a wonderful experience for those of all our relations who could avail of it.

NEWS FROM ACROSS THE SEA

My news: "Margery, you will never guess the news I have for you?"

"Don't keep me in suspense," urged my daughter as she fed her baby.

"Well it's this, Leo and Joey are expecting a baby in a few months."

"Isn't that good news?"

"It is, Mam."

"They think sometime in January, they might have a New Year's baby.

But as it turned out, it was a Christmas Eve baby girl they got. It is another granddaughter for me. They named her Kristina, a lovely name. Uncle Michael and a friend of Joey's are her godparents. "Well Margery that was some Christmas present for Leo and Joey to get. God Bless them."

"The next thing now Mom, you will be flying to N.Y. to see your latest grandchild."

"With the help of God Margery, I will."

AN AWARD

I got an invitation from the Girl Guide Area Commissioner Eileen Carrick to come to the Guide centre in Bohermore. Regional Commissioner Jane Thornbull was also there and a few more Guiders; it looked like a party was in preparation. Then, out of the blue, Jane Thornbull began to speak, "About the Guider who had done so much work in her area for Guiding, and tonight we are honouring her with the Lady Baden Powell Award." Eileen took a lovely Plaque and handed it to Bernie Higgins, who reached her left hand to me, saying, "It gives us great pleasure, Margaret Dowling, to present you with this award."

I almost fainted; I never expected such a prestigious award. I was thanking and thanking them for their thoughtfulness; we had a lovely party and as always when a few Guiders are together, plans are made for the next Brownie/Guide activity. It was a wonderful surprise; the plaque now hangs on my sitting room wall for everyone to see.

1991 – JANUARY, A DISMAL MONTH

The start of a new year, and I'm feeling melancholy as I sit by the warm range. I'm in deep thought. I say to Poochy, "What is wrong with me today?" She wags her tail. I know she wants out, but it is a bad day out there. "OK," I said, "come on but only down the garden path, Pooch." Afterwards, we came in and I towelled her dry; she hopped up on the chair at the other end of the range, "Now Pooch," I say, "It's just the two of us," as she settles down to sleep;

I go back to my thoughts. I can just imagine my late husband Mike Beggen in his grave, 3000 miles away in St. Raymond's Cemetery, The Bronx, N.Y. Covered in snow; it is snowing heavy over there. Twenty-eight years you are laying there, my poor young husband, R.I.P.

THE GRAVE ACROSS THE SEA

In a lonely grave across the sea,

There you lay "Mo Stor mo Chroi"

Our life was short and sweet together

I'll not forget you ever.

Although my heart within me cries, I wear

A smile for my two small boys.

As the years go slowly by,

And the time comes for me to die,

I pray God in his mercy and love

will unite us in heaven above.

Brooklyn is still home to Leo and Joey with their new baby daughter Kristina. No doubt Leo will be on the lookout for a house for his family too, but it is early days yet. Mike and Mary with their two sons are living in their new home comfortably in Long Island, Eugene and his wife are living in Rahoon Park, Galway. Geraldine is in Donegal visiting friends, daughter Margery is married to John Ruffley and living with their baby daughter Lisa, who is eight months old, in a house in Cook's Terrace, Bohermore. Daughter Caroline is off with her two friends Shirley McEntee and Lorna Folan. I know I will soon hear the door open and the three of them will come into the kitchen. Caroline will fix a tray of food and they will go into the sitting room to eat and at seventeen, I can just imagine their conversation will be 'Boys, Boys and Boys'. As they're leaving, they shout, "Bye, Mrs Dowling," I shout, "Bye, Bye,"too. I'm with a sleeping Poochy.

"And you, Paddy, sleep in a grave in Bohermore," as I reminisce on the thoughts you used to share with me. When all the children would be out for an evening, and you and I would be sitting on our own by the open sitting room fire. "Mags, you would say this is how it will be when they are reared and gone, you and I will be sitting here on our own growing old together."

"Oh! Dear, it wasn't to be. You were a handsome man with your premature grey hair and dark brown eyes, a look-alike for the well-known Egyptian movie star, Omar Sharif. But you left me at the young age of fifty-seven. It goes to show, 'Man proposes and God disposes.' R.I.P. Paddy. That's enough, I had better make myself a lunch from the New Years' leftovers and add on another pound or two."

I'M PLANTING VEGETABLES

Instead of working on my flower beds, I have turned my hand to vegetable planting; for the past few years, I have had great success in growing two ridges of potatoes, Kerr's Pinks and Golden Wonders. I spread the manure after getting the ridges ready, took great care spreading the slits, and as they grew and flowers came on them, I watched for blight and was sure to spray them in time.

With an old cap on my head, an oversized rubber apron and wellingtons on, holding a galvanised bucket and a long bristle whitewash brush, I did the job of spraying my garden of lovely spuds. "Paddy," I said, "you have taught me well." Cabbage, turnips, parsnips, onions and brussel sprouts were a success so long as the white fly didn't destroy the cabbage. I don't know what secret Paddy had with the perfect carrots he could produce; I have no luck they are eaten by some carrot-loving creature; I can't complain; I have had a few satisfactory seasons. But getting a pain in my right hip when I dig was telling me to go easy. I asked a man if he would carry on working in the same small area of the garden. He would be glad to he said, but his price for a few hours' work was too much for a widow with a small pension. Well, if the pain goes away, I may be able to plant again next spring.

FLOWER GARDEN

Daffodils and narcissi grew in abundance every spring in the flower garden at the front of the house. I was unsuccessful in growing tulips. But primroses along by the wall, all a plain yellow, were eye-catching. The scent of the wallflowers hit you as you came in the gate; their little petals were like velvet to the touch in their many colours, and pansies with their little faces looking up at you. The beautiful pink peony rose that lasted year in, year out. After a strong wind, the petals would fly around the yard like confetti. The blue grapes that Paddy brought the roots of from the back yard of Grant's Barbershop and planted in a damp shady area near the chalet, were a lovely camouflage in a ugly spot. The phlox that was growing in a corner outside the playschool window was beautiful and the scent was intoxicating.

When Cain Finn's Daddy, Alex came to pick Cain up from playschool, he would take photos of the pale lilac flowers. Alex loved the natural way these flowers grew. One of my most favoured flowers was the red dahlia. My Aunt Mary brought a root to me from Clare in 1965 when she came to see my newly-built home. This flower multiplied and I was able to give some roots to friends. The light green laurel hedging I planted between my house and my neighbours, the Concannons, gave some shelter. I let it grow very high; it eventually it fell in across all the flowers and broke some of the taller ones like the lupins and the blue monkshood which found its way to my garden from Paddy's home in Monasterevin. I broke the wooded part of the hedge and the sticks made good kindling to start the fire with; the roots stayed in the ground and the laurel grew in a shade of a paler green. The hybrid roses escaped. But in time, something killed them off; no matter what I did the leaves rusted and they died. I planted sweet william, more wallflowers, and the old reliable, marigolds that took root and did not need replanting. All those beautiful flowers needed very little attention, unless an occasional bit of weeding.

ANOTHER GRANDDAUGHTER L.I.

It is November the sixteenth and I get an early phone call from my son Mike in Long Island. "Is everything alright? Mike, you are phoning very early?"

The excitement in his voice tells it all, "Mary has had the baby."

"Thank God, Mike."

"A little girl, Mom; a little girl."

"Oh! I am so happy for you all."

"You're the first one I've told, Mom; I'm still at the hospital in the blue gown and cap; I must phone Mary's parents now, then go home and tell the two boys they have a sister."

I am so happy now I have three granddaughters and two grandsons. Going downstairs to the kitchen to make a mug of tea and toast the new baby, I can't wait to tell Margery and Caroline they are aunties again.

Just before Christmas, Mike calls me to tell me that the baby will be christened in the New Year.

"I guess you won't be able to come over for it?"

"I wouldn't miss it, Mike."

"Is your passport up-to-date?" He asks.

"I'm almost sure it is, I will book my flight straight away; thanks for letting me know."

Passport is in date. There was no problem with booking, and I got a flight for New Year's day.

ST. PATRICKS BRASS BAND

Pat Folan, who was very involved with St Patrick's Brass Band, invited me to their New Year's Eve recital in the Bandroom in the Fairgreen, Foster Street. I am looking forward to it. I went with Pat, for as well as playing music with the band; she will be making the teas tonight, so I will be there to help. On our way to the hall, I tell her my news about flying out in the morning to the States for my newest granddaughter's christening in L.I. She was delighted and wished me a safe and wonderful time.

"I guess you are packed?"

"I am indeed Pat."

"How are you getting to Shannon?" She wanted to know.

"By bus," I said, "there is one that will take me to Ennis, change there and get one straight to Shannon airport."

"Martin will take you to the bus."

"Thanks Pat, I was going to get a taxi." The band director was Mr Tommy Joyce. They played carols and ballads, some opera tunes and traditional music; it was a lovely way to see out the old year and sing Auld Lang Syne, while standing in a circle with the arms across the body, holding hands with the one each side of you and sing in the New Year. Tea and the Christmas cake, which Pat made herself, and plenty of other goodies, made for a very enjoyable New Year's Eve. I was so grateful to Pat for such a lovely evening.

1992 - KENNEDY AIRPORT

On my arrival, I was welcomed by a beautiful day in January. Meeting me at the airport was my daughter-in-law's parents, Paddy and Jane Moran. I noticed Jane's arm in a sling. "What happened to you, Jane?" I asked.

"I was here a few weeks helping Mary with the baby, and somehow I tripped and fell so I won't be here for the christening, I have to go home tomorrow."

"Oh, why have you to leave?"

"My arm is paining me; I'll feel better when I'm at home."

I was sorry for her. Meeting everyone was great, but meeting my little granddaughter was the icing on the cake; a little beauty and so content. A lovely Chinese meal was waiting for me. When I lived in the States, my late husband Mike and I would go to the local Chinese restaurant on a Sunday for a chow mein meal; this brought the memory back to me. I had the regret that he wasn't here to meet his latest grandchild. I wanted to cry, but no, everyone is happy, I'm not going to spoil anything. After I had congratulated everyone, my son Mike asked if I would stay a few nights with Leo, Joey and their little one until after the christening as his house was full. I said I would love to, so it was arranged that I would be back to stay with them for the second week.

After work, Leo came to pick me up. I was happy to see Joey and little Kristina, who was now able to walk. In the evening, Uncle Leo and his wife Josephine came for a chat; it was great. Uncle Leo, described himself with a laugh, "I'm a granduncle now." Joey said, "This is going to be some christening, all the relations are invited, your Aunt Margie and her daughter Maureen is asked as well." Mike said he could not leave out his old grand aunt; "She is a great grand aunt now," I interjected. During the course of conversation, I discovered my grandson Michael had been to Ireland and I hadn't seen him. I was disappointed on hearing this; I guess there wasn't time for him to visit me.

AN AMERICAN CHRISTENING

It was a beautiful day in the month of January; the sun was shining; it was like the middle of spring. The baby looking angelic in her beautiful white christening robe. Her godfather was Aquinas McKenna, and godmother was Teresa McCourt. So many relations were present; starting with her great-grandaunt, Margie Callaghan and her daughter Maureen Doerr, the baby's Uncle Leo, his wife Joey and cousin Kristina, there were also grand-uncles Packie, Felix and Leo Beggan with their wives and families; also friends and neighbours. The church was full and then the house. My son Michael had his photo taken with his godparents, Packie Beggen and Maureen Doerr, next the four generations, grand-aunt Margie, me, grandmother, Mike, her father, and then baby herself, who was christened the lovely name of Cassandra Jane Beggen, there was photos of her and her two brothers, Michael, aged ten and Gary, aged five. I was pleased to have a while with my Aunt Margie, for I wouldn't be visiting her in the Bronx this time. Everyone had a great time and as everyone was tired, they began to say their goodbyes to the happy family.

We were all tired and ready for bed. Next morning, Mike was up early for work, Michael for school and, as Gary was in kindergarten, I walked him there; it was about a half hour walk. Before leaving him into school, I asked him for directions to go home. "If I go up that street, will it take me back to your house?" I asked.

"Check it out Granny, check it out," were the advise my wise five-year old grandson Gary gave me. I loved him all the more. Mary was resting whenever she could, after having the baby and the big christening party. I collected Gary from school; the weather was changing and getting very cold. On one occasion coming home Gary and had wet his pants. I said, "Did you use the toilet in school?" He said, "No, Granny." Next day when I went to collect him I asked, "Did you use the toilet today?"

"No," he answered.

"Well, come with me; you need to go before going out in the cold." As I was helping him with his buttons, he said,

"I can do it."

"Let me help you," I offered.

"Chill out Granny, chill out."

I did chill out; I couldn't wait to tell his Mam what a smart little son she had; we had a good giggle.

I was finally ready for home. My son Leo and family came to say goodbye. I had a great time and arrived safely home to Galway on a lovely sunny day, Caroline and Poochy were happy to see me, and I them. She couldn't wait to hear all about the American Christening. In the evening, I had to repeat everything for Margery who came in to hear my news, and of course I had plenty of photos to show and give away.

COMMITTEE MEETING

There is a lot of post left on the kitchen table for me. I go through it and toss the bills one side; it's too soon yet to look at them after having such a good time. There is one from the Ballybane Community Centre to attend a meeting; "So early in the year; they're ambitious to get started," I think to myself.

Chairman Paddy O'Brien opens the meeting and tells us a booking officer is needed to take the bookings and also to hold a key. I was proposed and accepted both jobs, stressing it would be just for a year. It turned out to be three years. Making up the committee were three people, Treasurer, the cleaner and me, Margaret Dowling, key holder plus booking officer.

I was taking the bookings at my house and passing the information to the chairman Paddy to inspect. It was a demanding voluntary chore.

NO END TO PREGNANCIES

I am still enjoying the excitement of my granddaughter Cassandra Jane's christening. I pay a visit to my daughter Margery in her new home in Coole Park, Bohermore. In between admiring her lovely house and telling her about her new niece, she has a surprise for me.

"Hush a minute, Mom, I have news too; a little brother or sister for Lisa is due in November." I sat with my mouth open. I wasn't prepared for this good news. "Well, God bless you both," I tell her.

New house, new baby.

November, and baby Rachel arrives. She is, of course, another pretty granddaughter for me. Lisa, now aged three, is happy to have a sister. The families come together for Rachel's christening in St. Patrick's Church. Ann Marie Ryan is meant to be godmother, but her mother, Peggy stands in as proxy and Brian Ruffley is godfather to baby Rachel. We go for a very nice meal to celebrate and then leave the family to enjoy their latest addition.

1993 - THE LATE BRONWYN

Everyone was saddened to hear of the sudden death of a lovely little Brownie who fell from her pony. It was indeed a shock to us all in Guiding to hear of such sadness, and our sympathies were with her parents, Pat and Monica O'Leary, and her brother Derek. Bronwyn's mother was a Girl Guide leader.

Brownies, Guides and leaders attended her Mass in St Patrick's Church, Forster Street, and made a guard of honour to her burial in the New Cemetery, Bohermore, Galway. Monica and Bronwyn often came to my house and she would do some colouring with Caroline's crayons and books, while Monica and I planned a Guide camping break. That is the lovely memory I have of a lovely little girl.

A GARDEN OF THISTLES

The weather is beginning to get nice, and I am sorry to have changed my mind about planting vegetables in the garden. It looks like a forest with the tall weeds, nettles and thistles. I ask my brother Paddy for the loan of the scythe to cut down the weeds and thistles. He offered to do it for me, as the scythe was very old and needed sharpening.

I was very glad off his offer for I would be exhausted by the time I had cut a quarter of it. As he cut away I came behind him, raking up the cut weeds. "What will I do with them?" I asked.

"Put them into a couple of heaps and they will rot away."

"Do you see that side?" I pointed to a small section of the garden; "It's not so bad; I'll clear it myself, who knows I might put in some vegetables there." While we were having the tea, we talked about Mother and how adept she was at using the scythe, cutting down the hay in the upper field, holding the two short extending handles, and keeping the sharp, bow-shaped instrument facing away from her. Every so often, she would use a large sharpening stone to hone the scythe blade, then continue on cutting the hay. She would get Eddie and I to rake it up into heaps to dry, saving it a cosy bedding for under the fowl in the winter time. "I have to tell you this," said Paddy, "it is the last time it will do any cutting, it's finished."

"Oh dear," I said, "Is it my fault?"

"No, its days are numbered, guess how old it is?"

"About forty years."

"No, it is over sixty years and very rusty."

"What will you do with it?"

"I will hang it up high in the shed."

"Thanks for doing that job for me." Looking out the kitchen window, I wondered how I would manage the next year.

GRANDDAUGHTER KRISTINA

Kristina is coming to Ireland with her mother Joey. I am so thrilled with this news. "We are coming in June," said Joey, "We will come via Dublin and stay with my family for a week, and then come to you."

"I can't wait to see you; tell your mother I'm inviting her to come with you to Galway, Joey."

"I will Peggy; she will love that." Now to get ready clean the house, make up beds and shop for the meals; then, when they are here I will have plenty of time to sit and chat. I picked the three of them up from Ceannt Station, Galway. There was great excitement. Kristina was taller than I expected. It was lovely hugging her little chubby body. Everyone is looking great, although Joey's mother Madeleine was only a few weeks after a hip replacement. She stressed, "I want no special treatment."

I had plans made we would go to County Clare to visit my relations. The little Morris Minor was full that day, heading to Moygala, Six-Mile-Bridge. Joey, her mother, my daughter Margery, Lisa, and Kristina. And me driving. Little Rachel was only one and a half years old, so she stayed home with her dad. I was making sure Anne Hurley, my late Uncle Paddy's wife, wouldn't go to too much trouble cooking for so many of us, but typical of her hospitable nature, she had a dinner of roast chicken, carrots and beautiful mashed potatoes, and a sweet; a big bowl of custard and jelly; such a big dinner she laid on for us. I had told her, "Just boil the kettle, Annie, we will bring the rest," but she wouldn't listen.

Everyone was glad to meet up. I had told Joey so much about my Clare relations and how they were all farmers. Our next destination was to my first cousin, Maureen Lyons; she lived about eight miles away up a hill and it was slow driving to her house. After meeting Maureen, two of her daughters joined us, Geraldine and Linda. We were brought into her kitchen where the table was set for dinner; her husband Paddy came in from working out in the land and he shook hands with a hard working hand. Madeleine said as she took his hand, "I don't need to ask what kind of work you do." He was a nice, tall, jolly man.

"Sit into the table, let ye," he said, as he sat down himself. It was roast beef in this house, the beef was their own kill. "You kill and cure you own beef, Paddy?" "We do," he said. Again, more vegetables and the floury potatoes; we didn't know where to look, and the food was so tempting, we just had to eat it. There was great fun when a pet lamb strayed into the kitchen. Kristina and Lisa wanted to bring him home with them. The lamb ran out the door and the two girls ran after him up the yard; we had a job to bring them back. I regretted not having brought my camera. It was a great day and beautiful weather. After our deep gratifying thanks for everything, we were on our way again. Our last stop was Tulla, to cousin Ann Flower. We apologised for our late visit, but the kettle was put on and the table set for tea; I was so glad we had brought some cakes and biscuits with us. Anne made tea for us.

Our time with my County Clare relations was so very welcoming, but they were only a few; we would need two weeks to go around them all; and with all the rich good food we got in the three houses to eat, we thought we would never fit into the car. The next day was a late rise in the morning, so we took it easy. No one was hungry. The week flew and very soon I was leaving them back to the train again. "Call me when you are in Dublin."

"We will," promised Joey. They all had a fabulous time in County Clare, but Kristina and Lisa couldn't stop talking about the lamb that came into cousin Maureen Lyon's kitchen.

SET DANCING

Set dancing was being taught in the Bandroom at the Fairgreen. Chris Langan and I thought we would give it a go. As we approached the hall, we could hear the music playing loud and clear. "That has a good sound," said Chris. The hall was full of four couples to a set. Michael Carrick and his wife Eileen were the set dancing tutors, and boy but did they know how to tutor those steps and figures; Chris and I were soon teamed up with three more couples.

It was hard learning the various figures, but we persevered and soon knew the Galway set, next came the Connemara set. My favourite was the Kerry Polka; I loved the steps and the figures in it. Chris and I met up twice a week to learn what we could of the sets. Michael and Eileen were brilliant tutors, remembering and teaching the intricate steps and figures in the sets. Chris and I remained set-dancing partners for a year, having lots of laughs, especially when we made mistakes.

Chris's husband Sean returned after his course was finished. Chris had her partner now so this left me out on a limb. I would wait to be teamed up, but each time it would be a different person. It didn't stop me learning the set dancing. A workshop weekend was organised. Salthill was the venue and I booked into the Banba Hotel for the weekend; it saved me driving there and home the three days and trying to find a parking space. People were coming from all over the country to learn the sets. The chief teacher was a Kerry man by the name of Connie Ryan. It was from him I learned the Clare lancers set. I loved that set and would be in a state if I wasn't out in it. Seapoint was not the only venue booked, the Sacre Coeur was also busy.

I had such a good time. When I came home I said to my daughters, "You two should take up set dancing."

"Us, is it?" They echoed.

"Yes, it is part of your culture," I tried to preach, "You did learn to play the traditional music on the accordion and tin whistle."

"That's different and we were younger then, now we have other commitments," was the answer I got.

BRINGING SOME OF MY PATCHWORK TO THE STATES

I was taking a couple of week's holidays in the states to visit my son Mike, his wife Mary and family. "You're going to America again, so soon?" says Caroline, in amazement. "I suppose I'm stuck with minding Poochy."

"Don't put it like that, you know you love her, anyway she will mind you too." The weather was going to be hot so I did a light packing, except for two patchworks quilts which I had made for my two grandsons' beds. Grandson Michael was learning to play the guitar and I made his quilt depicting five guitars, making them from a brown and cream material that suited guitar colours. I then stitched my creative work onto my already-made quilt. Gary was into the latest craze at the time, 'Ninja Turtles', so I worked at making Ninja Turtles to suit his quilt. "I have presents for you," I said to my grandsons and I handed each of them a wrapped parcel. "Open them," encouraged their dad. Having opened their parcels, their eyes almost popped out of their heads. "They are handmade quilts by me for your beds."

"Put them on your beds," said their mother. They were thrilled with their bed covers. "Mine has guitars," said Michael.

"And mine is my very favourite, Ninja Turtles," said Gary as they hugged me. "Thank you, Granny, that's the best present ever." Mike and Mary could not get over my gift at making patchwork. "Don't look too closely at them; I am no artist," I said.

As usual on my visits, Mike would ask was there anyone I would like to call. I said, "I would like to call my second cousin, Kathy Maloney." Kathy and I had a great chat and I had a wish to meet up. Kathy arranged that we could have a get-together in her sister Jeanne's house, which was a few blocks from where Mike lived. I was delighted with this suggestion; it had been a long time since we had all been together, and this was an opportunity not to be missed. So with Mike and Mary and their three children, we prepared to meet at Jenney's house. Kathy and her husband Joe, and their two children were there. Joseph was the same age as Cassandra, about four years old, and his little sister Megan was three. Jeanney and her husband John had three children, John, ten, Jenny, seven, and a young baby. They had a wonderful welcome for us and were glad in meeting the Beggen cousins, and vice versa.

There was a lake at the end of their long garden where John moored his boat. He treated the children to a trip around the lake. Michael and Gary loved it and so did their little sister, sitting on her daddy's knee. Jeanney had a barbecue meal for us. I was so happy when the third sister Christen arrived; she was at work and was worried she was going to miss us. It was a joyful day; I was overjoyed to meet Jenney and her husband John. I had been at their wedding in 1983 and now they had three children. We had a great day and I was so thankful to Kathy for arranging this come together. I will have news to tell Margery and Caroline when I go home. Driving back to Mike's, there was lots to talk about especially the novelty of the spin around the lake in John's boat.

THE CHOIR NIGHT OUT

St. Bridget's Choir, Ballybane, prepared to have their annual meal out, this time in Park House, Foster Street. Pat Folan, director and Joan McCormack, organist had everything under control and most of the members were available for this relaxing occasion away from the formality of rehearsals and hymn singing. The priest was unavailable to come with us. The brainchild of our choir, director Pat Folan, was to reward a member who attended regularly at rehearsals for the Sunday Mass and seasonal feasts. Sometimes there could be up to four recipients being given recognition for their dedication at the end of each year with a presentation of a plaque inscribed with the relevant details. No doubt the members would be honoured in receiving this memorial gift, which would keep them in mind of this wonderful choir, founded in 1984 by seven parish members.

At this dinner, there would be a surprise for Pat and Joan, for they were being honoured for patience and perseverance; each of them would be presented with a plaque that they well deserved. Through the years the choir grew with five male voices and twenty-five females. Through time, and as priests came and went, the choir kept the singing going and we knew we were appreciated by the applause from the congregation after Mass. We were blessed with every change of priest, who served in St. Bridget's Church. The choir was losing some of its members through death, moving house, family commitments etc. By 2005, we were down to seven dedicated ladies after approximately twenty-four years. "We were no longer needed," we cried, and that was the end of our choir days in St Bridget's, Ballybane; what a sad change.

1994 - DAUGHTER CAROLINE DOWLING

Caroline is going to America. I have the house to myself and my constant companion Poochy. I am still holder of the Community Hall key and taking bookings. But, having a sore throat, I'm unable to do this demanding job. I called Dr Michael O'Flaherty; he came to the house and examined me and diagnosed I had inflammation in my chest and a septic throat. "Stay in bed and keep warm; get someone to pick up this prescription." I thanked him and wondered who I could call. With luck my good neighbour Pat Folan had seen the doctor's car in my drive way. Calling in, she asked, "Are you sick, Margaret?"

"Very sick," I said; she went immediately to collect the tablets and at the same time she brought me a cup of warm soup and hot sweets to suck, then filled a hot water bottle for me. I was so grateful to her.

The chalet is making a little money. Two college students are renting it, nice lads from Ennis. I have to go downstairs to answer the phone in the hall (I am the only person privileged to own a house-phone in the locality). I tell the person who wants to book a room in the hall that I'm not well and gave him Paddy O'Brien, the chairman's, address. The phone rang many times but I was unable to go down stairs to be answering it, and to take out the booking diary to mark in the bookings.

Pat Folan would call in to make sure I was taking the tablets. I was feeling very guilty as Pat had her shop to run. "I am taking you away from your business, Pat; you are spending so much time attending to me."

"Martin is there to look after it," she said. She never rushed off but sat on the bed listening to my laboured breathing. Her profession was nursing. Early morning, she would be back with a piping hot mug of tea. At the weekend when the boys in the chalet were going home, they would come to the backdoor to pay the rent. This Friday I could hear them knocking and knocking, when I didn't answer they came to the front door and rang and rang the bell. I crawled out of the bed and down the stairs, when I opened the door and they saw how sick I looked they got a shock. "We are sorry to disturb you."

"It is alright boys, I have a bad dose of a cold."

"We will be back on Sunday evening. Leave your back door unlocked, I make nice vegetable soup," said the blond one, "I will fill a mug for you and leave it on the table." I was very grateful to them for the soup. It was the only substance I was able to take.

In time I was getting better and was able to dress and make a meal, but the weather was very cold. My daughter Margery came every second day and set a fire in the sitting room; it wasn't easy for her as she had two small children.

SON MICHAEL APPLIES

Michael applied to the renowned Esteé Lauder Company, New York, a legendary name in the world of cosmetics. He applied for a cost accountant position; he was lucky and was hired. He worked at audit accounting for this company in New York, and advanced into global inventory and promoted to cost manager; he worked in this position for a number of years. I was very proud of him as he had studied very hard to get so far, and he was still only a young man in his earley forties. He had to retire on disability as cost accounting manager. His career was cut suddenly short. I toasted him even though he was over three thousand miles away.

1995 - I AM PLANING ANOTHER HOLIDAY

I am going to get ready and take a trip to Brooklyn, N.Y. to see daughter Caroline, and son Leo, and family. Also Mick and family living in Long Island. And my long-time friends Mike and Clare Burke and their two grown children, Michael and Mary Ann living in New Jersey.

But first I must let Margery know she will be minding Poochy. "She's a nuisance, I know, but can you mind her?"

"Sure I will mind her, what about your small animals, Margery?"

"They will be safe in their hutch." Lisa and Rachel are playing in the back garden. Margery calls them in. "Lisa, tell Granny your news."

"Nanny, I'm starting school in September."

"That's great news; what school are you going to go to Lisa?"

"The Convent of Mercy."

"That is big news, Lisa."

"Thanks, Nanny," says my granddaughter, they both skipped out the door to continue with their game.

"I don't know how I will manage taking the two of them down to the convent, it's a good walk. The stroller is falling apart. I have tried to get a twin buggy but they are all too wide to get in the front door," complained Margery.

"Well, this is only June, someone might have a pushchair to give to you before September," I said encouragingly.

Back home in the kitchen I'm talking to Poochy. "Aunty Margery will be minding you for a few weeks, so be good for her." Then I get a fright from Martin Folan as he comes in the open back door. "It's all right," he tells me, "they say people go like that in their old age."

"Martin, knock next time please; who knows, I could be talking about you." "Here, I caught a few fish and there's a couple in that for you."

"Oh Martin, you are a sweetheart; you don't need to knock."

"Go on out of that with your ould blarney," said Martin as he went out the door. Martin and his wife Pat were very good to me and lived next door. There was a gap in the wall between the two houses where the children climbed in and out when Martin's brother Joe and his family lived in that house. Joe, his wife Jean and their four children immigrated to Canada. They were good friends of mine too, and I missed them when they left. Martin, Pat and their children moved into Joe's house. Martin and Pat rented out their house and shop.

A PLEASANT FLIGHT

Having settled Poochy in with Margery, I was ready for the bus to Shannon and board the plane. I said to myself, "I hope I sleep now," and I did. I came alert as the plane was descending to land at Kennedy airport. Waiting for the carousel to bring my bag around seemed for ever, then, grabbing it I hurried to the checkout. My son Leo was waiting for me; we had hugs and were glad to see each other. "I will just drop you off at the house and go back to work; I'll see you this evening."

"Thank you very much, son." Joey and Kristina were waiting with open arms; it was good to see them. Hugging Joey, I thought she was a bit heavy,

"What is going on?" I ask, "Don't tell me I'm getting another grandchild? She laughed.

"Well, you are, next October."

"Well, God bless you," I say. "You are going to get a little sister or brother, Kristina."

"I know," she answered, "and I'm going to school too," she let me know.

"You are a big girl now."

"I am," she agreed.

After a welcome mug of tea and a salad, I asked when Caroline would be in.

"After six," said Joey, "herself and Leo come in about the same time."

The excitement and chat was great; we had a lot to catch up on. Caroline told me she was minding two big dogs, and as she loved dog's they were in good hands. Leo and Joey were excited about their coming event and so was Kristina, who would be five years old on Christmas Eve.

"This baby," said Leo "is due at Halloween."

"You won't have any excuse to forget their birthdays Leo."

"Have you any plans Mom?" asked Caroline.

"Well, I would like to spend a few days in Massapequa Park with Mike and family."

"We are going there on Sunday," said Leo.

"Oh, lovely," I was delighted.

There was plenty of fun in Mike's as he had a swimming pool in his back garden. Kristina and her three cousins, Michael, Gary and Cassandra played in the pool. After an overnight stay and plenty of card-playing it was time for Leo, Joey, Kristina and Caroline to head back to Brooklyn. I stayed on with Mike and family. Mary and I did some shopping. Mary bought craft material. As we sat having a chat in the sitting room, Mike asked if there was anything special I would like to do.

"I would like to go to New Jersey for a couple of days to my friends, Mike and Clare Burke. I wonder how I could get there?"

Mary said for me to arrange it with Clare.

Clare said I could get the train to Manhattan, and her brother-in-law, Peter Joyce would meet me at the hotel where he works. It's beside the train stop.

I was glad to see Pete. "I have the car here, so hop in. I'm just finished work." Pete Joyce, a Connemara man, was married to Clare's sister Dell. Peter was interested in how things were in Galway; I told him it was prospering from the tourist trade.

"Much better than when I lived there," he commented.

"You are right there, Pete." It was great to see Clare and Mike; we had a lot to catch up on.

1995 - ATLANTIC CITY

Clare and Mike were on the ball. After the usual big welcome, Clare told me they made arrangements for us to visit Atlantic City the next day. "Oh, that is great, Clare." We boarded the bus next morning; it was full of elderly people, all with the same thing in mind, winnings! As we approached Atlantic City, a lady came onto the bus with bags of change to hand to everyone to use in the slot machines. "Do I owe for this?" I asked Mike.

"No," he said, "they do that for the older people to keep us coming," he said with a laugh, "so use it you could be lucky and win a fortune." I did spend it, and once in a while I would win $5 and spend it again. Mike had tokens accumulated for free meals; you could eat all you wanted. Mike kept gambling away. Clare and I walked the boardwalk; it was a beautiful day, the blue of the sea and the blue of the sky matching each other; one just did not want to leave. I bought some souvenirs. Back on to the bus, tired and happy, but without a fortune.

Next day, Clare had a little job helping an old lady. I decided to walk into Dumont, the local town. It was about a mile of a walk. I went in the cool of the morning. I liked browsing through the stores. Walking down the street, I suddenly stopped; there, on display was a twin buggy, one seat in front of the other. I thought, "It's perfect for what Margery needs and only $90." I went in and asked about it and as it was on shop display, and the last one they had, they sold it to me for $88, but the tax brought it to almost a $100. Still it was a bargain. I wheeled it up the town, home to Clare's. There wasn't an ould fellow on the street that couldn't resist having a go at me. "Are you going to fill it? How will you do that now? Aren't you on' a bit, to be thinking of having twins?"

"Ah, leave her alone, can't you see she's in her second spring," chipped in another smart alec.

"Oh God help me let me get home quick," I thought, "Those devils have to be Irish."

Mike had to put his bit in. "Margaret, did you wheel it up the town?"

"I did, Mike, and don't you go adding to it."

Clare was home and had made a lovely light meal. We talked about how things were in Ireland. Clare and Mike were from Tuam; they thought it was a shame the sugar factory was closed down; so many of their relations had to go to England to try and get work; I agreed it was a shame. Then, my girlfriend of long past, Clare's sister, Maureen Buckley/Farrell came to see me. We had plenty to reminisce about, especially the years we worked together in the agricultural college, Athenry. It was great meeting up but my time was coming to an end. I was very grateful to Mike for folding and tying up the buggy. Clare and her daughter Mary Ann drove me back to Massapequa. I was so thankful to them for the good time I had; the few enjoyable days flew. After a quick cup of coffee with Mike, and Mary, Clare and Mary Ann left for home.

Me, Mike and Claire Burke.

ARIZONA

"Listen to this, Mom," said Mike as he answered the phone call from Caroline, "she has a great surprise for you."

"What is it?" I was excited to know. Her surprise for me I would not have guessed in a million years.

"How would you like a trip to Arizona to see your aunt Margie?"

"I would love it, but there is no chance of that."

"Well, I have booked a flight for you in a few days time," said Caroline.

"Oh dear God, have you? I can't believe this, thank you, Caroline I love you." "Mike will take you to Kennedy airport and you can pick up the tickets there. Take down these numbers and pass them in at the departure counter."

"How long will I be in Sedona?"

"A week, then you will be back to Mike and Mary for a day before you fly back to Shannon airport again. So have a great time with your aunt."

"You have it all laid on for me; indeed you are so good, thanks Caroline."

"When I was talking to your cousin Maureen on the phone telling her you would be coming to visit them, she was screaming with excitement in my ear," said Caroline. It was good to have a while with my son Mike and Mary. The children, Michael, Gary and Cassandra, were out in the swimming pool with their friends.

"I have your cousin on the phone, Mom."

"Thanks, Mike. Hi Maureen, I cannot believe my daughter has done this for me," I gushed.

"She is a good daughter Peggy, Mam is really excited to be seeing you."

"And so am I looking forward to seeing her!"

"Joe and I will be at Phoenix airport to meet you."

"Thank you, Maureen."

As Mike was leaving me to Kennedy, he said, "This is a short flight now to Phoenix. Call us when you are in Maureen's."

"I will, to be sure," I promised.

Like Mike, said it was a short flight, but my wait for Maureen and Joe to come and collect me was very long. I waited hours; I was sure I would be going back again to L.I. Finally, I hear her shout,

"Peggy, I am so, so sorry; the car broke down on us; we had to get it towed to a garage to get it fixed; we are all night on the road, I know you are dead tired Peggy from the long wait," said my cousin all in one breath.

Arizona

"I'm alright now, Maureen." I tell her, "You are looking well."

"You are too, Peggy. I feel terrible for leaving you waiting so long."

"We are together now Maureen, there's Joe."

He is also apologising, "It is no problem," I tell him. "How far to your house, Joe?"

"About three hours. We will drive on now, and you go to sleep." I lay down in the back seat and the next thing I know, Maureen is shaking me awake. "We are home Peggy, and you are very welcome to Sedona."

WELL HERE WE ARE

"Here we are!" said Maureen, pointing to their brand new, beautiful house.

"Oh, what a house Maureen; it is something out of a picture book." Maureen explained that it was a one-level house. "A bungalow," I tell her. She laughs, "That is what Mom calls it too."

Showing me to my bedroom, which was like a shrine to John Wayne, the great movie star of the 'Quiet Man', his profile was on cushions, pillowslips, the quilt, the wall over the bed was lined with plates with pictures engraved with many of the movies he took part in; the last word was the large effigy of him standing by my bed. "You must really love him, Maureen."

"It was here in Sedona most of his cowboy movies were made."

"And you have made a shrine to him."

"Come to the kitchen, Peggy, it's time you had something to eat; I have a hot lunch for you, and after that we will go to see Mom; she is in residential care".

"Is she happy there?" I asked.

"I will let you judge for yourself when you see her."

Seeing my aunt brought so many memories to my mind. I was so glad to see her looking so good; she still didn't need a hearing aid or glasses and she was all of ninety-five years of age. She was wearing a lovely summer dress. I looked around her space; she had her own bed and the bedclothes from her apartment in the Bronx, and many pictures, including her wedding photos hanging on the wall. She saw me looking at them. "Yes," she said, "I brought Dan with me; I couldn't leave him behind." Dan, her Scottish husband had passed away in 1968, about twenty seven years ago, but she still talked of him with affection. We held each other and hugged, and hugged; it was so good to be together again.

She explained how independent she was. "I fix my own breakfast in here and sometimes my dinner; the carer comes in everyday to ask me where I want to eat my lunch. Sometimes I will eat it in here, other times I like to eat with the other residents in the dining room. We have everything here all under the one roof and still independent."

"Do you like it, Marg?"

"I do, Peg. And Maureen comes every day. We are never alone here; we are taken out sightseeing and for lunch and to concerts, those of us who are fit to travel."

"Do you go, Marg?"

"I never miss a trip; everything is laid on for us and very comfortable. It is not so cold here; the weather is mild all year. We have a movie palace here, where we can spend an afternoon watching the old movies of our time, after that we are treated to cake and coffee."

"Oh Margie, you have it nice here."

"I have Peggy; what I like most is I'm never alone."

"Thank God for that, Marg."

"We will take Peggy for a drive around Sedona; are you all right with that, Mam?"

"I am, let me get my pocketbook." I see sights I would never see in Ireland, the cactus growing as high as oak trees. "They are endangered species; anyone caught touching one of them is fined a lot of money," said Aunt Margie.

My first day with Aunty was wonderful. "Do whatever ye want tomorrow, I won't go with you but come in later."

Arriving back at Maureen's house, Joe had a nice tea ready for us. "How do you think your aunt looks?" He asked. "She looks great, Joe; she is much better than she was when she was in the Bronx."

"Your cousin was very worried about her there, on her own at her age. Most of her Irish friends in the Bronx have passed away or moved to the country with their family, so she had no one there."

Aunt Margie Callaghan, her daughter Maureen and husband Joe Tully.

"You did a wonderful thing for her, Joe."

"She is a wonderful woman, your aunt. Go to bed, Peggy and have a good sleep, for tomorrow, Maureen is taking you sightseeing."

I was very tired and slept till late next day. A late breakfast of homemade pancakes was, as they say, what the doctor ordered.

SIGHTSEEING IN SEDONA

The weather was very hot, but the air conditioning in the car kept us cool. Maureen brought plenty of cold water to cool us down. Each time we stepped out of the car, the heat would hit us with a blast.

Maureen brought me to see a beautiful church built straight into a rock; it was magnificent. Some people named it Cathedral Rock, others the Chapel of the Holy Cross. It was the brainchild of a Marguerite Brunwig Staude in 1956. She was a disciple of a famous architect by the name of Frank Lloyd Wright. There were no regular services held in this church like the Mass, for it was not consecrated. The building of it didn't go through the proper channels like the building of a Catholic Church. It was laid out like a regular church, inside an altar, seats and statues. People were welcome to stop in and meditate and say a quiet prayer. "You made a good move after retiring out of the police force Maureen, to come and settle here in beautiful Arizona."

"It was Joe's idea; his Mam and Dad came here on their retirement too. I met Joe in the force; he was also a cop. I met him there after my husband Henry dying. Of course, I said I would never marry again".

"You had to follow in my footsteps, Maureen."

"Tomorrow we will spend time with Mam; I know you both will like that. Is there anything you would like to do or see?" She asked.

"I would like to visit a quilting and patchwork store."

"I know just the place; I will take you there now."

I was gobsmacked to see both men and women sitting around tables, cutting and stitching scraps of material to form their artistic work into patchwork quilts. Their work was fantastic. I could have stayed all day. By buying the fabric there, you were taught the craft for free. I bought a pattern, "Turners Wedding" and some fabric.

I learned that during the great Depression of the 1920/30's, people had to find ways to make a living out of old cut up fabric/rags to create patchwork quilts, cushion covers, tea cosies, aprons and lots more to sell; that way they could keep bread on the table during the tough and lean years. Today, it is done to pass the time, have conversation and compare their craft work while keeping occupied in their retired years. They raffled their fabulous craft work to raise money for the poor and destitute.

"Thank you so much for bringing me here today, it's a heaven I would like to be a part of."

"Move over here so you can be a member, Peggy," she chided. "We will have something to eat and go visit Mam."

"I'm looking forward to that, Maura."

My time spent with my aunt Margie, those days are among my best memories. Maureen made sure we had a day to ourselves. Aunt Margie and I linked arms, as we walked around the grounds admiring the cacti beds. "You won't find many flowerbeds here." We sat on a bench, she took on a faraway look in her eyes; her thoughts were of Kilnacree, County Clare, where she was born and reared; where she emigrated from in 1928/29. She wanted to hear so much about her old home; it is gone now, but not once did she mention the Bronx where she had lived for sixty years. Maureen came to find us. "Come on, you two, we are going to have honeycomb ice-cream."

"I never had honeycomb ice-cream, what is it like?"

"You will love the flavour of the ice-cream, especially when you eat it with a piece of honeycomb dipped into the ice-cream and scooped up to lick it off the honeycomb." It was delicious even if it was a bit messy; I could feel my waist expanding.

We leave Aunt Margie and a kind of loneliness came over me; I felt like crying. We were in Maureen's when the tears began to flow. I thought my heart would break. "It's alright to cry, Peggy." Then she was crying, too. Joe turned on the TV and we watched a funny program. I fell asleep halfway through it.

On Sunday, we went to Mass with Joe's Mam and Dad. After Mass, we went to an all-day breakfast restaurant high up the mountains. Joe was driving miles and miles, up and up we went to a place named Flagstaff. Tall cacti grew each side of the road. The restaurant was laid out with tables that were laden with food of every description, and people filling their plates many times. There were some very tall people and some very obese, but not the company I was with.

I was in a bad way; my nose started to bleed from the high altitude. I had no comfort eating. The piano player asked me, "What song would you like to hear?"

I said, "Galway Bay," which he sang and played to perfection. He was partly Indian and white and a beautiful singer.

Maureen decided we should leave. When we were outdoors, my nosebleed gradually stopped. They gave me a choice to go to visit the Grand Canyon or the Indian Reserve; Maureen and Joe were going to the Reserve so I went with them. It was an eye-opener with the thousands of Indian handmade jewellery and shawls for sale. The colours of the shawls brought to mind Connemara. I bought some jewellery to bring home for my daughters. I took out my camera to take a few photos. An old Indian man came up to me, "No camera, evil." Maureen explained I was from another country and didn't know the rules; I said "sorry" and put my camera away. A half a mile away, I was approached by another Indian man, "You have camera, you take picture of my jewellery." I was just getting it ready to snap, when he said, "Only $10."

Maureen saw the look on my face, "Come on, Peggy, it is time now to go home."

Next morning, I could not believe my wonderful time was over and I would have the goodbyes to say. Only this time my sadness would go deeper into my heart. I had my carry-on bag all packed; because of the heat I needed only a few light clothes to wear. Maureen called my son Mike to let him know the time I would be arriving at Kennedy airport. This would be my last call to Aunt Margie. She was preparing a lovely tea for us. "I'm sorry I'm not dressed yet; give Peggy a cold drink there Maureen, while I take a quick shower."

As she went into the bathroom Maureen made a suggestion, "Go in and tell her you will help her with her shower." I washed her back and shampooed her hair, rinsed her down and dried her old body; she had perfect skin, not a blemish, but as she was a strawberry blond in her young days, and spent a lot of time in the sun at Archer Beach in the Bronx, she had a lot of freckles, but never got skin cancer, or any kind of cancer. We sat quietly having the tea and cake she had prepared for us. I tried to keep my spirits up. I knew they were doing the same. I ate a big chunk of the rich, creamy cake; it was nice. It was time for goodbyes, hugs and kisses. "You'll be back, Peggy."

"I will Marg. I will." We had our last hug and kiss, then it was time to leave. I sat into the car and dared not look back.

We are now on the road, and there is so much to see, I am distracted. Joe stops the car and gives me a good look at the wild horses roaming the plains. "This is where the John Wayne Wild West movies are filmed," he said.

We are at Phoenix airport. We make quick farewells. I have so many wonderful memories and so much news for my son Mike, who will be waiting for me at Kennedy. I had a satisfied feeling as the plane landed, having been with my dear Aunt Margie and of course my cousin Maureen and Joe. I was happy to see my son Mike waiting for me.

Here in New York, the rain is coming down in torrents. "I have to take a detour home," he said, "the roads are flooded." We talked and talked about my holiday and he told me about the time he worked in Tucson. Mike was delighted to hear his dear old grandaunt; Margie Callaghan was well and happy. Mary was ready to hear all about Aunt Margie too and of course Maureen and Joe Tully. "I could go on for ever and I still wouldn't have told you everything," I said. "I have only one more day of this brilliant vacation left, and then I'm on the move to go back home," I moaned, "but thanks to you all. I have had such a wonderful time."

"Thanks to your daughter Caroline," Mike reminds me. Now the time has come to do the last bit of packing. Mike has the twin buggy left by the door. "Thank you for everything," I said to Mary, as we hugged goodbye, then kisses and hugs to grandchildren Michael, Gary, and Cassandra. At last, I'm on my way to Kennedy airport and a quick goodbye to my son Mike.

RED CLAY

My memory is of gazing at the red clay in Arizona; I couldn't help wondering how vegetables, flowers or trees could grow in it. Travelling around Sedona in the car with my cousin Maureen, I observed many trees, like the rich green pine, oak trees, sycamore, maple and mountain mahogany. In one field, I saw a mass of beautiful yellow flowers growing; they were asters. My cousin Maureen would point out the massive rock formations, and told me some of their names; looking closely you could understand why they got their titles, Coffeepot Rock, Courthouse Rock, Bell Rock, Merry-go-Round Rock. These rocks were sculptured by nature. Modern man came to find this a place where he could write books. Robert de Niro was inspired to title his book 'Midnight Run'. The Oak Creek Canyon inspired many writers in naming their books, like Zane Grey naming his book, 'Call of the Canyon'. Maureen was telling me many things about Sedona; the best time of the year is the season of spring when the fields are a mass of bluebells. "Next time, come in the spring; you won't find it quite as hot."

It is unreal that a country could be blessed with so much of nature's own gifts. Creeks, wildflowers, rocks that are named, and the clay so red. What a wonderful creator God is.

There was so much to tell; every now and then I would remember something greater to talk about. Explaining about Maureen and Joe's lovely house, I was making sure I filled everyone in on Maureen's shrine to John Wayne; so much to tell and repeating it to Caroline on the phone. "Make sure you tell Leo and Joey I had a wonderful time."

"I will," she promised.

SHANNON AIRPORT

Looking down on an oases of green, I said, "My homeland, dear old Ireland, I wouldn't swap you for all the red clay in the world." I found my bag and spent almost a half hour looking for the precious twin buggy; it was the last item to be taken off the plane. Boarding the bus for Galway, I sat down and thought about all the relations and places I had seen and travelled in the space of a month.

I was glad to see "Rock Dale", my home, and I'm ready to go pick up Poochy from Margery's house and give everyone little American gifts. Poochy licked my face all over. After a nice tea with Margery and telling her about what a wonderful time I had, I was ready for home and bed. I was keeping the twin buggy as a surprise until September when Lisa would be starting school.

1995 - SEPTEMBER

I put the buggy into the car and drove to the Ruffley's. There is great excitement in the kitchen; Lisa is ready in her Convent of Mercy navy and blue uniform and her school bag in her hand. Her dad opens the door for her to go out, but first I take a photo of her. Out in the hall she sees the twin buggy. "Mam," she calls, "where did you get that?"

"What is it?" Asks her mother.

"Look," she says. Margery puts her hand to her mouth, "Oh! Mom, you didn't."

"Well, I did."

"Thanks come on Rachel until I put you into it, and Lisa you sit in the front seat this is going to make life easier to walk to the Convent, and look there is a canopy to cover them over in case of rain. Now John you, what do you think of that?"

"It's great, thanks heaps," said John.

"Bye Mom, we will be up to see you soon." I was indeed very pleased with myself.

ANCIENT ORDER OF HIBERNIANS

Mike phones me. "Did you get home alright Mom?"

"I did Mike thank you."

"I meant to tell you when you were here I joined the Ancient Order of Hibernians (AOH), Division Fifteen, in Massapequa Park.

"Explain what that means, Mike."

"It's a Catholic Irish-American FraternityBrotherhood Organization, founded in New York City in 1836. It was founded to protect the clergy and Church property back then, and the Irish emigrants fleeing the famine; it still continues to help Irish Americans and introduces them to Irish culture, dance, music and sport."

"It sounds like a great organisation."

"It is Mom, and it has thousands of divisions throughout the country. The men are mostly retired. We have our own lovely hall where we meet once a week to play cards, celebrate birthdays and occasions like that."

"It sounds like a very practical organisation to be attached to Mike."

"It's better known by the initials AOH."

HERE I AM AND BLESSED

With another grandchild on the way and I am looking forward to whatever God will send. It's October and the weather is lovely here. I'm awakened by the ring of the phone in the hall; I hurry down the stairs, at the same time wondering who is calling at this hour. I pick up the receiver and in an unsteady voice say, "Hallo."

I hear a shout, "Congratulations!" You have another grandson; born the thirty first of October."

"Oh Leo, God bless ye, how is mother and baby?"

"They are fine, and will be coming home tomorrow,"

"That is great news. I will call Joey in a few days." I put down the phone and bless myself. I won't go back to bed now.

A few days later, I get a phone call from Caroline. She is talking about coming home; she doesn't like it in the States. I say, "Caree, I didn't like it in America either when I first went over, but Aunt Margie coaxed me to give it a few months longer and I did. Now I'm saying the same thing to you, give it another while, you might get to like it."

"I will Mom, but I know I won't"get to like it here.

"That's alright dear; I will phone you in a week or so, mind yourself."

"I will Mom, bye for now."

CAROLINE COMES HOME

Margery comes to see me. She has a look on her face that says, 'there is something you don't know'. I ask, "Is something wrong?"

"No, nothing is wrong. Caroline wants you to pick her up from Shannon airport tomorrow morning."

"I will of course; why didn't she call me?"

"She is worried you might be disappointed she didn't give it another chance and stay in the States, like you were saying to her."

"Oh! For God's sake. I was repeating what my Aunt Margie said when I was giving up all hope of wanting to stay there. What suits one won't suit another. I will of course pick her up, call her and tell her I will be at Shannon."

"And come to my house after you pick her up; I will have a meal ready for you," suggested Margery. It was a very happy daughter I held in my arms at Shannon airport. And true to her word, Margery had a lovely tea ready, but not before the sisters hugged and kissed.

Margery's husband John and their two little daughters Lisa and Rachel had their own welcome home to give her. Then she handed out some gifts. "Poochy will be happy too, to see you Caroline."

"I know she will, but in comparison to the two big dogs I was minding she is going to look so small."

"She will make up for her size when she welcomes you with her licks around your face. Eat up; I'm sure you are looking forward to a good sleep."

SAVED BY A DOG

Caroline and I talk about America and the jobs she had. I told her how worried I was about her minding the two Rottweillers."You didn't have to worry, Mam. I'll tell you this about the dogs. One day I was going to light the outdoor gas barbecue; the sun was shining very strong. I didn't realise it was already lit as I put the lighter to it, it made a loud bang; I screamed, one of the Rottweller's jumped up and shoved me back to a seat, then he licked my face and stayed beside me until I was alright, I wasn't hurt, I just got a bad fright." "You never told me that."

"There was nothing to tell. I loved the dogs and taking them for walks, but a time came when I wanted to move on and do a bit of exploring in some other kind of work."

"What will you do now you are at home?"

"I will apply to Standard Printers; I might get hired in there again."

"That is very sensible of you Caree, good luck to you."

LEO NEEDS A FAVOUR

Leo's phone call took me by surprise. "Is everything alright, Leo?" I stammer.

"Everything is alright here, Mom. I must ask you for a favour. While Joey was pregnant, I got sad news from her sister Anne in Dublin, their mother is dying of lung cancer, and has a short time to live, but they didn't want Joey to know until after the baby was born. Her sister called her this morning and told her the sad news. The baby is only two weeks old. Can you come over to mind him and Kristina for a couple of weeks, while Joey visits her mother? I can't take time off work; if I do I will lose my job."

I am so saddened not only is Joey losing her mother, but I'm losing a good friend. "I will book a flight today; I should be there in a couple of days."

"Thanks, Mother."

"I'm glad to be able to help, son."

I rush around packing a bag, making sure my passport is in order. I phone Fahy's travel agent; no problem with securing a seat this time of year. "I will be down to pick up the ticket shortly."

"It will be here waiting for you," said the travel agent. I phone Joey to tell her, "I will be there in the morning and Leo can book your flight."

"I am so grateful to you, Peggy."

"I am so glad I can do it, but are you fit to travel? The baby is only two weeks old, is it too soon for you to fly?"

"My doctor said I am fine," she answered.

I have to tell Margery and Caroline, and of course Poochy needs minding.

MEETING MY GRANDSON IAN

As I arrived in Kennedy airport, Leo was waiting for me. "Thanks for coming, Mom. Joey is very upset."

"I am sure she is. Indeed, I am too. Madeleine is a lovely woman; I hope God spares her."

"According to the family she hasn't got long."

"We must pray for her, Leo." As we park outside the apartment block, Joey runs down the stairs to meet us and she gives me a hug. Leo turns the car around and heads straight back to work.

I am looking forward to meeting my latest grandchild, little Ian and my granddaughter Kristina, who was making sure I understood he was her brother. Joey was prepared for her sad journey back to Dublin the next morning. Leo picked up her bag and they left for Kennedy. I kissed her and wished her a pleasant flight. It was a sad trip for her to make.

Before leaving, she gave me instructions about the baby's feeding times and asked me to sleep in their room next the cot. Leo would sleep in the guest bedroom. Ian was a good baby, but poor Kristina had a bad chest cold and did a lot of coughing. I gave her plenty of warm soup and spoons of honey. She had a good appetite and was not sick. Eventually one afternoon, the mucus all came away. I was glad she would be better when her Mam came home. Kristina helped with feeding baby and giving him his bath in the little bath.

Son Mike, Mary and their three children came for a visit one evening. I was overjoyed to see them as I wouldn't be able to visit them this time. Kristina and Cassandra were almost the same age, and had great fun playing. Michael and Gary sat watching TV. I was glad of this distraction for Leo.

We looked forward to Joey's return. As she arrived back, I said to Leo, "Joey is not looking so well; her face is very flushed."

She had a worrying time with her Mom and is upset, she knows she won't see her alive again."

"Tomorrow we will take you out to dinner and tonight you sleep in the guestroom."

"There's no need to fuss about me, Leo." Early morning Leo wakes me up;

"I need you to come to our bed and mind baby Ian. Joey is very sick with a pain in her leg. I'm taking her to the doctor now."

I can only wait and pray, for I know it can't be good. I hear them coming back and rush to open the door. Joey was a tall and well-built girl. Leo was out of breath from trying to carry her into the apartment. It's thrombosis.

"I guessed that, Leo."

"She must stay in bed; we need to raise her leg, she has to take these tablets day and night and get her to drink plenty of water."

For the next week, we helped her in and out of bed; she was not allowed to put her leg on the ground. Leo had to go to work. I slept with her and took care of the baby with Kristina's help, who was five years old, and would hold the bottle to his mouth at feeding time, while I looked after her Mom. The district nurse came to see Joey. She raised her leg higher on extra pillows along the back of an upside-down chair placed on the bed. The nurse was quite pleased with Joey's progress; her temperature had gone down and she allowed her to get up for an hour. This made Kristina happy.

My time for going home was drawing near; the four weeks nearly up. Joey had to make a visit to her doctor before I left. Leo was on the phone to Joey. "Tell me what the doctor says when you get home, Joey."

"I will, Leo."

After the doctors' check-up, I knew by the look on her face coming in the door all was not well. "I am so sorry Peggy, I have to go back to bed for another week," said Joey in tears. "I must let Leo know." She handed me the phone, "He wants to talk to you, Peggy." I take the phone. I can guess what he wants.

"Can you extend your stay for another week?"

"I can, Leo," I said. The extra week made a big improvement in Joey.

It is coming up to Christmas and snowing. Kristina and I go for walks in the evenings to see the Christmas lights in the houses. "Let us amaze our eyes," said my granddaughter.

I was all ready for leaving. Having a large brown paper bag, I was joking with Kristina telling her I was taking little Ian home with me in the bag; all I would need for him is in the bag, a nappy and his bottle. She gave me a steady stare. "You cannot take him," she said.

"Why not?" I asked.

"Because he is my baby brother."

That set me straight. Joey hugged me tight. "Thanks Peggy."

"Enough of the thanks; I am glad to help any time." It was Kristina's turn then with her little hugs. "I will miss you, my pet."

"I will miss you too, Granny," she said. Now a last kiss for a sleeping Ian.

It was Sunday and Leo left me to the airport; he was thanking me; I said,

"I was glad to be of help."

"Call me when you get home."

"I will." Then we kissed goodbye.

LANDING AT SHANNON

The weather was mild but I missed seeing the snow. "You are in Ireland," I said to myself, "and thank God"; I slept most of the way home on the bus.

And as always, old faithful Poochy was wagging her tail wild with happiness to see me. Caroline was at work, but had a warm fire on in the range; the kettle was boiling and the kitchen was cosy. I made myself some tea, I wondered if there was bread in the house; there was, so I made some toast. I heard the door open and in walked Caroline. "Welcome back."

"Thanks," I said.

"Tell me how is Joey?"

"She is fine again; I guess she should not have gone flying so soon after having the baby. The baby is so good and so is Kristina. As for Leo, he was a very worried man, but all is well now. Thanks be to God."

"We will have to do something for the Christmas. Margery is inviting us down to their house for Christmas dinner."

"Oh, how nice, I must buy some presents; I had no time to go out to the stores in Brooklyn."

A WEDDING ANNIVERSARY

My niece Ann Egan invites me to her father and mother's fortieth wedding anniversary; they are celebrating it in the local, 'The Lantern'. I said, "Thanks Ann, I will be there."

"Bring a friend with you," she included. I thanked her again. After putting down the phone, I remember my own wedding on the seventh of May 1955, when we became Mr & Mrs Michael Beggen, and my brother Eddie's in September of the same year, when he and Honor Carrick also became husband and wife, forty years ago. I know I am not going to like wedding anniversaries for I won't ever celebrate such an occasion with a party.

I invite my friend Mary Sugru to come with me; she understood I needed a friend in the same position as myself, for she would never celebrate her wedding anniversary either; her husband had also passed away. It was a lovely occasion and it was nice to see my brother Eddie and his wife Honor here to celebrate it together with their family. I got over it, but it was hard. I went with my friend Mary to her house and together we had a good cry.

CHRISTMAS IN MARGERY'S

Caroline and I went to midnight Mass in St. Brigid's church; there was a rich atmosphere of Christmas and our choir added to it. Christmas day and we are on our way to Margery's for a Christmas dinner of turkey and Margery's homemade stuffing. There were lots of good things to eat, including her specialty, the Christmas cake. We complimented her. "It came out well for you," I said. There were plenty of Christmas gifts for Lisa and Rachel from their Aunty Caroline and myself; everyone was excited opening theirs. "Open yours, John," we urged. "What is this?" he asked.

"Leo sent you a Hawaiian, colourful shirt. Will you wear it?"

"Will I wear it? You can bet I will wear it." We had a great day talking about Joey, the baby and of course her dear mother Madeline.

"Will you go to Dublin, Mom, to see her?" Margery asked.

"I will next month. It is lung cancer; poor Madeleine, she liked her cigarette." It was time for home and everyone full of turkey, thanks to Margery and John. We opened our gifts when we got home.

1996 - A SAD JOURNEY TO DUBLIN

As I boarded the train at Ceannt Station, Galway, my thoughts were with Madeleine O'Connell; this lovely warm person, so near to her last days, a friend you might say to everyone, but especially to me. As the train pulls into Heuston Station, I see her husband Pat waiting for me. I am glad to see him. "You are great to come, Peggy, it will give my wife a lift."

"It grieves me, Pat," I say.

"I know; she has had the cough a long time." We arrive at 55 Old Cabra Road, their home. Pat leads me into her bedroom. She is propped up on pillows; as soon as she sees me, she reaches out her arms. We both embrace. I feel the weakness in her once-strong body, we have a cry. Pat comes to the rescue, "Well Peggy, you're not long back from your visit in the States. Tell Madeleine all about the Beggen family and their new addition."

"He is a lovely little boy, quite a bit like his mother Joey."

"I won't ever get to see him," said Madeleine as tears come into her eyes.

"You talk away while I make the tea," says Pat. I told her everything; how good he was and Kristina loving her baby brother; there was nothing said about Joey not being well. After the tea, Pat showed me the little single bed in the corner of her room. "That's where I sleep, but Madeleine would like you to sleep in the room with her tonight."

"Thank you so much," I try to say against the lump in my throat.

"I don't be far away when she needs me."

"He doesn't sleep at all," said the dear lady affectionately. She coughed all night; in the morning she went to sleep from exhaustion. I spent the day with her; she wanted to hear the same story over and over about how the Beggen family were, and I kept her going with good news.

In the evening, I was lonely at the thought of leaving her. Her daughter Mary came to stay with her while Pat took me to the station for the lonely trip back to Galway. I said goodbye to her; even though she was coming to the end of her days, she had a spark of fun in her. "I will surprise you and be at your door someday," she laughed, "don't get a fright."

"I love you, Madeline."

FEBRUARY - ESKER RETREAT

A three-day Retreat was on in the Redemptorist Father's House in Esker, about ten miles out from Galway. Breda Brennan, who was organising a group of Ballybane women to attend a women's prayer weekend, invited me to join the group of about ten women. I thanked Breda for letting me know about it. I said, "It couldn't come at a better time; I will be praying for a dear friend who is very sick."

There were various groups from other parts of the country taking part in this solemn occasion at Esker House. There was Masses, gatherings for prayer, discussions, breaks for coffee and biscuits, walks in the beautiful grounds, and lovely dinners served to us.

On our second day, we were seated to lunch, when a phone call came for me. I wondered what it could be about. I tried to make a joke, "Maybe Poochy is missing me."

My daughter Caroline was trying to tell me the sad news as best she could.

"Go on, Caroline, and tell me."

"Mom, there has been a bad accident down in Clare."

"Who?" I asked.

"It's Cousin Pa Jo Hurley, he was fixing something under his van, and whatever way he had it propped up on stones, it fell on him and killed him."

"Oh, dear God. When did it happen?"

"This morning. Another cousin, Michael Hurley, phoned to tell you."

"Thank you, Caroline. I must leave." Breda put her arm around me as I tried to explain what had happened. One of the priests advised me to wait until the next day as I have had a shock and it would be better not to go driving straight away. I did what the priest said and I left early next morning.

Caroline was waiting for me. "Your brother Eddie wants you to give him a lift to the funeral."

"OK, I will pick him up, but I will be staying the night; do you want to come?"

"No, I have work and I will mind Poochy." I packed a bag with a few things and left to get Eddie. I got a surprise; his wife Honor, and daughter Ann were coming too, I wasn't sure if my old car could take the four of us; it was on its last days.

1996 BROKEN HEARTED FAMILY

After arriving in Six-Mile-Bridge, we went straight to the funeral parlour where we met his broken-hearted mother Anne, his wife Eileen and sons P.J. and Justin, also his two sisters, Sister Margaret and Margie Sheerin. It was a very sad thing to have happened; a 'freak accident' is what they called it. I looked at Pa Jo in his coffin and the memories of when he was a baby came back to me. How I used to love to hold him in my arms when I was a young child myself. I talked to him in my mind, "You were born in the house I was reared in, Pa Jo, only fifty-three years ago."

The parish priest and some neighbours came to his poor mother to give her the sad news. He was her only son. We stayed in cousin John Hurley's house for the night. He made us a nice breakfast of rashers and eggs before we left for the funeral. There was a big attendance for his funeral in St. Finnucane's Church, Six-Mile-Bridge. Pa.Jo was well liked and had a good singing voice; when out on the farm he could be heard belting out a song; he was always a happy lad. After the burial, we went to his mother's house where a dinner was laid on for family members. I said to Eddie, "He will be missed by his mother; he did many jobs for her."

"I know," he said. Some people left to go home. I drove back home to Galway in a daze. Could all of that have happened in such a short space of time?

MADELINE'S LAST FAREWELL

Early in the morning, the phone is ringing. "Who can that be?" I say to Poochy. As I answer it, I get a shock to hear Madeline O'Connell's voice, "Peggy, I am on my way to the hospice and I am walking to the ambulance on my own." I'm stuck for words. I can't answer her. "Goodbye now, Peggy."

"Oh Madeleine, I will pray for you." She hangs up. I go out the back door and walk up and down the path crying my heart out. A week later, Pat, her husband phones me. "Peggy," he says, "We buried Madeleine yesterday; you were the last person she spoke to."

"Thanks, Pat." I hang up the phone. I have no more tears. It's early morning in America, but I make the dreaded phone call. Leo answers. "You know," he says. "I do, Leo, how is Joey?"

"She is good; she wants to talk to you."

"How are you, Joey?"

"I am fine with it now, the short while I was with my Mam when I went home for the two weeks is helping me; I am going to get on with life now, Peggy."

"Good for you," I say as we hung up our phones. I said, "That is what I am going to do too." Madeleine O'Connell was seventy years of age, R.I.P. She was one of the nicest people I ever met.

GRANDDAUGHTER LISA

It's a big day in Roscommon for Irish Girl Guides and Brownies. President Mary Robinson is invited to do the honours of opening their new IGG Centre in Moate. It's a lovely day, and Guides and Brownies with their leaders are neatly togged out in uniform for this momentous occasion. As my granddaughter Lisa's mother was working, and could not be there, I offered to go in her place. A Lady Bird was needed to present the President with a bouquet of flowers. Commissioner Jane Thornbull chooses Lisa Ruffley. I was a very proud granny and Lisa was a proud Lady Bird carrying out this official honour, presenting the President on behalf of the regional IGG with a bouquet of flowers. This occasion has gone down in guiding history (Lady Birds are the youngest section of IGG).

FEBRUARY

It is very cold and I am in the chalet giving it a good clean and making up beds for two lady students, who will be coming to rent it until the summer. I have the heat on, saying to myself, "This will be a cosy home for the two girls." When I finished I locked the door and went up the path to the house, at the same time I was hoping my daughters would have a good fire on in the sitting room going into the kitchen. I could hear them talking as they sat each side of the cosy fire. Their conversation stopped when I walked in. I made a joke, "Were ye talking about me?"

Caroline said, "I have news for you."

"Tell me your news. She was hesitating, "Go on, tell me," I encourage.

"You are going to be a granny again, Mom."

I look at her, "Is it yourself?" I ask.

"It is," she replied.

"It's a surprise, when are you due?"

"Next August."

"You are three months gone, why didn't you tell me sooner Caree?"

"I wanted to make sure first, Mom."

"Have you been to the doctor?"

"I have."

"Well," I said, "I'm glad I kept your big pram and it is still above in the attic." She smiled. "How do you feel? Have you morning sickness?"

"No, I feel good."

After a while, I say, "I could do with some tea; cleaning the chalet has made me hungry; make us some tea Marg, and cut a few slices of currant bread. Would you like some, Caroline?"

"I would love a slice."

"Everything is going to be alright." I gave her a hug. Marg brought in the tray of tea and currant bread; "I was ready for it, Marg," I said, "You are going to be an aunty."

"I know," she answered. We sat and talked about the students that would be moving into the chalet and the preparations that had to be made. Margery then said, "It's time for me to go home, we will be seeing you, thank you for making the tea."

1996 - ART CLASS

I tell Caroline about the art class starting in the Ballybane Resource Centre. "Will we join it? It will shorten the winter months, and we have plenty of paint brushes from your school art class." It was a cold evening we set out for the centre; thankfully it was a short drive and the hall was nice and warm.

After the initial stages of how to treat your canvas, we learned how to mix various colours of paints to get the right colours and consistencies for to use; this took some time. At last we are ready; the art teacher passed out to the class of ten pupils pictures to choose from. Caroline and I chose a sunset, so we started with the basics. We were coming to the end of the two months, I was finally grasping the lesson but it took the two months with many bad strokes across the canvas and needing help. With water colours, it was easy to do. Caroline on the other hand had turned out a masterpiece. She gave a helping hand to beginners. We had a show and tell evening. I was proud of my sunset which I have framed and hanging on my landing.

A WEDDING INVITATION

If it's not new babies and christenings, it is wedding invitations; this one is from my niece Marie Nally. She is getting married to Declan Moran, also in August. I said to Caroline, "That wedding is at the same time as your baby is due."

"Don't let that stop you Mum, you go and enjoy the wedding."

AN UNFORGETTABLE DAY IN AUGUST

I phone my very good friend Maureen O'Neill/Costello who lived in Shannon, County Clare. We have been close friends since 1938 from the day she first stopped at Kilnacree to bring me to school, faithfully taking me by the hand across the bog to Oatfield School and bringing me back home in the evenings. I was a small six-year old toddler. Maureen was five years older than me, and like a big sister. Most

Saturdays, I would stay at her house, two miles over the road in Reinaskomoge, when my Aunt Mary went to Limerick shopping.

As I left Galway to drive to Shannon, I was basking in this beautiful day in August that we had picked for our day out together. When I knocked at her door, she answered with a big happy smile on her face, for this coming together after a long time apart, we hugged each other tight. "What will we do first, Maureen?"

"I would like to visit my Mam and Dad's grave." First, we went to Ballysheen, Six-Mile-Bridge to visit her parents' grave, the next grave to visit was her husband Joe's, and then to visit my Aunt Mary and Uncle Jimmy Hurley's grave. After praying for the dead, we were feeling hungry. Maureen treated me to a lovely lunch in a small neat café in the bridge; before we left we paid a visit to St. Finnucane's church, where we were brought to Mass many a Sunday in the pony and trap.

Now we are on our way to Reinaskomoge to visit Maureen's old home, bringing back the memories of our childhood playing together, reminiscing on how the two of us would ride on her donkey's back around the field; I sitting behind her, holding on tight. "I guess that old donkey is well dead and gone by now, Maureen."

"Indeed he is, Maggie; I cried the day he died; it was the end of an era. My brothers buried him in the far field under a hawthorn bush. Many a time I would go visit his grave and stand and remember how patient he was with the two of us on his back. I would put a bunch of daises on the mould of clay covering him, 'Sleep well,' I would say."

It was seven miles from Six-Mile-Bridge, as I have said before, all uphill. I was getting more excited the nearer we were coming to the old road to take the turn in for Maureen's old home. "It is thirty years since I travelled in this old road to your house Maureen. Do you remember the winters, Maureen, when it would be flooded?"

"I certainly do, and the floods of water coming down the mountain and the rapids every few yards apart, streaming across the road, flowing in under the ditch and disappearing, and we would splash through it in our wellies/ wellingtons."

"The old road hasn't changed."

"No," she said, "and when you see the house, it hasn't changed either. I am so looking forward to this visit."

I stopped the car at the entrance to the yard; the little thatched house was at the bottom of a deep slope. When in my young days, coming to stay on the Saturdays, I would run down and hit the half-door with a bang. Maureen's poor Mother (RIP) would say, "God Bless us all, Maggie, you nearly gave me a heart attack."

There is a change. Maureen's brother Mikey is married and they have a daughter. Today when we arrived, they are in the kitchen. As we enter, Maureen says, "Mikey, do you remember little Maggie Abberton?"

"Indeed I do," he said as he stood up from where he was seated by the open fire. He hugged me tight saying, "You haven't changed, Maggie."

"I'm a lot older, Mikey." It was then my tears began to flow and so did everyone else's. I could picture their Mam and Dad sitting by the fire. Their Dad, Johnny, sported a moustache curled up at each end, and he smoked a pipe. I missed all those things as I looked around.

Philias, Mikey's wife, made the tea and cut and buttered the home-made brown bread; their daughter Ann set the table with the best cups and saucers. "Sit in now and eat and no more of that crying," said Philias. We sat in and many things of the past were brought to mind. One of my many happy memories was the picking of the hurts, a blue fruit that grew along the thick hedges at the side of the road past Maureen's house. Maureen and I would bring an over-flowing bowl of them to her mother, who would wash them and divide them into dishes, then cover them with rich cream; we would devour them. I said to Maureen, "You remember?"

"I do well remember, and do you know them same hurts are now called 'Blueberries' and are flown in from other countries; you could not afford the price the supermarkets sell a little fistful for."

Time was moving on and Maureen stood up, "We will have to leave. Maggie has a long drive ahead of her back to Galway." On the way back to Shannon, we agreed we had the most wonderful day of our lives.

"Maggie, I don't think it will ever happen again."

I agreed, "Not as good as this turn anyway."

Reaching Shannon, Maureen invited me in for the last cup of tea I would have between Shannon and Galway. I thanked her sincerely for showing me the way to her old home, for I would never have found it without her. "I don't go up there very often," she said, "so I was glad of this trip, thanks to you Maggie; my two sons Martin are away working, I don't have a way to get there." I looked at my watch, it was 10 p.m. I'm glad it's a fine summers evening, and won't be dark until after eleven. I will be home by then. We hugged and kissed and shed more tears, "Bye Maureen."

"Bye Maggie." What a lovely day that was. "Why does life have to change?" I ask myself. I was met at the door by a very happy Poochy. "I'm home and glad to see you too." I had a fantastic day, thank God. I was truly glad of meeting Mikey O'Neill, for soon after I heard the poor man passed away (RIP). It was a day I will never forget.

POOCHY'S NOSE

Poochy's nose is knocked out of joint, with this new arrival in her space. I said to Caroline, "I know you like big dogs, but did you have to get an Alsatian? I understand he is a small, cute pup now but overnight he is going to be a big dog, and a lot of work."

"I will look after him, don't you worry."

"There will be a time and you won't be able to," I remarked. Poochy barked and snapped at Levy; while Levy pranced around her thinking she wanted play. As he was fast getting bigger, one day he pranced on top of her. That was when I saw red. Poor Poochy was hurt. "Caroline," I said, "that dog has to go."

"We can put one of them out in the garage."

"Well, it's not going to be Poochy, she was here first." As time went, on this purebreed dog needed injections. Taking him in the car to the vet, I said "He will soon be the full of the car."

"Mom, will you please stop complaining about his size. I have asked Mickey Ward to build a fenced-in-space out in the back where Levy will have plenty of space to run and be safe out of the way."

Before her baby was born, Caroline ordered stakes and wire to have the enclosed space built for Levy. Mickey set to work digging holes and putting down the stakes, and fastened wire to them. Mickey asked us to look at it, "Well," he said, "are you pleased?"

"It is great," said Caroline; "Levy will have plenty of room to run around in it, what do you think, Mom?"

"It's like a corral, Caroline; you could keep a small pony in it."

"He is not going to get that big," she snapped.

"Sorry Caree, it is fine for him."

1997 - ANOTHER LITTLE GRANDDAUGHTER

The months were flying; soon I would be getting another grandchild. It was the twenty-fifth of August and Caroline went into labour. I said, "It is time; we will go to the hospital." Margery came with us and we waited at the Regional Hospital all that Sunday morning, for to be there when the baby was coming into the world. We got so hungry; we decided to go to a nearby café for a meal. On our return to the maternity ward, we met a nurse and asked, "Any news yet?"

"There is, but she wants to tell you herself; go in and see them but don't stay long."

"Well, mother, what did you have?"

"A little girl."

"God Bless her," I said. Margery and I held her for a little, while we kissed and congratulated the new mother. Before we left. Caroline said she would like her baby christened in the hospital. The nurses prepared everything and asked the hospital chaplain/priest, who was very willing to baptise the little baby. We dressed up, and John and Margery Ruffley were her godparents. The priest was very nice and took his time talking to the new mother. She named her baby after herself, "Caroline." Her godparents gave a lovely pushchair as their gift, and Mother Caroline was happy with this surprise, and as it was summer time; she couldn't wait to push her baby out for walks in it.

NIECE MARIE'S WEDDING

On the same day as my niece Marie Nally was marrying Declan Moran, I brought my new family home from the hospital. Margery and I went to the Galway Cathedral to attend their marriage ceremony. It was a lovely day and I said to Margery, "Marie is a beautiful bride."

"She is," agreed Marg.

I explained to my sister Mary I had just become a granny again. "The birth of Caroline's baby daughter has clashed with your daughter's wedding." When we came home, mother and daughter were cuddled up in my double bed. There appeared to have been trouble in the kitchen; Levy was lying down and looking very guilty, little Poochy was, lo and behold, out in the garage. "Oh dear, you are coming to the kitchen and that Levy is going out into his 'Corral'."

There was a great welcome home for Caroline and her baby. Many of our neighbours came with gifts and sat chatting and wanting to hold the baby. I was like a servant girl serving up teas and cake, but I was not complaining. It was so wonderful. I was in disbelief as to how the beliefs of Ireland and the Catholic Church has changed. I thought back to the years when unmarried mothers gave birth to a baby, and immediately the little baby would be taken from the poor mother who would be left grieving for the rest of her life. The very thought of it sent shivers up my back.

1998 - THE BIG PRAM

Baby Caroline is coming up to one year old and her Mammy has gone back to work. The weather is beautiful. I find it hard wheeling the pushchair and anyway the baby would be facing away from me; I prefer to be able to see the baby. On such a beautiful day, I am itching to take the big pram down from the attic. Well, here goes; I gave into temptation and very soon the pram was like new again, after I gave it a good clean up, then I strapped baby into it. Her mother won't approve, she had already told me to leave it in the attic.

I placed Poochy at the foot of it and Levy on a lead, then off we went out the new by-pass. It was great, baby is sitting up high and looking all around her. When mother came home the pram was in the kitchen and baby was up in her cot asleep. My daughter looked at the pram, then at me. "You didn't take my baby out in that thing, did you?"

"If it was good enough for her mother, it's good enough for her daughter. She loved it, Caree; she was sitting up and viewing the world around her. I can't wheel the pushchair, anyway all the babies can see in them things that are so low to the ground, are cars, and the dust from the road flying in on them."

"Have it your own way, Mom, I won't be taking her out in it."

FEELING SORRY

I felt sorry for Caroline. Levy was getting sick a lot and today we must take him once more to the vet. "Well, what had the vet to say this time, Caree?"

"He said pedigree dogs like Levy are prone to disease; their own system produces it."

"What will you do?"

"He is costing me a lot and the vet thinks this could continue, when it happens again he will put him down for me."

"Oh! Dear, poor Levy, it will be better than looking at him so sick."

When the day came, I waited outside the vet's surgery talking to baby Caroline. "He was a very big dog, your Mammy loved him but it is best this way. Caroline came running out of the vets, come on Mom, drive; I want to get away from here quick. Is the vet going to dispose of him for you?"

"He is keeping the body for research."

In a matter of days Caroline had the fence taken down and sold to a local farmer. "I am so sorry for your loss."

"It's fine, I have the baby to fill my time."

"Good for you, Caree," I agreed.

1997 - THEIR OWN PLACE

"I have found a nice house close-by; I will be moving into it soon."

"You don't need to do that, Caree. There is plenty of room here for all of us."

"I would like a place just for me and the baby. You will need your own space, and I hope you and Larry have a nice time together, I'm sure the dancing will take over. I will drop the baby into you on my way to work each morning."

"That will be fine, Caroline."

"I need you to help me move my stuff into the house this weekend then you will see what it's like."

"I'm glad you are so near to us, Caree. And by the way, Larry has a variety of hobbies."

"I can see that Mom, do you mind?"

"Well, I did think he would be around a bit more."

1997 - AN ACCIDENT

One morning, I get a phone call from my friend Elsie O'Dea who lives near Caroline. "Now, don't get frightened," she says. Her next words were, "Baby Caroline has had an accident; it was just a fall down the stairs."

"Oh; dear God, is she badly hurt?"

"Her little leg might need attention; they are here at my house."

"Thank you, Elsie, I will be there in two minutes." As I arrive, there was an upset baby but a more upset mother. "I think there's a bone broke, I heard a crack as she hit the last step," said her mammy in tears.

At the hospital, an X-ray showed a bone in her thigh was damaged. The little dear was put into a cot and her leg was strapped up high; she was roaring with pain. The doctor advised against giving her a painkiller for twenty-four hours in case the baby would go into shock. Her mammy spent the night with her listening to her scream. Margery came and stayed for a while, but Caree told us both to go home, as she would be staying to give sips of water to the baby.

It was a relief in the morning when the doctor gave the injection to ease the pain; after a while the little one relaxed and went to sleep. It was a relief to everyone. I said to a very tired mother, "Go home to bed, I will stay for the day with the little patient."

She was a good patient. We were finally allowed to bring her home. She was left in the hospital cot with her leg in a plastercast and tied up to a hook attached to a bar, then attached to the cot and wheeled into the ambulance to bring her home to "Rock Dale". We would keep her in the kitchen during the day; she could watch her favourite TV programs, and her mother would wheel her into the sitting room for the night. It was more convenient for them to move back to my house again. Caroline's leg was strapped up for six weeks. She pulled and shook the leg so hard, we were afraid she would damage it worse. She was a great little patient.

The plaster cast on the little leg caused an itch which was making her cry.

At her next check-up, her mam told a nurse about the itch, the nurse gave her a large jar of Vaseline. "Coat the leg as far as you can reach inside the plaster, then with a knitting needle, gently rub it up and down, it should help ease the itch." She did that and it gave comfort.

The day of removing the plastercast has arrived; the doctor explained to her mother that it would take some time before the little one would be able to walk on the leg again; Caroline said she would put her into her playpen until she had the courage to put her weight on it. "It is going to take time, Caroline."

"I know it will," said her mam. First day home and she is placed in her playpen. Caroline has the ironing board set up, near the playpen. Talking to her baby, she says, "I'm going to do some ironing, so be a good girl for mammy." While she is busy ironing, she thought she felt Poochy sniffing around her legs. She bent down to look and there was her daughter standing, holding on to her mam's skirt. She had climbed out over the playpen and walked the few steps to her mom. We were both speechless. Picking her up, her mammy was in a worried state.

"Mom, do you think she has damaged her leg? Phone the hospital and find out if you can take her in now for them to look at it."

We were allowed to go straight to the hospital. Rushing to Merlin Park, we had only the one thought on our minds; "Did she damage her leg climbing over the playpen?"

When baby Caroline saw where we were going, she roared crying. The leg was X-rayed straight away. We waited and got good news; there was no damage done to the leg. We came home smiling. Her next appointment was in six months' time.

1998 – FEBRUARY, THE PASSING

The passing has ocurred of our dear Aunt Margie/Margaret Hurley/Callaghan, in Kachina Point Nursing Home, Sedona, Arizona, USA. She is survived by her daughter, Maureen Tully, son-in-law Joe, three granddaughters and great grandchildren. She is the last of the seven Hurley siblings to pass away. I am heartbroken, for I know I won't ever see her again. My visits to the States will be empty not to see her or hear her voice. She was a jolly, happy, welcoming person. I phone Maureen to ask if her mother had an easy passing. She said, "She went quietly in her sleep and Peggy I know you will be happy to hear, I was with her to the last."

"It was hard on you, Maureen, you being her only child."

"It wasn't too bad, I came home after and cried on Joe's shoulder. She was cremated, Peggy. How are you with that?"

"I don't know; she must be the first member of our family to be cremated."

"I will tell you my reason; she wanted to be buried with her husband Daniel/Dan, my Dad. It would be very expensive to have a casket flown to N.Y., then to rent a hearse to bring it to Dad's grave in St. Raymond's in the Bronx, N.Y. There would be the opening of the grave; I could not afford the cost of it all; this way I will carry her ashes in the urn the next time I visit my daughters in L.I. We will drive to the grave and place it into Dad's grave, and I know they will be both happy again."

"Thank you, Maureen, I am happy now too. God Bless you."

1998 - FIRST COMMUNION

My first grandaughter, Lisa Marie Ruffley, would be making her First Holy Communion very soon. Her mother Margery was fussing about getting the perfect dress suitable for her petite daughter. On one of my trips to County Down, it was uppermost in my mind to be on the look-out for a Communion dress. At last I saw one. I phoned her mother. After getting Lisa's measurements, I bought the dress; I was sure it would be perfect.

I was very excited when I got home, taking the dress out of the bag, I placed it on a hanger and hung it in the kitchen for everyone to see. I phoned my daughter telling her I was home and had the dress. "We will be up straight away," she gushed. The dress was facing them as they came in the door; as soon as Margery saw it, the first thing she said was, "It's gorgeouse , Mam."

Lisa slipped into it as if the dress was made for her; she just loved it and rewarded Granny with a big kiss. "Well, Lisa, you are all set to receive Our Lord."

"Almost," she answered.

"First Holy Communion day is such a big day, not just for the First Communion children, but the family too."

Lisa looked a picture in her pretty dress and veil over her pretty dark hair, joining her hands so angel-like at the altar rails to receive Our Lord. Her parents were very proud of her, especially her mam. Then, home to where her mammy had a lovely dinner prepared. As Lisa sat to the table, she was the happiest First Communion girl of all.

THE DEATH OF OUR COUSIN

Our first cousin Tess/Teresa Hurley Higgins died aged 58. Tess, as she was known, lived in Parteen, County Clare, with her husband Terry and family. Tess was the first of our first cousins to break the link. She was a lovely, gentle lady. When I heard she was ill, I called to see her; she was at home and preparing the dinner and also made tea for me. I thought she looked well, although a bit thin. Shortly after my visit, Tess passed away; she is sadly missed by her husband, children, and her sisters and brothers, her cousins and indeed, all who knew her. I was glad I had the opportunity to have tea with her, and attend her large funeral. RIP Tess.

1998 - IN TODAY'S IRELAND

There are many changes, and for us who are unacquainted with some of these changes, it's an education when we come face to face with some issues unexpectedly, which we know happen, but believe it won't come to our family. I was brought to my senses when my daughter Margery came to tell me that herself and her husband John had decided it was best for them to separate. "Why?" I ask.

"Don't you get upset, Mom. It's a big decision to make and a trying time for everyone, it is best for the children too."

"Have you both talked about this?"

"We have decided to part amicably."

"It's sudden, isn't it?"

"Not really, Mom." I try not to cry. I make some tea; we sit quietly for a while. "The children, Marg?"

"Yes, they will be with me during the week and their dad at weekends and during holiday time, so they won't miss out on either of us. I'm very sorry Mom, to bring you this news."

I hug her tightly, "God guide you both, I say." As she is leaving, I remind her to call me any time she feels she needs me. "I will, Mom," she says.

I think about the many people here in Ireland I know that have separated; it would not be allowed years past. And I guess that was not a good thing, either.

1998 - I AM ECSTATIC

I am ecstatic, for I receive an invitation from the crowned Miss Ireland, Vivien Doyle, a stunning twenty-one year old blonde-haired girl, a native of Ballybane, who had beaten sixteen other contestants from various other counties to represent Ireland in the Miss World Competiton. She had been a past Brownie/ Girl Guide in the Ballybane IGG company. She was a diligent worker in each of the groups and got involved in all activities. But true to her teachings, she didn't forget her past childhood days in Guiding and invited me as her Girl Guide Captain to City Hall, Galway as a guest. Mayor Angela Lupton was presenting Vivien with gifts and compliments on her successful win as Miss Ireland, and wishing her the best of luck when representing her country in the Miss World competition in Seychelles. This occasion was a great honour for me.

1999 - IT IS FIRST COMMUNION DAY

Rachel looked so pretty in her full-length Communion dress trimmed with lace and a floral crown decorating her long, thick brown hair, reminding me of how much she is like her mother. I was happy to see both her parents at the church for their daughters' special day, having compromised with each other in taking their daughter for a treat. Her many Ruffley relations were giving her the first Communion money, it made a good day for her. At home, her Mam prepared a special dinner of roast chicken, potatoes and vegetables. Sitting into the table, Rachel joined us and told us about her big day. I was glad the day went so well. I keep praying for the parents.

JOINING THE RENMORE ACTIVE RETIREMENT

I joined the Renmore Active Retirement Association (RARA). It was a good idea for me; on my first day, I found it had a great buzz; there appeared to be forty exciting things happening all at once. A diary of activities was listed out. Guest speakers, table quizzes, Easter bonnet competitions, and in some cases spot prizes. Also, a walker's group. Joe McCarty was lining up a singing group for some act or other; the list was endless. I knew I was going to enjoy this club; there was great camaraderie among the people. I had joined up a few months before their Annual General Meeting (AGM). I accepted the proposal to go on the committee and this kept me busy; I learned how to organise events. I took part in the training for gentle exercise with my long-time friend Bernie Higgins. A Halloween party was suggested by the chairperson, Ethna O'Toole, and the plans were set in motion; the committee encouraged members to participate by coming in fancy-dress for Halloween. There would be prizes for the scariest. I had created a one-woman show some years before. I often acted it out for club's entertainment. It was called 'A Cameo of a Farmer's Daughter'. I decided to give the RARA members a laugh. As I recited the different parts of the girl's life and her dreams of what she wished for, I would remove a layer of clothes depicting that wish. The one depicting a nun was the favourite, for I looked like a Reverend Mother; the group enjoyed it and laughed a lot at my performance.

2000 - ELECTED CHAIRPERSON

Getting elected Chairperson of the RARA was something I did not anticipate, even though I put my name down for it. This was a big club. I was sure there would be plenty of names to select from. I was proposed and seconded and applauded. I protested, but to no avail. I agreed to take it on for a year, even though it was a three-year commitment. With everyone's help, I got to enjoy the job. The year went fast, and I wasn't sure now about stepping down. Joe McCarty was vice-chairman, he encouraged me to stay on, so I agreed.

ZIMBABWE

I read in a magazine that women in Zimbabwe were losing their eyesight at a very young age from picking sea shells along the beaches. As the bread winners, it was their job to go out on the beaches each day to pick shells to sell. The intense whiteness of the sand/stones was blinding these poor women. This meant they would have to give up this essential job. The request in the magazine was for discarded eyeglasses.

I immediately put it to the floor for people to bring in the eyeglasses they no longer used, for this worthy cause, with or without the cases. A week after this request, the members brought in two and three pairs, and sometimes more; they were glad to know the glasses were going to be put to such good use. Very soon I had over 500 pairs to pack into two cardboard boxes.

I wrapped the boxes in brown paper and wrote the contents and the Zimbabwe address which I had copied from the magazine. They were quite heavy. As it was for charity, I was told there was no cost needed for posting. I went into the G.P.O in Galway. They were weighed and I was told I would have to pay the postage which was a lot; I brought them home again disappointed. On a trip up the north, first thing I did was take the two boxes to the nearest post office in Newry, County Down. They were weighed and left to be sent away without charge; I was so thankful.

I didn't collect any more used eyeglasses; I was glad to hear Specsavers were doing it. I was very pleased with that charitable effort, thanks to the generosity of Renmore Active Retirement Assocation, Galway.

MEETING COLM

Margery's new man was a tall young fellow; I took to him straight away, but I couldn't resist saying the following: "It didn't take you long, Margery. I hope all goes good for you and the girls."

"There is something else," we are going to have a baby."

I'm staggered, of course. I say, "You're not."

"I know you don't believe me, but we are."

"Aren't you rushing things a bit?" I ask. Then in the heat of the moment, I vent on saying a bit too much. I have upset her; they leave. What am I to think? I thought I gave her the same teaching I got myself. "Dear God, may all go well for them," I repeat the prayer. I know, I know times are different now. It's their life, I can't live it for them, I must look after myself. To thine own-self be true. Still, how do you connect the way we were brought up and today's way of thinking? Maybe now she won't talk to me. We meet in the town and it's as if nothing happened, so I make a vow I will keep my thoughts to myself in future. "When is the baby due?" I ask.

"April," she replied.

"You will let me know when you are in hospital."

"Colm will call you." We part friends.

I phone my son Mike in the States and I tell him about Margery and John's marriage break-up, and how they both have new partners, and that I am to be a grandmother soon. Mike tells me to slow down, "It is all very sudden for me too," he says. Mike asks,

"Have you met her new man?"

"I have and he seems a nice fellow."

"Don't worry, Mom, everything will be fine."

"Thank you, Mike."

"Do you see Margery's two daughters, Mom?"

"I do; I pick them up from school most days and bring them home for their dinner. They are often with their Aunty Caroline and play with her daughter. They are fine, Mike. Lisa is very smart and Rachel is a great Irish speaker. I was at an Irish play, which they were both took part in, in the Taibhhearc (that is an Irish Theatre), they were a credit; the way the Irish flowed fluent with them. Margery knew I would enjoy their performance. They are attending an all-Irish speaking school, Gaelscoil Dara, Renmore.

MY SON MIKE

My son Mike has some good news for me. He phones to tell me their son Michael has graduated from Farmingdale High School and will be attending Nassau Community College; he will be studying to be a high school teacher. "My other good news, Mom, is that he has qualified with a four-year scholarship from the Ancient Order of Hibernians (AOH), Division Fifteen, Massapequa Park." I am enclosing a picture of him with the board of directors receiving the scholarship from the President, Richard Ryan.

"Now, Mom what do you think of your grandson?"

I can barely answer with the excitement of such an honour to my grandson.

"You and Mary must be bursting with pride."

"We sure are, Mom."

"Thanks for that good news, Mike; I will be telling Margery and Caroline." Michael's first school was Sun Valley. Apart from his usual studies, he played football and learned how to play the electric guitar. He was a very dedicated student and he went on to graduate from Columbia University, New York with a Master's degree in education. He continued with his teaching career. Michael attended a six-month course studying the language of Arabic in Egypt; on his return, he went back to teaching the subject of history in high school.

In time, my ambitious grandson discovered he had other talents. He moved to Raleigh, North Carolina, and turned his hand to opening a business there with his friend, Richard Conroy. Their business was a success from the start, selling Italian flavoured ices/sorbet. It is titled "Sweet Water Ices." It is a much appreciated cool-downer in the hot climate of N.C. Their trade mark is two bicycles with little carts attached, plus two large pink brollies.

On their business stand, Michael can be seen standing beteen one of the bicylecart and their brand new delivery van, in downtown Raleigh.. When the colder weather sets in, and cold ices lose popularity, Michael returns to his teaching.

RENMORE ACTIVE RETIREMENT

Going to the club and chatting with the members is good for everyone. As chairman, I opened the morning session with the usual welcome. "We have a speaker on gardening this morning, advising us what to plant in our gardens now as its spring time." I appreciated the information, having a big garden like mine and plenty of ground to till. The most suitable vegetables and flowers to plant were described and informative leaflets past around. I was in a hurry to get home and down to gardening.

Gardening was a therapy I enjoyed; digging and preparing a couple of short drills for potatoes, cabbage and onions. I called on Mattie Walsh for farmyard manure, his son Richard brought me the usual load and I gave him the usual few euros. I was complimenting myself in succeeding and following my late husband's guidelines. Looking up towards the heavens, I whisper, "Paddy if you were down here, you would be proud of me."

MORE ACTIVITIES

There were more activities for the actively retired to get involved in. The club had a visit from Ms. Mary Sural, who had come from UCG with a plan for older people to become involved with younger people. She had in mind students in their transition year (TY) in secondary school and asked for some of the Renmore ARA members to get involved with the Presentation Convent students, to take part in sessions such as storytelling, old time songs and more modern ones to swap around, and even to create a play. Mary took some names and I signed up too.

This was a new adventure. We would meet each Friday in the Presantaintion Convent Hall. An exciting time getting to know the girls; some were from other countries. I made friends with a Nigerian student. She told me she loved Ireland because the people were very friendly. Each year as classes moved on, we would befriend another group; it would take time for the youth to bond with us older people but eventually we would come together. Short plays would be produced with many laughs. I was involved for at least three terms each year getting to know more new faces.

The play that remains with me is the one about meeting American visitors arriving off the boat for the Christmas holidays. Props were required. I loaned my old brown suitcase, which I bought when I was immigrating in 1952 to the USA, to a student. She was meant to be my sister and as she was coming home, I would meet her off the boat. We did a great bit of acting, she putting on the American accent and I hugging her with a big welcome home and then helping her to carry her heavy case. There were many short acts performed, songs were sung and music played. This particular play was performed in the Taibhdhearc, the national Irish theatre, Middle Street, Galway. I am so proud to tell my friends that I sang two verses of the *Isle of Innisfree* on the stage of the Taibhdhearc, where greats like Siobhan McKenna and Mick Nally put on great plays. I had an inner feeling of greatness that night.

End of the year, we are parting and saying goodbye with a party and discussing what we had achieved. I eventually had to tell Mary I wouldn't be back next term. She appreciated the amount of time I gave. We said our goodbyes and I told her I enjoyed my time with the young students. One day I met a friend, and she asked me if I had seen the magazine 'Galway Now'.

I said, "No."

"You should buy it," she said. I thanked her, and when I looked through it, there was a big picture of me in my acting costume and my name under the picture; I was gobsmacked.

ANTICIPATING COLM'S PHONE CALL

I was almost afraid to answer the phone. "What's the news, Colm?"

He tells me, "I have a son." He was unable to hold back the excitement in his voice.

"God bless him," I said, "and how are they?"

"They are both fine."

"I'm glad to hear that; congratulations on being a daddy, Colm; I will see them this evening. Do the girls know they have a brother?"

"They do, I brought them to see him this morning."

I was overjoyed to see my new grandson. I knew by the look on Margery's face that she was pleased and relaxed now that they had a little son. I said Marg, "He looks like his dad." she agreed. I was thankful to God they were all well.

KALLUM'S CHRISTENING

This was a joyful time for Colm; having a son fulfilled his dreams. It was a happy occasion for both the Dowling and Fahy families. Kallum was christened by Fr. Willie Commins in Mervue Church; his godparents were Valerie and Gerry Conneely. We celebrated with a lovely meal in the parents' house.

2001 - POOCHY GONE TO DOGGIE LAND

My poor little dog is not well for over a week; she is fifteen and a half years old. The vet shakes his head; he tells me he could give her an injection to carry her on for maybe another week, but that she would be as bad as ever again.

"What are you telling me? Is her time up?"

"I'm afraid yes." I start to cry.

"She is over fifteen years of age. That's over 105 in man years, what do you expect?"

"Put her to sleep so, I will wait in the car." As people were going in to the vets, I hide my face; they will think I'm cracked crying over a dog, but no, she was a big part of the family. The nurse brings her little body out wrapped in a pure white tablecloth, gently placed in a box; it was so sensitive of the kind nurse. We buried her at the back of the chalet where we had already interred a pet rabbit and a cat. Poochy had won many trophies and rosettes at many Agricultural Shows for her elegant strut around the rings; she was also a winner in the Ballybane fancy dress dog show. "You are missed Poochy, no dog will replace you."

SAD NEWS IN BALLINROBE

My son Mike phones to let me know that Marys Pop/father has passed away in his home in Ballinrobe. "He was sick a long time, Mom."

"May he rest in peace Mike, how is Mrs Moran?"

"She is sad; she will be lonely now that Paddy is gone; they were together a long time." I went to the wake. Patrick/Paddy Moran was very thin, but at the same time he looked peaceful. After the funeral, I sat in the church with his wife Jane. For a long time, she was silent, then she said, "Margaret, you have been down this road twice."

"I have," I said. "When Mike and Leo's Dad died, I was only twenty-eight; it was tough going." We knelt down and said a few prayers together.

"I would like for you to come and visit me, Margaret."

"I will, Jane," I promise.

A TALENTED LADY

The news of the passing of Patricia/Pat Folan was hard to digest; she was such a talented lady. Pat had her finger in every pie in the Parish of St Bridget's. From the choir, of which she was a founder member, secretary of the Ballybane building fund, and also an experienced musician with St. Patrick's Brass Band. With her husband Martin, they ran successfully their local grocery shop while rearing their five children.

Her profession was nursing in the Regional Hospital, Galway. She was at everyone's beck and call. I was sorry when she moved from living next door to me. Her new home was a mile up the road; not far, but being used to her next door, it might as well be five miles away. Of course, we met twice a week for choir. We would also meet at the monthly meetings in the Ballybane

Resource Centre for community business. She was secretary and I was recording secretary, and as the population was growing more activities had to be proposed and sounded out for the area. The time came when Pat fell sick; prayers were offered and many Masses said for this wonderful leader of the Ballybane parish. Her illness rapidly took over. It was a sad privilege I had spending a night in Galway Hospice with my dear friend who passed away at the young age of fifty-two; what a loss to many, especially her family.

OUR WEEK ENJOYING THE RACES

My son Mike was having a wish fulfilled to attend the Galway Races; he hadn't been to them in about fourteen years, not since he and his family went back to live in America. He has let me know he is coming this year and I am overjoyed. His wife Mary and Cassandra will stay that week in Ballinrobe with Granny Moran. Mike and my grandson Gary who is fourteen, will be with me.

The weather is beautiful for the racing festival and Ladies Day; I tell Mike I will be wearing my hat. "I don't care about hats," he says, "I will be backing horses." The usual rush was on to be down the Racecourse for the first race, putting me in mind of when he lived here, and himself and his stepfather, Paddy, would be rushing to be there to back the favourite to win in the first race, "as they hoped." Having race cards and the newspaper, Mike was finding it difficult to see the horse's names. "Promise me Mike, when you go back home, the first thing you will do is get your eyes tested."

"I will; I know I need glasses."

We went five days and Mike had a few wins that kept him happy, and bringing his son Gary to the Galway Races was another plus. They had lots to tell Mary and Cassandra when they came to bring them to Ballinrobe for a few days, before flying back to N.Y. and then meeting up with their son Michael, who had a job and didn't come to Ireland this time. Looking at my granddaughter Cassandra, I could not believe how tall she had grown, and only nine years old. "She is going to be tall, Mary."

"I know she says, not like me, barely five foot." I was sad to see them leave. We had a fantastic time together. We hugged and kissed. "Call me when ye are back in L.I." They answered with their usual promise, "We will Mom," as they drove away.

2001 - AN AUGUST I WON'T EVER FORGET

Mike and his family are only a few days home in Long Island, when Mike phones me with news I was not indeed expecting. "I had my eyes tested."

"Yes," I say, "are you in need of glasses?" I ask.

"I don't have good news, Mom."

"Why Mike, what is it?"

"I have a brain tumour, Mom." It didn't register with me for a while, I stammered, "What is going to be done, Mike?"

"Emergency surgery tomorrow morning."

"Oh, my son; will I go over?"

"No Mom, don't do anything until you hear from Mary." We put down our phones. I am so stunned. One week we are having a great time together at the Galway Races, the next week we are facing uncertainty. I try to cry, but it won't happen, neither will my efforts to pray. Caroline comes in from work. I am so glad she is here with me. I tell her the bad news about her brother; she cries. Now I must tell Margery; I go to her house. It is so hard to be telling such news to his siblings. She asks through her tears, "Have you told Leo, Mom?"

"Not yet, I don't know how I'm going to. I will call him the weekend. We must have a Mass said."

"We will," she says, "the more Masses the better.

Phoning Leo is so hard to do. They were not at home. I leave the message on his answering machine. I put down the phone, then I think maybe I shouldn't have done that. In the morning Joey phones me, "We got your news, Peggy. Leo didn't go to bed at all; he sat on a chair all night. He phoned Mary before he went to work, they were just leaving for the hospital."

"Oh Joey, I am so sorry for leaving that news on the answering machine."

"It's alright Peggy, you are in shock. I am taking the kids to school and I will go into Mass and ask the priest to remember Mike in the Mass, we just have to put our trust in God."

I phone my sister Mary but she is away. So I tell my sad news to her husband Jimmy Nally, he is speechless. "I'll tell her when she gets back Margaret," he says. I know he is upset. Soon, my brothers Eddie and Paddy and their wives Honor and Theresa call to to console me. They will pray for him; all the prayers are needed now. It was a few days before my sister came to visit me, after our hugs she asks, "Any word yet?"

"No Mary," I tell her, "and there is no one in their house, the children must be staying with neighbours. Cassandra is only nine years old, Gary fourteen and Michael is nineteen and attending University, they are so young. Their poor mother is working in Aer Lingus." I'm getting no news; I don't know how Mike is. I pick up the phone to call his brother Leo, but the phone keeps ringing and the answering machine comes on. I leave a message, "Will you please call me Leo." I put down the phone. Sometime later, I was walking out the hall when tightness came in my chest; I never witnessed so frightening a sensation before. I was near the sitting room; I walked in and lay down on the couch for a few hours until I felt better. I get up and went to the kitchen to make a pot of tea. I kept telling myself, "The tightness is gone, thank God."

SON LEO PHONES

He is in Mike's house with the three children. "I just have a chance to talk while they are watching some program; the news is that Mary wasn't allowed to see Mike for about four days; it was hard on her each day going to the hospital." She phoned me today saying she finally got five minutes with him and to let you know, he gave her hand a squeeze. "It was about a twelve-hour operation; the tumour is growing through an artery in behind his right eye that is the reason he was losing his sight."

"How are the children, Leo?"

"They are coping; they have to go to school, and their Mam talks to them on the phone. I am staying the weekend with them, their friends come to play games and talk with them. Their mother is hoping to be home with them soon, and she will phone you then."

"Thank you, son. God is good, Mike will be alright."

SURPRISE VISITOR

It is a beautiful sunny Sunday. I am sitting in the kitchen looking out the window at the horses grazing in the next field. I say to myself, "I'm going to go for a walk." Just then, the doorbell rings. As I open it, I stand and gaze in surprise. "Yes, it is me, Maggie." P.J. Hurley, my young cousin, has come from County Clare.

"Come in," I say at the same time hugging and telling him how welcome he is. "What a lovely surprise, P.J."

"Sit down, while I make the tea." He agreed he could do with a cup. We sat having tea and cake and shared gossip. I told him about the ballroom dancing competition in the Corrib Great Southern Hotel in aid of cancer. I asked him to come with me.

"I will," he agreed, "but I'm not much of a dancer."

"Don't worry about that P.J., we can sit and watch the competitors. He enjoyed it, saying, "Now I will have to take lessons in dancing."

P.J., a talented young tenor was studying singing and music with Olive Cowpar in Limerick. I said, "At present, you have plenty on hand." We spent a wonderful day together.

Back at my house, while I made the dinner, he sang 'Danny Boy' for me. It was a treat I have treasured ever since. I kept from telling him about my son Mike's brain tumour until the last minute.

"I have news P.J. that is not so good, I don't want to spoil your day."

"Share it with me, Maggie." Telling him about this sadness in our family was not easy. He was quiet for a while, then in his strong Clare accent he said,

"We don't know what to expect from one day to the next, but we have to face into it."

"Thanks P.J. That's a great Clare saying and that's what we have to do, like you had to do when as a very young boy you were witness to seeing your poor dad killed when the van fell on him outside your kitchen window. Maybe I shouldn't be reminding you of that tragedy, but I stand in admiration of your courage to be making something of that beautiful voice you have. Your dad, Pa Jo, would be so proud of you."

We had another cup of tea but, as he said himself,

"I have to hit the road."

"Did you enjoy the day?"

"I did, Maggie. I will remember Mike in prayer." I was very lonely to see him leave. In time, I attended some of his concerts in Limerick. He came to Galway where I had the priviledge of meeting him again and hearing him sing in St. Nicholas' Collegiate Church, Market Street, Galway City.

Another occasion in Clarinbridge he took part in a musical in aid of the Christian Brothers Charity, and he also sang in the St. Augustine's Church, Middle Street, Galway. He now lives in Germany, and it's a long time since I heard his beautiful voice. I think back to the day he surprised me and I had him all to myself for a short while.

2001 - MY PRAYERFUL THOUGHTS

I think of Mike's father (R.I.P.) and ask God not to send my daughter-in-law Mary the heavy cross he sent to me. "Please leave her husband and the father of their children with them" (My prayer has been answered so far for as I write; it is 2017, sixteen years hence). At last the phone call I have really been waiting for, "Mary, my love, how are you?"

Mary, always upbeat, says, "I'm well; well, you know how it is. I would need a holiday, but I can't think of things like that; I have to take all the work I can get for soon the bills will start coming in. I took the children to visit their dad in Stonybrook hospital; it was a short visit. He spoke to each of them by name, so his memory is not affected, but he will be a long time in recovery and then he will have to attend rehabilitation. He has a little vision in one eye, but he won't be able to drive a car; he has given up his accountancy job."

"How about Michael's college fees?"

"His scholarships are covering them."

"When can I go over, Mary, to see Mike?"

She says, "It's better to wait until he is home; I will let you know."

"Thanks Mary, we will keep praying."

2001 - THE SADDEST SEPTEMBER

The weather is beautiful, and the Renmore ARA is on a break in Achill Island. We are out soaking up the beautiful sun. I hear someone calling me; it is Maureen McCarty. "Bad news," she says.

"What?" I ask.

"The Twin Towers are gone."

"What do you mean?" I ask. Her husband Joe says they have been attacked and razed to the ground. We hurry to the hotel we are staying in. The awful news is shown on TV. It is true. "Oh, God help us."

At least three U.S. planes were hijacked and headed straight into the Twin Towers, destroying the buildings. It's hard to see what is happening with the massive clouds of dust. President Bush orders a shutdown of New York; the Trade Centre in Lower Manhattan is under terrorist attack. An attempted attack on our nation. My son Leo works in Manhattan; there is no way I can contact any of my family in N.Y. The buildings tumbled down, killing and injuring hundreds of firemen. I pray my cousin's husband who is a fireman, is safe.

Next day, our holiday in Achill Island is over and we go home. There is no Poochy to welcome me. My first concern is to phone family members in N.Y. but the phone lines are still shut down. "Please God, let Leo be safe."

It's four in the morning and the ringing of the phone wakes me up. I hurry to answer it, hoping it is Leo; and it is. "Hi, Mother."

"Oh, son, I was so worried."

"I know, Mom, and so was Joey, the store where I work was in lockdown, no one could contact their families. We are not allowed to drive our cars for another while. I had to come home by subway. I was so happy to see Joey and the two children."

"Thank God you are safe, Leo. I'm sure you are tired."

"I'm in need of a good bath and a meal; I'll talk to you later."

"Have a good sleep, Leo." I join my hands and talk to the picture of the Sacred Heart. "Thanks," I say, "a thousand times thanks."

I phone my son Mick, it is good news, for he is at home, and Mary gives him the phone so we have a short talk. He is saddened over what has happened in N.Y. "I will be over to see you in a week's time."

"Can't wait, Mother."

"Me either, Mike."

One more phone call to make. My cousin Maureen; I pray her son-in-law is safe. She answers her phone. "It is good to hear from you, Peggy," she says, but there is a tone of sadness in her voice.

"Is Joe safe?" I ask.

"No Peggy, he was one of the 350 firefighters that died."

"Your poor daughter," I said. Kathy has her two children, Joseph, aged nine, and Megan, aged seven, who is getting ready to make her first Communion next year. Joe was looking forward to that big day. Tall, dark and handsome, loud, boisterous Joe, he was only forty-five years of age and over six foot tall. Joe's parents were from Cavan. Joe was the hatchet man with Ladder Company Three, Manhattan, N.Y., who used to sit on the back of the fire lorry, ready to jump off to break windows with the hatchet, to save a life from flames.

"Peggy, many is the life he saved."

I will never forget Tuesday the 11th of September 2001.

"How is your son, Peggy?"

"He is home from hospital, and I am going over to see him in a week's time." "Thank God you still have him."

"I do, Maureen. I will call you when I am in L.I. Bye for now."

IT'S MY FIRST VISIT

It is my first visit to see Mike after his major brain surgery. It is a very sad year, but I am thanking God I have my son Michael/Mike. I am looking forward to seeing him. As the plane lands at Kennedy airport, the amount of security to be seen there was scary. Our bags are searched thoroughly, going through the scanner twice. I am OK. I leave the airport and take a taxi to Massapequa Park. The driver and I don't have conversation. I pay him, then get my bag and go up the steps to Mike's front door. I wonder how things are inside.

Mary opens the door, she looks a bit stressed but is in good form. I am told to keep my voice down for any little noise hurts Mike's head. Mike is all smiles to see me but his head hurts. I look at him; I don't see a mark.

"Where did they open your head, Mike?"

"They didn't; they went up between my gum and lip."

I know I must not ask too many questions; while I'm having some tea, Mike sits next to me. He tells me the tumour is growing through an artery and while they were trying to get the root he says, "I started to haemorrhage and suffered four strokes on the table. As you can see, I don't have much power in my left arm or my left leg, but it is coming back, Mom. That was the reason Mary was not allowed into see me for four days, I was like a time bomb ready to go off." He gives a low laugh.

I go to the bathroom to cry. Mary takes my hand. She says he is trying to handle it, but his head hurts; the least little sound hurts. I pull myself together; it is so easy to cry. The two youngest children come home from school and they talk to their dad, and tiptoe down to the den to start their homework. Mike just stays sitting and tries to keep his head steady. Mary and I talk to him. We try telling him the surgery is very new and it will take time. Their son Michael comes in from college. He is suddenly a young man, I hug him and say, "You're all grown up, Michael".

"I am almost twenty," he tells me. He has a quiet word with his dad, then walks quietly to the den. "He is all grown up, Mary."

"God bless him, he is." I am glad Mary has him for support; he is a good son. When my two weeks stay was up. I didn't want to leave but Mike was assuring me he was alright. Before leaving, I phoned my cousin Maureen, her life is turned upside down too. Her daughter Kathy is taking her husband's death very bad. The terrible way he was taken from his family. I left with a heavy heart. Leo drove me to the airport and promised to keep me informed if anything came up. We said our goodbyes. I was glad to be home. Margery and Caroline had to be filled in on the news off their brother Mike. I had to tell them that I was worried. "Mom," they remind me, "he has had a brain tumour operation."

"You are right," I agree.

I tell them about Joe Maloney, who they met in Westbury the year we spent a week's holiday with my cousin Maureen. He would come and pick up Kathy to take her out on a date; that was twenty years ago, in 1981. We have good memories of him; he was great crack. He is gone with 349 other firemen. They cry as they think of his wife Kathy and his two young children, Joseph and Megan.

2001 - TRYING TO RELAX AT HOME

Even though I'm tired, I have no desire to go to bed.

I take pen and jotter and start my usual therapy; writing a few lines of poetry; it might soothe my aching heart.

UNWELCOME GUEST

On a beautiful, August week in 2001. At the Galway Races we had such fun.

The horse you picked won the race. At times you could not see your pencil trace.

My horse romped home, but my winnings I can't see to count, you'd moan.

The holiday over, it was grand, now it's back to your home in Long Island.

It's the ring of the phone I hear, but in your voice a tone of fear.

I've had some tests; the news is bad, you will be sad.

Oh! Mike my son, tell me do, the trouble that is troubling you.

It's big a growing tumour inside this head of mine, I want to burst out cryin.

Your only forty-five, my son, what is going to be done?

Tomorrow a brain surgeon, in operation urgent. I have such fear, I will pray my dear. In prayer, palms pressed together, words won't come; this is my darling son.

There she is, the girl he chose for his bride, always by his side, three pairs of eyes with tears a-glisten, but they don't cry, our dad, why oh, why. Having borne a baby boy, we had such happiness, your dad and I. We were so blessed. Little baby, chubby cheeks your dad would tweak and tweak, while holding you to his breast. Now we have this awful unwelcome guest.

2001 - ONE MONTH LATER

I get a phone call from Leo. "Is something wrong, Leo?"

"Mike took bad with his head, and had to be rushed to hospital where he underwent another operation; he is much better after it; when you get a chance give Mary a call, she will fill you in."

"Thanks, Leo. How are things in Manhattan?"

"Not good, some funerals have taken place, but there is many more. They are still searching in the rubble for bodies. There is a big hole where the Twin Towers were, it is now called 'Ground Zero'.

"Mind yourself, Leo. Cousin Maureen's son-in-law, Joe the fireman, lost his life in it, pray for his family, Leo."

"I will, Mom."

"Leo, how is the job getting on?"

"We are very busy with turkeys and hams; the Americans stock up early for Christmas and the people are trying to make the effort to carry on as usual. Kristina is an angel in the school play, and Ian is going to be a shepherd in his class. Joey, well, she is spending my money on gifts for everyone." It was so nice talking to him.

WILL DEAR MARY HAVE GOOD NEWS?

I phone her and wonder what news would she have to tell me this time? Her news is half and half. But first, she explains how Mike took very bad one night with the pressure in his head and she had to rush him to hospital, as there was pressure on his brain. He was taken for surgery immediately. She explains the nature of his tumour; it is growing through the pituitary gland at the spinal top; the operation is done up through his nose. It is a tricky method, but he is in the hands of a very qualified surgeon, Mr Rosello, who is a specialist in anything to do with the brain.

"We have Dr. Vinnie, our local man just across the street from us."

"Thank God for that, Mary. How is Mike now?"

"Here he is, he will tell you himself."

"Will I need to whisper into the phone?"

"No, you won't." There is a cheerful, "Hi Mom?"

"Mike, my son," I shout without thinking. "Oh, I'm sorry for shouting."

"Doesn't worry, no amount of noise bothers me now. The doctors expected this to happen, but they didn't tell us. I am fine now and the kids are glad they don't need to tiptoe around their dad anymore. But I will be in need of rehab treatment for a long time. You remember I told you that when we moved to Long Island ten years ago I joined the Ancient Order of Hibernians (AOH), it is an Irish-American Catholic organisation with mostly retired men. The men have made up a rota and they will take it in turns to stay with me during the day, and that gives Mary freedom to go to work. If she is needed they will call her."

"How long will they be doing that good turn, Mike?"

"For as long as is needed, I guess the rest of my life!"

"Oh dear, Mike."

"Yes, but we are facing it together day by day."

"God bless you," I say.

"We don't have to worry; the men from the AOH take me four times a week for the rehab treatment."

"My dear son, I am very happy for that news."

"The men are doing a rota, two to be with me every day."

"I will pray for you and the good men. And your surgeon."

2001 - JOINING LADY BIRDS

I was real pleased when my young granddaughter, Caroline, told me she was going to join the Ladybirds in Mervue. Its the youngest division of IGG. "I am so proud of you, Caroline; your mother was a Brownie and Girl Guide and your granny here was a Brown Owl and then moved on to be a Girl Guide Captain. You are third generation in our family Caroline, getting evolved in such a worthwhile organisation as Guiding."

Six months later she comes to me, "Mam said to tell you I've left Ladybirds."

"Oh that's alright, maybe at age five/six, you are too young. When you're seven/eight, join the Brownies, you will be old enough to enjoy them."

2002 - REMEMBRANCE MASS

I set to arranging a remembrance Mass with Fr. Gearoid O'Greafa P.P. of St. Brigid's Church, Ballybane for the late Joseph/Joe Maloney and his family. I explain to him my plan in having a 'fireman's memories' presentation of gifts at the Mass, presented by members of our family. I would be inviting family members from around the country to attend, and also members of the Galway Firemen's association and ask for the fire engine to be parked outside St. Brigid's Church, and I would like the choir to sing. Family members would do the readings and prayers of the faithful.

Fr. Gearoid was delighted with this plan, and we would remember all firemen heroes who risk their lives in saving others. My next job was to call into the Galway Firehouse and make my request for a representative to attend the Mass. They said they would be happy to be there, providing no emergencies occurred. I thanked them, and as I turned around to leave, I see a framed pictured on the wall of the lost firefighters who died in the Twin Towers and Joe Malone among them. I pointed him out to the fireman I had been talking to. He sympathised with me and promised to do their best to be at the Mass and offered me a fireman's helmet, which was presented to them by the N.Y. fire department some years ago. He was apologising for the dust on it. I said, "You won't recognise it when it comes back." He smiled at my half-joke. Our family members were well represented in celebrating Joe Malone's Mass, coming from the four corners of the country, all his wife Kathy's Irish cousins. The Galway Fire Chief, John Shaughnessy, was represented by one of the three firemen who attended. We were proud of the fireman's helmet which was brought to the altar by a member of our family, borrowed from the Galway Fire Brigade.

At the end of the Mass, I thanked Fr. Gearoid for the beautiful, sensitive touching and holy way he celebrated the holy Mass at this very sad time, I also thanked the choir, and the Galway Fire Department, and all the family who took such a big part in the Mass. Especially our cousin, Sr. Margaret Hurley of the Blessed Sacrament

Convent, Dublin who came such a long journey that morning. I also thanked granddaughter Lisa Ruffley, who acted as Mass server for this very special Mass. "Rock Dale" was a full house on that cold Sunday Morning, 13th Janurary 2002. It was also my late husband Paddy Dowling's fifteenth anniversary, coinciding with this sad occasion.

Cups of tea were called for as the family members kept coming in the door. Margery and Caroline set to getting the food of roast beef, potatoes and vegetables up on tables and everyone helped themselves buffet style. There were salads and chicken legs, glasses of milk, beer, wine, and bottles of Guinness for the men. The dessert was my specialty, the old reliable, a large bowl of sherry trifle, and ice-cream for the children, then plenty of cake and biscuits, and pots and pots of tea. The morning went well, but Joe's young family was the main topic and all who were killed in this terrible atrocity. I was very glad there was such a great turnout of family members for this special remembrance Mass.

HIGHEST AWARD IN GIRL GUIDES

At the age of twelve, my granddaughter Lisa Ruffley joined the St. Nicholas' Collegiate IGG. Lisa proved herself a worthy Girl Guide, working diligently to gain her badges; each one an interesting challenge. She enjoyed these tests, persevering to please her Guide Captain, Ann Walton, who was very proud of her. In 2006, Lisa was the only Girl Guide from St. Nicholas' Collegiate IGG to qualify and be accepted to gain her Gold award, travelling to Dublin with the Mervue IGG, who were also receiving their awards. This was the highest award in Guiding for continous achievement, at age sixteen. She was a very happy Girl Guide on that day. Lisa continued for another two years as a young leader and helped younger Guides on how to earn their badges. I was very proud of her as was her mother Margery who had also been a diligent Brownie, Girl Guide and also trained to become a young Leader.

GRADUATING FROM COLAISTE COIRIBE

At age eighteen, Lisa was pursuing her studies and could not commit her time to Guiding. She was sad to leave, but would never forget her wonderful time in IGG. Having graduated from Colaiste Coiribe, Lisa was setting her mind on what she would like to do in her future. Her love for music was uppermost. Her mother bought her a keyboard to tap out some tunes on; her wish was in time to learn to play the piano. She applied for a job in Specsavers and was accepted. She worked there for two years, and benefited from what she learned. She turned her hand to many things, one of which was teaching English as a foreign langue (TEFL). She did waitressing in the Salthill Hotel, another couple of years working in Launderland. Then came her twenty-first birthday and, with a few of her girlfriends, she had a good time celebrating it in Barcelona. Her real ambition was to study music.

For a while she studied Tai and Yoga. Having some money saved, she travelled a little of the world, Portugal, Spain, Italy and Holland. After these adventures, it was time to take her ambition studying music seriously. She returned to the teacher who had been teaching her for about five years, Petra Carrick, and now at last, in 2015, she is excelling in music composition (with a Distinction). With the keyboard having run its course, she was given a piano. She will now do serious practicing. I am so proud to give this young ambitious girl a chance to achive her goal, which she will.

Lisa Ruffley rests by her piano.

MY VISIT TO MORAN'S

Phoning Mrs Jane Moran, I apologize for not getting back to her sooner. "Are you coming?" She asks.

"I will come tomorrow, Jane, if that suits you."

"It will, Margaret, come early, we will have lunch here in the house together."

"I will Jane, see you then." Now I must phone her daughter Mary. Speaking with Mary, I ask a delicate question. "Mary, I hope you won't mind me asking you this. I'm going to visit your mother tomorrow." Big pause. "Have you told her that Mike has a brain tumour?"

"No, Mom, I don't know how I'm going to tell her."

"I will mention it to her if you like."

"No, don't. I am going over next week and I will tell her in person. Pray for me."

"I will, love."

Jane and I had a lovely day together. We talked about her career as a registered nurse and the number of hospitals in various states of America she nursed in. She had to sit an exam in each state. "You had no trouble with that, Jane."

"No," she agreed. Then we talked about her late husband Paddy and how he liked to fish. He took his grandson Michael with him and also for trips in his boat out on the lake. We had a long discussion about the disaster of the Twin Towers. Her husband's cousin, living next door, served us with a delicious dinner and lovely home-made brown bread, finishing with sponge cake. We ate in silence for a little while. The cousin returned to collect the tray and we thanked her sincerely for the lovely meal. Jane told me how happy she was when her shy daughter, Mary was so lucky to meet a fine boy like my son Michael. I could have screamed even cried out loud, "Oh Jane," I thought, "if only you knew the news Mary will be bringing you next week!" I knew both of Mary's parents adored my son Mike.

Too soon my time to leave was up, but I promised to come soon again. We hugged and hugged and then said goodbye. I could hardly see to drive on my way home for the tears coming down my cheeks.

Mary phones me, "How is Mam?" She asks.

"She is good, Mary; we had a lot to chat about. The cousin who lives next door brought us in a lovely meal."

"You didn't say anything about Mike?"

"No, Mary, not a word."

"Thanks, Mom, I will call to you after I tell her next week."

"Do that, Mary, God give you strength, bye for now."

SAD NEWS IS HARD

Sad news is hard to deliver especially, to a mother. That was what my dear daughter-in-law Mary had to do, telling her mother that her young husband Mike was not well.

After the day Mary broke the news to her mother about Mike's illness she came to see me on her way to Shannon. "Mary, how are you? How is your mother? Was anyone with you, Mary?"

"No, it was better on my own."

"You poor girl."

"I managed alright. Poor Mom, she is very upset; I didn't like leaving her but she understood I have to get back to Long Island."

I walk with her to the car she has hired out for this sad journey. "It is a hard world Mary, we can only keep praying."

We said our goodbyes, "Phone me when you get home."

"I will," she said, as we waved to each other.

I AM THINKING OF MRS MORAN

I feel its my duty to visit her, after the sad news her daughter came from America to tell her about her son-in-law. I am on my way to Ballinrobe. Coming nearer, I keep praying that poor Jane is alright. I steady myself before reaching the door. Jane is very happy to see me. It brought tears to my eyes when she said, "Your dear son, Margaret."

"I know Jane, but how are you?"

"Not so well. I spend my time praying."

"So do I." She told me where the kettle was I made tea; together we sipped it with some bisuits. We sat a while in silence, each feeling our own inner pain; I made some small talk. I was glad she could talk about Mike and how herself and her late husband Paddy loved him. We talked about things of the past and the sense of humour Mike had. She paused, "How will his family get on now he is unable to work?" I remind her of the strong daughter she reared in Mary. I didn't know how I was going to leave her. Then I said, "Jane, I will have to leave, but I will be back soon, if its OK."

"Margaret, there is people coming in to look after me."

"That is good." We kissed and said goodbye. It was the last time I saw dear Jane alive.

2002 - CHURCH FLOWERBEDS

I was tired of looking at the three large flowerbeds in the church grounds of St. Brigid's; there was a heavy overgrowth of heathers. I mentioned it to Fr. Gearoid; "What would you put there instead?" He asked.

"I have a lot of flowers in my garden, I am going to thin them out. If it is alright with you Father, I would like to plant them into the three beds, but the wild over grown heathers will have to be removed."

"Leave it with me Margaret; I will get rid of them." A week later I was glad to see the heathers were gone. "How did you get it done so quickly?" I asked.

"McGaugh's Nursery; they came and cleared the three beds with a rotary plow and took away the heathers."

"I will get started now," I told him.

"They're all yours," he said. The flowerbeds were very large, but being raised a couple of feet and the clay plowed, made planting easy. The weather was mild and I was able to work at a steady pace. I put in a variety of daffodil bulbs for spring flowering, snapdragons, primroses, marigolds, and winter-hardy geraniums that bloomed with blue flowers all through the month of June. I also added seasonal flowers, such as Michaelmas daisies, and did the weeding.

It was a labour of love. As the weather was fine there was very little growth of weeds so I relaxed my attention on the flower beds for a time. One afternoon

I paid a visit to see how the church flowerbeds were doing; they were overgrown with weeds. I was so disappointed. It would be hard work to get them looking nice again. I decided to leave them until after the winter, when the growth would have died back and I might be able to get them back to normal.

REACH-OUT

Fr Gearoid O' Griofa Parish Priest St. Brigid's Church, Ballybane; set up Reach-Out, a structure for parishioners to take part in the religious events taking place in the Church. He called a meeting and was pleased with the good turnout of people. He opened the meeting with a prayer. Discussions took place on appointing various groups in supervising the religious celebrations in St. Brigid's. There were the Eucharistical Ministers, literature readers, adult and junior choirs, baptismal preparations, first Holy Communions, Confirmations, and much, much more. Leaders were appointed in taking charge. This is necessary, as priests today are on the decline and assistance from the laity is needed.

I continued as minister of the Eucharist, reader and choir member. The choir had reduced in numbers, but still we continued with our rehearsals and sang at the eleven a.m. Sunday Mass and the church feast days, sometimes at a funeral. We were requested by our youngest choir member, Ann Kirwan to sing at her wedding; this was a great honour. She made a beautiful bride in her lovely white wedding gown. As she walked up the aisle on her father's arm, we also sang, "Here Comes the Bride."

TAKING MY SON'S ADVICE

I thought about my son's advice to sell "Rock Dale". I visited an auctioneer to make the necessary arrangements. In no time, a 'For Sale' sign was erected at my front wall by Sherry Fitzgerald auctioneers. Looking at it, I said, "I didn't think I would ever do this to you, "Rock Dale", almost forty years sheltered by you, you have served us well. You understand I am getting old."

Daughter Margery comes in the door. "Mom, you are selling "Rock Dale", you never said. Oh Mom, you will be sad."

"Now Margery, don't get me started; it's not sold yet."

Caroline adds her bit, "She didn't tell me either, and I living here."

AN OFFER

One day two men came to the door, one I knew quite well; he introduced the man with him telling me at the same time, this man is interested in buying the house, and could he have a look around at it?

I said, "Of course he could." Going round to the back of the house, he had a good look at the extent of the garden and he spoke a few words to me. "I will let you know my offer."

"Thank you," I said, and both men left. On a miserable winter's day, I was sitting by the warm fire in my sitting room, thinking, "How many more fires will I light here?"

The ring of the doorbell interrupted my thoughts. On answering it, I was surprised to see the man I knew standing there, whose friend was interested in buying my property. He began by reminding me about the man who came to look at my property is interested in buying it. It was very cold standing at the door, so I invited him in. We went into the sitting room, but he declined to sit at my offer of a chair, he was very busy with paperwork. "This man is making you a good offer for the property, and I think you should take it for you won't get much more. I have €300 of a deposit here for it, and you can put your name down there." He was showing me a sheet of paper to sign. I didn't look at the paper, I just said, "Sorry, I won't be signing it."

"You won't?"

"No."

"What are you expecting for it?"

"My sons have valued this property to be at least ten times or more than what your man is offering."

With that news, he sat down. He had no more to say but got up and left. I couldn't believe this man who knew me, and whose wife I was friendly with was trying to pull a fast one on me. What a cheek, without even a mention of a solicitor. I told my sons about my experience. "A cowboy for sure," was their response.

2003 - GETTING THE KEY

My daughter Caroline had her name down for a long time with the Corporation to get a house. At last, word came from City Hall for her to go in and collect her key; it was her birthday too, what a gift. The house was in a new estate and like all estates, the houses were semi-detached. Caroline was pleased with her house. The neighbours were young mothers like her with one or two children; she had great enjoyment furnishing it. As the years went on, her next-door neighbour, who had two small children, became unneighbourly. This was becoming unsatisfactory and was a very disagreeable situation for her and her child to be in. I was worried about my daughter Caroline, who needed to be up early in the mornings for work in the Galway-Mayo Institute of Technology (GMIT) in the Student's Union, plus she was studying and caring for her young daughter, getting her ready for crèche after a sleepless night. Due to her neighbours' late night loud music and loud talking, she found it difficult to be alert in the mornings. She was unsuccessful in her request to the Corporation for a transfer for herself and her child. She tried to turn a deaf ear, but this was easier said than done. Caroline studied hard to get a degree and to secure herself in a satisfactory position.

GRADUATING

My daughter Caroline received a national certificate in Business Studies and Office Information from the GMIT. She continued her studies in there while working in the Student's Union, working hard to gain her B.A degree in Personnel Development, while also bringing up her young daughter, who was attending school in Renmore. Caroline would lend a hand in providing sponsorship of the annual gala Christmas cabaret in aid of Croí. She was always willing to give retired teacher, Ms Mary Cunningham, her support. A very successful coffee morning was organised by the GMIT. It was held in the front of the Galway Advertiser's office and the staff served up coffee to hundreds of people in aid of Croí; also lending a hand was Caroline Jr, with two of her little friends dressed in nurse's uniforms. There were musical concerts held in the Radisson SAS hotel, and Caroline was on hand selling tickets for the many exquisite hampers and prizes raffles held in aid of charities.

A BIRTHDAY PARTY FOR ME

It is September and I'm throwing a big seventieth birthday party for myself in "Rock Dale". Little did I know at the time that it would be the last party held in this good house. I invited many of the friends I made in the Renmore Active Retirement Club. It was a great evening of singing and joke-telling.

Tom Talbot and Joe McCarty sang amusing songs; Frank Hanrahan stood up and gave a monologue about a train. Everyone of course sang me a happy birthday and wished me many more. The family had a cake made for me with my photo on it. The kind people gave me nice gifts too. There was lots of food and drink, and I took many photos and put them carefully into an album.

NEXT DOOR NEIGHBOURS

My neighbours join with me in selling their house. It is six months up for sale now and Sherry Fitzgerald were urging me to be looking for a place to move to when the house was sold. I was in no hurry for I didn't think it would go so quick; only a few buyers showed interest. Events took a turn though as my neighbours, the Concannons were interested in joining with me, to sell the two houses together. All was in agreement with my selected auctioneer and solicitor; everything was carried out legally. The only thing to do was to wait for the right buyer to come along.

A BEAUTIFUL SUNDAY

Such a beautiful day; the sun is shining brightly, what a pity not to be out enjoying its rays. I get dressed up and put on my sunhat, then drive out to the Claregalway Agricultural Show. There are lots of stands with home bakery, home-grown produce and flowers, all in competition. There were also some lovely hand-knitted garments, plus cushion covers. Out in the fields, the dog show is in full swing. It was bringing to mind my little Pomeranian. "We won't be strutting our stuff today, Poochy, you are in doggie heaven." There was a varied class of lovely fowl to admire, more competitions out in the fields, great big bulls, and different breeds of cattle, pony and donkey shows.

Coming near the end of the day, I saw a section where about a dozen ladies were dressed lovely and sitting on chairs. As a chair was vacant, I too sat down. A lady came to me and asked if I had paid my fee. I asked, "What the fee was for."

She said, "Aren't you entering the best-dressed lady competition?"

"No," I said.

"But you must; it is only a couple of euros, do give it a go."

"Alright, I will," and she pinned a number on the back of my dress. As we paraded around in a circle, we were finally asked to sit, then five of us were called to walk around again, two were asked to sit and three to remain standing. Of the three, I was the winner, the Best Dressed Lady at the Claregalway Agricultural Show. I got a beautiful trophy and a large shield to bring home (which was to be returned at next year's show), with my name on the shield. There was a photo of me on the City Tribune. This was unbelievable; I had no notion of entering any competition. What a lovely day.

LAUNCH OF BALLYBANE ACTIVE RETIREMENT

Ballybane Active Retirement Association is to be launched in the Ballybane Resource Centre.

Having served as chairperson of the Renmore Active Retirement Association, I was inspired to open one in the parish of Ballybane, which was closer to home. After a year of trying to recruit the required number of people to set one up, I was very lucky in finding four enthusiastic people to form a committee, Chairperson Margaret Dowling, plus Activities Organiser, Treasurer, Bobby O'Reilly, Secretary Eleanor King, and committee members, Mary McDonough and Larry Doyle. With the increase of the numbers, the Ballybane Active Retirement Association (BARA) was officially launched on the 23/9/2003 by the National President of Active Retirement's Mrs Eithne Carey, with the Assistance of the Development Officer, Ann Goodwin.

The club flourished for over 12 years. It was one of the happiest and most vibrant clubs ever set up in the Association. Among the numerous activities the members took part in during the twelve and a half years were, art classes, silk painting, Yoga, swimming, aqua aerobics, and our own stories by seventeen enthusiastic writers, adding their past histories to a book titled, *'Down Memory Lane'*, with help from local Historian William Henry. It was launched in the Ballybane Library by Deputy Mayor Collette Connelly in December 2007. A big turnout of club members and residences of old Ballybane, who had also contributed to *'Down Memory Lane'*, attended this occasion. Classes also included digital camera training by Lorraine McManus, VEC, and some of the lessons took place in the Merlin Woods. We learned about close-up on flowers, light and dark, focus near and far, transferring to the computer, deleting etc. The club birthdays were celebrated each year with a cake. Some individuals like Bobbie O'Reilly and Larry Doyle celebrated their combined 80th birthdays. Jimmy Rainbow always brought a cake to share on his birthday.

End of each year there was an enjoyable Christmas dinner with P.P Father Gearoid O'Griofa taking part, adding to the fun by joining in the dancing to lively music. The children of the poorest countries were not forgotten and the Christmas gift shoeboxes were well filled to be sent out to the poorest countries. Easter bonnets brought glamour as well, with the winner getting the largest Easter egg, while everyone else got a small one. Halloween brought laughter in dressing up. There were outings and holidays, too numerous to mention, occasionally joining with sister clubs. Indoor mat bowling was set up in 2005 by Larry Doyle, who was a member of the Renmore Bowlers. He checked first if BARA members would be interested, they were very willing to take part in this new activity. We set to work on getting grants for mats, bowls and all equipment needed with the help of Minister Frank Fahy, who procured a sports grant of €5,000, and so bowling took off, with many enthusiastic BARA members willing to learn and even enter club competitions. On one occasion two of our men were winners against two opponents from a competitive bowling group. There was an annual bowling week set up in the month of February for enthusiastic bowlers in the Castlecourt Hotel, Westport, County Mayo.

We had our share of sadness with the passing of dedicated members. Our first secretary, Eleanor King who was a founder member, and dedicated to the club, she always had her minutes up to date. She lived in Ballybane until her health began to fail. Eleanor passed away June 2012 in her home place in Leenane, County Galway. Some members representing BARA attended her funeral, it was touching to see the book *'Down Memory Lane'* placed in her coffin and opened at the page where she had written her life story.

A money-savings club was set up for the members to put aside money for holidays and outings; in charge of this task were two dedicated women, Mary Brennan and Pat Fortune. Sadly, Pat passed away in 2009. Her replacements were Sister Delia and Mary Scanlon. Leading the weekly walkers was Joey Reed who also served a term as club treasurer. With the recession and grant aid cubacks, mnembers of Active Retirements were invited to model some very fashionable Anthony Ryan clothes on the 'catwalk' in the Ardilaun Hotel, to help raise money towards regional expense. You can imagine my excitement when I got a call to join the Grey's Anatomy and strut my stuff. First, there was a fitting of the style to suit the 'model', then there would be three different outfits to change into and then swank it on the 'catwalk' for the audience to admire. I really enjoyed this adventure. The Western Region of Active Retirement would benefit from the proceeds.

It was a glamourous evening with photographs taken and chocolates being served, such a lovely memory, thanks Betty O'Flynn I was especially happy to see my daughter Margery and her husband Colm, dear sweet Colm with his serious illness, to have made such a big effort to come and watch me parading up and down the ramp.

Without the grant aid from the VEC, Galway City Partnership, St Columba's Credit Union and Minister Frank Fahy, many of the activities I set up for BARA would never have happened. I was constantly on the lookout for the grants and when and where to apply for them. BARA received a Community Awards gift of €500 from St. Columba's Credit Union, Mervue. All moneys were spent on the programs they were applied for and much appreciated by the members. The last event I did was to hold a morning's remembrance in 2013, dedicated to the seven club members who had passed away. I set up an altar, putting up photos of each of the seven members, a lighted candle for each one and a little vase of flowers to adorn the altar. Seven club members each read a short prayer in the memory of our friends past and gone.

Mayor of Galway Terry O'Flaherty sat with us to celebrate this remembrance.

Launch of Bally Bane Active Retirement

National President of Active Retired Eithne Carey and development officer Ann Goodwin with Chairperson Margaret Dowling after launching Ballybane ARA 2003.

AGM

At the AGMs the three main officers would hold their seats for the specified three years, and a new committee would be elected according to who wanted to step down. I continued to remain on as Activities Organiser.

I let it be known I was having health problems and explained I would be stepping down for some time for a badly-needed rest. Everyone was very kind in wishing me well, telling me not to be in any hurry back, "but they would be missing me." A new committee was elected. Some months later I met a lady from the club. I asked how it was doing. She looked at me in surprise, "Don't you know, Margaret?" She says, "Within the year, it was closed unceremoniously." Do I need to say how I felt?

2004 - "ROCK DALE" IS SOLD

With the two neighbouring properties combined, the Dowling and Concannon spaces made for a larger area for building apartments. We sold to a builder just one year after the 'For Sale' sign went up in my garden. Now the rush was on for me to leave my dear home that I had seen forty years ago being built. It was a comfortable home for me and my two sons. In time I met Paddy Dowling, a widower also with two small children. We got married, and Paddy with his son and daughter moved in to "Rock Dale". In due time, we added to the family, having two daughters. It was a full and busy home. I had never anticipated selling "Rock Dale". But times and circumstances change people.

"Rock Dale" was a good investment. And now I could help my family financially. Luckily, I found a lovely, smaller home in nearby Ballybrit.

I loved it at first sight, the beautiful sitting room, fireplace, and nothing but a small patio at the back, convinced me to buy this house. There was a disadvantage with not having a gate to open or close when I parked my car at the front of the house. I had never lived in an estate and I wondered if I would be happy here, but that thought was put to rest when my next-door neighbour came and welcomed me. During our conversation, I discovered I went to school in Briarhill with his mother. Having got rid of most of the "Rock Dale" furniture, which was by far too big for my new residence, I set to buying new furnishings. That was the fun part.

TAKING A TRIP TO SEE MY SON

Mike has had another hard year of treatment to try and stop the growth of the tumour without surgery. The treatment this time was thirty days of computer technology, radiation treatment. His wife Mary had to drive him each day to Stoneybrook Hospital for this treatment. I am going over to see him and praying this treatment is doing a good job.

It paid off and he got a few years relief from surgery. I was worried as to how he would be when I arrived. Thanks to many prayers, he was in very good form and so were the family. Mary, a true Irish tea-drinker, had a pot made and on the table when I arrived. Leo and his family came from N.J. to see us and stayed the night. Leo had ambitions of looking further afield in his line of work, the food business. "Is New York not suitable?" I asked

"It's a long drive in each morning to Manhattan, houses are too expensive. Joey and I don't want to rear our children in an apartment for the rest of their lives."

"I know what you mean," his brother Mike agreed, "that is why Mary and I were lucky in buying this house here in Massapequa Park when we did, if it was now and with the cost of my operation and treatment we would never be able to afford it."

Leo and family left in the morning. I spent a nice two weeks with Mike; we had the house to ourselves while Mary was at work, Michael in University, Gary and Cassandra in school. As it was coming into the hot summer, I said, "Mike I'm looking forward to going home, the July heat is killing me."

"I know what you mean, Mom. I used to feel the heat the first years when I came over. I'm used to it now." Back home again I'm telling the girls how well Mike was, but the tumour was still there, it is dormant for now.

KEEPING ME UP TO DATE

Mike's wife Mary would call me to let me know how he was progressing; most of the time he was in good form. In one of Mary's calls she had surprising news for me. "Guess what, your grandson Michael is going to Egypt to study Arabic."

"Oh dear, Mary, Egypt. It's a long way away. How old is he?"

"He is twenty-two."

"How long will he be there?"

"Six months."

"Are you worried about him?"

"Egypt is safe right now and he will be with other students in his own league."

"I will pray for his safety."

"Thanks, Mom."

"I will call you next week, Mary."

GRANDSON GARY

Grandson Gary phones. "Hi Gran."

"Hi Gary, how are you?"

"I'm fine, Granny. My friend Nick is coming with me to Ireland next week, can we stay with you?"

"Great news, of course Gary; I would love to have you here, how long will you be staying?"

"Two weeks, first week with you, the second one with friends of Mam's."

I was so happy to see two very tired boys at my door. I was granny to them both. Gary, in his shy way handed me a bunch of flowers. I was so grateful to the two boys who were only seventeen years of age being so thoughtful. After their journey, they were hungry, so a big fry-up, an Irish breakfast, for them was the order of the day. After they had enjoyed the meal, I showed them to their rooms. It was late evening when they surfaced, coming downstairs well-rested, they asked, "Is the store far from here, Gran?"

"I'll show you where it is, are you going grocery shopping?"

"We are, would you like some pizza?"

"No thank you, Gary."

"You won't mind if we cook it in your oven?"

"Of course I won't, enjoy yourselves Gary." He thanked me with a kiss on the cheek, of which I got many during the week, so much affection. I was being spoiled. Gary, being six foot tall, had to bend a long way down to me, while Nick had a good laugh at him. "What are ye doing for the evening?"

"My cousin Alison," said Gary, "is meeting us in the city and we are going to hang out with her for a while."

"Very good," I say. The shopping done and the strong aroma of the pizza cooking in the oven, I thought I was in Italy. I asked, "Have you plans for tomorrow?"

"No," they both answered.

"Well, Caroline is inviting you to her new house; she is cooking dinner for ye." They were delighted to hear that. In Aunt Caroline's there was great fun with young Caroline, aged seven; as a matter of fact the three of them could be taken for three seven-year-olds with all the running in and out of the house, and up and down the stairs, having fun. It was time to sit to dinner, all three puffing and panting. "Well, that has given you an appetite for your aunty's big dinner of spaghetti and meatballs with plenty of sauce." After which they were not able for the dessert of home-made apple pie with ice-cream.

When it was time to leave Caree didn't want them to go. "We will be back if you promise to stop crying," said Gary.

"I will," she said in between sobs. It was an enjoyable evening. "Your Aunt Margery would like if you can visit her tomorrow."

"We would love that," said Gary. "I want to see Lisa and Rachel." It would be his first time meeting their half-brother Kallum, aged four. We went in the evening and Gary met everyone and introduced his friend Nick. Margery had a cold meal ready and, as she said, "I don't think you boys drink tea, so there's Coco Cola for you." The boys had great chats with Lisa and Rachel. Kallum showed them his football. It was another nice evening spent with family members. Coming back to home, Gary said, "The girls are getting big, Lisa is fourteen and Rachel is coming twelve. How time flies." Our last night together and we decided to play a few games of cards. Their time with me was up and now their have packed for their second week's holiday with the Harte family. They hugged me and thanked me for the best week ever. I wished them a safe journey. And as always, I am lonely when they leave.

MORE EXCITING NEWS

Mike phones me with news that his son Michael has completed his six months study in Egypt and he is coming home by Heathrow, U.K. "Mary and I will be there to meet him we will come to Galway. Michael and I will be staying with you for a week. Mary is going to visit some of the friends she was in college with."

"I'm looking forward to having you here, even if it is only for a week." I am thanking God in my heart that Mike's doctor considered him well enough to fly those long distances. When they arrived at my door it was wonderful to see them looking so well. I did say, "Michael, you lost some weight."

"I did Granny; the food in Egypt was hard to get used to. We also had to walk most places to see many old Egyptian ruins, it was a wonderful experience. I am just happy to be home and looking forward to a good Irish dinner. I'm in need of a shower first."

"We will wait for you, Michael. You are leaving them with me, Mary?"

"I am, Mom; will you be able to put up with them for a full week?"

"Don't you worry; I will mind your two men while you enjoy yourself with your friends. How are you travelling?" I ask.

"To make the travelling easier for Mike, we hired out a car in Dublin."

"That is good; you won't be depending on public transport." There was a lot of resting done during the week, Michael was catching up on lost sleep; his dad would also be in need of rest as he tired easy. But when they were up they liked to see the town and the Ballybrit Racecourse. The week went fast; it was then time for Michael to visit some of his friends before he would return to L.I. He brought me a souvenir from Egypt, a mug which has taken pride of place among the many souvenirs my children and grandchildren have brought me through the years. Of course, the visits with Margery and Caroline and their children were happy occasions. It has to be said their joy at seeing their brother Mike so well was an endorsement. And cousin Michael's travels in Egypt were interesting to hear about. As always when in parting we are sad, but happy that we had time together, and none as happy as I to have my son for a while with me.

NOMINATIONS

For the Mayor's Award, I picked up a form in the Ballybane library and showed it to my daughter Caroline. "Will you nominate me for this award Caroline?" I asked. She wonders if a relation can do that. "Try it anyway, sure all they have to do is scrap it." Caroline filled in the necessary details as to why I should receive an award, i.e. because I did community voluntary work. I left it into City Hall, College

Road, Galway. "We will never hear from that," I thought, but we did, and Caroline and I had a lovely evening in the Black Box Theatre, where wine was served and plenty of finger food. There was a big crowd of supporters as well as the recipients. When my name was called, I was very excited being presented with a certificate of recognition for voluntary community work. The presenter was Councillor Catherine Connolly, Mayor of Galway City. I walked away very proud.

2005 - LEAVING NEW JERSEY

Leo was itching to leave N.J. He phoned to tell me of his latest intention to move. I asked, "Where are you going?"

"To North Carolina."

"And what type of work will you do there?"

"I will be still involved in the food business, but it will be more up-market."

"Are you staying with the same food company?"

"No, the name of this company is Harris Teeter."

"What does Joey think of this move?"

"She says she will miss her friends in N.J., especially Clare and Mike Burke. But after our trip to N.C. a couple of weeks ago to suss the place out, she thinks herself and the children will like it. Especially the house."

"The house?" I repeat.

"Yes, we bought a great big house; we can move straight into it when we are ready."

"How did you have the money, Leo?"

"Remember you said you could not afford the price of one in N.Y. or N.J.?"

"That is right, I couldn't. The house we bought is three times cheaper in N.C. and Joey will love the country atmosphere. When you come over you won't want to leave. Here, talk to Joey."

"Joey, how do you feel about moving so far away?" I asked.

"When we get settled in I know I am going to like it. It is a big change. One thing that is working out for us is Kristina and Ian will each have their own bedrooms."

"Good luck to you," I say, as we hang up the phones. Talking to my son Mike, I ask what he thinks of his brother's big move. "I'm going to miss him, and Mary will miss Joey."

"They will miss you all too."

"It feels like they will be at the other end of the world."

"How far are they from you, Mike?"

"It is about an hour and a half by plane from New York to Charlotte."

"I guess when you say it that way it can't be too far."

"Well you wouldn't walk it, Mom."

"You are smart; well the best of luck to them."

"That is what I wish too, Mom."

I AM ONE YEAR LIVING HERE

Cnoc na Cille, for sure it is a nice estate. But it is surely in need of a facelift.

I visit Councillor Tom Costello, who has meeting rooms in the Ballybane Resource Centre for people to come to him when they need advice. Tom, a very welcoming man shook hands with me and invited me to sit down. He sat back in his chair and folded his arms. "Well what can I do for you, Mrs Dowling?"

"It's not for me; it's the estate where I'm living." He took out his pen and book and began to write the list of things required; double yellow lines, white line going out on to the main road, stop sign, 'Beware Children Playing' signs, ramps and the grass cut. He took note of it all. "Councillor, there is another addition, a deep dyke along by the marine wall between our estate and the next one, it is full of rubbish and needs clearing and the dyke filled in." He came to see the estate and took a good look at its needs. I had asked the residents of the twenty-three houses to come out and talk to him. "Do you have a residence committee?" he asked.

"No," I said.

"Form one now; there is enough of you here. You take on as Chairman, Margaret." I was proposed and accepted, we needed a treasurer and we got one and the election was held out on the green in 2004.

"Now you have the start of a committee. The next thing is to call a residents' meeting and elect more people to form a full committee. You can apply for the Maintenance Grant and work from there."

Within the year, most of the requests we made were fulfilled, thanks to Councillor Tom Costello. I try to call a meeting each year and about the same four people attend. The spring clean-up is well-attended and our estate is kept neat and clean. The council cuts the grass about four times in the summer. The children are the best workers and helped to create a flower garden. I also work with them doing crafts.

WEDDING INVITATION

I open the wedding invitation from my nephew Seamus Nally's girlfriend's parents and on reading it, I could not help thinking back fifty years when I was a bride on that same date, fifth of May 1955, in St Anthony's Church, the Bronx, N.Y. Now Seamus Nally and his fiancée Deborah Lyster are marrying on the fifth of May 2005, fifty years later, adding to that, Seamus is my godson. I tell my son Mike and his wife Mary who is coming from Long Island to their wedding. "Would you believe it, Mike? Your dad and I got married fifty years ago on that same date in 1955."

"We will have to have a toast together."

"We will, Mike." There is something else, the Abbey Hotel, Roscommon where the reception is being held, is right next door to O'Keeffe's, the house I worked in when I was very young. "You are going to have some memories brought back to you on that day, Mom."

Their Nuptials will be taking place in the Sacred Heart Church, Roscommon town, where I attended Mass back in 1948-1951. Seamus was looking very handsome in his black tuxedo, grey waistcoat and matching tie. Deborah beautiful in a white off-the-shoulder white gown, a pretty tiara holding her veil over her pretty red hair, and carrying a pretty bouquet of pink roses set of with green fern; they made a lovely couple.

After the reception and having a quiet time to myself, I took a walk around the area. The Abbey Hotel was home to the O'Connor family back then. O'Keeffe's house had been a two-story thatched house in my time; now it is a tiled roofed bungalow. Yes, I had a triple remembrance on a life so long past, so much has changed and I have too. My son Mike and I toasted my fifty years. Mike and Mary had time to stay a few days with me before flying back home to Long Island.

I WAS NOT AWARE

As the day was fine, I was about to take a refreshing walk but instead, decided on paying a call to my long time and very good friend Bernie Higgins, who lived in Mervue. Bernie and I had been in the same class in the Convent of Mercy. As happens in life, we parted ways for a number of years. The setting up of Irish Girl Guides IGG brought us back together again. I was Brown Owl to the young Guides known as Brownies, and there was a little girl in my Brownie Pack; her name was Alice Higgins. When my mother, Mrs Abberton died and I told the Brownies I would be missing for one week, of course they told their parents that Brown Owl's mother had died. At the next meeting when the parents came to collect their daughters, Alice brought her mother to meet me. "This is my mother Bernie." Bernie reached her hand to shake mine.

"Margaret Abberton, do you remember Bernadette Ryan going to school in the Convent of Mercy." I opened my mouth wide; "You're not her?"

"I am!"

"Oh Bernie, I am ever so happy to meet you again," and we hugged and promised to meet up. In time, Bernie became involved in Guiding too. We took part in Guide leaders training together. One training course was an outdoor camp, pitching tents in a field in Moycullen, after a day's session of training on how to pitch a tent. We learned how to prepare the ground to light a fire, and clear away the ashes when cold; leave the place as we got it.

After such a busy day, we were very tired and settled down in our tent for a good night's sleep. The ground was sloped where I slept on my lilo, and wrapping myself cosy in a blanket, I settled down for the night. Bernie settled herself below me in a more even spot. Sometime during the night, she woke me with a shout, "Maggie you have slipped down and shoved me out of the tent, I'm perished with the cold and my blanket is damp."

"I'm sorry Ber. You can have my blanket."

"Thanks, we will have to put the lilos together and sleep next to each other; we won't tell any of the others or they might think us a strange pair." It was the last time we slept wrapped in blankets. We bought two good warm sleeping bags, a great comfort for the next many number of times we went camping. Bernie and I became involved in the Renmore Active Retirement and attended many training sessions. A very beneficial one was gentle exercise classes for the club members. We attended many socials together and Christmas dinners. When things were quiet, we would call to visit each other in our homes and share the latest gossip over a glass of wine. We had shared a similarity in our personal lives too, we were married twice and both of our husbands passed away and are buried in other countries, we each married a second time and both of us had two children by our second marriages. Sadly, we each buried our second husbands too. On this day, I was heading to tell Bernie about my son Mike's progress. As always, we were glad to meet up. This time Bernie had news to tell me first, news I was not ready for. "Margaret, I have something to tell you."

"Shoot, Ber."

"I have lung cancer."

"Who did you say has cancer?" I asked in disbelief.

"I have," she said. I started to cry. "Don't cry, Margaret. I worked hard to get this, you know how heavy a smoker I have been. The doctor told me years ago to give them up and now this is the way I am, but I will fight it."

"Oh Bernie, my best'est friend, I will pray hard for you." We hugged tight.

"Sit down Margaret, and I will ask Alice to make us some tea." Alice came with a tray set with tea and a big slice of cake each. I was unable to eat mine, I felt so sick at heart.

I struggled to walk home. Sitting in my kitchen, I cried my heart out, and forgot about everything else.

I HAVE ANOTHER SURPRISE

My life is full of surprises that I'm never ready for. It is late in the evening and the doorbell rings. There is a shout, "Hi Mom," coming in the hall. There is only one person in the world with that greeting, my daughter Margery. She walks into the kitchen, Colm right behind her. "Ye're welcome, sit down." Margery, never one to start a conversation with a bit of trimmings attached to it, she comes straight to the point. "Mom, Colm and I are getting married next year; my divorces will be finalised by then."

"That's great news, the best of luck to you both."

"Thanks, Mom." But they have another piece to add. "I don't know how you will feel about this, Mom."

"Go on tell me."

"We are going to have a civil ceremony in the Clarenbridge Hotel, by a licensed registrar who performs marriage ceremonies."

"How does it work?" I ask.

"Almost in the same way as a church ceremony, with witnesses. But there is no priest."

"It will be nice for your son Kallum for you to be married." We have tea and more talk about this kind of ceremony. I tell them I would be in favour of the parish priest giving them a blessing.

THE PHONE IS RINGING

I say, "Hold your horses." It is Mike, "Hi, what's new, Mike?"

"Sad news, Mam, Mary's mother passed away this morning."

"Oh, God have Mercy on her."

"We are ready to fly over now; I will let you know about the funeral arrangements in Ballinrobe later."

"Thanks Mike, I will see you there." I put down the phone. I wish I had visited poor Jane a bit more often. God have mercy on her, she is with her Paddy in heaven now.

The funeral parlour was full when I arrived. I look into Jane's coffin; she looked very peaceful, in my mind I say, "Sorry Jane, I meant to visit you more often." My poor daughter–in-law, Mary was crying. I try to console her. "Mary, you did all that you could, your Mam and Dad are both in heaven together." I remember the first and happy time I was in this, the Church of St. Mary, Ballinrobe. "What a beautiful happy day that was, when my son Michael and your daughter Mary became husband and wife. Theirs was a lovely wedding. The next time it was the christening of my first grandson Michael. Then the funeral of your husband Paddy, this time it's yourself. R.I.P. Jane."

THE MAYOR'S AWARD

I suggest to Bobbie O'Reilly, if you nominate me we might be lucky and be eligible to receive the €500 for our BARA. We set to work writing what we thought was a good account of why our club should be awarded the prize. We received notification to be present at the Black Box to receive the certificates and awards. We were in anticipation as we sat and waited for our name to be called. Margaret Dowling was called and I went on stage, as I thought to be handed a cheque, but to my great disappointment I was for the second time presented with a certificate, by Councillor Brian Walsh, Mayor of Galway City and another photo was taken. I accepted it with a big smile. Going back to my seat I could see by Bobbie's face; she was as disappointed as I was. We watched while some groups were presented with Galway Crystal and the €500 cheque. We wondered why we missed out. We enjoyed the evening and the refreshments.

2006 - FIRST CIVIL CERMONY WEDDING

My daughter Margery and husband-to-be, Colm Fahy, will be making their vows today. "Are you a bridesmaid again for your sister?" I ask Caroline.

"No, not a bridesmaid. I'm acting this time as a witness. How do I look?" She asked, wearing a white jacket and fitted black dress. "You look lovely, but don't worry, its Margery everyone will be looking at."

I'm very curious as to how this ceremony will be conducted. I was more accustomed to the religious ceremonies. Both families were well-represented at this happy event, to wish the happy couple good luck, and it was a prayerful occasion; I was happy with that. Margery was a pretty bride wearing a beautiful full-length maroon gown, Colm in a dark suit, pink shirt and pink striped tie, Margery's two daughters in pretty outfits and Kallum in black pants, white shirt and waistcoat. He had fun with his cousin, young Caroline for the day. A lovely meal was set out for us in the Harbour Hotel where we passed an enjoyable, relaxed evening.

As time went on Margery, confided in me that Colm was not well. "What is wrong with him?" I ask.

"He has an incurable disease called 'Colitis and Crohn's'."

"I never heard of it Marg, how does it affect him?"

"It eats away at the intestines and affects many young people; there is no cure." My heart broke for her. We will offer prayers for the poor fellow. There is no Government funding for this illness. As I was writing a book at the time I promised when it was finished I would donate the proceeds to the Society for Colitis and Crohn's (SCC).

WORKING AT SURVIVAL

Survival of the toughest and that is what this year is about. I get word that Colm is going for one of many operations. Margery is trying to go to work everyday. I take Rachel and Kallum to and from school for her. Lisa is attending the Irish secondary school, Colaiste Coiribe, only a walking distance from her home.I am having a lot of pain in my right hip and waiting for a call from Merlin Park hospital for the hip replacement. Finaly it comes. I meet the surgen Mr O'Sullavain who fills me in on the proceder "Thank you, doctor." A nurse takes me to a ward I undress and go into bed. I am given a light sedative to keep me calm. In the morning I get a stronger one this reley relaxes me. Laying on my side on the operating table the last thing I remember is the prick of a needle in my back. Waking up to no pain was a gift. With ten days care in the Merlin Park Hospital and two weeks in Carol Haven nursing home, it was the best holiday I ever had. Coming home on two crutches, I had to take it easy. This was the advice of the hospital's physiotherapist Liam Concannon, who patiently showed me how to take my first steps after this big operation. While I was in hospital, I was sorry to hear my neighbour Bobbie O'Reilly's husband, Willie had died.

Colm is in good form after his operation. "I will be able to go back to work soon," he says. His job was letting in the oil from the oil tankers coming into Galway Docks and filling the oil tanks at the Galway Docks. "It is easy", he says just the turning of a key.

GRANDSON GARY

I get an early phone call from Gary letting me know he is on another one of his trips to visit me and bringing his girlfriend. "You are both very welcome," I tell him. Now I must get to work and prepare two bedrooms. I had met his girlfriend on my last trip to L.I. I found her a nice, pleasant girl. But still, I was a bit shy at the thought of her coming to my house, and would she like the meals I cooked. They arrived, and I was doing my best to please, there was no need to fuss, and Gary by this time knew his way around Galway very well. They travelled by bus to and from the city. They took a trip down the country and did some sightseeing, then back to me for the last night before heading to Dublin for their flight back to N.Y. I asked Kim what she thought of Ireland and the little she had seen of it. "It is a lovely, quiet country and of course with beautiful shades of green."

"Would you come again?" I asked.

"I would but for a longer stay, you don't get to see much in a week."

"I'm glad to hear you say that."

"We are both in college and as there was a cheap flight, we said why not take advantage and see a little of Ireland."

"It was a pleasure having you," I said as I hugged them both when they were leaving. I always miss Gary when he leaves; he is a lot of fun and seems to have grown taller each time I see him.

BOBBIE AND I TAKE A HOLIDAY

Bobbie O'Reilly's husband Willie had worked for many years in the GMIT. On his retirement, one of the many gifts presented to him were two tickets for a free round trip to America.

On one of my many visits to Bobbie's house she explained to me about the two tickets presented to her husband and now he has passed away before the time to use them was up. Bobbie wanted to use them. It would be convenient for the two of us to travel to Long Island together. Bobbie's daughter Bríd and my son Mike lived only a town from each other. I said I would be glad to travel with her. She had the name changed on the ticket that her late husband would have used. I was very thankful to Bobbie for giving me this chance of free travel. I had made many trips to visit my son Mike. We headed off on a lovely day in September. Her daughter Bríd met us at Kennedy airport with her three young sons. We stayed the first week with Bríd and her family. Bríd gave us a big treat when she took us with the children for a hay ride in a very country area. There was apple and pumpkin picking; we were supplied with large baskets to fill. Another treat Bríd took us to a Japanese Restaurant; here the chef cooked our meal on a hot table in front of us. It was a treat watching and listening to the food cooking right beside us. At the end of the week I got a bad attack of vertigo. After a day in bed I improved, if still a bit giddy on the legs. I made sure I took my tablets. I had a worry, as I had booked a return flight to North Carolina for the two of us to visit Leo and family; for a while I was afraid I wouldn't be able to make it. I improved in time to fly.

OUR N.C. HOLIDAY

Bríd drove us to Kennedy airport for our trip to North Carolina. Joey and my two grandchildren, Kristina and Ian had a big welcome for us. It was my first time seeing their new home after they left N.J. I was in awe at the size of this house. "You went for a big one, Leo!"

"I did," he said, "a far cry from the small apartments, Mom."

"It certainly is." Joey was doing her best to entertain us, taking us on shopping trips and the odd meal out. She took us to Sears, a very exquisite jewellery store where she had applied for a position as sales lady. She hoped to start working there soon. We admired the very expensive trinkets in this store. Joey told us how they were living on the Bible belt. "You won't see any stores or restaurants open here on Sundays, it is a complete day of rest, the parents take the children to the park."

"Do you miss New Jersey, Joey?" I'm worried as to her answer.

"I did for a while, but I have got used to here and I keep busy. We are two years here and Leo is happy in his new job and the children are much happier in school. The cost of living is much lower, too." She showed us the childrens' two bedrooms, one each, "Now no more squabbling about lights on or off," we laughed, typical of children. "It's what you always wanted Joey, with plenty of closet space." Kristina and Ian would have friends in and go upstairs to a large room that I called a cinema with a big TV screen where they played games. Leo worked late hours all week. Having Sundays free, it was nice all the family to sit together for dinner.

It was soon time to pack the bags again and leave this lovely setting and the mild weather. The week came to an end too fast and Joey left us back to Charlotte airport. We said our goodbyes to her and the children.

Coming back to Long Island, Bobbie spent the last week with her family, and I with my son Mike and family. We broke it for one day when Mary and Mike took the two of us on a trip to the Shrine of our Lady of the Island. It was a beautiful day's outing. And about our last one on holiday; the time flew and soon we were back to Shannon where Bobbie's son met us at the airport. It was a very enjoyable holiday.

CALLING TO SEE BERNIE

I went to visit my friend Bernie Higgins. Her news was not good. We are in her kitchen. She makes a big effort at making me tea and she won't let me help, it was a lovely cup of tea and the last one we had together. Her daughter Alice phoned me to say her mam was now in the hospice and if I could to go and see her. I sat with some of her family, spending a while of the night with her. I went home with a heavy heart. She passed away quietly in the cold month of November. She had a warm send-off with many tributes paid to a lovely lady who gave her time to her family and the youth of the Mervue parish, RIP.

JOEY SALES LADY

I hear from Joey, the excitement in her voice tell it all. "Peggy, I am now sales lady in the high-fashion Sears Jewellery department store," she said in delight. "You sound so happy, Joey, I am happy for you. You must find working in such an exquisite place with jewellery exciting."

"I do, but it took me a while getting used to the till, it's different from the one I used in H. Williams supermarket in Dublin."

"I bet it is, Joey."

"The supervisor is very nice and helpful showing me how it works. Leo is glad I'm not in the house all day."

"I am happy for you too, and this glamourous job suits a glamourous lady like you."

"Thanks Peggy, you pay the nicest compliments."

INVITATION

An invite to Áras an Uachtarain. Ballybane Active Retirement receives an invitation to the Áras an Uachtarain, courtesy of Frank Fahy, Minister of State. We were looking forward to this treat. It was a lovely day's outing with tours of the Áras. We viewed pictures of our many presidents displayed in the entrance hall. We met Enda Kenny, Leader of Fine Gael and shook hands and I got my photo taken with him. Little did I think I was talking to the future Taoiseach, (Prime Minister) of Ireland, I was chuffed to be meeting someone of importance. It was a very interesting and educational day, I would love to go there again and dwell longer on the many portraits of famous dignitaries who visited our country from overseas. We sat to a lovely meal in the company of our host Mr Frank Fahy. We asked him many questions; I don't know if he got answering them all. It was a day to remember.

MAYOR'S AWARD

Hoping for a third time lucky on this occasion with Michael Ford who one year acted as Chairman for the Ballybane Active Retirement Club. Together we nominated BARA in the hopes we would be on the list for the cheque of €500, but once again I was presented with a certificate by Galway City Mayor, Niall Brolochain.

CREATIVE WRITERS

When I heard Galway City Council was sponsoring a Writer in Residence in the Ballybane Library on weekends, it gave me an idea to join this writer's class, as I liked writing short stories. I knew I was no expert and these weekend classes would be very beneficial to me. Our tutor was Poet Michael O'Loughlin, who came down from Dublin each weekend.

Our group was small, give or take about six ladies, with so few, each one got a turn to ask Michael for advice. It was a two-year course. While I was there I continued writing a novel, 'From Clare to Texas'. I told Michael how his tutoring had inspired me on in my effort writing this novel. He asked to see some of my work and he spent some time reading it. I had a feeling he might tell me to scrap it. Instead he gave me some useful tips, telling me to continue on as I was going. In the second year, he suggested we write a piece for a book he was preparing with another class he was tutoring in the City.

2007 – ST. BRIGID'S CHURCH

Fr Gearoid P.P. called a 'reach-out' meeting to plan a celebration for the twentieth anniversary of St. Brigid's Church, Ballybane. There was a big attendance. Everyone was making suggestions. It was scheduled for Friday the 20th April. We will hold a Mass first, then a buffet in Flannery's Hotel, and it was suggested a raffle to be held. I volunteered with a few others to get some prizes. I was very successful, for most of the business places I asked a gift from were very generous. When I had about seventy-two piled up in my sitting room I said, I have enough. On the evening of the celebration I would take them to the hotel and John Rabbitte was the person in charge; he would know what to do with them.

At five thirty p.m. on the Friday, I was all dressed up in my pink full-length dress and Bobbie O'Reilly came in and sat down. We were chatting about the evening. When the phone rang I answered it, it was my son Leo. "Hi Mom," he said, "are you on your own?"

"No," I said, "Bobbie and Larry are here."

"Sit down Mom; I have something to tell you." Without drawing a breath, he said, "Joey died this morning Mom."

I was stunned. "Oh Leo," I said, then I started to cry and couldn't talk. Leo hung up the phone. I could hardly get my breath; I tried calming myself as best I could.

I immediately phoned my poor son back. "My dear son, that was sudden."

"It was; she died in the hospital from thrombosis."

"Oh, God help us."

"I was talking to her yesterday she said she had a pain in her leg and went in for a check-up and would be coming home today."

"How are the children, Leo?"

"They are upset and crying."

"Leo, I will get back to you after I call and tell the girls." I called Margery and Caroline; they both came to the house very upset and we hugged and cried. I said, "First we must book flights for tomorrow to fly over to be with Leo and the children." While the girls were doing that, I called Fr. Gearoid to tell him of our sad news and that I wouldn't be with them at the church celebration. He was deeply shocked and said he would pray for us all at the Mass. I thanked him and told him about the prizes for the night, my daughters would take them up and leave them in his house. "That is alright, John Rabbitte will look after them."

I called Leo and told him the girls had booked a flight out and we would be with him next day. I could feel the relief in his voice.

JOEY'S FUNERAL

We boarded the plane early in the morning at Shannon Airport. It was as sad a situation as my own when I buried Leo's young father in 1962 at the age of 35. My beautiful daughter-in-law Joey is only 45, leaving her brokenhearted husband, her daughter Kristina aged 17, and son Ian aged 12. I thought of Joey; for eighteen years she was trying to make small apartments spacious and comfortable for the four of them; now with a beautiful big house and everyone having their own room, she gets only two years to enjoy it. God called you to himself, Josephine/Joey.

Her funeral was well-attended with her family from Dublin, ourselves from Galway, Leo's relations, his brother Mike and wife Mary with their family from L.I., Leo's Uncle Leo and cousins, who live in other part's of the states and many of Leo and Joey's work colleagues. I will never forget how beautiful she looked laid out in her casket/coffin; she looked so beautiful and peaceful. During the Mass, the priest offered many prayers for her husband and children, for God to give them the strength they need now to carry them through this hard time. Josephine Beggen is buried in Forest Lawn Cemetery, N.C. Each time I visit N.C., Leo brings me to pray at her grave. I am on the same duty when in N.Y. My son Mike and his wife Mary bring me to St. Raymond's Cemetery in the Bronx, where we pray for my late husband Michael Beggen. When Leo comes to L.I it gives himself and Mike the opportunity to go to their Dad's grave; being so far, it's not often they visit it.

A REMEMBRANCE MASS

It is June and I have been waiting for a chance to book a remembrance Mass for Joey. After arranging with Fr. Gearoid and telling him the Mass was for my daughter-in-law Joey, he asked what procedure I would be taking. I will be inviting family members to come, and take part in the Mass, the readings, prayers of the faithful, and the bringing up of the gifts of bread and wine to the altar. "That is nice Margaret; you had a big procession of gifts for the fireman's Mass; it was a wonderful remembrance for a fire hero."

"Thanks Father," I said. It was a lovely Mass for Joey; her two sisters Mary and Ann and brother Martin came from Dublin. Her sister Ann Roberts and Leo's cousin, Tommy Beggen did the readings. Prayers of the faithful were by Leo's sisters Margery and Caroline, nieces Lisa and Rachel Ruffley. Bread and wine was brought to the altar by Joey's sister Mary Quinlan and me. Fr. Gearoid gave a tender homily in Joey's memory. "It is always very sad to hear a young mother being taken from her children and husband, but God's ways are not ours. Mass and prayer will help see Leo and his two young children through this difficult time."

The Mass was well-attended by family and neighbours. We finished up with a simple meal in Flannery's Hotel. Joey was well-known to my family, having been on holidays with me in Ballybane. Joey's brother Martin O'Connell went home to Dublin after the meal. Her sisters Mary and Ann stayed with me for the night and we sat and talked about Joey into the early hours of the next morning.

KRISTINA AND IAN

My two grandchildren came from N.C. to stay a few weeks with their mother's family in Dublin. On their trip to Galway, their aunty Ann accompanied them on the train where I met then. I was happy to see them; as it was school holiday time they would be spending a few weeks with me. They said goodbye to Ann who went right back to Dublin again. It was good to have them and make distractions, at the same time their Mam was often mentioned. Their Dad and Diana, a friend of the family came home to take a break also. I was working out in my mind what to do. Caroline worked for the students' union in the GMIT and one of her jobs was hiring buses to accommodate the students to various functions. I asked her to hire out a minibus and I would take the family on a sightseeing tour of the country.

I was glad to see a beautiful sunny day for this treat. We visited the Cliffs of Moher, then on to Bunratty Castle where Diana and Leo enjoyed a pint of Guinness. It was a lovely day and the Irish countryside was at its best. I asked the bus driver to drive us to Doolin, for I knew everyone was ready for a good meal by this time. We found a great restaurant. The choice from the menu was bacon, cabbage and mashed potatoes for the adults, while the children choose chips and burgers. Leo washed his down with a glass of Guinness and so did Diana. A real American, she loved the Guinness; Margery and I had tea and the children preferred to stop along the way home for ice cream. It was a good day's outing, with plenty of distractions; everyone was tired after the County Clare tour. It was soon packing up time again for the train to head back to Dublin to spend a few more days with Joey's family. I was sad to see them leave. The year dragged on and I would be keeping a promise I made my two grandchildren when they were in my house. I was going to go over to N.C. and spend Christmas with them.

I BOOKED THREE MONTHS

Flying out in October to North Carolina, I was hoping they would be in fair form. Leo and my two darling grandchildren met me at Charlotte airport. Leo of course, was happy I would be with his children, as his work in the food industry and especially coming up to Christmas, kept him working late hours. Kristina would have her girlfriends in, they were rehearsing for a school play. It took up a lot of time and was part of an exam. Kristina wanted it to be perfect so their group would get the highest marks. She would wait up to tell her dad when he came home from work how well their play was progressing. They had to make their own particular costumes and some money was required to buy material. She would tell her dad how much she needed and he would give it to her. She was very busy as she played the saxophone in the school band. Ian, on the other hand, played the wooden flute and sometimes the trumpet. Kristina made sure he practised his music for the Christmas play. I found the days very long, so I decided to continue writing my book, a novel. I kept adding to it. One day I let Kristina read some of it. "It's good, Granny, I can't wait for you to get it finished." She gave me the encouragement I needed.

OCTOBER

While I was in N.C. Caroline phoned me with her exciting news. "Mom, I have graduated from the GMIT with a Bachelor of Arts in Personnel Management." I was so happy for her. I asked, "Who was with you when you received it?"

"My daughter Caroline, you will love the photo of the two of us, me in my cap and gown, and her wearing a big smile."

"I can't wait; keep one of the photos for me."

"I will Mom, but I wish you had been here."

"You had your daughter; that was more important, I'm going to tell Leo and Mike about your success. I will see you in a couple of months."

Caroline Dowling holding her Degree in Bachelor of Arts, accompanied by her daughter Caroline.

NOVEMBER IN AMERICA

The last Thursday in the month is a national holiday. It is a day America celebrates Thanksgiving. When I lived there in the 1950/60s it was celebrated like Christmas, with family dinners of turkey and ham, there would be no exchange of gifts. But gifts of food were given to the poor.

Here in N.C. in 2007 I learned something I won't ever forget. As my son Leo worked for the leading food stores in the USA, Harris Teeter, like all Businesses in the States, Harris Teeter would close for that day. But the staff didn't get the day off. Instead, a large enclosed arena was hired for the day. The staff set to work in groups at special stations. They prepared food for the poor of the city. Many hot tables were carried into the arena. Turkeys, hams, vegetables, large dishes of mashed potatoes and sweet potatoes and large jugs of gravy. The meals were served on a strong type of plastic plates with plastic cutlery. The desert was pumpkin Pie with cream or ice cream, a speciality served for this celebration. The coffee and tea urns were positioned around the arena and the people helped themselves to these beverages.

The employees only drank water, for they were kept busy serving up hot food to the poor people from ten a.m. to six that evening without stopping. The employee's children also gave up their free time to do this act of charity, as did Leo's children. I was happy to be counted as one of the helpers too. My job was to hand out the ice-cold drinks and make sure the bin was kept filled. The tiredness I felt at six o'clock that evening was satisfying.

This is how the Americans celebrate the harvest and I can boast I once took part in it. We served up to seven hundred poor people on that day.

There was one rule; no one was permitted to bring in a bag with them; the food was not to be taken out of the building. It had to be consumed only inside, this was done so everyone who came in got their Thanksgiving dinner.

Driving home to Leo's house, he suggested that, before we cook our dinner,

"I want everyone to take a shower and freshen up after ye're hard days' work."

Indeed it was very refreshing. We prepared a dinner of mashed potatoes, roast chicken, vegetables and corn muffins. Dessert was ice-cream. God Bless America.

Christmas was fast approaching. Leo didn't neglect to put up a tree and decorate the house with the help of his two children in celebration of the festive season; the holy crib was also to be seen. We all went to Midnight Mass. The priest, after saying Mass, would call out, "Happy Birthday" to anyone who had a birthday that night. This time Kristina's Beggen's name was called and everyone sang 'Happy Birthday' to her, she was celebrating her eighteenth birthday. I asked her how she was feeling. "I am sad Mammy is not here," then quickly she turned and said, "Dad and Ian are sad, too. We are so glad you are here, Gran."

Christmas dinner was quite a big spread. Leo invited his good friends who are there for him and his children at all times, taking them to school, band practice or anything they needed when he was at work. I was happy to meet with Diana again and then I had the pleasure of meeting Gill and Gale, these three people were Leo's wonderful friends; they were there for him and still are his constant friends.

It was a double celebration for Kristina, her dad had a big birthday cake for her and we sang 'Happy Birthday' as she cut the cake. There were tears in everyone's eyes remembering her dear mother. On St. Stephens's Day we went to visit Joey's grave, no doubt it was a sad time. We prayed and thanked God she didn't suffer.

Larry came over for the New Year and we sang *Auld Lang Syne*. Before we left to come home, we helped with the taking down of the decorations. I was very sad to be leaving them, but I knew they would be fine having so many nice, caring friends near them. Hugging my two grandchildren, I didn't want to let them go.

Leo left us to Charlotte airport for the long flight back home. Even though it was cold when we landed at Shannon, we were glad to be back and I had a satisfied feeling to have been company to Leo and his children at this lonely time. And also having the experience of serving food to some of America's poor.

2008 - RETURNING HOME

I said to Larry, "I left in 2007 and in three months I'm back in 2008, what's another year?" The house is very bare; I wonder how it felt having no Christmas celebrated in it. "Did you have a good Christmas, Larry, with your family in the North?"

"I did, we had Christmas dinner with my daughter Evelyn and family; they send their condolences on the death of Leo's wife."

"I will thank them. I was afraid the roads would be too frosty to drive down to Galway and I might miss my flight to the States, but it all worked out well." "How did you like it in Leo's?"

"He goes the full hog with the decorations and celebrations."

"You noticed that, he did it for the children's sake. Did you see how Kristina was laughing when herself and Ian was playing the carols for us?"

"I know they will be fine, Leo has a lot of nice friends to help them."

BOOK LAUNCH

Since the two years we joined the writer's class in the Ballybane Library, many things happened, some traumatic. The sudden loss of my beautiful daughter-in-law Joey, weighed heavy on me. I was very glad of the two hours attending the writer's class once a week. I was trying to finish my book and getting advice from the tutor; he was valuable help. Our group were compiling our own stories to add to Michael O'Loughlin's writer-in-residence book, 'Galway, a City of Strangers.'

The launch of this book would be taking place in the Town Hall. The

Ballybane group would meet the other groups of writers, most of whom were from about twenty other countries. It was most interesting; they spoke in their own languages, but had a good smattering of English. Hence, the book title 'Galway, A City of Strangers'. Cllr. Tom Costello, Mayor of Galway City launched the book and took special notice of the title, saying as we have many cultures welcomed to our fast-growing city, the title of this book is appropriate. It gives me great pleasure in launching, 'Galway, A City of Strangers'.

My personal piece was titled 'My Story'. I was telling how I found Galway when I returned home in 1963, after over eleven years living in America. I didn't find much change, my mother still had no running water, there were very few cars to be seen driving on the road, buses only did long journeys, there was very little change made in the years from 1952-1963; people were still struggling. Country people came to the town in horse and cart or cycled carrying their heavy shopping on the handle bars of their bicycles, those who did neither like my mother, walked the three miles to Galway every Saturday, pushing the old pram she kept after the babies had out grown it. She brought her eggs to the market in it to sell. Then she filled it with groceries and pushed it back home again. The launching of the book was a lovely social occasion and while having refreshments, the two groups had a chance to mix and share ideas.

KALLUM

My grandson Kallum is getting ready to make his first Communion. His mother is trying to keep their spirits up because Kalum's daddy is back in hospital and we are praying he will be well enough to see his son making his first Communion. Margery tells me, "If Colm is still in hospital I will bring him to the church in a wheelchair; this way neither he nor his son will miss out."

"That is a good idea, Marge." The week before the first Holy Communion Sunday, Colm was well enough to be allowed home. Marg. set to work getting Communion outfits and it was a father and son look-a-like in the suits, shirts and ties. It was a happy dad being present at his son's First Holy Communion in the Holy Family Church, Mervue. Colm's sisters and brother were pleased also to see this answer to prayer. Sadly, the Fahy grandparents, Johnny and Maureen had recently passed away. A very nice afternoon was spent in the Claregalway Hotel celebrating with a lovely meal. It was a happy occasion for Kallum and his Daddy.

NEXT DOOR NEIGHBOUR'S FIRE

I am finishing off my book of 'Fireside Nostalgia Poetry' in the hopes of launching it in the Ballybane Library in May, and this is April. I'm sitting at the kitchen table reading over the poems. In a day's time, I will be taking it to the printer. As I sit and continue reading, I hear crackling behind me. I think it's the radiator but it is a hot day and there is no need to turn on the heat. I look out the back door and as I do the next-door neighbour's patio door bursts out with a shower of black smoke. Going back to my kitchen, my neighbour is there.

"Call the fire brigade," she tells me, "my house is on fire." I tell her to wait at the door. The City Fire Brigade is not available to come. We wait for the one ten miles away. "We will be there in ten minutes," the fireman I'm speaking to tells me, I give the details and go outside, closing the door behind me. A lot of people have gathered. One man tells me to move my car. As I open the door to get the car key, a blast of black smoke hit me in the face; I run in and get the car keys and I move my car to the next street, feeling very sick and faint. I had swallowed the smoke. A neighbour, Maureen Joyce took me into her house and gave me a few glasses of water to drink. I felt better and left.

Going towards my house, the fire brigade is there and the men won't let me in until the fire is out next door. When Larry comes from pitch and putt I tell him what has happened. My house is destroyed with black smoke. I call my insurance company. Two insurance men come to inspect my house. I am told we must find accommodation straight away for the next two months at least. I phone my friend John

Rabbitte; he is great help and knew a man who was after renovating his house about ten minutes' drive away from my house. John immediately contacted the owner of the house who was willing to rent it to me for the two months while the insurance company secured a company that would take on the big job of clearing out what was destroyed, and redo the entire inside of my home, which I had bought and lived in for only four years. Our clothes were destroyed; the black smoke did untold damage. I was told how wise I was to have house insurance. I could not understand why my insurance should cover the damage when it was not my fault. I was told that, that is the way the law works. While the men were getting my house back to normal, I busied myself finishing my poetry book.

LAUNCHING 'FIRESIDE NOSTALGIA POETRY'

Was this to be a new adventure or challenge in my life? All of my life I loved poetry, especially the verses I would write for my own satisfaction. My daughters Margery and Caroline, on finding them when I was selling "Rock Dale," insisted I should put them to a book. I had never or even thought my poetry was worthy of publication. With their encouragement, I decided I would give it a try.

I got so much help in preparing a little book of poems. The layout and typing was done by Martina Derrane, Ballybane Resource Centre, front cover by Artist Pearl O'Kennedy, Shantalla. It was printed by Ace Printers. The launch took place in the Ballybane Library on the 26th April 2008 and the welcome introduction was carried out by the Ballybane librarian, Siobhan Arkin.

The launch of my very first book ever was performed by Mayor of Galway Councillor, Tom Costello, *"Fireside Nostalgia Poetry."* Mayor Costello paid me many compliments and wished me luck in writing more; he also presented me with a Galway Crystal Plate with his name and year inscribed on it. Many people attended, to name a few, P.P. Fr. Gearoid O'Griofa, Galway Historian Peadar O'Dowd, included were my daughters, Margery Fahy and Caroline Dowling, my brothers Eddie and Paddy Abberton, my sister Mrs Mary Nally and little grandnephew Luke Nally, grandchildren Caroline Dowling and Kallum Fahy, also Teresa Abberton, sister-in-law and her daughter Rose Walsh, Larry Doyle and daughter Ursula O'Kennedy. Photographer Joe Shaughnessy took many photos which appeared in the City Tribune, plus many friends and neighbours who bought several books. There was tea, coffee and cake for everyone; it was one great day, I was so happy I made up a lovely picture scrapbook of that memorial day, that went so well for me. My daughters didn't forget to have their little joke. "Isn't it a coincidence that you are launching your *Fireside Nostalgia Poetry Book* now?"

"Why?" I ask.

"Well you're not in your house because of a fire," they say with a giggle.

"Very observant of you," I retort.

Launch of "Fireside Nostalgia Poetry"
With my sister Mary Nally and brothers Paddy and Eddie Abberton

EMPLOYED

Caroline is employed by Collins McNicholas in Galway city. Parking space is difficult to find and she applies to Sim2Learn and is hired, and, as its outside the city, parking space is fully available. But one year here and the company is about to go out of business. Caroline applies to C&F and is successful here, she likes the job but again she would like to return to Collins McNicholas. As it happened, Collins McNicholas Company transferred to Briarhill Industrial Estate, where there was no shortage of parking spaces.

Caroline soon received a call from Collins McNicholas requesting her to return to her previous job with their company. She accepted and returned after giving in her notice to C&F.

RETURNING TO CNOC NA CILLE

I return to No. 12 Cnoc na Cille after the fire. It was June, two months after the next-door neighbour's house had gone on fire and caused a lot of damage to mine. As I was living in a terraced house, I got the dirty, black smoke right through to it. Now it is back to itsself again, I am still nervous. The insurance has come through and the bills are coming in eating it up. The workmen are paid, the laundry and dry cleaners are also paid and before moving in, I have to buy four new beds, also the landlord whose house I rented for the two months has to get his rent. Plus, I have to replace our clothes that were damaged for me and Larry. Most important, winter coats, jumpers and pants. But I thank God the fire didn't happen during the night.

ANOTHER PHONE CALL

Getting phone calls from my cousins in County Clare always makes me feel uneasy; until I hear the tone of the person's voice I can immediately detect the nature of their news.

This time it is sad the death of my late uncle Paddy Hurley's wife Annie. Even though she had been a long time suffering, she was always cheerful when I would visit her at home or in the hospital, mostly at home as her daughter Sister Margaret had compassionate leave to take care of her mother. Annie was one of the best friends I ever had. When trouble hit me, I would get into the car, drive to

Moygala, County Clare and pour out my woes to her; she would console me and give me encouraging advice. I will miss her. God finally called her home; she was ninety-one years of age. An elegant strong lady, who for years cycled her bicycle to Limerick to do her weekly shopping, to Six-Mile-Bridge on a Sunday for Mass, through rain or sunshine,. She was not without her crosses. Her husband Paddy died suddenly twenty-five years before her, also the sudden death of her daughter Margaret's husband, Brendan Sheerin, and the death of her young son Pa Jo at the age of fifty-three in a freak accident. This was a great shock to her. As she would say, "Prayer will get us all through it." She is laid to rest with her husband Paddy in Kileen Six-Mile-Bridge.

2009 - THE WEDDING RECEPTION

The wedding reception of my nephew Christy Abberton and his wife Michelle was held in the Shannon Oaks Hotel, right next to the Shannon waters on the 17th January 2008. It was a very stormy day, the wind was blowing wild. Getting out of my nephew Patrick's car at the hotel door, but for the help of the doorman I am sure I would have had a cold dip in the Shannon waters. I was due a hip replacement three days later; even with the aid of a walking stick I was unable to keep my balance. However, I enjoyed the evening's entertainment and as can be expected, the bride and groom were elegant in their wedding attire. Their wedding was filmed for those who were unable to attend the nuptials. Michelle's figure-hugging off-the-shoulder gown was beautiful, as was Christy's suit and classy yellow tie; they made a handsome couple. The music was tempting but because of my painful hip I had to remain sitting.

LEFT HIP REPLACEMENT

This was an operation I welcomed after suffering two years of pain. I knew on waking up I would be free from such agony, and thank God, I was. My gratitude is due to Mr O'Sullivan for the second successful hip replacement he did for me and to the wonderful staff of the Merlin Park Hospital for the ten days' care they gave me. The physiotherapist Liam Concannon helped me back to mobility again, although I must go at a slow pace with crutches. Then, a week in Mystical Rose nursing home for more recuperating. Back home and with the help of my daughters Margery and Caroline whenever they could, it all helped my fast improvement.

GRANDCHILDRENS LETTERS

As always, I get excited when I receive a letter from one of my grandchildren. This one is extra special; from Cassandra Beggen and as I am just over a hip operation her news is cheering me up. She writes that she, with her mam and dad who are invited to attend an orientation dinner in the Molloy College Campus, Rockville Centre N.Y. where she is accepted, giving her an opportunity to meet some of the professors and check out the college. She writes, "I've met the track coach of the college and he is interested in getting me on his team. I have had a great season on track for my High School Farmingdale team and I'm captain of the long jumpers, I'm also among the top three sprinters and made it to state, qualifying for the 400-metre sprint in relay." Such wonderful news from my talented granddaughter.

She continues on to tell me that a big party was held in their team's honour. Herself and her mother Mary are busy preparing to march on St. Patrick's Day with the Tara pipe and drum band "This will be our sixteenth parade, Mother is playing pipes and I the snare drum. Our section won first place in the Rockaway parade and received a big trophy last year." I love to get her enlightening letters and she never leaves out asking about my health. And always ends with love from Cassandra and plenty of x's.

KILLARNEY

Ballybane Active Retirement were planning their spring break to Killarney. I have a worry; will I be able to go after having recently had a hip replacement operation? I was feeling well and having no club responsibilities, I said I would chance it, so I brought my trusty walking stick. I was glad I went, for Killarney was a beautiful place to have a holiday. The hotel was comfortable and we were in luck with the fine weather. We took lots of sightseeing trips. The days the group did walking trips, I sat reading in the hotel. Three months later it was an

outing to Connemara. Kylemore Abbey was very popular with lots of tourists. We decided to have our lunch there and then visit Killary Harbour.

A TRUE MEMBER PASSES AWAY

One of our stanch members sadly passed away, Kathleen Connolly. Kathleen attended all of the activities and functions I organised for the BARA Club. She would always encourage and compliment me on my efforts. Even though she was age eighty, she didn't look a day of it; she was a vibrant person and was indeed sadly missed, by her family and especially me.

COMPUTER SKILLS

There is a lot of talk about the importance of learning how to use the computer, and although I have made an attempt by attending various computer classes for the older generation, I cannot get the hang of it. Each class I attended there was a different tutor with their own idea of training. I would like to get repeats of the piece of what I was trying to grasp, but that was not happening, so I gave up.

WORKING HARD

I am working day and night to get to the end of the novel I started two years ago *'From Clare to Texas'*. I am hoping it will be ready for launching early in next year. I hear that a six-week Computer Course by Age Action for senior people who want to learn Computer Skills, is coming to the Ballybane Resource Centre, where a computer room is set up with about eight computers. Some members from BARA took up the offer and a grant was on hand to cover the cost of the course. We learned first how to turn on a computer and how to use the mouse, which kept flying all over the page every time I touched it. I have convinced myself that it is all too complicated for me.

By the end of the six weeks, I had mastered the use of the mouse, but with only two tutors and eight beginners, I decided that I would need a one-to-one, which would be too expensive. I was almost giving up hope of ever learning. The constant talk about computer skills seemed that it was a must in a person's life. I was told of classes in the Age Action centre at the other side of the city near the small Crane. The problem with that was parking the car; it was almost impossible. The tutor Patricia who was teaching me was a very patient lady, and would repeat every detail a number of times which I needed. I got a copybook and began to write down what she was teaching me. By now I had my own laptop which my daughter Caroline purchased for me online. "What does online mean?"

"Never mind, learn a bit first."

There were times I would get up during the night and work until I got the subject right.

PATRICA MADE A SUGGESTION

In time and with the problem of parking the car, Patricia Knight invited me to come to her house where she would teach me through Age Action and I could park outside her gate. It was a good move and I made good friends with her lovely, elderly mother Mai Knight. This was a wonderful move and Mai would have tea and cake ready every

Monday morning for me. I would say, "You are spoiling me, Mai." Then we would have a chat and finally Patricia and I would get to work, bringing my laptop with me to use made the learning easy.

FLOWER GARDEN PRIZE WINNING

Ballybane community form held a flower garden prize day to be presented to the winners in the Clayton Hotel by Councillor Declan McDonnell. The prize winners waited in anticipation to hear Chairman Tommy O'Flaherty call out the winner's name. I was very proud to be a winner in the first section and accepted a beautiful plaque. It meant a year of hard work cultivating with attention to colour, height and thought as to the flower garden size and grass margins. Prizes were selected for all areas of Ballybane that entered.

2010 - LAUNCH FROM CLARE TO TEXAS

Is almost ready to send to the publisher to check over the book and return to me for a re-read and get my daughters Caroline to perform her English skills in corrections, and Margery to read it word for word. Margery's young husband Colm is not improving and we are praying for him. Margery tells me she will probably have to leave her job as a Down syndrome carer to look after Colm full-time. "I guess it's a choice you will have to make."

"I guess it is, Mom."

"Call me when you need me."

"I will," she says. I am so saddened for her lovely husband to have this incurable disease, Colitis and Crohn's disease. Now that *'From Clare to Texas'* is ready, I have booked the Ballybane Library again, the next items on the list are, to contact the City Mayor, order refreshments, contact the newspaper and Galway Bay F.M., then send out invitations to family members and friends.

I will be making a donation in aid of Colitis and Crohn's Disease. I was very disappointed that the Western Reign had no support group in Galway for this disease to accept the donation. Tom Duggan of Renmore gave me the Dublin area address. I wrote to Elizabeth/Betty Lattimore, honorary secretary, based in Dublin and explained what I was proposing to do. I also included an invitation for her to attend the launch. She promptly replied and thanked me for my kindness and said she would gladly be with us on the day.

Everything is in place and I am as nervous as a kitten. The book is at last ready and several boxes have arrived from 'Choice Publishing', Drogheda, County Louth, and the books look well. My daughter Caroline is wearing the green coat and carrying the old-fashioned brown suitcase, all of which I used when emigrating in 1952 to the U.S.A. She posed as a girl looking out to sea about to emigrate for the photograph on the front cover of the book, *'From Clare to Texas,'* The photo was taken in Ballyloughane by Michael/Mickey Ward, Clare View.

This book was launched on the 3rd July 2010 in the Ballybane Library. County Librarian, Pat McMahon, on welcoming me, gave a nice talk about the book. "A novel can either be a success or a failure; I can safely say this one is going to be a success." His words were gratefully appreciated. Ballybane librarian Siobhan Arkin also commented on my efforts. Councillor Terry O'Flaherty, Mayor of Galway City launched *'From Clare To Texas'* and gave many accounts of me whom she said she knew, from her mother Bridie O'Flaherty's time. Bridie was elected Mayor of Galway City a couple of times. For the launching, I had a ribbon fixed for my grandson Kallum to cut which he did. I was pleased the honorary secretary, Betty Lattimore and her friend Mary Dunphy were able to come from Dublin. They presented me with some T-shirts with the logo SCC; these I shared with family. Betty gave a talk on the history of the Society of Colitis and Crohn's Disease there was a support group set up in Dublin, it served many young people who are affected with such a painful incurable disease. She said the donation they will receive from Margaret will be very welcomed. Also attending were historian Willie Henry, Tom Duggan, Renmore, my daughters Margery and her son Kallum and Caroline, our cousins the Cooney's from Clare, Jammie and Irene with their two young sons, Noah and Harvey who stole the day with their trilby hats. Many friends and neighbours attended and bought lots of books from Caroline and Bobby O'Reilly for this worthy cause. Everyone enjoyed the refreshments laid on. I was, as always, so grateful to the staff of the Ballybane library and the many friends and relations for their support.

JOINING THE CREATIVE WRITERS

I joined a creative writer's group in Croí Na Gaillimhe, Mill Street, Galway. This was a regular Friday get-together with at least eighteen enthusiastic writers sitting around a table for two hours with Mr John McGinty, volunteer facilitator. Of course, there was time for a chat around the kettle while it boiled for the tea or coffee. John gave instructions as to how to form your creative piece tirelessly, giving pointers and handing out helpful leaflets to take home and study. Each Friday he would suggest a certain project to write on, then end by saying, "Or anything of your choice, but always write about something." The following week, we would read our story then wait for his comments which sometimes could be challenging; then you felt you had caught his attention. In my three years attending I had written many short stories, these I compiled in book form, eventually launching it in the Ballybane Library. I invited Councillor Terry O'Flaherty Mayor of Galway City to do her second launching of a book for me. For this book, I would donate the proceeds to Leigh McCann, chairman of Galway Autism Partnership (GAP). Leigh spoke on behalf of GAP and gave an account of the number of children who suffer with Autism and the pressure on families. I was able in time to donate over €3000 to this worthy cause. Having family relations whose children suffer with Autism, I was glad to help in some way. Leigh was very grateful to me. I thanked the staff of the library who are always so helpful, especially the executive librarian, Siobhan Arkins. I thanked the large crowd of people who attended this launching; after the long afternoon, the refreshments were welcome.

SOME SAD NEWS

It is going to be a hard winter and starting early. Water pipes are freezing. One day as I'm talking to a plumber, a friend of my brother Eddie Abberton, he asked me how is Eddie. "He is fine," I tell him.

"Oh," he says, "he is OK again."

"What?" I said, "Was he not well?"

"I heard he had a little turn."

"Thank you for telling me." He didn't say what was wrong with Eddie, and when I hadn't heard from his family, I was thinking it can't be too serious.

It was coming very close to Christmas when I got a phone call from Eddie's son Gerard. I was surprised to hear from him so late in the evening. "Is everything alright, Gerard?"

"Dad is here in Merlin Park Hospital; he told me to let you know."

"Thanks, Gerard, I will go up straight away to see him." The hospital is only about one mile from my house. My brother was in bed; he had a very swollen hand stretched out from him. "Did you break your hand, Eddie?"

"No, it has been paining me a few months. I have been in and out of hospital a few times."

"My goodness, Eddie I did not know."

"Well here I am now. My hand was a lot more swollen but it is gone down now," said Eddie.

"Will you be home for Christmas?"

"I think I will, with the help of God."

"I will call to the house to see you."

On my way home from the hospital, I thought it strange no one told me poor Eddie was so sick.

After Christmas, I called to his house to see him, his wife Honor opened the door and we wished each other a happy Christmas. I asked how Eddie was.

"He is in the sitting room, go in and talk to him."

"Hello Eddie, how are you?" We kissed and wished each other a happy Christmas. He tells me he is feeling good but has to get treatment. I hoped he would continue to get better.

As time went on, he was in and out of hospital and on one occasion when he was at home I called to see him. I told him I would be going to America as my son Mike was having his gallbladder removed; he was sorry to hear his nephew Mike was having so many operations. The next time I went to see Eddie he was in the hospice and walking around. "My legs," he says, "are getting weak and you know with all the hurling I did, they were the strongest part of me."

Today is his eighty-first birthday. I am so happy to have this time with him and I have a small, expensive little box of five chocolates for him. I said, "This is what a prince would receive."

"Well this Prince will eat them when he comes back from the hospital. The ambulance will be coming for me and they will take me, chair and all." As he was leaving we shook hands and kissed. I said, "I am going over to see Mike tomorrow."

"Good luck Maggie."

"You too, Eddie." It was the last time I saw him alive.

2011 - I FLY OUT

I fly out to be with my son Mike in Long Island for a few weeks. I am pleased with his progress and tell him about his Uncle Eddie. Eddie's son James, his wife and two children live in Boston. Mike gives me their phone number. "Would you like to call him?"

"I would, please." I was glad to get talking to James.

"This is your aunt Margaret."

"Thanks for calling, Margaret," he says. "I am in a hurry to get the next flight home. Dad is in a coma. I hope to make it in time."

"You will James, please God. I won't be at the funeral James; I am here with Mike."

"I understand," he says.

Eddie Abberton passed away on the 15th September 2012. Caroline phoned to tell me, I ask her to represent me at the funeral and to get a flower wreath from us and a Mass card. "I will," she said. I put down the phone and cried. My brother Eddie is gone to heaven. Mike and Mary comforted me; I am thankful to them for their company. We spent the day talking about the sport of hurling that Eddie lived for. Mike had many memories of his Uncle Eddie when he was a small boy after coming from America. How Eddie would make up funny songs about himself and Leo without an air, making us laugh. "You remember them silly times, Mike?"

"I do, they are stuck in my mind, Mom. May he R.I.P. now."

MY FIRST VISIT TO MY BROTHER

Eddie's grave. Arriving in Shannon, I was in plenty of time for the bus to Galway. It was good to be home. I said to Caroline, "After I have a rest I would like you to take me to visit Eddie's grave."

It was a sad moment, a bit hard to grasp, as I was unable to attend the final farewell to my dear brother.

"Thank you, Caroline for representing me at his funeral, it cannot have been easy for you."

"I was fine, Mom," she assured me. On the way home she filled me in on the big funeral he had, the Castlegar Hurlers, Corporation road workers, the men that worked on the Quincentennial Bridge where he worked as foreman, his card-playing mates in Flannery's Hotel, the many parishioners from Mervue and Castlegar, and many of his hurling mates, all who knew him.

"He is happy now, Mom."

In a few days' time, I will call to see Honour. I know she is missing him. When I got the opportunity, with my friend Larry, we called to pay our respects to Honor and also met her son Eammon. I sympathized with them on their sad bereavement. I felt a deep void in the house. I said to myself, "He is really gone, but my memories of him will always be with me." We talked fondly of him and also of my son Mike's good progress.

CÚIRT FESTIVAL

International Cúirt Festival of Literature was featuring worldwide, with authors and poets. I was in the Ballybane Library changing a book, when the librarian, Siobhan Arkin, asked me if I would like to host the festival, as the organisers were looking for people to play host to kitchen poetry reading. "Would you be interested in taking it on?"

"I said I would love to, what do I have to do, Siobhan?"

"Just boil the kettle and have mugs on the table for tea and coffee. Invite a few of your friends; the duration is about two hours. Some of the library staff will bring the guest and his/her followers to your house in the morning. This was a new challenge for me but as a lover of poetry, I was looking forward to meeting well-known poets. A lady poet was first, Yvonne Cullen, accompanied by a violinist and there was a combination of poetry and traditional music. This was very entertaining. Playing host was fun to a full kitchen of enthusiastic listeners. The library staff served up tea, coffee and biscuits and my homemade lemon drizzle cake; my treat for everyone. All enjoyed a relaxing morning.

It was the first of five yearly sessions playing host to literary readers in my kitchen. I enjoyed the privilege of meeting famous artists.

2012, and I'm again being host to a session of poetry and music. Robin Roland read some very sad verses from her book, one of my invited guests cried. She said, "Don't worry, I am a weepy for anything a bit sad." Robin was accompanied by harpist Kathleen Loughnane and she played and sang beautiful Irish airs. The morning ended with tea, coffee and my lemon drizzle cake, a pleasant ending.

2013, this was a very exciting morning, for we had the well-known author/poet, Michael Harding. This was a real privilege. The kitchen was full, people sat on the floor and anywhere they could find a space. Michael told us of the many traumas that haunted his life but he always worked through them as best he could. I felt like crying. I told him a few details of my own traumatic life, he shook my hand and said, "Life is a test." The two hours were over and the tea had to be rushed, but everyone got a slice of lemon drizzle cake.

A sombre morning, 2014, and I'm busy making the annual lemon drizzle cake. Our poet this morning is a young man, Dave Lordan. I welcomed him. He had very few people with him apart from a few of the library staff. I invited ten people but only two came; even so Dave was not deterred. He read some funny articles he had written, an entertaining morning with plenty of time for the tea, coffee and lemon drizzle cake.

2015, and "Who are we having this year?" I ask Siobhan.

"You're hosting for Little John Nee and Sarah Clancy." I knew we were in for a lively morning. Again, a full kitchen and with Little John who brought a peculiar musical instrument, a type of organ which he would wind up, then sing or tell one of his many funny jokes. Sarah walked around holding her book of stories as if she was reading it, but really, she was reciting from memory. It was a hilarious morning and was over far too soon.

While the entertainers packed up, the library staff did the usual of serving tea and coffee, with yes, some lemon drizzle cake slices. I enjoyed such kitchen entertainment each year and met many people I may never meet again. I wonder will they remember me for my lemon drizzle cake.

I'm pictured in my kitchen with author/poet Michael Harding.

BALLYBANE ACTIVE RETIREMENT

We are into another busy year with art, the art tutor is Pearl O'Kennedy; it's a big class with ten members, taking all of the three hours for Pearl to get to each one. It was a six-week course, with everyone pleased with their finished masterpieces. Mine was of a little boy playing in a puddle of water in front of a thatched cottage. I framed it and hung it on the landing.

SPRING BREAK

The BARA members were busy deciding as to the best area to have their spring break, many brochures were passed around, and no one would agree on one particular place, resulting that the deposits would be in too late so it had to be cancelled. The leader of the walker's group, Joey Reed, was organising where they would have their annual lunch. A few members who were not at the launch of *'From Clare to Texas'* were keen to buy a couple of books after the club morning was over.

Today I must hurry home, for the painter is coming to paint the outside of the house. It won't be as costly as having "Rock Dale" painted and won't take as long. No wooden windows to contend with. Coming into spring and everyone is talking of the work that must be done outdoors, putting the disappointing decision of the club's spring break, well into the backs of our minds.

FOR A LONG TIME

I have been itching to pay a visit to see the Agricultural College, Athenry, County Galway, where I was employed for a few years as a waitress before immigrating to America in 1952. I had started writing a book about my time there; although I had a store of memories, I felt in need of a recap. I had the notion the only way to do that and fulfil a longing I had, was to go back and visit the college where I worked over half a century ago. That makes me sound very old, which I am, and proud of it.

On a very cold, wintry day I ventured to drive the twenty miles to see the place. It took courage, for I didn't know what I would discover after an absence of so many years. I pulled up at the gate, which had not changed in that length of time, but it was the last of the familiarity. I walked into a whole new era; I knew there would be changes, but in what way? Would the whole place be boarded up?

Walking around the college, I discovered the huts that accommodate the young farmers in my time were gone and grass grew where they once were. There were people employed there, and I was worried I would meet someone who would tell me I was trespassing, and I would have to leave before I accomplished the mission I came for. A young man saw me and came to ask if he could help. I explained my reason for being there. He shook hands with me and asked if I would like to see inside the college. I said I would love to. He brought me in and introduced me to the workers who were sitting at computers, photocopying machines, etc, a big change from my time working there, when this room was a kitchen containing cookers, pots, pans, and the Aga Range where the cook, my Aunt Mary Hurley took her place each day to cook for many people, with her kitchen assistant, Maureen Buckley. Everything to do with the domestic life was the rule here in my time, now it's converted over to electronics. It was a great experience, if a sad one.

I thanked everyone for their welcome and decided to go home and continue to write the book I had started. Much research was needed to be done. I knew I would enjoy going back to meet relations of the people who worked in the college/farmyard in the early 1950's. I was delighted to meet Bobby Gardiner who worked at the college in the 1950's. He gave me Mrs Monsey Kennedy's name, a retired librarian; she in turn passed the names of people who I could contact for the necessary information I needed. The Dobbyns, Somers, Kellys, Burkes and Ward were some of the names I was glad to get. It was sad for me, discovering many of the people I had known while working in the college had passed away, some at a very young age.

BOOK SELLING IN CLARENBRIDGE

As I had done in the past few years, selling crafts at the annual one-day Craft Fair in the church grounds, I booked my spot to see if I could sell some copies of my novel *'From Clare to Texas'*. I set off with a few bags full of my books in the boot of the car with a little table (my stall) and hoped for the best.

I find my number and set out my stall, my moneybox and my poster identifying my charity purpose. This was Colitis and Crohn's Disease. The market was very busy with many nice, friendly people setting up their stalls on this lovely day. Selling starts at about nine a.m. and goes on until six p.m. It is a long day but when you make a sale it is worth it. I am very lucky in selling about a dozen books; the people buying tell me their sad stories about family members suffering with serious Crohn's Disease. Before I leave for home, I go to the Poppy Seed restaurant and have lunch. At home, I put away the unsold books for another day, then sit down and count the takings of the day, €180 less the fee for the morning. I'm pleased. Now I soak my feet and watch T.V.

Photographer Stan Shiels, while taking a photo of me selling my books he had to make a comment, "So you're peddling books." Cheek!

WHAT WILL THIS YEAR HOLD

What will the year hold for us? Especially for poor, sick Colm Fahy. I visit my daughter Margery, she tells me Colm took bad during the night, and she had to call for an ambulance which took him to the Regional Hospital. He is in the cancer ward. The poor boy has cancer with the Crohn's. I try to comfort my daughter, I tell her I am praying for him. She says, "I am too, Mom." I don't like to see her so troubled. I ask for Kallum. "He is with his cousins, the Fahys; it is best for him."

In a few days, I go to see Colm and I put on the blue gown and cap and wash my hands going into his ward. Margery is there. She gets his attention, "Look, Colm, Mom came to see you." He is sitting on the side of the bed. It is so hard to know what to say to such a young man who knows he has a very short time to live. We say a few funny things to each other. As I'm leaving I tell him I'll be back to see him soon again. But I never did, he passed away in the hospice on the 11th of July 2012, aged thirty-eight years; a young man who was once a professional kick-boxer and ambitious for life.

His funeral was well attended, as befitted a person so young. Family came from far and near; my son Leo was lucky in getting a flight from the States, landing in Dublin and taking the train to Galway, where his sister Caroline picked him up, and coming to Mervue Church in time for the Mass and burial. It was sad for Leo, bringing back memories of having buried his young wife only a few years before. Colm's resting place is in the Bohermore Cemetery where Margery and their son Kallum visit and tend his grave.

2012 - REMEMBRANCE MASS

I am arranging with Fr. John Keane P.P. St. Brigid's Church, Ballybane to hold a remembrance Mass for my brother Eddie, who went to his redeemer five months ago. I explained how I was in America with my son Mike who had undergone another operation at the time of Eddie's death. Fr. John said he would be happy to celebrate the Mass. I phoned Eddie's family and let them know about the Mass and tea after in my house. I also put the notice on the local paper, as I did when I held a remembrance Mass for Joe Malone, a fireman who died in the Twin Towers, USA, and for my young daughter-in-law Joey Beggen, who died suddenly.

Fr. John said a lovely Mass and mentioned Edward Abberton by name many times. After Mass, I read a poem I had written in celebration of my brother Eddie's life and his love for his family and hurling. Some people came to sympathise with me as they had missed his funeral. Eddie had many friends. May he rest in peace. I went home feeling so lonely and sat down to cry. Still, I felt a deep satisfaction with the Mass in his memory said by Father John Keane.

I CONTINUED TO ATTEND

The Creative Writer's class in Croí Na Gaillimhe. We were given exciting news that there would be the launch of a book with the publication of our written work. We were asked to submit our contributions in prose, poetry or stories. We set to work. My three submissions were a poem, *'Eyre Square back then'*, two stories, *'Busybodies'*, and one with a little romance in it, *'The Love Seat'*. The launch took place in Croí na Gaillimhe. As this establishment was beside a river, the book title was appropriate, *'Reflections by the River'*. It was a most exciting day for eighteen of us scribes mostly in our senior years. We were very much in appreciation of the instructions we received from John McGinty.

EYRE SQUARE BACK THEN

Running down, the road, from three miles out,
Drawing near we hear the music blare,
Announcing the carnival in Eyre Square,
A shilling & sixpence in my pocket
For a bumper ride, and a swing boat spin
Well that was the way 'back then'

Drawing close, get the diesel smell
Hear the engine's roaring sound,
Rubbing hands along the iron rail,
That hugs the carnival ground,
Crushed, in the queue to the ticket stand.
Holding the shilling, tight in hand.
For a go on the Bumpers, or a swing boat spin.
That was, the way back then.
Such a magic feeling, a toffee apple we will share,
a bottle of lemonade too. Rush to the next stall,
What can we afford there?
A slab of ice-cream between wafers thin
It was fun back then.

Slowly homeward bound, far too tired to run
Chair-o-plains, swing boats and bumpers too.
We've had our share of fun.
My sister six years old, and I just ten.
That was way back then.
Our time of youth has swiftly past
Eyre Square changed far too fast
Fond memories linger in an old timer's eye.
Memories so fond and true
The curious visitor ne'r shall view
Visions related to kith and kin.
Of Eyre Square way 'back then'

2013 - THIS WILL BE AN EXTRAORDINARY

year for our humble family. Two of my granddaughters are graduating from universities in the USA. But first, I am happy to have accomplished writing my memories of the Agricultural College, Athenry, County Galway. I enjoyed a most beneficial journey of two years retracing my steps, driving regularly out the fifteenmiles to Athenry, meeting people who were related to the people employed in the Agricultural College in my time. They were generous with photographs to be included in the book and lots of information.

THE LAUNCH OF 'RECAPTURING BYGONE DAYS'

At last, the book is ready and plans are laid for launching in the Raheen Woods Hotel, Athenry. Councillor Thomas Welby, Mayor of County Galway did the honours of launching the book. Among the many compliments the Mayor paid to me, was my idea of bringing out a book evoking memories of the college, which was almost unknown to the local people, except for being referred to as the 'Farm Yard.'

The number of people who attended from Athenry, Renmore, Ballybane, Dublin, my family and cousins from County Clare was gratifying. Among the invited guests were Fr. Benny McHale, C.C. St Mary's Parish, Athenry, Councillor Peter Feeney, Bobby Gardiner and Monsie Kennedy, Athenry. I would be making a donation from the sale of the books to the Western Region Brain Tumour Support Group, Galway. I also invited Anne Buckley, Chairperson, Western Region, Galway, to give a short description on the work they do to support the person and their family, when someone is diagnosed with a brain tumour. She spoke of her trauma when she learned of the sad news and how her family suffered, but thankfully, twenty years on she is here to tell her story and promote the Western Region Group of Galway City. It's a place for people who have or had brain tumours, to come to have refreshments and chat. My daughter Caroline and granddaughter Caroline were very busy as book sales-ladies for the day. In the evening, it was relaxing to enjoy refreshments. Many stories were shared about the 'Farm Yard'... enough to fill another book.

The launch of "Recapturing bygone days"

GRANDSON KALLUM

Kallum has completed attending Renmore Primary School. I was happy to see my grandson Kallum being confirmed with a large number of children in St. Oliver Plunkett's Church, Renmore. The next step in his life is attending Claregalway secondary school. Here he works at his studies. But, being an avid soccer player, he joined the Cregmore Soccer Club where he started training early in 2013. He was made captain of the Cregmore team and played in Eamon Deacy Stadium, where they were successful in winning the cup final. This was a great break for Kallum. Kallum played with Cregmore from 2013 to 2016. He joined Salthill-Devon under-18's where he again played as a goalkeeper.

In April 2017, Kallum was asked to start training with the Galway United squad every Thursday and Sunday. Also in 2013, he joined Annaghdown Gaelic Football as goalkeeper. While he was training with Annaghdown, his coach put him forward for trials to play for the county in the under-16's, these trials took place in Mountbellew, Co. Galway and Ballinhaunis, Co. Mayo where every county and city gaelic team put their best players forward to be selected as goalkeeper. Kallum wasn't confident of being picked as there were a great number of goalkeepers in the trials. But he got selected to be goalkeeper for his county, a great achievement for Kallum.

WHITE COLLAR BOXING

My daughter Margery Fahy trys her hand/fist at white collar boxing in aid of Autisem herself and her opponent spared each other around the ring with out ever touching each other and finished up exausted after the five minutes, they had a good time and raised a few hundred Euro for this worthy cause.

White collar boxing- Margery in red.

MEDJUGORJE

My son Mike phones to tell me his latest exciting news. "Mom I have been to Medjugorje!"

"Wonderful Mike, how did that visit come about?"

"Every year the late Mrs Cooney would select an invalid person with long-term illness from the parish, and take them to Our Lady's Holy Shrine in Medjugorje. Andy Cooney the great singer and musician, and his sister, but mostly his sister, in remembrance of their late mother, is carrying on her voluntary good work. So this year I was selected from the parish, having this long-time brain tumour meant that I qualified."

"God bless them, Mike. How did it feel to be in such a holy place?"

"I felt Our Lady's presence near me all the time I was there. Andy and my wife Mary helped me to walk up the many steps to the apparition hill, where Our Lady Queen of Peace in 1981 appeared to six young children, asking them to tell people to pray for peace. I found the walk very hard work, but with their help I made it up and down. It is a wonderful place; the lovely nuns and priests and helpers were looking out for us. The numerous Masses and prayers to Our Lady were a real blessing, I prayed for you Mom, and lit candles at Our Lady's Shrine for all our family."

"We appreciate that son, thank you."

"I want you to pray that next January when I go for the Brain Magnetic Resonance Imaging (MRI), we will get good news."

"I will of course Mike, like I always do, son."

USA GRADUATIONS

Two of my granddaughters will be graduating from universities in the States. I told their parents I would like to see them in their hats and gowns. "You are very welcome to come, Mom," said both my sons. Both graduations were in the month of May. I was anxious incase the dates would clash; thankfully there was more than a week between them. Early in the month of May, I set off for Charlotte, North Carolina, accompanied by my young granddaughter Caroline Dowling. My son Leo met us at the airport. "This is great, Mom; Kristina is happy you will be present at her graduation." I was happy to be present at this momentous occasion. I know I won't take the place of her dear mother who will be watching down from heaven.

IT WAS A LONG AND BEAUTIFUL DRIVE

Kristina Beggen attended the Appalachian State College, miles from her home in Charlotte. It was her first choice. She shared accommodation with two other students in a very old-fashioned, elegant house. On the eve of her graduation, my son Leo told me we had a long drive ahead of us. "We will be climbing up, up into the Appalachian Mountains. You and Caroline might get air-sick as the higher we go, the thinner the air gets."

I said, "Don't worry about us." It was a beautiful day, with the warm sun beating down on us, my son Leo seemed to be driving up to the heavens. "I see what you mean," I said. Travelling along, Leo pointed out the scenic views, the Blue Ridge, the Old Smoky Mountains with a blue haze visible across the ridges. He stopped the car so I could get photographs of them. I thought I would capture the blue mist, but it didn't show in the developed photo.

Leo shortened the journey by telling us how this was one-time Indian country or Cherokee Land. Around 1829, newspapers described how vast areas of these lands held gold. Thousands of miners flocked to here with dreams of getting rich quick. The Indians knew about the gold, it didn't mean as much to them as it did to the white settlers, who drove the Cherokee out of their land. The poor Cherokees harnessed up their horses to their caravans, while the women sat on the backs of ponies and donkeys with their babies wrapped beneath colourful shawls (like our tinkers/travellers, long ago). They were forced to march to Oklahoma, and during bad winters many Cherokee people died along the way. That road is known today as the Trail of Tears.

AT LAST, WE HAVE ARRIVED

Driving down a side road, we came to a beautiful log cabin that Leo had rented for the night. As he showed us into this most charming setting, I was in awe; it was superbly equipped, from the smallest pot to the largest bath towel, supplied for our comfort.

The cabin looked out over vast fields going right down to the calm sea waters. Granddaughter Caroline asks are we going to be staying here. "We are," said her Uncle Leo; "sadly only for one night."

Later Kristina, her brother Ian and Leo's friend April arrived; they had Yoshie, their pet dog with them. My bedroom was downstairs, while the girls slept in the loft, but not as we know lofts. Leo and his son bedded down in the living room. Next morning, I was told no one could sleep as Yoshie barked all night; I hadn't heard a sound. After breakfast, we got ready for the exciting day ahead.

KRISTINA

Kristina looked elegantly studious as she joined about five hundred graduates wearing their mortarboards/caps and gowns, walking up the aisle of the Appalachian State University to receive her degree as 'Outstanding Senior in Sustainable Development,' for which she had studied for five years. Her daddy, Leo was very proud as was her brother Ian; there were tears in our eyes remembering her dear mother Joey (RIP). Kristina explains the backbone of her studies involves re-writing cultural stories and ideologies, so as to produce more sustainable outlooks and thus yielding more actions for continuity.

After the excitement of the morning with hugs and kisses and plenty of memorable photographs of this great day, we were very hungry. We were led to a massive hall where many long tables were set up to seat hundreds of people who attended their children's graduation. There was a large selection of meals for the variety of cultures attending the college. It was all self-service, you had your choice; ours was potato, beef and vegetables; Kristina's was the same except for the meat, she is a vegetarian, there was also a variety of creamcakes, etc. We finished our meal, and more photos were taken of me and my beautiful graduate.. Kristina and her dad went to meet with her professors to show their appreciation and thank them for Kristina's successful graduation. They in turn complemented Leo on his excellent, scholarly daughter. Our stay was filled with wonderful experiences, including the log cabin which we were reluctant to leave.

Dad Leo Beggen, me, Kristina Beggen, cousin Caroline Dowling and Ian Beggen.

KRISTINA'S ACHIEVEMENTS TO DATE

Kristina was born in Brooklyn, N.Y. on Christmas Eve 1990, to Leo and Joey Beggen. She attended kindergarten public school 190. The family moved to New Jersey in 2002; here she attended Selger School, until once again the family made another move, this time to North Carolina. Now aged fourteen, it was somewhat daunting for her. She had left her familiar friends in N.J. She was thinking about how the N.C. girls would accept a N.J. girl. She had an outgoing and friendly personality and fitted in well in Sun Valley School, making many friends. Apart from her many studies and drama, her chosen musical instrument was the saxophone. Moving up to Sun Valley High School, she joined the High School Band. I was privileged to witness her playing with the Sun Valley High School marching band, leading their school football team onto the field to challenge a rival team in American football. From here, she graduated and spent her next educational years in the Appalachian State College.

Kristina's chosen career is organic farming/gardening as an outlet for positive change. In 2015, she moved and worked on the Mescalero Apache Native American Reservation in Southern New Mexico for three years. Whilst there, she managed a small educational farm that not only provided the community with fresh local organic produce, but also helped to educate the people on good dietary habits.

At present, she works on an organic farm in North Carolina while attending graduate school. Her ultimate goal is to teach sustainable development at a collegiate level. In her relaxing time, she plays her saxophone. She recently told me her good news: she has been accepted to a graduate college in the Oregon State, her aim is to become a professor and teach environmental studies for the good of people's health. Her belief is this subject is not promoted enough. Kristina is a determined lady and I know she will be successful. Her only regret is Oregon is so far away from N.C., and she will miss her family. I console her saying, "It is not forever."

"I know; thank you, Gran."

AFTER A FEW DAYS' REST

Caroline and I fly to N.Y., where grandson Gary meets us at Kennedy airport with welcome open arms. "This is a great time for us," I say to Gary, "attending two graduations in the one month."

"It is," he agreed. "When my brother and I were graduating things were a bit different; our Dad was not well with the brain tumour."

"That is understandable, Gary."

"Dad talks about how he missed out on important things in our lives."

"I know that, Gary."

"He makes a little joke by saying we don't hold it against him. But seriously, he is always there for us."

"Well it is good to make a joke, Gary." We arrive at the house and Cassandra is waiting for us in the kitchen. "I have only a few days left before my graduation."

I ask, "Are you nervous?"

"No," she says, "but Mom is." We have a laugh.

Her brother Michael has arrived from N.C., taking a break from his business for a few days. The morning is finally here and we are all ready for this great occasion which will soon be taking place in the Molloy College, St. Agnes Cathedral, Rockville Centre, N.Y.

CASSANDRA JANE BEGGEN

Before the graduation, Mass was celeberated. Molloy College was founded by the Dominican Sisters of Amityville, and continues in the Dominican tradition. This has been the way since the college was founded in 1955. On this beautiful day with many graduates prepared for whatever the future holds, they will have the blessing of St. Dominic. Cassandra's proud parents and brothers plus granny, me, and cousin Caroline join in, in attending the Mass with the parents of five hundred graduating young people. We stand and clap the loudest as Cassandra walks up the aisle to receive her degree in finance, after much snapping of photographs, handshakes, everyone trying to hug Cassandra on this great day of all great days. We were led into a large hall where beautiful food is laid on, indeed we were ready for it. Afterwards, Cassandra's parents Mike and Mary went to meet the priest, who said the Mass and Cassandra's professors to thank them for the success of Cassandra's passing and receiving her professional degree in finance. There was an extra person to meet, her athletics coach, who encouraged her all the way in earning many scholarships.

Knowing Cassandra since the day she came into the world, I knew she was destined for a promising future. From an early age, she learned Irish dancing at the Inishfree Irish Dance School, Massapequa. She attended for thirteen years. Her great ambition was to dance at championship level in her solo dress; this she achieved twice and earned a scholarship. She loved music and participated in senior orchestra and senior recorder ensemble in Farming Dale School. I was lucky to attend one of her school recitals and hear her playing the violin. I was also lucky to watch her kicking American football for her school, Farming Dale at about aged nine and be present to see the team winning and receiving beautiful trophies. She was classed as having a 'never give up' attitude on the field.

Her talent showed up early as far back as her kindergarten days when she attended the Albany Avenue Kindergarten School. The children learned many creative activities; she liked making and designing a seven-foot teepee made from sticks and paper; she showed her skill in painting it in various zigzag colours. Her mother Mary designed a plan for an igloo. She likes sculpting in cardboard and paper or any scraps she can find and passing on creative ideas.

In Cassandra's years attending Molloy College she was a star student, successfully attaining many honorary awards and each year receiving a stripe until she had all four stripes to show, and also gaining scholarships. She was/is a super athlete; while a freshman she won for her college the triple jump, breaking her own record by 10.5 metres at the Lafayette Rider Winter Games 2010.

Today her parents Michael/Mike and Mary Beggen are proud to see Cassandra Jane graduate with an honours degree in finance from Molloy College, Rockville Centre, N.Y. And I, her old granny bursting with pride. Right after graduation, Cassandra applied for one of fifty internships at the New York Federal Reserve Bank, and was selected from an estimated five thousand; yes, I said five thousand, applicants. Her photograph was framed and displayed in the bank for three years with the caption, 'Go Ahead Start; Something you can Bank On.' Our day ended with toasting Cassandra and her father who was so overjoyed he was able to attend this momentous occasion.

Our wonderful three weeks flew, and it was now time for Caroline and I to pack our bags for home after all the celebration of photos, handshakes and super meals and the wonderful memories we brought home with us. But most of all the memory of the graduation of two of my granddaughters. We were both happy and sad leaving. Daughter Caroline was waiting at Shannon airport to drive us back to Ballybrit, and there was much for us to relate.

Michael Beggen, parents Mary and Mike Beggen, Cassandra Beggen, Me, cousin Caroline Dowling and Gary Beggen.

THEIR DADDY'S REWARD

The girls' dads rewarded their successful graduated daughters to a holiday in Ireland. Cassandra came first; it was lovely meeting up so soon again. I took her into Galway City to show her some of our historical buildings including St. Nicholas' Collegiate Church dating back to about 1320, Lynch's Castle, now A.I.B., telling her the Lord Mayor of Galway long ago hung his son out of one of the windows. "He was a savage man, Granny." I said it was long years ago. "Today's Mayors are a little more civilised."

I then took her to see St. Patrick's School & St Joseph's Secondary School (the Bish), where her father Michael Beggen got his education; these were places she always wanted to see. We went to see the newly-established art museum down by the Spanish Arch. Here we met and shook hands with Douglas Kennedy who was visiting Galway on the fiftieth anniversary of his uncle, the late president John F. Kennedy. He was delighted to talk to us and mentioned his late famous Uncle John. Cassandra told him she was

American and never shook hands with a Kennedy until she came to Galway; Douglas said it was "his pleasure."

It was time to move on as granddaughter Caroline said she was hungry. Chips and beef burgers were on hand in Quay Street. Sitting outside a restaurant eating in the sun; it was like New York. The time was flying and Cassandra had other friends and places to go and visit, so we hugged and said goodbye. I say to Caroline I will miss her.

"I will too," she said. I am preparing now for Kristina's visit.

Me, Rowen and her dad Douglas Kennedy, Cassandra Beggen and Caroline Dowling.

A WELL-EARNED BREAK

Kristina is on her way from Dublin where she has spent a week with her late mother's sisters and uncle. She will be here in Galway shortly on the train. It is exciting to be meeting up so soon again and the weather is keeping nice. We meet with hugs and kisses. Driving home, she tells me about the lush green grass she admired on the way from Dublin, the cow's grazing and a wide stretch of land where she could see a lot of horses. I tell her, "That is the Curragh of Kildare and they were probably racehorses you were admiring." The country is full of scenic views all the way from Dublin.

Now we are at my house in Ballybrit. "You are welcome, my love. I have dinner ready."

She looks at the plate of food, "I know you are a vegetarian," I tell her, "This is a plateful of spuds and veggies."

"Oh, thank you Gran, you remembered."

"We will take a spin out to the Agricultural College in Athenry tomorrow."

"I would love that," she says. She was surprised at the size of the college.

"Do you think it is big?"

"I do," she admits. Its holiday time so the yard is empty. We walk around and I show her the sheds and tell her where the animals were kept when I worked there. "You will have a memory of where your Granny worked when you look at yourself in this photo standing next the college." She wanted to see the little town of Athenry. I brought her to the Heritage Centre. "It is a lovely place Granny, why did you leave it?"

"Money, Kristina, and the need of it." As we set for home, she asks me to stop; she wants to look over a wall to see the sheep. "Could I take one home?"

"You need a bigger suitcase," I tell her. Next, we will meet the two Carolines in the city and have dinner in Cactus Jack's restaurant. "This was just what the doctor ordered," she laughed.

Next day it was a spot of shopping. I was hoping to buy her a dress, but after trying on a few she decided not to bother. "It will be adding weight to my bag for the plane." That sums up my wise Kristina. Only another few days left, so I take her to the Spiddal Craft Village. She is fascinated with the Irish words and buys home-made soaps and candles; the scent puts her in mind of palm trees. Coming through the city, I drive by St. Patrick's School. "That is where your dad Leo went to school, Kristina."

"Oh thank you Granny, for showing it to me."

"Then he went to the Christian Brother's boarding school in County Carlow; it's a long way from here."

She invites me to come back to Dublin with her; of course, I am happy to go. We stay a night with her aunty Anne and husband

Damien; they have a lovely home and two lovely dogs that give us a big welcome. Anne is busy dishing up a sumptuous dinner for the hungry travellers. Sitting in to dinner, Kristina keeps us entertained about her farming work in the States.

"How did you get interested in that type of work?" Damien wants to know; "Wouldn't an office job be nicer for you?"

"I could not sit at a keyboard all day. I love the great outdoors and the feel of the clay running through my fingers," she answered, "Indoors all day? No thank you!"

Next day I ask Anne to drive us to Malahide to visit my cousin Sr. Margaret Hurley. She would love to meet Kristina, for she was well acquainted with her dad Leo when he was young. This was a nice treat and Sr. Margaret had a lovely lunch prepared for us. It was a chance to snap some photos of them together. Back again to Raheny and tonight we will be staying with Kristina's aunty Mary and her husband Billy. We had a pleasant evening of chat. Kristina and I shared a bedroom. "It's a long time since we shared a bedroom, Kristina."

"It is," she agreed, "not since I lived in New Jersey."

Morning came too soon and I must be on my way back to Galway. Anne is driving me to Heuston Station. Kristina comes too; they walk me to the train, and we say our goodbyes. I'm lonely to be parting with Kristina. I stand and watch as they walk to the exit, after every few steps, Kristina looks back and waves, and I wave back. Soon they disappear out among the crowd. I board the train, take out a magazine and try to read it. At home, I suddenly remember I never thought to bring Kristina to see St. Mary's College, Galway, where her dad graduated from in 1980. Well, the next time, please God.

SOMETHING GOING ON

There is something going on and I am not being told what all the fuss is about. Caroline is searching for photos and information of my past; she tells me it is for an essay for young Caroline. I help her all I can.

As time is passing, I ask her has she enough. She says, "Leo is going to call you soon, he has something to ask you."

"What does he want to know?"

"I don't know," she says, as she runs out the door. I soon find out; Leo tells me, "The family are going to give you an eightieth birthday party and I want you to give Caroline names and addresses of people to invite."

"Oh, dear God, you're not doing that, it's too expensive; no Leo, I won't do that!"

"You will have to; everything is booked for it now."

"So that is what Caroline was doing all the fussing for?"

"It was; so get busy."

"Leo, I'm sure to leave someone out." I get busy and give a big list to Caroline, "Is that too many?" I ask. I'm sure to leave someone out. Caroline creates a beautiful invitation with a photo of me when I was sixteen. "Give me some information on what is going on," I beg.

"It is in the Harbour Hotel; Neil Diveny is making the cake depicting the books you have written, its buffet, hot food and a piano player. It's all done, so get yourself a pretty dress."

A PARTY

It was a party fit for a queen. Son Mike and Mary Beggen came from the States and stayed with their friends, the Harte's. My house was full with cousins, and son Leo and fiancé April. In the morning, Caroline brought four of us ladies to the hairdresser. While we were there, I missed my daughter Margery's visit; she had come to the house. Herself and Leo had time for a nice chat together. She had gone home when we came back. I was sorry to have missed her. Later she phones me; I am so glad to hear from her. She wishes me a happy birthday. "Thanks Marg. I'm just coming out of a bad flu," she says.

"I'm sorry Mom, I'm not able to go to your party."

"Oh Marg, you will be missed."

"I know Mom, I am very sorry."

"After we hang up our phones, I have a cry. Shirley McEntee is ready to do my makeup; she has my tear-stained face to sort out first. The day is flying on and I'm heavy of heart. But Leo is hurrying me on to get ready. "Hurry," he says, the taxi is waiting."

"I don't see a taxi." Then I see it; a limousine. "Leo, you have gone too far."

"It's not only me," he says, "It is your family putting this party together for you, Mother."

The chauffeur opens the door and I sit into luxury and meet more members of the family. There's a table with bottles of champagne and glasses. "Here, Mom," says my son, "drink up, you might need it."

Drawing up at the Harbour Hotel, I see a red carpet laid out with lighted lanterns each side, with glasses of wine and juice being passed to each guest as they entered. Caroline has created a 'Friends Tree.' Each guest dipped their finger in special ink and put the mark next to a branch and wrote their name beside it. It is now having pride of place hanging in my kitchen.

The next surprise was the screen on the wall with my life history on it; this was Caroline and Leo's work. So many people kept coming in and sat at tables and meeting up with friends they hadn't met in a long time. Mike walked around and thanked each one for coming to see our mother, who was entering her octogenarian year. Although his eyesight was poor, he still recognised some of the old neighbours. Then there was the cutting of the cake, the 'Happy Birthday'

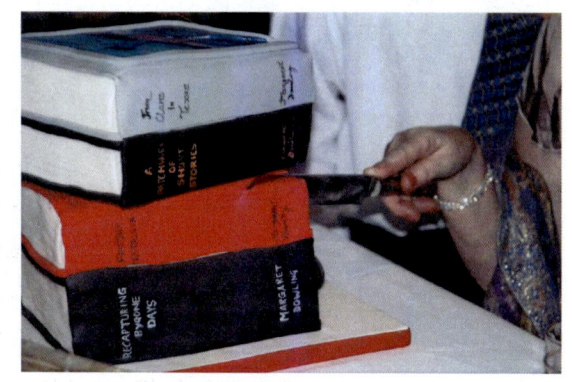

Birthday cake

song, and photographs taken of the family for the paper by Joe Shaughnessy. There was a phonecall from the grandchildren in the States to wish me happy birthday. I was so happy to hear from them. Although Margery phoned me during the day, I missed her presence and, of course her family, at my party. Many beautiful gifts and vouchers were presented to me. Caroline and April had their arms full coming home. The night finished with a sing-song. Mary Beggen and Trish Carrick rendered classical tones. Next day the family and friends said their goodbyes before returning to their homes. It took at least a year for my feet to touch ground again; what a wonderful family to give this old lady such a magnificent party. God Bless you all.

argaret celebrates 80th rthday with her family

celebrate her 80th birth-y Margaret Dowling of 1oc na Cille in Ballybane Id a gathering at the Har->ur Hotel, attended by her family, relatives and friends. Over the past 40 years Margaret has been involved with local groups in the Ballybane area where she also founded the Active Retirement Association 11 years ago. She has had four books published over the past six years with proceeds from their sale going to charities.

Margaret is seated with her granddaughter Caroline and daughter Caroline Dowling. Behind are her sons Michael (left) and Beggan, Michael's wife Mary (left) and Leo's fi April Will, who lives in United States. Missing the photograph is Mar garet's daughter Marge Fahy.

2014 - A MIRACULOUS MIRACLE

It is January and I phone Mike in the hope he has word of the MRI results. "There is a heavy snowfall here in L.I., Mom," he says, "It's impossible to drive the car the long distance to Stoney Brook hospital. It will be another month before we get the news, Mom."

"Please God, it will be worth it, Mike."

The phone is ringing; with fingers crossed, I answer it. It's Mike. "Sit down Mom, until you hear the result of the MRI - my surgeon, Mr Rosello could not believe his eyes when he looked at the result.

'Mike,' he says, 'there is no sign of the tumour.' He called two other doctors who agreed, the tumour was gone."

"Thank God, Mike."

"Thanks to Our Lady, Mom."

"Yes, Mike!" I want to clap my hands and shout Hallelujah. "How does Mary feel?"

"She is overjoyed and can hardly wait to tell the rest of the family."

"Neither can I, Mike."

"Just one MRI a year now, to keep a check that it's still gone. It's a miracle."

"It is, Mike." (It is now 2017 with no sign of the growth returning, thank God). Mike told his good news to his brother Leo, and I gave the same good news to his sisters Margery and Caroline, and to everyone who asks for him. We offer prayers of thanksgiving to Our Lady for this wonderful gift for my dear son Mike.

MIDNIGHT MASS

My daughter Caroline phones to ask me if I would like to go to Midnight Mass in Castlegar with her and her daughter.

"What time is it at?" I ask.

"10 p.m.," she says.

"I would love to."

"We will collect you."

"Thank you for telling me," I said, "See you then."

I walk into the church that was once a big part of my young life, until changes came and bishops had ideas to switch people from one parish to another. The church is changed a bit; the gallery where we sang in the choir is missing, but everything else is much the same. It took me right back in years to when I was very young. It's in this church that I was confirmed at age eleven with my brother Eddie, by Dr. Michael Brown, Bishop of Galway. In more recent years, Paddy Dowling and I were united in matrimony by Canon Hyland. Here my children were baptised, made their first Holy Communion, my son Michael served Mass, as did his uncle, Eddie Abberton, in his young days. My mother was buried from this beautiful church. It holds so many wonderful past memories for me.

I am so grateful to Caroline for bringing me here to Midnight Mass. Celebrating the Mass was Canon Michael Reilly. The resident choir sang beautiful Christmas carols accompanied by music with a variety of instruments, all adding to the splendour of the holy season. I have continued to attend Mass in St. Coloumba's Church and meet many friends from my old school days. I am back to my roots. I also try to attend the weekly Holy hour as often as I can.

JOINING THE ST. JOSEPH'S

I had often heard of the St Joseph's Young Priests Society, and had a wish to join. My chance came in St. Coloumba's Church, Castlegar, when leaflets were being handed out, and a member of the Society told me I would be very welcome to join their Castlegar branch. The monthly meetings are presided over by P.P. Canon O'Reilly. The meeting is held in a comfortable room in the priest's house. Special prayers are offered for vocations. And many dates of Masses and upcoming events are given to us by the secretary, Bernie Tully, and an annual collection is taken up to alleviate the cost of education and ordination of new priests. There is a devout and relaxed presence at these meetings and always prayers are offered for vocations. There are many branches of the Society open in Galway.

MAYOR'S AWARDS AGAIN

I am almost apologetic to my daughter Caroline; "This is the last time I will ask you," I promise. "Will you write a piece for the Mayor's Award; we might have a good chance this time to win the €500 for the Ballybane Active Retirement club?"

"Oh Mom, you are wasting your time!"

I say, "Haven't you heard, 'Try & try again and you will succeed at last?'" We did try, but once again it's a certificate like the other three for community voluntary work, presented this time by Padraig Connelly, Mayor of Galway City. Now the four of them are framed and displayed on my kitchen wall.

Margaret Honoured

Margaret Dowling, Ballybane, was among the recipients of this year's Mayor's Award for her outstanding community work in Ballybane and also for her generosity in donating the proceeds from her books – From Clare to Texas; 'A Patchwork of Short Stories and a true story of her like in Recapturing Bygone Days in the Original Agricultural College Athenry – to charity. Margaret has donated over €10,000 through the sale of these books to Irish Society for Colitis and Crohns Disease, Galway Autism Partnership and The Western Brain Tumour Support Group.

Mayor's awards again

MEETING A FIRST COUSIN

This was an exciting day in the family, thanks to cousin Sr. Margaret Hurley. I always wondered where cousin Bonnie Hurley/Dignan and her brother Mick Joe lived in England. Then came a great surprise when Sr. Margaret phoned to tell me she was coming to Galway, and would be bringing someone I wanted for a long time to meet. "Don't tell me its cousin Bonnie?"

"The very one."

"That is wonderful news. How is she?"

"I think it is going to be a bit strange after all these years to be meeting her close relations for the first time."

I prepared a banquet to make her welcome. The doorbell rings and I rush to open it. "Now," says Sr. Margaret, "look who is here." I look Bonnie up and down, then I say, "You're a Hurley to the backbone!" We hugged and laughed and were soon sitting at the table telling each other of our past and not knowing where to begin. We wished her brother Mick Joe could have joined us.

"He sends his apologies and best wishes," she says. Bonnie told us she married a very nice Tipperary man. "I wish you could have met him. We have three grown-up children. Sad to tell Denis got sick and spent a long time in a wheelchair, and he passed away in 2007, aged seventy-nine."

"Thank you for the photos you sent me; he was handsome, even up to his last days, sporting his stylish white moustache." Now we have met, we are making up for lost time by corresponding to each other. We were surely very grateful to cousin Sr. Margaret for this momentous occasion.

First time meeting cousin Bonnie. Seated Sr. Margaret Hurley, Bonnie Dignan Standing Margery Sheeran, Me and Granddaughter Caroline Dowling.

LOOKING TO BUY

I know Caroline is anxious to move from her present residence. I see on the local paper where a house is for sale in Old Mervue. Don Colleran Auctioneers has the sale of it. I tell Caroline about it. "I'll make arrangements to view it, and if the price is right I might buy it," she says. It will be sold at auction and some other viewers are coming to see it also. On the day of sale, I was so happy Caroline's bid was accepted. She set to work decorating this lovely old house to her liking; it took a few months. There was no rush as I had the company of her and her daughter with me and their two cats. It had the latest in a kitchen stove for solid-fuel heating, making it warm and comfortable.

Caroline is ready to move into their palace with her daughter and three cats; it took them no time to settle right in. With the large site of ground stretching down the back, Caroline was making decisions about where she will plant the first crop of potatoes and a variety of vegetables. I have picked a section at the end of the garden to create flowerbeds. I would enjoy designing and planting colourful blooms.

ANOTHER GRADUATION

This time my granddaughter Caroline Dowling, aged eighteen, is graduating from Galway Community College, Móinín na gCíseach. She has picked a dainty little pink dress for the occasion and I am looking forward to this day. Her mother and I enter the college and are shown to our seats with many other parents and grandparents. I ask my daughter Caroline if she remembers her own day when she graduated from this same College. "I do indeed, and I remember the dress you made for me." The place is changed since my day. Now they have an auditorium well set-up for these occasions.

Soon the ceremonies begin with a big welcome for the twelve girls and twenty-five boys. The principal in his speech is telling the parents the pride the school had in this group of graduates. A few pupils were invited to give a short talk on their teacher, each one going up to the podium to make his/her speech. One boy had some jokes about his teacher, and while we laughed, the poor teacher stood red-faced; it was a relaxed and fun graduation. My granddaughter Caroline was one of the pupils that said a prayer. Her mother and I were proud to see Caroline receive her graduation certificate.

The evening ended with lovely finger food. Caroline and I then came home while her daughter Caroline went celebrating with her friends.

Caroline's next step was entering the Galway Technical Institute, GTI. During her year there, she trained in a little photography. 2015 and she was accepted to the Galway-Mayo Institute of Technology, GMIT. Her first summer job was working in a very busy nightclub. During the Christmas holidays, she also worked as saleslady in 'New Look' Ladies Fashions. Some of her past achievements included, at age six she joined the weekly art classes after school, in the Paint Box studio at Terryland Shopping Centre. She painted an abstract picture and proudly presented it to me. It has hung in my hall for the past fourteen years. In 2007, Caroline joined the Mervue Order of Malta, learning First Aid. She also tried a bit of kick-boxing. She successfully won a scholarship, and spent a month in Connemara, learning the Gaelic language, to speak in our native tongue. She also made many friends from various parts of the country.

MODEL PLANE FLYING CLUB

Grandson Kallum Fahy gets his first remote control plane and joined the Galway Model Flying club in Carrowbrowne. He also became a member of Aeronautics Council of Ireland. In between his hobby and playing soccer, there are school studies and soccer practice a few evenings a week. He is lucky in having a private chauffeur in his mother Margery. In June, Kallum was awarded the under-fourteen Manager's award in soccer. Kallum was accepted to attend trials for the Galway Academy Gaelic football and played for County Galway. He also took part in the Ted Web Talks. Playing against Mayo, they got to the final, but sadly they lost. In December, he started goalkeeper training with just four keepers; this is football language.

A MOST PLEASURABLE INNER FEELING

With the successful book sale of *'Recapturing Bygone Days'*, I lodged over €3,000 in the bank for the Western Region Galway Brain Tumour Support Group. I received a lovely invitation from the chairman, Anne Buckley inviting my daughter Caroline and I to meet herself and Teresa Lawless in the Menlo Park Hotel and to bring the oversized bank cheque with us and one of the books (*Bygone Days*). We went along on the evening appointed and were delighted to meet Anne and Teresa again. "What is this all about, Anne?" I asked.

"You will see," she said. A table was set with some lovely cakes for high tea. Photographer Joe Shaughnessy arrived.

We posed for a photograph holding out the large cheque between us, and with Caroline holding up the book, but the greatest of all was the massive bouquet of flowers that was presented to me by Anne and Teresa, which indeed I did not expect. Joe took the photo for the City Tribune and left. We sat into the table. I said, "This is so thoughtful of you. Caroline and I are very thankful."

"You are both worth it," said Anne and Teresa. We came away with such happy feelings; such a lovely thought. A very pleasurable evening. The flowers lasted for months. It was such a big bouquet I divide it with my book saleslady, Caroline.

CHRISTMAS HOLIDAYS

In the U.S.A. I am scouring the shops in Galway week after week, to buy what I think each one would like. Daughter Caroline and granddaughter Caroline are doing likewise. I tell them that I have so much bought and packed I won't have space for my own clothes. We will be staying Christmas week in North Carolina with my son Leo, Kristina, Ian, Leo's fiancé April and her daughter Ivy. New Year's and we will be in Long Island with my son Mike, his wife Mary and their family Michael, Gary and Cassandra. We agreed we would pack light, a few changes of clothes for day wear, and a couple of changes for evening wear. Caroline has booked our flight online so I have only my passport and insurance to see to.

DECEMBER

The three of us are all packed for USA. We pile our three bags into the boot of Caroline's car to take us to Dublin airport. The car is safely parked in the long stay area, and we each take our bags and get into line to have them checked in. We would be changing at Heathrow to get our next flight to Charlotte, North Carolina.

After boarding the plane for Heathrow airport, we get the declaration forms to fill in. Caroline checks that she has a bottle of whiskey. At Heathrow, our bags are checked and granddaughter Caroline and I are allowed to go straight through. Daughter Caroline is kept back and interrogated about the whiskey. Where did she buy it? She tells them at the duty free. "Was the bottle opened?" She answers no, then we lose sight of her; where is she? "We will miss our connecting flight to Charlotte airport," and we did. Caroline came up beside us. "What was that all about, dear?" I ask.

"I don't know, Mom; I must let Leo know we are going to be arriving late. Thank God for the mobile phone." We are very late arriving at Charlotte; Leo is waiting patiently for us. We apologise. "Don't worry, you are here now." He hugs the three of us. "Where is your luggage?" he asks. There is no sign of it, we check with the airport staff, but they can't help us, only suggesting two things that might have happened, it was either put on the wrong flight or it is still in Heathrow.

We tried to relax in Leo's. But we couldn't help wondering where our luggage, with all the Christmas gifts were. Leo gave Caroline money to buy what we needed, he then took us to the store. I bought a camera as I would like to have photos of our Christmas holidays together. Caroline was frustrated from phoning airports for any sign of our three bags. It was almost Christmas Eve. I was near out of my mind as Caree kept phoning Heathrow airport, each time describing the three bags to the girl at the other end of the phone. Then a breakthrough came with a different girl who said she thought she saw bags that description left by a wall in the airport. "I will send them on tonight," she said.

"Thanks," said Caroline.

Next morning, Christmas Eve, two bags arrived to Leo's house. "Where is the third one?" he asked.

"I was told two," muttered the delivery man. I was raging; it was young Caroline's bag that was missing; she was crying that her party clothes and gifts was in it, what could we do? Her poor mother was on the phone to Heathrow again in an angry voice and she asked about the third bag, but the person in Heathrow was unable to help her.

When I opened my bag, the wrapping on the gifts was torn off and things were pulled apart. Caroline's was in the same mess. I rewrapped the gifts and after midnight Mass we came home and passed around the Christmas gifts. I was aware Caroline Jr. was near to tears as she hadn't her gifts to give her cousins. To enliven the atmosphere, April's sister Cynthia, an artist had planned an evening of art. She supplied everything from paint brushes to the canvas and easels. She had done a sample for us if we wished to copy, *'Christmas trees by the beach'*. Those of us less experienced followed her instructions and it was a wonderful distraction; for hours we mixed paints, dabbed it onto our canvas to create something spectacular. We worked until our masterpiece was done, then looked for Cynthia's approval. The ten of us were treated to glasses of wine while we complimented each other's work. I felt my artistic effort was the best. We retired to bed and had a good night's sleep.

Next day, we woke up to the smell of turkey wafting through the house. Leo was chef, while April was setting up a beautiful Christmas dinner table. We enjoyed a rich, sumptuous dinner with all the trimmings, the wines, glasses of water, Christmas plum pudding with lashings of custard and cream, ending with the pulling of Christmas crackers. Then numerous pots, pans, platters, cutlery and glassware to be washed and put away. "Don't worry about them," said April, "the most of them will go into the dishwasher."

"Oh, thank goodness for that; I thought we would be standing at the sink for hours.""Mom," said Leo, "you are in America."

Visitors were calling in and wishing everyone a happy festive season over glasses of wine. And still no sign of the third missing bag.

We are ready to leave for Long Island, and Leo and April promised if the bag came they would send it on to us immediately. We thanked them for a delightful time. Leo drove us to Charlotte airport; while there, we enquire about the missing bag, there is no sign of it, we wave our goodbyes to Leo.

2015 - WE ARE IN LONG ISLAND

It is now 2015. It is good to see Mike, Mary and family. We greet each other with Happy New Year hugs. They know about the dilemma of the luggage. The three cousins make a big fuss of young Caroline. "We are going to have a very happy New Year," sang Mike. Caroline and I passed around our gifts and I felt very sorry for granddaughter Caroline, for the tears were ready to flow, her bag hadn't arrived and the presents for her cousins are in it. Indeed we thought we would never see it again. After a dinner of honey-roasted ham, potatoes and all the vegetables we could eat, accompanied with wine; apple pie and a variety of ice-creams were the finishing touches.

With the dishwasher filled, and everyone sitting down, the Beggen family passed around their Christmas gifts. Caroline got so much nice girly stuff from her cousins, she didn't have time to think of her lost bag. The day before we were to leave for home, a taxi-man arrived with the lost bag, announcing that he was asked to collect this bag from Kennedy airport, it was Caroline's bag. Mary paid the taxi-man and young Caroline jumped up and down to finally get her bag. She hurries to open it; her clothes are all in a mess, the heels of her party shoes are broke, and more upsets - her gifts for her cousins are there, but open and pulled apart. Her cousin Michael says, "Sit down everyone; Caroline has gifts to give out." This made her laugh and she set to passing out the unwrapped presents. In a joking way, there were complaints, "Why didn't you wrap my gift?" and, "What were them security people looking for?" We were insured and had kept all our receipts to be sent off and were refunded after a long wait. But no amount of money would compensate for what we went through.

We enjoyed being with both families for the festive season. Caroline's car was nice and handy to have waiting for us at Dublin airport and we arrived home safely. We could not understand why our bags were so carelessly left at the airport in Heathrow with our name and address tags on them, and to be ransacked; no one had an answer for us. All three bags had to be replaced.

PREPARING FOR A MEMORABLE WEEK

This will be Leo's first time at the Ballybrit Races in over forty years. His fiancée April Worten is accompanying him. He is pulling out all the stops and has Caroline booked to help with arranging where the four of us will spend Ladies Day. "I don't want to be sitting in the ordinary Grand Stand," he says. Caroline lets him know that everything else will be expensive. "Go for it," he tells her. So she booked the Galway Plate Suite on the second floor of the Killanin Grand Stand.

I was so delighted. Both Leo and April had arrived; their stay was just for one week, however we intended to make the most of it. Their first day home and I explained that Caroline and I were invited to my nephew Michael Nally's marriage to Elaine Burke in the Mervue Church. We were going for the marriage ceremony and not the reception. We would come home straight after the Mass. This I had explained in the acceptations card to my nephew Michael. Leo of course would like us to attend the reception. "Don't worry," I said, "I have it sorted out."

The wedding was lovely and bride and groom looked a handsome couple.

On the way home after the marrage cermoney, I said to Caree, "I wonder what our visitors would like to do."

"We could take them to Cong to visit Ashford Castle and have dinner there." "Good idea," I agreed.

This was a real treat and Caroline did the driving. Her daughter also joined us; it was a fabulous day. Next day, Sunday, it was gift shopping in Galway City, but I stayed home to cook dinner. They were tired from the shopping. Leo could not believe how crowded with people Galway City was. "It's Race Week," I remind him, "rest for the evening, for tomorrow we are going by bus out towards Connemara to Dan O'Hara's Cottage."

DAN O'HARA COTTAGE

Dan O'Hara's Cottage proved the right spot for tourists. The bus was full mostly of German tourists accompanied by an interpreter. We were the only three English-speaking people travelling in the bus. Before visiting the cottage, we had a lovely tea in the Dan O'Hara Café. We were called to board the bus, which turned out to be a broken-down bus pulled by a tractor up a rocky hill. It was great crack/fun, with us there was twenty German tourists. The interpreter was kept busy translating to their language while the tourguide related the history of poor old Dan O'Hara's fate.

The main attraction was the cottage situated in this historical area. I noticed it had been given a facelift. A short history of poor old Dan's life was told. The landlord threw Dan and his wife with their six children out on the road, because Dan had added an extra window to the little cottage and as the rent of the

Leo Beggen and April Worten standing by the Dan O'Hare Cottage.

cottage was paid by the number of windows, which were small, about two-foot square, letting in very little sunlight, poor Dan was not able to pay the rent increase. It was during the Famine times in Ireland. Relations in America helped to bring Dan and his family to America. Dan spoke only Irish, so he could only get a job selling boxes of matches on the streets. A sad but true story. Everyone was given a short swig/small taste of poitín. Some liked it, others made a face. It was time to board the latest in transport as it rattled its way down the rocky road. "Now, April," I said, "You will have something to tell the family back home in the USA." She was enjoying every minute of the day. Our bus was waiting at the gate. By the time we reached the city we were feeling the pangs of hunger, and a meal in Park House took care of that.

JULY 30TH

At last it is Ladies Day at the Races. These three ladies are smartly styled in gorgeous dresses, high-heeled shoes, sunglasses and of course to top off the ensemble, our hats. Not to be outdone, topping off his smart attire, Leo sports a trilby hat and dark sunglasses. "Who is that Yankee Boy?"

Before we started to make our way to the Racecourse, we take some snapshots of our stylish selves. Caroline acting as chauffeur again, we head out and join with the cavalcade of cars heading to the Races. Leo stands to admire the Killanin Stand. "I don't remember an enclosed glass building like that the last time I was here," he says.

I tell him, "It is very new and modern."

"Wow, it is grand," he exclaims.

"We won't be in there," said Caroline as she leads the way to the second floor to locate the Plate Suite, where we were comfortably booked for the day. We enter wearing our guest badges and are greeted with glasses of champagne, then led to our table. We see the name, Beggen, in big print on a card. "We won't miss our table!" laughed Leo.

The backing of horses could be done from the table, as the waiter took our bets to place them. There were times we won and times we didn't. The four-course dinner of one's choice was sumptuous, with plenty of top-quality red and white wine. This treat was expensive, at least €450 per person. It was worth it, thanks to my son Leo. Among the privileged guests in the Galway Plate Suite, there was just the one person I recognised, that was Mr. Pat McDonagh of Supermacs. It was a wonderful day; we enjoyed watching the races on the TV without moving from our table, and also had a good view of the ladies parading, as they showed off their delightful hats and style.

Leo was indeed amazed at the amount of people attending the seven days of the Ballybrit Galway Races. But he missed the open stalls, where the women from Dublin would sell their fruit and chocolate bars, the big Guinness tent out in the field, and the boys with the three-card trick, who would catch out many an unsuspecting fool/person, while at the same time keeping on the look out for Garda attention. I go to the Races every year and enjoy them, but this was a day that will go down in my memory for ever.

THE FASTEST WEEK

On the morning before leaving, Leo needed Caroline to go shopping with him. Some gifts to take to the States, I presumed. You can imagine my surprise when they arrived in with a new television set for me. Leo ordered Caroline to dismantle my very, very old one with the five channels. I was objecting to the expense Leo was going to, but no one was listing to me. "Now, Mom, you have a choice of programs to watch." I was indeed thankful for such a gift but still grumbled about the cost. It was now time to be on the road again; Caroline is chauffeuring us to Dublin airport. We had our final meal together and stayed the night in the Premier Inn Hotel. Six a.m. departure time was fast approaching. Our goodbyes said, Leo and April boarded the plane for N.C. and Caroline and I drove home to Caroline Jr. On my kitchen table was the price of a recliner chair. "Oh, Leo love, thank you so much."

AFTERNOON WALKS

Like many of the locals, I was on one of my constitutional walks, when I met James/Jim Cotter. After a few pleasantries, he asked me if I would like to join their musical group in the GAA hall on Friday evenings. I said, "Thank you, Jim, but I don't play a musical instrument."

"But you can sing a song," he said.

"Gosh," I said, "I would love to join." I had been very sick for a few months during the year; my doctor put it down to a viral infection that affected every part of my body, but the worst was my voice. I was talking like Donald Duck, and my doctor advised me to give my voicebox plenty of exercise, to talk, or sing and to keep at it and take an antibiotic, which I did. Gradually, there was a little improvement; I could talk better.

On my first evening at the traditional musical session, I was sitting listening and enjoying the music, when Charley Davis, whose job it is to call the next tune or song, called on me to sing.

I had a big problem; I could barely sing a note, or remember a line of a song I had known for years. I was mortified, but everyone was nice and continued on playing music, so I began to relax. As the months were passing, I was improving. I observed two people playing bodhráns and I'm thinking, "I could play a bodhrán" (a circular instrument with a treated goat skin base, kept in place with a surround of wood, and beaten in time to the music with a tapper, a short, specially-made piece of wood). Next step, buy one, and with it I received a learner's DVD.

I began regular practice in how to hold the bodhrán and the tapper/stick from the DVD. I also got tips on the way to hold and beat it from the bodhrán players in the group. Now, I join with the group playing a musical instrument.

2016 - WONDERFUL NEWS

I get wonderful news from North Carolina; it was one of the best phonecalls I ever got. Son Leo is telling me that he and April have set the date to get married. "This is the news I have been hoping for, for a long time Leo. And I hate to say this Leo, but you are following in your mother's footsteps, marrying for a second time." We both laughed.

"You will need to book your flight early and let me know how many of you will be coming." I ask family members how many of them will be free to travel. Daughter Caroline and her daughter will book online to fly over. My granddaughter Lisa Ruffley is free to come. She is very excited about the chance. I tell her I am booking her and I together. Daughter Margery won't be free to come with us as her son Kallum will be going to Germany at that time with his school. And granddaughter Rachel Ruffley says it's an inconvenient time for her as her Aunty Caroline helped her prepare documentation to attend the GMIT to study Culinary Arts and Management. If she was away she might miss her place. That all settled, it turned out that there are four of us going.

I AM BOOKING THROUGH FAHY TRAVEL.

While I wait for my flight to be sorted out, I have a word with one of the girls working there. I ask if any member of the Fahy family works in the business now. She showed me a dark-haired girl who was busy working on a computer. "That is Maura Fahy, go talk to her." I said thank you. I continued by explaining to Maura how, in 1952, I booked my passage through the Fahy Shipping Agent when I was immigrating to the States. I said, "Miss Fahy was very helpful to me." Maura was so pleased to meet me and said, "I'm Kate's grandniece."

We shook hands and I told her how I had forgotten her grand-aunt's name was Kate. I always called her Miss. She apologised for not been able to talk to me as they were very busy, such was the life of the Fahy Travel Agency. She asked me to write some information on my experiences of emigration and of travelling back in those years, and leave it in to her. I said that I would. I wrote quite a piece on my experience, of how tough it was in 1952 when going to America, and how particular the American authorities were back then for immigrants, that they must be of good standing before allowed entrance to the USA.

I left it into Maura. Six months later, Maura phoned me. "Margaret," she said, "I am sending a reporter to you; he needs your phone number to call you and make an appointment; can I give it to him?"

"Of course you can; actually, Maura I had forgotten all about the piece I wrote and left in; did you read it, and is it alright?"

"It is Margaret, and thank you."

A few days later I got the phone call and I gave the reporter my address. Answering the door, I immediately recognised him. "It was on your desk in the Connacht Tribune office, that I used to leave my news items on Scouting and Guiding."

"It was," he agreed. We sat and talked over cups of tea. It was time to take the photo. He wanted one of me holding my 1952 passport. As he was leaving, I remembered to ask why he needed this information. "For the paper," he replied. "The City Tribune maybe?"

"Both City and Connacht," he said, as he was going out the door.

"But I will be in America then."

"I will have some sent to you."

"Thank you, Brendan," I said. Before I departed for the States, I asked my neighbour Mary O'Connor to get a few Tribunes for me. I didn't want to miss out on this bit of publicity.

I RECEIVE SAD NEWS

I hear that my good friend, and computer skills tutor, this lovely and patient lady, died very suddenly. The shock of hearing this sad news was like losing a family member. For over five years, I went each Monday to her house where her dear mother Mai would spoil me with tea and cake. "You are going to make me fat, Mai." She would laugh and say, "eat up". Patricia would set to work calmly teaching me the skills of the computer. I learned well from her.

Patricia Knight taught voluntarily through Age Action and was also into Animal Rescue, while taking care of her elderly mother Mai. I will always miss her kind ways and our chats.Patrica was just coming up to fifty-one years of age. May she rest in peace.

ON THE GO BUS

up to Dublin airport was a handy way for the four of us to travel. We boarded the Boeing 757 jet for the eight-hour direct flight to Charlotte airport. There was no worry of losing our luggage this time or the precious wedding gifts.

The two Carolines sat together and Lisa and I sat behind them. It was a lovely flight and drawing nearer to our destination we were feeling the heat of the weather. On landing, our baggage was almost the first off the conveyer belt. Two cars were waiting for us, Leo with his and April driving hers.

Arriving at Leo's house, we received a big barking welcome from Yoshie the dog, while pussy waved in around our legs. After a welcome cold drink, April showed us to our rooms and we unpacked and hung up our wedding attire. A shower, then a quick change into our shorts and light t-shirts. This was refreshing after the long trip. Down in the kitchen, a delicious lunch was very welcome with plenty of cold drinks. We go out to sit in Leo's latest addition to the backyard, a fantastic gazebo. We sat and felt a cool breeze wafting in around us. Outside, the temperature was high but we didn't mind; we welcomed a bit of heat. We are the first of the house guests to arrive.

MEETING OUR NEW RELATIONS

April's parents are due any minute and I'm sitting in suspense for this first meeting. How will I greet her dad? He is a Baptist Minister.

"Just call him Chris, and Mam is Becky," smiled April.

At last the suspense is over, and I find that they are very ordinary people like ourselves. Later when Becky and I were having a quiet chat, she says, "You won't believe this, Peggy, I wasn't sure how you would react to us."

"Well that makes two of us, Becky," we laughed as we held hands.

It was a little late when my son Mike, his wife Mary and their three grown children came storming in the door. There were loud greetings from us as we all kissed and hugged. It had been a long time since Michael, Gary and Cassandra had met their cousin Lisa; they almost ate her up. I glanced at April's parents a few times. I was afraid they might have thought Leo's family was a bit mad. Leo's son Ian and daughter Kristina arrived and so did April's pretty blonde daughter Ivy, who I would be adding to my list of grandchildren. She already refers to me as granny and I love it. Also present were April's sister Cynthia, and last but not least, their married sister Sarah and husband Josh Rogers. I turned to April's parents and said, "After all that yelling, I must apologise."

"Not at all," said Chris, "We loved the wild greetings you all had for each other." His answer put me at ease.

INSTRUCTIONS FOR THE BIG DAY

With so many people coming to stay in Leo's house, the young people have been accommodated in Morehead Inn. This was once an old building known as the Charlottean's House. It was built in 1917 by Charles and Marjorie Coddington, wealthy people, owners of all the Buick dealerships in Carolina and the WBT Radio Station. WBT was their slogan (With Buicks Travel). The house was designed by William Peeps of London, England. It was located in Dilworth, Charlotte's oldest neighbourhood. In 1984, it was converted to a stately Inn and remains as Charlotte's most unique southern estate. Leo and April choose this beautiful location to accommodate their overflow of wedding guests, with all expenses paid by the hosts. It was close to St. Marys Church where the nuptials would take place. Preparing for the wedding rehearsals, the family members who had the comforts of staying in Leo's house were now told to pack up our belongings. We would also stay on the eve of the wedding in the Morehead Inn convenient to St. Marys Church.

From the outside, it looked like an old ruin. We were in awe of the old-fashioned splendour of the rooms; the furnishings and the atmosphere were astounding with an area of flowers and gardens surrounding the outside of the building. My bedroom and living room had an old-world décor and an old-fashioned type bathroom with the old-fashioned windows and net curtains. My bed with the iron head and footstead reminded me of my bed (albeit a much, much smaller version) in County Clare. I did not want to leave this haven.

THE WEDDING DAY

The day was beautiful. Of course, the sun always shines in Carolina. St. Mary's Church was decked out in sweet-smelling flowers. Everyone was groomed to do their part at the proper times for the wedding cermoney. The bride in her long white gown with her long brown hair draped around her shoulders, walked up the aisle with her mother. Her bridesmaids Ivy and Kristina came next. Leo in his dark suit was looking so happy as I walked with him to the altar, where his beautiful bride-to-be stood smiling as she waited for him, it was a touching scene. I remembered his heartbreak nine years ago, when his lovely wife Joey passed away so suddenly. And here he is with his handsome son Ian, all six foot of him towering over his dad, acting as his best man.

The marriage ceremony was performed by April's father, a Baptist minister. It was all new to me having attended so many weddings in Catholic churches, also having witnessed my daughter Margery's civil ceremony when she married Colm Fahy. This was different; the bride's father marrying them; still the blessings were the same. I, as mother of the groom, was honoured to do the first reading. "The Lord said, 'It is not good that man should live alone; I will make him a mate.'" Second reading was read by Leo's sister Caroline, and April's mother Becky did the final reading. The ceremony went well and Mr and Mrs Leo Beggen kissed and everyone clapped, photos were taken as the happy couple walked down the aisle and out into the church grounds.

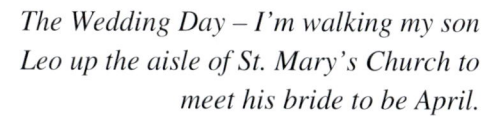

The Wedding Day – I'm walking my son Leo up the aisle of St. Mary's Church to meet his bride to be April.

THE WEDDING RECEPTION

The reception was held in the Morehead Inn. The meal was sumptuous. When the music started, the groom took his bride onto the floor with their arms around each other and they danced the first dance. The groom then took his mother on to the floor dancing to the tune of 'A Mother's Love is a Blessing.' The bride's parents, Chris and Becky also waltzed. Leo's daughter Kristina had a very appropriate speech prepared, welcoming her new-found family and how very happy she is now to have a sister in Ivy. Ian gave a short talk and Ivy tried to add her welcome to the Beggen's, especially to her new sibling's Kristina and Ian.

The Wedding Ceremony.

She became a little emotional and as happens at weddings, she had a little cry.

I had written a poem to welcome our new relations into our Irish family. It was a splendid event. I was introduced to many of the relations who were very genteel people. As the evening drew to a close, many of the guests went home. The overnight residences didn't have far to go. The young people stayed up late and, as Caroline brought her accordion she gave a few rousing tunes while Lisa played the piano. I went to bed and so did my bodhrán.

GRANDCHILDREN'S AMAZING CAREERS

Sometimes I am amazed at the careers my grandchildren chose in their lives, but my grandson Ian Beggen's is the most intriguing of all. His chosen profession is studying archaeology and is looking to graduate from the North Carolina State University with a degree in this field. His ambition is to be a professor of archaeology. "God bless you Ian, I hope I will be around to see that day."

He hugs me and tells me that I will. "Why did you pick such a way-out subject?" I wanted to know.

"I like analysing rock formation, taking part in digging/trampling for skeleton bones, both human and historic animal." As he continued to try and explain his ambitious choice in simple language to me, I did my best to understand the basics of what we talked about. "Keep me up to date, Ian."

"I will, Granny," he promised. He continues telling me of his next venture. "I will be going to Vancouver, Canada soon to make a presentation at the Society for American Archaeology, and when I return I will be going to South America, to Bolivia for two months to bring back their ideas to my professor in the North Carolina College where I attend".

"You are very ambitious Ian, how is all these expenses covered?"

"I won a scholarship from the College I'm attending, Granny, so I am not out of pocket.

It covers my travel, study and accommodation."

"I will be looking forward to hearing from you Ian, love."

MASS IN ST. PATRICK'S CATHEDRAL

Next morning is Sunday, and everyone up early, regardless of the late night; we eat breakfast and get ready to be in time for Mass. The Baptist family came with us and we all prayed together as one family. I was so happy with this uniting of religions.

To see this large cathedral filled to the doors on an ordinary Sunday morning with young and old, was encouraging for the Catholic faith of North Carolina. I was told the number of priests is steadily dropping, while the number of Catholics is skyrocketing. People are asked to pray to St. John Vianney for vocations. Before I left, I walked around this magnificent church. Then it was back to Morehead Inn, we gather up our bags and everyone heads back to Mr and Mrs Leo Beggens home.

IT WAS A WEDDING WEEK

We will remember that week for a long time. All good things come to an end. My daughter Caroline and two granddaughters are packed to fly home to Ireland, as they have work next day. Goodbyes had to be said and once more Leo is heading to Charlotte airport, dropping people off for departure this time. Son Mike and wife Mary are ready to fly home to Long Island and I will be with them for three weeks vacation. Their son Gary and daughter Cassandra had also departed for L.I. and, as their son Michael had his own business in N.C, he departed with a cheery, "I'll see you soon Dad." Leo's son Ian, daughter Kristina and his new daughter Ivy had said their goodbyes to their dad and mum and left also for work. "You will have an empty house now, Mr and Mrs Beggen," Mike reminded them, as they left us to Charlotte airport and quick goodbyes were said.

2016 - GOING TO NEW YORK

Going to New York from Charlotte was a little different. Simple enough if you know the way and Mary knew the way. First, we had to take the elevator up a couple of flights, then step out on to the train platform, then board the Sky train, which took us over what seemed to be a city. Alighting from the train, we are now in the airport for our flight to Kennedy; this was only about an hour. At last we are in Mike and Mary's lovely home in Massapequa Park. Over tea we cannot stop talking about his brother's wedding.

A BLUE MASS

It is Sunday and Mary is driving us to Mass in the Church of Our Lady of Lourdes. Mike asks me if we have a Blue Mass back in Ireland. I said no but I didn't ask what he meant by a Blue Mass. As we enter the church I soon found out. I see a number of firemen, police officers, sheriffs and hospital representatives, all in their blue uniforms in the front seats. It is September and this is a remembrance Mass for all who gave their lives trying to save people during the Twin Towers devastation. I remembered my young cousin's husband, Joe Malone, one of the many firemen who died that day. The priest prayed for all who were involved in Nine Eleven. The readings and prayers of the faithful were done by the men in blue. It was a sad Mass but one that is said annually, keeping the brave people who lost their lives always near.

Here in Massapequa Park I am having a wonderful rest and also many walks with my son Mike.

QUEEN'S COLLEGE

I am looking forward to my Grandson Gary bringing me to see Queen's College where he has graduated from. It is a massive building, spreading out almost across the Borough of Queens. When I lived in N.Y. many years ago, little did I ever think back then I would one day have a grandson a graduate of Queen's College, with a

Master's Degree in Physical Education, and teaching at the same college.

Next, he takes me to see the massive gym to meet many of his students. They call me Granny; what a lovely group of young people. Gary was already experienced in teaching; he had taught at the Helen Keller Academy for blind and partially-blind adults and children, swimming in Sunny State University, New York. his sister Cassancra would some times assist him giving the swimming lessons,

Gary asked, "Are you hungry?"

"We sure are," echoed his mam and dad. He took us to a Brazilian restaurant with the name, 'Churrascaraon,' try getting your tongue around that one! The food was in massive big pots laid out on long tables, it was self-service and we walked around with big plates in our hands, filling them up with pasta and the biggest variety of vegetable that was ever grown in the ground.

Queen's College – Gary Beggen holding his signature plate

Everything was on the plate except the meat, a waiter came to the table with three swords with a choice of meat on each one, and a carving knife, you made your choice and the waiter carved the meat with a sword. I was amazed at this unique way of serving the meat.

Gary talked about his move from Long Island to Queens, saying he had to make the move from home because of the distance. I said, "It's understandable why you needed to get an apartment near your work, you had a long drive to and from home each day."

"You can judge for yourself; the traffic is bumper-to-bumper all the way and cars swinging in and out in every direction."

"It was a good idea. I wish you every good luck, Gary." He thanked me with a hug.

A BIRTHDAY PARTY

I get a birthday party to celebrate my eighty-third. "I wasn't expecting this, Mary," I said. A group of friends from the A.O.H. came with food, each one bringing their own speciality. One lady made two cakes, a coffee cake and an ice-cream cake with eight candles on them. They also brought their musical instruments and played some rousing Irish tunes and sang many old-time ballads. I got the courage to join in playing the bodhrán with them. "Mike," I said, "this must be the fifth birthday party you have put on for me, not counting the big one back home."

"Mom, you know the time of the year to come, when it is your birthday."

The three weeks had come to an end fast and I was trying to pack my case, but as it had been damaged the year it got left in Heathrow, Mike said, "Dump it, I will buy you a new one."

"You have done so much for me on this vacation; I don't expect you to buy me a travel bag." He bought me one I could roll along on four wheels; I called it my 'four-wheel drive.' It was easy to pack, close and wheel.

At Kennedy airport Mary got me a wheelchair, then handed me over to an attendant. We made our goodbyes and I was wheeled to the departure station and was first on the plane. It was a beautiful, smooth flight across the Atlantic; I slept most of the way. Landing in Dublin on a lovely day; in a couple of hours I would be in Galway by the speedy Go Bus, then get picked up by my daughter Caroline and safely home again, Thank God; after a wonderful time with my sweet and wonderful families.

A LARGE HEADING

When I was a few days home, my neighbour Mary came to see me, carrying a ream of newspapers. "Welcome back," she says.

"Thank you, Mary. What have you got there?"

"Have you not seen the large heading on the Tribunes yet?" Opening one of the newspapers she said, "Look at that."

"Oh, it's the piece about me; look at the heading in big black capitals."

'Atlantic Crossing,' the piece is taking up half the page. I never expected that. What a write-up they gave me on my 1952 emigration.

"Thanks for keeping the papers for me, I will have a great read this evening."

ODE TO PATRICK KAVANAGH

The poet Patrick Kavanagh was born in 1904 in Mucker, County Monaghan. He left school at the age of twelve to pursue his love for poetry. Although uneducated, he wrote excellent verses.

His genius is celebrated by the Monaghan people yearly. And, as Galway people marry Monaghan people and dwell in Galway, a group assemble together to celebrate Patrick Kavanagh week, which is now in its eighth year. I attended their yearly celebrations held in the poet's honour in Galway City. Listened to his published poetry being read, I enquire if the people who came from Monaghan knew the Beggen family from Scotstown; most of them did and I would tell them of my connection with Monaghan. My late husband Michael Beggen was a County Monaghan man.

I was keen too, to learn more about Kavanagh. In 2016, Des Kavanagh, (no relation) organiser of a Kavanagh evening in the Galway Mechanics Institute invited me to create a verse or two in celebration of Kavanagh. I did my best with *'Ode to Patrick Kavanagh'*. It was greeted with applause on the night, and my daughter Caroline rounded it off by playing 'Raglan Road' on the tinwhistle. We were very proud of our effort. It was a very successful and enjoyable evening, listening to the many dedications from followers of Kavanagh. There was a big attendance

2017 - THE GREATEST SHOW ON EARTH

Recently I heard announced on the news that Barnum and Bailey are coming to the end of their time as the greatest show on earth. Hearing this announcement triggered a memory in my mind from formative years. It was in 1961 that my husband Mike and I took our son Michael and his friend Maureen McAndrew to Madison Square Garden, New York to see the Barnum and Bailey three-ring circus.

What a happy day that was. We saw the ringmaster come into the ring in his red wagtail coat and top-hat, walk around the rings cracking his whip while calling out in that particular voice that only a circus ringmaster possessed, as he welcomed everyone, especially the children, to see the spectacular performances of the daredevil trapeze artist, the beautiful horses with pretty ladies standing on their backs, then somersaulting while the horses galloped around the ring. Sitting in the front row, we had a close-up view. The massive big elephants came out, obeying their master by standing with their four big feet fitting on the bottom of a small, round box. Everyone was clapping as their trainer bowed.

But the greatest of all were the colourful clowns, in suits and shoes three sizes too big, red noses, big lips, red cheeks and funny hairstyles. They would argue and slap each other around the place; squirting water towards the audience, making the children scream. When the lions came on with their deep roar, Michael and Maureen climbed up on our laps, we held them close as they were afraid. The lions also performed their act to perfection while trainer took a bow. The juggler entered the ring, juggling so many balls you would swear he had four hands. With the three rings in action, it was hard to watch what was going on in each one. At the break, ice-cream servers came through the rows of stalls selling iced drinks and a variety of ice-creams from trays hung around their necks. We were glad of the refreshments and the children licked their fingers. The Barnum and Baily Circus had been in existence since the 1800's, entertaining the world with wild animals tamed out of their natural existences. How many people took heed back in 1961 of the suffering these huge wild animals must have endured to perform such extraordinary acts. Well, we didn't; it was an afternoon of entertainment for hundreds in Madison Square Garden with two performances a day. The change in times will have a good result for the wild beasts.

And as I listen now, the time is coming for the greatest show on earth to cease. I think back to that day when we sat watching the many performances, not giving a thought to the endurance of these poor creatures. All we knew was, we were entertained. The animal rights movement is showing the world how unnatural this has been for wild beasts which belong in the wild.

MOTHER'S DAY

Ireland celebrates Mother's Day in March. The USA celebrates it in June. I have the benefit of being reminded twice a year that I am the best mother in the world, from two countries. This year I'm expecting the usual call from my two daughters. I get the hugs and kisses, beautiful cards with tender inscriptions of being the best mother in the world, flowers, and a lovely china tray and mug from my daughter Margery, suitable for my cuppa while I watch TV (in June I will get the same cherished greetings from my two sons in America). Daughter Caroline is not telling me much, because she has a surprise for me. "Get packed," she tells me.

"Why?" I ask.

"Because I am taking you out to Delphi for a weekend as a Mother's Day treat."

"You are too good, Caree; I am looking forward to that break. Thank you so much."

Delphi is a beautiful, relaxing, peaceful country resort in Leenane,

Connemara, County Galway. The ideal place for the tired worker or stressed-out mother to rejuvenate and unwind, a wonderful, safe place for families. A quiet place if that is your choice. My daughter and I availed of the pampering end of it. She treated me to seaweed baths, massages, facials, foot saunas and of course, the pool and sauna, also beautiful food. My daughter treated herself to surf-boarding and bog challenge. We had a wonderful time and came home rejuvenated.

CLOSING MY LIFE STORY

On that relaxing note, I'm sure the good reader of this woman's life story had a little giggle, and at times shed a tear. But, dear reader, I rode out the storms and I have lived to write the tale. One way or another, it is very true.

Beavers Investiture
F.R: Michael Cummins, Trevor Condon, John Tierney, Paul Connolly, Lee Fleming
C.R: Wesley Shaughnessy, Ronald Ward, Kenneth Lydon, David Heaney, Sean Lally, Shane Cunningham
B.R: Darren Murray, Beaver helper Liam Concannon, Beaver Leader Paddy Dowling, Fr. Paddy Heneghan C.C. Ballybane and Des Murray Scout Leader Mervue

First Aid Recipients
F.R: second from left Margery Dowling, Iam directly behind her.
F.R: Centre, Captain Neville Breen, officer in charge, Dr. O'Conghaile Medical Officer and Instructor Margaret Mullgannon.

*Ballybane Mummers in competition in Ballyfae, County Galway.
F.R: Caroline Dowling, Pat Broderick, Seamus Nation.
C.R: Margery Dowling, Me, Anne Marie Broderick
B.R: Eamon Carr, Jim Cotter, Louise Walsh, Sean Kane, Organiser,
Marian Heneghan, Noel Spellman and Geraldine Heneghan.*

*Members of St Bridget's Choir Ballybane.
In dark jackets, Joan McCormack organist, Pat Folan director.
At end of back row Fr John Kane. I am second from right in front row.
Also three young mass servers.*

1976 Renmore-Merue Ladies Club Committee.
F.R: Mrs Mary Alone, Mrs Mary Williams, Mrs Sarah Mongan, Mrs Eileen Carrick, Presiden, Mrs Maura O'Brien and Mrs Margaret Dowling P.R.O.
B.R: Mrs Kathleen Dillon, Mrs Mary Browne, Mrs Sally Gallagher, Mrs Mary Linnane and Mrs Ethna Egan.

2007 pictured in Leo's house North Caroline with my family - Caroline Dowling, Leo Beggen, Mother, Michael Beggen and Margery Fahy

2016- I was privileged to have my photo taken with Bishop Fintan Monahan, native of Castlegar, County Galway. Ordained Bishop of Killaloe County Clare.

2016 Son Mike and I having a quiet time sitting at Leo's table.

Friends to tea Eileen Carick, Mary Lawless, Chris Langan and Sheila Hegarety

2017 – I'm cutting a slice of beef from the spears helped by grandson Gary (wearing glasses) and the waiter.

Here Mary Beggan holds her award presented to her for diligent
service to the Tara and Drum Pipe Band Long Island, N.Y.
Mary is an excellent Piper. She is accompanied by her family, son
Michael, daughter Cassandra, her husband Mick and son Gary.

1985 Ballybane I.G.G. were successful recipients of certificates after
completing a Red Cross First Aid course in Bohermore Guide Centre, Galway.
F.R: Lorna Folan, Jean Cooley, Caroline Dowling, Shirley McEntee
and Carmel Kelly.
B.R: Alice Higgins, Leut. Maura Kelly, Comm. Jean Turnbull and
Capt. Bernie Higgins.

Mrs Rita McDonagh and Mrs Kathleen Cooke busy with the little ones.

Mrs Teresa O'Connell helpful in the playground.

Cassandra Beggen with her Farming Dale school team, under 10's receiving their winning trophies.

Michael Beggen, standing betwe the bicycle trolley, pink umbrell (sweet water ice) and delivery va

1972 Me, Uncle James Hurley(Jimmy), Caroline Dowling and Barky. This is Jimn on his last visit to Galway from Co. Clare. He is wearing his I.R.A. Medal attached to his watch chain.

Best Dressed Lady at the Clare Galway Agricultural Show.

SALTHILL DEVON AWARDS

*Sathill Devon Awards – Grandson Kallum Fahy, 4ᵗʰ from left.
Receiver of two awards – the Annual Award and Player of the Year Award.*